THE LIFE OF WHITELAW REID

BY

ROYAL CORTISSOZ

VOLUME II

POLITICS — DIPLOMACY

NEW YORK
CHARLES SCRIBNER'S SONS
1921

Published March, 1921

Signing the Treaty of Peace between the United States and Spain, December 10, 1898.

After a wood engraving by G. Kruell

CONTENTS

CONTENTS

THE LIFE OF WHITELAW REID

THE LIFE OF WHITELAW REID

CHAPTER I

BEHIND THE SCENES

The year 1879 was a good year for the United States. Those timorous souls who had foreseen a disastrous crisis in the resumption of specie payment were well confounded. Business did more than weather the "experiment." It throve exceedingly, and the state of the national finances was as a symbol of restored health, lifted above the brightening horizon of private enterprise. It was at this time, too, that agricultural development received a new impetus. Like Greeley, Reid pinned his faith on the farmer, deprecating the excessive tendency of capital to gravitate into the cities, and regarding with enthusiasm every sign of widened areas of cultivation throughout the Union. He dilated especially upon the expansion of our foreign trade in farm products, seeing in it a promise that the country was destined to become for centuries the great food manufactory for Europe. The history of the war with Germany supplies interesting confirmation of these economic surmises of his, set down in print forty years ago.

The prosperity he hailed was based, of course, on things quite apart from the politics of the moment, and, in any case, he was never one of those who are fondly disposed to attribute the rainfall to the virtuous interposition of the party in power. Nevertheless, it was undeniable that the administration had been favorable to business and industry. Through the rest of its course he was one of its most generous supporters. After bitter discouragement in his fight for party reorganization he had won, through the cipher despatches, his hour of exultation. That success in his effort to close up the lines only spurred him to stiffer campaigning, in the hope of drawing them closer, and a marked trait in his personal history at this time is the eager swiftness with which he sought to ward off every possible setback. A typical instance dates from the spring of 1879, when Hayes was not altogether reassuring about that egregious army bill through which the Democrats, pretending to block military interference with the suffrage—a peril quite imperceptible, if not impossible—were really seeking to obstruct the operation of federal election laws. "I felt annoyed," Reid wrote to Evarts, "at the reports we had here that the Secretary of the Interior [Schurz] was giving the Democrats some reason to doubt the certainty of the President's veto. If we can't show a united front on the purity of the ballot box, nothing but a stroke of paralysis or of lightning could relieve us from Mr. Tilden as our next President." Evarts and the administration could always be sure of one thing, and that was that there would be no ambiguity about the words of warning received from their editorial counsellor in New York. He was bluntness itself in his communications with the secretary of state. In this case he had ultimately no complaint to make. Although it took about a month more for Hayes to get to the sticking-point, when he got there his gift for writing a veto was shown in full force. "I want in a word," Reid wrote to him, "to tell you how glad I am for the matter as well as the manner of the last veto, and to say how proud I am of the fact—now visible to everybody—that the Republican party stands united and solid behind its chief." Slow work it had been, and sometimes very hard, for them to get into really settled harmony, but it was done.

Hayes was as glad of it as was Reid. He had always been well aware of the value of The Tribune's support. The paper was, indeed, more important to the administration than any of the State leaders, a fact which Evarts once frankly admitted to Hay in a talk about "practical politics" in New York. Reid, he said, "had done the Republican party more service by the cipher publication alone than Conkling had ever rendered in his life." We have seen what Reid made of such tangible appreciation of his labors as was shown in the offer of the Berlin mission. He put it from him as an honor beguiling in itself but not powerful enough to draw him away from the work he was doing in his paper. On the other hand, while he would not accept office or ask favors from the administration, he was not ill-pleased when the latter leaned toward his friends, and there are some amusing passages in the story, as it comes out in his correspondence, of John Hay's relations with Washington in this period. Reid had tried in vain, we know, to persuade Evarts to transfer the Berlin offer from himself to his old comrade. Hay wasn't "politically" strong enough to suit! That mythical disability of the future secretary of state was an old joke between Reid and Hay. It turns up in a letter as early as this one:

New York,
January 22nd, 1878.

My dear Hay:

I have been meaning to write you a queer little bit of confidential gossip. An intimate friend of mine was recently invited to a long and confidential talk at the White House. Before he went, he and I talked over some things which it might be judicious to bring into the conversation. In the talk I made use of the hint you had dropped about not being unwilling to take a foreign appointment before you got to be too much of a family man, and took too serious views of life. So when the good President began excusing the foreign appointments on the ground that it was hard to get good men, my friend said: "Well, when you were casting about to fill such places, why didn't you happen to think of John Hay?" Now read, mark, and inwardly digest the answer, and if the iron doesn't enter your soul, then I am not yet revenged for your leaving New York. The President replied: "Why, don't you know, I have thought of it again and again, and would jump at the chance if it were not for the wretched fact that he has settled down in Ohio. What can I do in such a case?" Alas, alas, that I should have lived to see citizenship in my native state at such a discount.

Faithfully yours,

WHITELAW REID.

Confidential gossip naturally travels quicker than any other kind. "Thanks for your letter," replied Hay, "though I had heard the news last Tuesday. New York news is always stale in Cleveland. According to this authentic version, which was told me in public, as I stood with parted coat tails before my own drawing room fire, the Great Father said, 'I'd send him anywhere if he wasn't from Ohio,' and, sotto voce, 'I want the Ohio places for my own friends.' I am in an unaccountable state of mind in regard to this subject. I think I would like a small mission, and I know I could not accept it if offered. If you can understand this paradox, you can beat me. I will tell you in the strictest confidence, that Seward has written to me expressing his desire to have me in the service. I shall tell him when I get to Washington that I can't go—and so end the matter."

The matter of a "small mission" did end there, but not the matter of his becoming, nevertheless, identified with the administration. Reid never abated his conviction that Hay was exceptionally fitted for public service, and it delighted him to act as intermediary when nearly two years later the opportunity came for his friend to enter the State Department. He sent him the news in this letter:

New York,
October 13th, 1879.

MY DEAR HAY:

Secretary Evarts telegraphed me a week or so ago that he would be in town at the meeting of the Peabody Trustees, and was anxious to see me. So I invited him up to breakfast, and the result was a "session"—lasting from 10 till nearly 3. I couldn't make out any particularly important or serious business he had except on one point, and that was the first thing he brought up. What the Secretary wanted to know was whether in my judgment you would accept the post of First Assistant Secretary of State in case there should be any need of filling the vacancy suddenly. I told him I thought you would; that I was sure you would have done it at almost any time before the campaign, but that possibly the new political prominence you were getting now, and the certainty that you could go to Congress next Summer if you chose, might interfere. This seemed to make him a little thoughtful, but he was prompt in saying that certainly the Assistant Secretaryship would be pleasanter for you as well as more important.

The point in the case is that Fred. Seward (on account of illness in the family I believe) may insist upon retiring. The Secretary said there was a possibility that he might stave off the resignation, but he wanted to be prepared for contingencies. I think he had already settled upon you pretty positively but he asked my opinion of your qualifications. You may imagine that you didn't lose anything in the recital. There, file it all away in some inner convolution of the *pia mater,* and either burn this letter, or put it with your old love letters.

Faithfully yours,

W. R.

Hay was surprised by this letter and said so. It impinged upon him, too, at a moment when dalliance with a congressional ambition was distracting his mind. He confessed that he would find it difficult to reply if he were put in a corner. Shortly afterward decision seemed simpler. With the nomination to Congress practically in his hands he discovered, to his amazement, that he didn't want it. Evarts formally invited him to join the staff of the State Department, and he declined. But the secretary was not to be rebuffed. He turned again to Reid, placing offer and rejection before him, and saying:

"I wish you would write Mr. John Hay pressing him to accept and urging him to come on to Washington and see me before deciding finally. After election anybody can be spared anywhere. He will miss his figure if he doesn't take the place." The rôles of the two friends, as we have seen them when the German mission was to the fore, were now amusingly reversed. Then Hay had moved heaven and earth to get Reid to go to Berlin. Now Reid was as strenuous in urging Hay to go to Washington. Theirs was a kind of rivalry in good-will on which it is pleasant to pause, for the affectionate intimacy between them was one of the most characteristic possessions of their lives. Reid's loyalty to Hay was nothing less than fraternal, looking always to the best interests of his friend. I have shown how sympathetically and wisely he advised Hay when he brought him to the staff of The Tribune in 1870, making him an editorial writer in New York instead of a correspondent in Paris, as Hay had at first thought of being. Once more, in furthering Evarts's request, he spoke the right, decisive word. He telegraphed as well as wrote, to make the issue doubly urgent. "I don't fully understand the Congressional situation out there," he said, "but I do hope you will not let any consideration of mere business interfere with what I know has been an ambition of your life, and what I am sure would now prove a most agreeable stepping-stone to better things. Certainly, I would not say no finally without paying the Secretary the compliment of the personal consultation he asks. By all means come directly to New York, stay with me till you are ready to go down to Washington, or intercept him here as you may prefer. It is too big a thing to reject without the fullest deliberation and consultation—bigger a great deal just now and for you, as it seems to me, than any foreign offer could be." This appears to have ended Hay's dubiety. "Is the matter still open?" he telegraphed. "If so I shall be with you Friday A.M."; and when he got there a long talk with Evarts in Reid's library clinched the matter. A week later the appointment was announced in the press, to Reid's unbounded delight. If there was a single personal association of his with Hayes's administration for which he remained ever thankful it was this one, linked with John Hay's initiation into the governmental department he was long afterward to rule and to adorn.

There are a few other episodes of this period which, like the foregoing, have the unusual character of being without the mark of politics upon them. One, which I cite for its historic interest, relates to General Sherman. There was printed in The Tribune an article by George Alfred Townsend—better known as Gath—reporting some talk with ex-Senator Willard Warner, a member of Sherman's staff on the great march to the sea. Speaking of that event, Warner gave some reminiscences of Sherman's grief over the death of General McPherson, the best-beloved of all his colleagues, at the battle of Atlanta, telling how the weeping commander paced in his slippers up and down beside the body, and through his tears went on giving orders to the officers constantly arriving at headquarters. The printed story led to correspondence between Sherman and Reid, from which I take this fragment, exhibiting the emotion of a famous soldier in one of the great crises of his career:

HEADQUARTERS, ARMY OF THE UNITED STATES.
WASHINGTON, D. C.

March 12th, 1879.

MY DEAR SIR:

I don't think I was in "my slippers"—but I did doubtless pace that floor, to keep up with the thoughts whirling through my brain in the midst of a terrible battle, inaugurated by the sudden and unexpected death of one I loved, and on whose advice and action I leaned heavily. Realizing at that instant that Genl. Hood had begun his command by fighting outside his intrenchments, the very thing both I and McPherson had wanted, I saw vision of victory, but at heavy cost. Who could tell my thoughts, when I myself can hardly recall them or find words to describe them? I am more than willing that everybody should testify of what they saw, heard and felt—and even then we will fall short of giving a full picture of all the events around Atlanta on that eventful day.

With respect,
Your Friend,
W. T. SHERMAN.

It was in 1879 that Reid started a benevolent movement foreshadowing in its services to poor children the work of the Fresh Air Fund in later years. He was surprised one day by the visit of a stranger from New England, who handed him a thousand dollars in greenbacks and asked him to use it according to his own best judgment for the relief of cases of real distress in New York. They talked over various schemes, and finally found their inspiration in Greeley's celebrated admonition: "Young man, go West." Securing the co-operation of the Children's Aid Society, Reid organized the transportation of detachment after detachment of destitute boys from the slums of New York to homes readily found for them on the farms of Kansas and Iowa. The publicity he gave to the plan brought immediate practical recognition. One sympathizer after another followed the example of the New England philanthropist, making Reid their almoner, until several hundred boys and a goodly number of families had been sent West. The names of these generous men and women he was never permitted to publish. One particularly he would gladly have printed if he could have done so. It was that of a man who was living on a salary of only $50 a week, but who nevertheless gave $500 to the fund. In midsummer Reid himself got out of the city on an unprecedented holiday. "I am just going off on a three or four weeks' run to

California and back," he jubilantly wrote to Halstead; "my first trip to the real West, and my first absence of that length from The Tribune office in nearly eleven years!" He went with Collis P. Huntington, in the latter's private car, spent four days amongst the big trees and waterfalls of the Yosemite, was fêted by the editors of San Francisco, and returned with renewed health and a store of golden impressions—the unsuspected precursors of the new and more durable relation to the Pacific slope into which the Fates were presently to bring him.

He came back to a State campaign in which the Republicans were handicapped by mediocre leadership. A. B. Cornell received the nomination for the governorship, and how far he was from thrilling the political observer may be judged from the comment of Evarts: "A really brave and impressive nomination for Governor in New York," he wrote to Reid, "would have enabled us to shake the Democratic party to pieces in the whole country and close the politics of the Rebellion. But now, we must submit to the frog-in-the-well process for another series of campaigns. However, if it were best that everything should be done in a day, I suppose God would not have taken six to make the world." Reid, occupied like everybody else in making the best of an uninspiring nomination, was on the whole more sanguine than the secretary. Though he had no surprise, like the cipher despatches, to spring upon the Democrats and thereby repeat the strategic triumph of 1878, his opponents saved him the trouble by indulging in a party split in which he rightly saw the promise of their defeat. Election day more than confirmed his hopes. Cornell won in New York, States ordinarily "doubtful" fell into line, and in the general result, as The Tribune tauntingly put it, a solid North sent its greetings to a solid South. The victory was, indeed, so wide-spread that Reid confidently faced the future as belonging to his party. The contest of 1880, he thought, could now be opened with fair prospects. Unless the Republicans blundered most strangely they could elect the next President and shape the history of the country for the ensuing ten years.

It was a not unreasonable forecast. Without any fortuitous interference existing conditions should have promoted plain sailing for the new campaign. The return of General Grant from his European travels, however, supplied all that was necessary to complicate an otherwise simple problem. He landed at San Francisco a month or so before the State elections, naturally received the heartiest of popular welcomes as he came East, and with surprising rapidity was in pleased possession of a Grant "boom." I say "surprising," but the revival of his political fortunes was, perhaps, only to be expected. None of our ex-Presidents, with the exception of Theodore Roosevelt, has ever had a larger or more devoted personal following. By this time, too, "Third Termism" had lost its terrors for many of his adherents. Voters who had balked at giving him a third consecutive election were not unwilling to return him to the White House after an interim of four years. By some queer process of reasoning it was assumed that the interposition of the Hayes administration had taken the curse off a policy previously condemned. It was condemned again, of course, but not before it had caused a prodigious lot of trouble. In Reid's circle it raised anxious doubts. Hay was so far impressed as to say that there was no more chance of stopping the Grant movement by sober, serious, sensible presentment of the facts and reasons in the case, than there was of stopping the yellow fever with a brass band. If Grant lived, and wanted the nomination, he would get it. From a trustworthy source Hay reported what he considered a most disquieting feature of the business, namely, that Mrs. Grant had set her heart upon it, believing that the general would be unanimously elected by the whole electoral college. And, as Hay's informant remarked, "the General would rather offend forty million people than Madame." Halstead gave way to something like fury. "The damned farce of the American people prostrating themselves before Grant," he ejaculated, "is one of the most shameful chapters in history."

Shameful or not, it had to be reckoned with, and the interest in Reid's correspondence centres in the diplomatic activities, pro and con, which it set going behind the scenes. The special significance of the Grant boom resided less in the matter of his personal chances than in the effect it was bound to have upon the determination of other candidacies. "It is my judgment," wrote Halstead, "that the Republican leader who fights Grant first and hardest will win." The discussion amongst Reid and his friends revolved all the time around the question as to who the early and invincible gladiator should be. The name of John Sherman was on many lips. He occupied at the outset a fairly strong position. In November Halstead sent word to Reid that the secretary of the treasury, with the prestige of Resumption behind him, was cheerfully confident of his chances in the convention. Halstead was sure that he would contest every inch of the field to the last. I have a pointed souvenir of the statesman's indignation when, in the midst of the first skirmishes, he met Grant in Philadelphia, and was promptly represented in the press as having, under the softening influences of a luncheon-table, actually joined the Grant movement! To kill this astonishing canard he wrote to Reid as follows:

Fifth Avenue Hotel,
December 21st, 1879.

My dear Sir:

I wish very much to have an interview with you during my visit here, and venture to name today at some convenient hour to you. I will be at this Hotel at or after 3 P.M. or can call at your House. I take this occasion to say that the story I see in the "Herald" this morning is untrue in every material respect. I did see Gen. Grant at Drexel's Party on Friday evening but had no conversation with him or with any one about his Candidacy either in form or substance. On the contrary I am now, as four years ago, utterly opposed to the 3rd term and believe Gen. Grant would make a fatal mistake in accepting a nomination and the Republican party in offering it. While I do not care over my own signature to make this statement you are authorized to say so in The Tribune.

Very truly yours,

John Sherman.

The interview was arranged and, as was plain the next morning, The Tribune was only too glad to "say so," making the most of Sherman's sturdy challenge, and leaving no possible excuse for any further public misunderstanding as to his position. Nevertheless, throughout the period leading up to the convention, Reid appears to have had no illusions at all as to the potentialities of Sherman in the fight against Grant. He had the promptitude and the courage. He could count upon his State, Ohio. But the wider, national drift was not in his direction. Blaine, in Reid's opinion, was unmistakably marked for the critical rôle in the impending conflict. The only virtue of Sherman's boom, as he saw it, was that it might help to weaken Grant's, without hurting Blaine's.

On the verge of the presidential year Blaine himself was debarred by circumstances from mixing to any extent in the deployment of candidacies. The fall elections in his own State had developed a grave imbroglio, threatening the fraudulent reversal of a clear majority. A Republican governor was seated only after the supreme court had been called upon for a decision, and until that was rendered Blaine was too busy in Maine, as the mentor of his party, to work upon anything else. In his memoir of the statesman Mr. Stanwood says that he could not be induced to promote his own candidacy in any way at this time; he could not even be persuaded to leave Augusta before the judicial verdict had been pronounced, which was not until the middle of January, 1880. Meanwhile, however, there were others who were thinking of him in relation to the campaign. One of these was Halstead. He preferred Sherman as a candidate, but he was not at all unfriendly to Blaine, and he thought he saw a way in which the latter might aid in taking the bloom off the Grant boom. This was to be by the exertion of his influence in designating the place for the national convention. If Chicago were fixed upon, the complexion of local politics would be heavily in favor of Grant's backers. At Cincinnati those gentlemen would be ill at ease, if not in danger of political frost-bite, and Halstead bombarded Reid with letters urging that Blaine be persuaded to act in the matter. Ultimately these epistles were forwarded to him. They elicited a notable reply, notable for its manly revelation of Blaine's state of mind on the whole question of presidential ambition. I give it in full:

Augusta,
December 10th, 1879.

My dear Mr. Reid:

I have been so much engaged in fighting—or at least exposing—the Democratic conspiracy in this state that I have really given no attention to the possible action of the National Committee touching time and place of the Convention. And in fact my general conclusion, without going into details, that I had no special interest of a personal nature in the result, has tended to keep my mind off the matter.

Circumstances outside of my own original designs or desire made me fight an aggressive battle in 1876—against all the candidates combined, against the Grant Administration, against a hostile city

[Cincinnati] highly inflamed by the course of "those two d—d Kentucky papers," as an Oregon delegate styled the "Gazette" and "Commercial." I will never again fight an aggressive battle, horses cannot drag me into it, and as you well know I am literally doing nothing in the matter. Grant's friends are very active. Sherman's friends are very active. Mine are not. If I am taken it will be as an alternate. If I should go out actively in the fight I should very probably end with a combination of Grant and Sherman against me. That would not be half so unnatural a result as the coalition of Conkling, Morton, Hayes and Bristow at Cincinnati in '76.

Therefore my conclusion is that I ought not to attempt any intermeddling with the possible conclusion of the National Committee. I cannot be in Washington on the 17th and could do little by writing. I have not the remotest objection to Cincinnati being selected and yet if I should say so publicly it would require the space of a quarto dictionary to explain my position to my friends. I do not retain any soreness out of the conflict of '76, and least of all would I, if I could, do a resentful act towards the "Gazette" or "Commercial." While I think they dealt unjustly by me in '76, when I was on my back and helpless, I count that all as belonging to the Silurian epoch, and I never recur to it otherwise than I am now doing for cool comment. Both papers treat me very well of late and Halstead I think has gone out of his way to say kind and friendly things of me, and I certainly have no feeling adverse to friendly relations with him—entirely irrespective of Presidential plans and plots.

If I should say publicly that I am not anxious to be nominated in '80 it would simply be taken as a piece of affectation. Therefore I never say it; and yet if I know my own "true inwardness," I could say it with absolute candor. Not that I feel indifferent to the exalted position, with its mighty power, but because of the bitter struggle and its doubtful end at last—doubtful by the double danger of defeat at the polls and cheat in the final count. And then I have had one great ambition of my life filled. Many of those who aided in beating me at Cincinnati congratulated themselves that I was done for and ended as a public man, that I had lost my grip, and was injured in my character. I have lived to see some of the most malignant of these men relegated to private life—by no agency of mine—and I have lived, if it is a pardonable boast in a private note, to find myself with a larger personal following than any or all of those who combined against me. And I have not done it by demagoguery or double-dealing on any question or with any man. And now if the great American people don't choose to nominate me for the Presidency (as they almost certainly will not) you will not find me a fool, or a weakling, or a sorehead or a mourner—but I shall go into the campaign of 1880 for the candidate, with all the cheerfulness in the world.

I enjoy my place in the Senate and unless the deuce comes to be counted as the ace in Maine I can hold it indefinitely. Why then should I fret to get into a doubtful contest? Had I succeeded in '76 I would now be on the eve of "muster out" at fifty years of age, with the best part of my life—if I am to be blessed with length of days—to be passed as a walking gentleman in the play, like Fillmore, or as Justice of the Peace and Quorum, like Madison, or travelling the earth's surface after the fashion of the Wandering Jew, as Grant does. Frank Pierce once told me that God Almighty had permitted no torture to be invented so cruel as the life of an Ex-President; in fact, as he said to Gov. Shaw, "there is nothing left for him but to get drunk." As I have no taste for liquor even that resource would have been cut off from me.

Therefore, with all these warnings before me (like the English lady's horror of the bull fight and her eager desire to see one) it only remains for me to say that of course I would enjoy being made miserable after the pattern of those illustrious predecessors. But Heavens! What a letter I am writing, and with what reckless candor I am talking. But of course it is private for all the world except Phelps.

Hastily and truly,

J. G. Blaine.

P. S. In reading over my ten pages, written without looking back, it might seem that I had by some possibility manifested an unconcern for those who have steadily honored me with their friendship, "of whom you are chief." Of course you could not so understand me for indeed the friendship, attachment and love that have been shown to me and for me, by so many of the best and bravest, are as sweet to me as the "odors, which are the prayers of saints."

J. G. B.

He went on struggling with what Reid called "the Maine diabolism," but in January, as I have said, that was finally disposed of, and back in Washington he could see that he, as well as Grant and Sherman, had supporters who were "very active." Hay's letters constantly testify to this fact. It hadn't taken him long to recognize the superiority of his friend's judgment on the net value of Grant's prospects. "About that Grant boom," he writes in January. "I hear wonderful news this morning. Murat Halstead came to see me and told me that the jig was up, that the intimate Grant circle in Philadelphia admitted it and said that before long there would be an authoritative announcement to that effect. The thoroughbred stallion James Gillespie Blaine seems to be the favorite in the pools at this moment. Don Cameron's four-in-hand seems to be running away with him." The next day his conviction has gone a little deeper. "I think Blaine is the Bully Boy with the celluloid ear," he gleefully proclaims. All seemed then in train for the complete dispersal of Blaine's doubts and fears. But the allusion to Don Cameron's four-in-hand directs attention to the ambiguous, misleading movements which certain chariots sometimes make on the political highway. The hereditary "boss" in Pennsylvania, Don, son of Simon, was engaged just then in manœuvres upon which the supporters of the leading candidates gazed with emotions determined altogether by the degree of their acquaintance with his wily ways.

When Cameron was made chairman of the Republican National Committee John Sherman told Reid that he had favored the election "because he was by all odds the best man for the place," a comment made, as we shall presently see, with almost pathetic blindness. The Tribune's remark that the action of the committee would probably be regarded as a gain for General Grant proved in the upshot only too true. Of the three United States senators who were peculiarly active in bolstering up the candidate for a third term, Conkling, of New York, and Logan, of Illinois, were unquestionably powerful enough, and in the convention the first of these was to develop an exceptional influence; but while the grooming of candidates was going on Cameron was impressive in weight and mischievous intent. As chairman alone he counted to some purpose. With the Pennsylvania machine at his back his influence was doubled in force. This was to be made grimly manifest in the spring. In the preceding winter appreciation of what was sinister in his conduct varied, as I have indicated, with knowledge of the boss, his environment, and his antecedents. Hay, for example, required fuller initiation. Chuckling over Blaine's seemingly secure seat in the Cameronian equipage, he was still not quite certain of what was developing. In some bewilderment he informed Reid of a singular talk he had had with the great man. Don hadn't been entirely consistent and coherent, but the nub of it was that Grant was only his figurehead and Blaine really his man. If he were to be let alone and not antagonized by the Blaine men in Pennsylvania, he would give the Plumed Knight his fifty-eight votes. He said that the State convention would instruct for Grant—it had to do so as part of his plan—but Blaine would lose nothing by the process. Reid's reply is illuminating, exposing at once the motivation of insincere politics in general and the sweetly ingenuous art of Don Cameron in particular:

New York,
January 29th, 1880.

My dear Hay:

You have doubtless forgotten one point which I fancy you must have heard. When Cameron was driven out of Lincoln's cabinet John Sherman voted against his confirmation as Minister to Russia. When Cameron got back into the Senate he went to the record of Executive Sessions, and looked that interesting fact up. Don won't throw the vote of Pennsylvania for the man that voted to disgrace his Father—at least not while the venerable Simon could still reach for his scalp. So, if Don can't get Grant, of course he wants Blaine, or somebody else, to beat Sherman. I believe that's the true inwardness of his talk with you.

But his effort to get Pennsylvania to instruct for Grant is dangerous and ought to be defeated. I suggested very earnestly the other day to Blaine that his friends, if strong enough, should put through the Pennsylvania convention a simple resolution reaffirming their 3rd term plank of 1875—that and nothing more. No instructions for Blaine. Please talk with him about it. The thing seems to me of great importance.

W. R.

Blaine's friends in the Pennsylvania convention, held a week later, were not strong enough to withstand Cameron. He saw to it that the delegation was instructed for Grant, with orders, also, to vote as a unit on all questions. But he won his point on so narrow a majority that the repulse of the Blaine forces was more apparent than real. "It winds up Grant," was Garfield's comment.

When the Third Term movement was later successful in the New York convention, Reid recognized the fact that Conkling, who controlled that body, would be in a position to make serious trouble at Chicago, yet he still could not believe that at the crucial moment the hated scheme would go through. Republican leadership would see, he prophesied, the absurdity of embarking upon a losing fight. If Grant secured the nomination the party would be committed beyond all peradventure to a defensive campaign, and to the managers contemplating that suicidal course he commended the parable of the seeker after a trustworthy coachman. All the candidates were asked the same question: "Suppose that you were driving my carriage alongside of a precipice—how near could you go to the edge without going off?" The first named a limit of two feet, the second was content with only six inches, but the man who got the job was the one who said he should keep as far away from the edge as possible. Grant's supporters maintained, in effect, that they could take the Republican party within six inches of the abyss of defeat and still save it. Reid knew they couldn't do it, and said so from day to day with all the vigor at his command. To the remonstrances of those political leaders, some of them in his own State, who deprecated opposition to Grant, he retorted simply that a defensive campaign was, in the circumstances, a campaign thrown away, resting upon this broad principle rather than upon the advocacy of any other candidate. At the same time he gave them furiously to think by quietly printing certain facts in his news columns. These, gathered from many parts of the country, clearly showed the increasing popularity of Blaine.

In his December letter Blaine had declared that he would never again fight an aggressive battle. "Horses cannot drag me into it," he had said. As the winter waned it was impossible for him to resist the tide of political activity which eddied round him, and Walter Phelps, in March, gives the measure of Blaine's concern for his own candidacy as it throve in the atmosphere of Washington. "Blaine is very happy," he wrote to Reid, "and his home is in the fever of a perpetual exchange. MacVeagh said he doubted if I or any one else could see him alone. Blaine is at least hopeful enough to take an interest, and is himself apparently putting his fingers to the wire—certainly not publicly, perhaps not confessedly to himself, but he certainly is doing it. And this personal activity is one reason—I hope not the only one—why he is so cheerful." On the evening at Blaine's when he gathered this impression he also met Cameron, who, however, did not talk up the prospects of their host. On the contrary, he tried to convince Phelps that Grant's nomination was necessary, as he, and only he, could carry Louisiana, Virginia, or any other Southern State! A marplot, indeed, was the persistent gentleman from Pennsylvania. Writing to Reid at the end of April, Hay says: "I think Grant is not yet beaten but he is beatable, by a miracle or two. Don Cameron is the absolutely unknown quantity. He swears—profanely

—that Pennsylvania and New York will be solid, and that Blaine is a goner. He says if Blaine is wise he will take the Vice-Presidency. He even said so to Mrs. Blaine. You may fancy how it was received." If the astute Pennsylvanian thought that with desperate counsels he could "rattle" Blaine, he was, for once, a little too astute. Preliminary skirmishes had renewed in the Maine statesman all his wonted zest and resourcefulness. There are some revealing words in a long despatch of his to Reid, sent early in May. "The Grant forces are making superhuman efforts in Illinois," he says, "but up to this time I hold the lead. The fight, however, is desperate." That was the kind of fight to bring out Blaine's most characteristic traits, and he could display them with the knowledge that he had a growing support. A careful analysis which The Tribune just then made of the voting at a large number of State conventions showed that the set of Republican opinion was strongly in his favor. For one thing, a majority against a third term seemed already quite assured. On May 23d William E. Chandler, expert in reading the signs of political weather, was predicting that Blaine would have a plurality on the first ballot and would be nominated on the second. This was the view generally prevailing when the convention was organized at Chicago on June 2d. And everybody concerned was there to be taught anew the ancient lesson of politics—which is that it is the unexpected that happens.

One expectation of Reid's was in nowise disappointed. He said that the convention would bring up more contestable questions than any since 1864, and he was right. Trouble began even before organization. A resolution against the unit rule was introduced at a meeting of the National Committee. Don Cameron, as chairman, peremptorily refused to entertain it, or to permit an appeal against his decision. Whereupon he was hotly accused of using the high-handed methods of Tammany and threatened with deposition. From the compromise that was effected the anti-Grant men issued, however, with courage heightened and hopes not by any means cast down. In the upshot it gave them as permanent chairman of the convention Senator G. F. Hoar, of Massachusetts, who had no love for the unit rule, and under his impartial auspices there were much better chances for justice when the crucial battle opened. On the first trial of strength, a ballot on a resolution, the delegates ignored the unit rule, each man voting for himself, and this was a token of defeat for Grant. Reid hailed the omen. There was never a possibility, in his opinion, of the nomination of the general, except by the deprival of many of the delegates of their freedom in voting, and when the report of the committee on rules was called up he saw his liveliest hopes confirmed. The Grant faction strove mightily to bring about nominations before the unit rule should be formally smashed. It strove in vain. Garfield, in terse, telling sentences, and with great parliamentary skill, led the opposition to this intrigue, the convention played up, and the unit rule was thrown into the discard, where it belonged. When the nominations began it had taken nearly four days to clear the way for them, but a point of inestimable value had been made —the free and voluntary action of every delegate had been recognized and reaffirmed as the fundamental law of the party. In the process the Third Term movement had been smitten in its tracks.

Six names were presented to the convention at the Saturday-night session which found the delegates at last ready for their task—Grant, Blaine, Sherman, Edmunds, Washburne, and Windom, and on the following Monday morning The Tribune expressed the current opinion in saying that it was "anybody's race." But the first ballot cast on that day showed that the contest was essentially between Grant and Blaine, and this situation remained unchanged through two sessions. Twenty-eight ballots were taken without the making of a choice. On the other hand, they had left it fairly evident that neither Grant nor Blaine could win. I have indicated the personal significance of a State "boss" in a crisis of this kind in alluding to Don Cameron of Pennsylvania. To his assertion that "Blaine was a goner," an even keener edge was given on the scene of battle by Roscoe Conkling, of New York. In his speech presenting Grant's name to the convention, not content with uttering a panegyric upon his candidate, he went out of his way to make remarks which could only be construed as insinuations against the general's most dangerous rival. Never were sneers more grossly ill-advised. If they gratified Conkling's private spleen they also raised amongst Blaine's supporters an anger absolutely fatal to the plans of the vindictive orator. If forced to it, the Blaine men might have shifted to another candidate, but never to Grant. The two camps, antagonistic enough before Conkling spoke, were now mutually implacable. There was no mistaking this when the twenty-eighth ballot had been taken. It spelled a deadlock only to be broken by recourse to a third candidate. There seemed here a forlorn hope for John Sherman. Garfield had led the Ohio delegation in its devoted support of that candidate, presenting his name to the convention in a brilliant speech, one which, as The Tribune expressed it, was admirably adapted to make votes for his candidate, if speeches ever made votes. But through the long-drawn-out balloting of the first day the secretary, starting with 93 votes, ended with 91, and although, when the struggle to break the deadlock began, he jumped to 116 and subsequently made a trifling gain, thenceforth his strength gradually melted away.

It was on the thirty-fourth ballot that Garfield—as the "dark horse" that Conkling had protested against, and dreaded—came into view. The frequent mention of his name, early in the convention, as a possible compromise candidate, had seemingly made no serious impression, least of all upon Garfield himself. Through thirty-three of the apparently interminable ballots he had received the nominal honor of one vote, sometimes rising to two. Then, on the thirty-fourth, the germ of the final nomination was deposited. Sixteen of Wisconsin's twenty votes were cast for Garfield, and critical developments in the situation seemed imminent. Perhaps he vaguely sensed them, for when he rose in his place to address the chair he was pale with excitement. Senator Hoar, instantly alert for an infraction of the rules, sought to head off any personal explanation or declination, which would have been a clear violation of them. He did not succeed, altogether. Garfield pointed out that no one had any right to cast votes for a gentleman in the convention without his consent. "And that consent," he exclaimed, "I refuse." The matter was beyond his control. On the next ballot 50 votes were cast for him, and on the one that followed—the last—the trend in his favor was soon unmistakable. The Tribune thus described Garfield's demeanor as the taking of the thirty-sixth ballot proceeded, the Blaine and Sherman States began to pour in their strength, and the choice of the Ohio senator was clearly indicated:

There was a universal uproar; half the convention rose to its feet. While the building was resounding with loud cheers for Garfield there was a cluster of excited delegates about the General himself, who sat quiet and cool in his ordinary place at the end of one of the rows of seats in the Ohio delegation. He wore the white badge of an Ohio delegate on his coat, and held his massive head steadily immovable. But for an appearance of extra resoluteness on his face, as that of a man who was repressing internal excitement, he might have been supposed to have as little interest in the proceedings as any other delegate on the floor of the convention. He was in fact going through one of the most extraordinary experiences ever given to an American citizen. He was being struck by Presidential lightning while sitting in the body which was to nominate him. He was being nominated for President at half past one o'clock in the afternoon, when he could hardly have dreamed of such a thing at nine o'clock in the morning.

The situation was indeed not only dramatic but peculiar, as the report continued. Garfield had entered the convention as the loyal representative of Secretary Sherman, who was still a candidate. The Ohio delegates, most of whom were the warm friends of both men, were in honor bound to support Sherman so long as there was any possibility of his nomination. Like a truthful and honorable gentleman, Garfield had from the first set his face against all suggestions that he should himself become a candidate, feeling that any yielding to such suggestions would be rankly disloyal to the friend he had come to support. But now he was being forced into the field in spite of himself, and the indications were that his own vote would surpass that of his candidate. He passed Grant as the vote of Massachusetts was thrown into the balance and thereafter his lead was swiftly increased. When Wisconsin, that had set the ball rolling on the thirty-fourth ballot, once more came to the front, he could reckon up 399 votes, where only 378 were necessary for a choice. It was a fitting conclusion to a strange sequence of events. The Republican convention of 1880 proved true to its exceptional character. Sharply distinguished in the annals of the party by an extraordinary prolongation of factional strife, it wound up with a nomination unforeseen alike by the nominee and his fellow countrymen.

The convention did more than give the party a winning candidate. It squelched at last the Third Termers who had planned to control its deliberations, and in this circumstance, as the reader will doubtless have already surmised, there was a special balm for Whitelaw Reid. He had fought the abhorred heresy long and faithfully. It looked now as if he would never have to fight it again. The name of Grant no longer conveyed to his ears the sound of a hateful challenge. That it had done so through such an extended period, waking in the columns of The Tribune constant echoes of warfare, had led to the belief in some quarters that the course of the paper had been actuated by personal animosity. As a matter of fact, Reid had never in his life opposed Grant on any save purely political grounds. Rejoicing on the day after Garfield's nomination that not for a century could another successful soldier ask for a third term, he protested that by this he meant no reflection upon the great military leader he had always endeavored in his paper to treat with the admiring respect due to his noble service and exalted career. What he acclaimed was, simply, the settled judgment of the Republican party and of the American people that protracted terms of service in our highest office were not in harmony with the spirit of our institutions. As the subject disappears from these pages it is pleasant to recall the cordial—and not unamusing—circumstances in which he himself bade it farewell.

Just after the campaign, in which Grant had made a number of speeches for the candidate, giving him the most sportsmanlike support, the Lotos Club entertained the general at dinner. Reid presided, and when he rose to pay a tribute of welcome to the guest sitting at his right hand, there was not a man present who failed to realize the piquancy of the moment and the bristling nature of the hurdles which the speaker faced. He took them with candid directness, pausing only to eulogize the soldier and to recall his own observation of Grant's calm carriage at Pittsburg Landing. Then he plunged straight at the question which had so recently been occupying the American people, the question as to what was to be done with their ex-President. He spoke, he said, not as the general's partisan. That he had never been. Often, in civil affairs, he had not been able to follow where Grant had led, and a long laugh went round the tables as he expressed the fancy that the general would probably be quite willing to give him a certificate for having practised great freedom of speech upon that subject. But speaking confessedly as a political opponent he had a solution to offer for the problem that was in so many minds. It was that Grant, and every retiring President in the future, should be given life membership in the United States Senate.

In the debate on the subject which forthwith ran through the press there were signs that certain irreconcilable "Grant organs" found little to their liking in this suggestion. It had too much the air of implying, as Reid meant it to imply, that the Third Term hypothesis had been exploded forever. But it was as graceful as it was pointed, striking the right note for the occasion that brought it forth. There was nothing left for acrimony between the political adversaries of a long period, now breaking bread together in peace and amity.

CHAPTER II

THE CAMPAIGN OF 1880

From a friend of Garfield's who saw him at his home in the summer of the nomination I have received a brief but telling reminiscence. There was about him not a trace of the self-consciousness of a successful candidate. His happy spirit appeared to draw nothing of its vitality from the political situation. Sauntering arm in arm with his guest down the lanes of the Mentor farm, his easy, interesting talk was now of the prosperous fields on either hand, and now of bookish things. The impression he left was of a mind and a personality equally strong, original, and lovable. All of the private souvenirs that I have come upon in the Reid papers unite on the sheer human attractiveness of Garfield's character. Hay, for example, speaks of him as "so thoroughly upright and able, one who knows so much of men and books, who is not only a statesman but a good fellow besides." And the richness of his traits is shown by their carrying power, which impressed them upon people who had never seen him. Walter Phelps, travelling in Germany during the campaign, writes in one of his letters home: "White, in Berlin, was nice. I went with him to call on Auerbach, who lives in a handsome suburb. He's a jolly, fat little gentleman, who looks like Falstaff. He knew all about Garfield. He said he was 'a scholarly Lincoln.' Not bad, was it?" This observation by the German novelist had been anticipated by Whitelaw Reid in 1868, when he wrote "Ohio in the War." The biography of Garfield therein set forth discloses the remarkable range of Garfield's qualities, the moral and intellectual energy which carried him from the tow-path to academic distinction, made him not only a brave soldier but a brilliant chief of staff, and in political life won him the name of "Great Majority Garfield," the easy winner of one contest after another. When The Tribune published its campaign life of the candidate this memoir from Reid's book furnished forth the bulk of the pamphlet, requiring only to be brought up to date in order to show the American people what manner of man was destined to be their next President. Phelps then wrote of it: "You have no idea how graceful, complete and interesting that is. I'm hugely delighted. I read it through without pausing from beginning to end. And no one can rise from its perusal without thinking highly of Garfield. I think more of him, even, than I did. And the fact that he is photographed so nicely as he appeared then, when the photographer had no temptation in the fame of his subject, to powder or pose him, makes it remarkably effective." I cite the tribute not so much for its bearing upon one of Reid's literary productions as for the sake of the friendship to which it points. The tragic brevity of Garfield's service in the White House would in any case exclude from this chapter the history of "an administration." But all the circumstances of the period, from the nomination to the inauguration and after, emphasize the importance of markedly personal issues.

In previous chapters I have noted the close, almost fraternally intimate terms on which Garfield and Reid had long foregathered. The former was the older by six years, but under the pressure of the war, which had such an extraordinary power of turning youths into men, they may be said to have come to maturity together. They had the same principles and ideals, the same tastes in classical and modern letters. They were sons of the same State—a point of sentiment not without its value—and their attachment as men was ratified in the experiences determining their attitude toward the methods and aims of political life. Amongst all the presidential candidacies with which Reid had to do—and as the reader will have realized by this time, they formed one of the leading interests of his life—there was not one into the promotion of which he could throw himself with more heart than into Garfield's. The ticket, as a ticket, may not have been absolutely what he wished. In nominating for the vice-presidency Conkling's friend and adherent, Chester Arthur, the convention had caused many a stanch Republican to wince. Nevertheless, with a President like Garfield to elect, the question of the second office seemed then a matter to take with more than the usual philosophy. The nomination set Reid to work with literally unbounded enthusiasm. It placed him again, too, quite as much as in 1872, if not more decisively, in the rôle of counsellor. The interchange of ideas which had been going on between them through much of Garfield's congressional career took on redoubled energy and an even firmer status in the campaign of 1880.

It was a hot campaign, carried to a fairly close decision. Tilden's withdrawal before the Cincinnati convention undoubtedly relieved the Democrats of an embarrassing handicap, and they framed a ticket which if in nowise formidable was not, either, to be altogether despised. The principal charge to be levelled against General Winfield Scott Hancock was that his experience had been purely military; as a candidate for the presidency he had had no initiation whatever into the civilian side of public life. From the point of view of political ability Mr. W. H. English, of Indiana, nominated for the vice-presidency, had not even Arthur's mixed claims. He was a mediocrity, pure and simple. But his influence in his own very important State was not by any means a negligible quantity. It will be recalled, also, that this was the campaign in which a plank in the Democratic platform demanding "a tariff for revenue only" supplied that party with a potential slogan, renewing the impetus of an agitation which was to carry far. Decidedly Garfield was not to have a walkover, and as the files of The Tribune register progress it seems, nevertheless, quite characteristic of Reid to revive, at the height of the contest, his accustomed warning against Republican overconfidence. However, the party made a hard and ever more assured fight. The earlier State elections were auspicious. Vermont gave cheering tokens, Maine was close but ultimately came up to scratch, and in October, when Ohio and Indiana rolled up solid Republican majorities, the final verdict to be expected on election day throughout the country could be regarded as settled—as it was. The eleventh-hour attack made upon Garfield through the famous forgery of the "Morey letter," meant to bedevil his chances with the labor vote, was as futile as any of the similarly scandalous charges flung at him on the opening of the campaign. He was borne to election as he had been borne to nomination, not only on a wave of good fortune but on his merits, a thoroughly popular victor. The Tribune laid stress upon the normal, wholesome manner in which the simple affirmation of the candidate's character, open for all men to see at his home in Mentor, where he had welcomed multitudes of friends and strangers, had grown upon the people. "The more they learned of his career, his studies, his ideas, and his daily life, the stronger he became." If the hearty acceptance of Garfield by the people were all with which the historian had to reckon, I could readily pass from his election to his few administrative weeks and the assassin's fatal shot. But none of our Presidents was ever made more sharply aware of the fact that in getting elected and forming an administration it is necessary to deal not only with the people but with the politicians, and from the very nature of the case I must treat in some detail of Garfield's struggle with the latter. It constitutes, indeed, the salient feature of his short occupancy of the White House, dominating if not completely filling that chapter in American history which is devoted to his presidency. All through this struggle he counted heavily upon the aid and advice of Whitelaw Reid. The interest of their correspondence lies largely in what it exhibits of political developments behind the scenes.

There is a passage in the biography from "Ohio in the War" that is apposite here. Garfield, it says, "once recorded his vote, solitary and alone, against that of every other voting member of the House, on a call of the yeas and nays. But he is not factious; and, without ever surrendering his independence of judgment, he is still reckoned among the most trusty of the Radical majority." In other words, a good party man, the friend of every party measure that seemed to him sound, sympathetic to a firm policy of party discipline, accustomed to work in harmony with party organization. Wherefore, with impish irony, the Fates decreed that he should inherit, as the Republican candidate, some of the bitterest factional dissensions that ever afflicted any party! We have seen how they manifested themselves at Chicago. The truce called with the adoption of a ticket was hardly more than nominal. It left unimpaired the cleavage in the Republican ranks which had persistently widened under the administration of Hayes. The Third Termers who had howled for Grant, the "Stalwarts," with the envenomed Roscoe at their head, continued to nourish hot hatred against the "Half Breeds" who had seized the balance of power. Now, in the domain of practical politics this boded ill for Garfield. If his administration was to be a success, if he was to put his measures through the legislative mill, he needed an infinitely more tactful understanding with Congress than Hayes had been able to establish. He had to beat Hayes in the difficult art of getting a united party behind him, to achieve this earlier and more durably, and as the convention broke up it was clear that he would be kept more than busy with the task. Hence the steady recurrence in his exchanges with Reid of a keen anxiety as to matters calling for judicious political management. Garfield had wisdom in public affairs. He had discretion, too, and the precious faculty of making friends. "Personally he is generous, warm hearted, and genial," says Reid, in the memoir aforementioned. "No man keeps up more cordial relations with his political antagonists." It was an open question as to whether he would be equally successful in his relations with the malcontents in the house of his friends, where, in fact, geniality needed to be tempered with a good deal of the ruthless wariness of the serpent. Hay went to the root of the matter in one of his humorous ejaculations: "As you will see Garfield before I do, I hope you will inoculate him with the gall which I fear he lacks."

The one thing which Reid and Hay both wished for their friend was a clear vision amid the plots and counterplots thickening around him. Their counsel was directed toward his obtaining the whip-hand over those selfish political influences which he could afford neither to accept nor to ignore. The measure of Reid's solicitude, and of the frankness characterizing their intercourse, is given in his first letter following the nomination:

New York,
June 12th, 1880.

My dear General:

You got away from Chicago much earlier than I expected, or I should have said to you what I now set down below. First of all, I beg of you to make no promises to anybody. Hundreds of others will probably say the same thing. I however have seen such misfortunes resulting from hasty promises by Presidential candidates that I am specially anxious to impress the point. Don't be misled by the idea that this man or that man is necessary to secure the German vote. Mr. X. will be especially earnest and prompt in impressing upon you his importance. I don't believe he has anything like the influence with which he is credited, and I am sure that the early promise he extorted from Hayes four years ago was unfortunate. . . . One final word; please don't make any journeys or any speeches. E. V. Smalley has just been telling me that you are likely to go on to Washington to close up your house. I hope that even this can be avoided. There is no place where you can do so much for your supporters and be so comfortable yourself, from now on until November, as on your farm.

Very truly yours,
Whitelaw Reid.

Garfield had to go to Washington just then, for papers which no one but himself could gather up, but, he added in telling Reid this, "I shall make the trip as quietly and quickly as possible—and you may be sure I shall continue as I am, wholly untrammelled by pledges." So precautionary a policy might seem incongruous enough, and even a little derogatory to the dignity of a presidential candidate; but in glancing, as I have said, behind the scenes, one comes closer to the human issues involved and learns something more of the problems with which a man in Garfield's position has to contend. Some commentators have thought that he "blundered" in the course of his duel with Roscoe Conkling. As a matter of fact, we can only wonder that he postponed open warfare as long as he did. In illustration of the ineffable Stalwart's statesmanlike conduct I may cite a single incident. When in Washington Garfield called upon him, but he was not at home. He returned the call, but in his turn found that the candidate was out. Garfield presently wrote, suggesting an appointment, but received no reply, and the explanation of Conkling's silence edifyingly illuminates his nature. It seems that on completing some business at the Interior Department Garfield quite casually fell in with Schurz, who was on his way to a cabinet meeting. They rode a short distance together, since they were both going in the same direction, and this, as it happened, was enough to breed trouble. Some zealous tell-tale rushed off to inform the senator from New York that at the very moment when he was waiting in vain on Garfield's door-step that heedless being was actually "riding publicly with Schurz," and the damning news drove Roscoe into the sulks!

Could silliness any further go? Yet, I repeat, the success of Garfield's administration hinged in a measure upon the pacification of that silliness. The New York delegation in Congress was an important factor. Conkling could be helpful or harmful, as he chose. Reid's exasperated comment recognizes the fact. "I know how trivial, beggarly things of this sort," he says, "have turned awry enterprises of great pith and moment in past campaigns." Practically all things were in train for victory in the State. Garfield, as he pointed out, did not need to do anything to secure the support of the Hayes Republicans; he had them already. All the Civil Service reformers, nearly all the Independents, nearly all the Liberal Republicans, most of the college-bred men, who formed the bulk of the scratching element, were with him anyway. But the Stalwarts remained incalculable, if not pretty certainly inimical. There was promise of an opportunity to smoke them out in August, when a joint meeting in New York of the National and Congressional Committees brought Garfield on to confer with the leading politicians of both factions. He hesitated at first about coming and asked Reid's advice. It was only grudgingly favorable to the journey. "In general," he said, "I don't believe in running after the malcontents. Let them run after you. More than enough was done for conciliation when Arthur was taken. They can't help themselves, and, if they could throw away the State they dare not. They want promises about office. They haven't any right to them. Nobody has." He reported Conkling as "behaving like a spoiled child." But he counselled his friend to make the trip, adding an allusion to a book of Froude's that they had both recently been reading: "Do you remember how Cæsar, during the campaign in Gaul, frequently had to accept situations which were manufactured for him by the commanders of his legions? He knew they were not the best, but circumstances made them necessary, and his genius made them the means of triumph." Garfield took the Roman's philosophy to heart. He girded up his loins. He came, he saw, he conquered. And Conkling promised to be good. Only he wasn't there to make the promise in person to the candidate, a circumstance adding one more cynically amusing touch to the story of his perfunctory relation to the campaign. Reid thus discloses the point after Garfield had returned to Mentor:

New York,
August 15th, 1880.

My dear General:

The newspapers will have shown you already that Mr. Conkling has announced his willingness to go to work, and that the date for his appearance in New York is fixed. One of his close friends, U. S. Marshal Sayre, told me yesterday that he had spent two hours with him that day, and gave me a summary of the talk. Briefly stated it was George William Curtis that drove him away from the conference; not Blaine or Sherman. These it would seem he could have stood, but the idea of "conferring" with Mr. Curtis was too much for him. Payn, Platt and others of his close friends have talked to him with great plainness, not to say severity. His answer is that he is in the hands of his friends and will do whatever they ask. They have already asked that he speak first here, then in Indiana and Ohio, and they are thinking of asking that he also go to Maine. This last, I suspect, would be a dose hard to take, and I doubt whether it will be pressed upon him.

Everything I have seen since the conference convinces me that it turned all our way, that every point was made, and that the only one in any way injured by it was Mr. Conkling himself. Energetic action on his part is now a necessity and so it may prove that his behavior at the time of the conference will after all result in real good for the campaign. He is undoubtedly of great value on the stump, especially in this State, and we shall now have him as active as he can be.

Very truly yours,

WHITELAW REID.

At last the hatchet was, momentarily, buried, and Conkling did excellent service with that eloquence of his, the virtue of which, as a political asset, nobody could deny. The Maine "dose" was, wisely, not forced to his lips. He spoke in New York, in Ohio and Indiana, and in all three States with effects to which The Tribune paid becoming tribute. But neither in that paper nor amongst any Republicans conversant with the inside workings of the campaign, was there any disposition to overestimate the weight of his influence or to accept the idea of it current in his own tabernacle. Hay, as always on these topics, is refreshing. "I have heard," he says, "some incredibly ridiculous things about Conkling's demeanor. He really thinks he is the Savior of the Situation, and makes no bones about it." He made no bones about it either before or after the election, but he was to discover that others besides Hay could take a view of his pretensions drastically divergent from his own. It is a subject to which we shall return.

The devotion to Garfield's interests which broadly marks Reid's private correspondence at this time is reflected in every issue of his paper, which performed really magnificent services for the candidate and the party in the campaign of 1880. "The Tribune," wrote Hay, "seems as incapable of fatigue or exhaustion as if it were made of steel." To Reid, both as a personal friend and adviser, and as an editorial supporter, Garfield was profoundly grateful, and after election their counsels were, if anything, closer than before. Walter Phelps, writing from Vienna, put into words the thought common to many observers of what Reid had done to help secure Republican success. "The various consuls are all eager over Cabinet appointments," he said. "When I see how much they make of it all, I catch myself wishing that you were personally and conspicuously to get some of it, for you have contributed wonderfully to the attainment of it. I wish there were left a conspicuous Tribune man, who could wear the crown for you. Or, if it were only known to a larger circle, that Hay was your old and intimate friend, he could furnish a nice conductor for your lightning. 'Oh, yes. Hay's in to represent Reid.'" But Reid had no favors to ask. The friendship between him and Garfield was never more disinterested, on both sides, than when the herculean task of forming an administration was faced.

Neither was there any other period, in their long association, at which Garfield leaned more confidently upon his old comrade for criticism and suggestion. He had need of both, a circumstance repeatedly receiving earnest attention in Hay's letters. After election, warning its readers against idle speculation anent the composition of the new cabinet, The Tribune added the assurance of one precious fact, that it would be Garfield's own, "not that of President Hayes, in whole or in part." Hay came upon this paragraph only as it was quoted in some exchange, with additions dragging in obscure implications of Conkling's having something to do with the matter, and straightway he clamored for information.

Washington,
November 6th, 1880.

DEAR REID:

What did you mean any how? If you have got a "straight tip" don't be mean about it—but divide. Has he given hostages? All the boys on the Row have Cabinets made—but your information is more direct than other people's and, I take it, was given you to use—hence, therefore, (as Henry Clews says) give me a wink.

Your announcement in The Tribune about the Cabinet taken in connection with the "Herald's" two columns of gibbery gosh has caused all the damfools here to think that Conkling is to name the Cabinet and run the Administration. Of course you meant nothing of the sort. As a general proposition, a new President should have a new Cabinet. But Conkling did not carry New York, as you know, and it would be a fatal error for Garfield to abdicate at the start. There is infinitely more reason why you should name the New York member than why R. C. should.

J. H.

Reid assuaged his anxiety, telling him that no man in the United States better understood than Garfield did how Conkling had tried to keep out of the campaign, and how he had only come in when he had found that the party was going on without him. "I am glad to hear you say that," Hay replied. "Conkling is not in the least formidable when opposed or ignored. He has not in the least embarrassed this Administration and could not embarrass Garfield's. Besides, he will not quarrel with Garfield. He has learned something in four years. But he will pull down any Administration that surrenders to him. The work of electing Garfield, after Indiana and Ohio, was in New York City and Brooklyn and Connecticut, and Roscoe Conkling clearly did not do it. If you go to Mentor give our great and good friend all the wisdom you have got on the cabinet question. He will need it. Every despatch I have seen from Washington, Columbus or Cleveland, on that subject, is not only unutterably base and grovelling in spirit, but portentous of disaster, if certain influences get control." As the weeks ran on his fears only increased.

In December he reiterates his adjuration: "I hope you will go to Mentor before very long—not for any special interest, but simply because this is the time when G. is making the future of his administration. Deadbeats and office-seekers there will be in plenty—but he needs to talk occasionally with a strong, disinterested friend, who knows men."

The foregoing remarks of Hay's date from a time when he himself was the object of flattering proposals from the new President, though he did not know it. While he was thinking about Garfield, Garfield was thinking about him, thus:

Mentor, Ohio,
December 7th, 1880.

DEAR REID:

I am more at a loss to find just the man for Private Secretary, than for any place I shall have to fill. The man who holds that place can do very much to make or mar the success of an administration. The position ought to be held in higher estimation than Secretary of State. There is one man who fills my ideal of the fidelity, comradeship, culture, statesmanship, acquaintance with men, and address required to make that place one of power and brilliancy. But I suppose he is wholly beyond my reach. I mean John Hay. I would not dare to ask him, for I know he deserves very much more. But he could double my strength, and give me a great sense of security on the most dangerous side of the White House. Tell me if it is altogether preposterous to think of it as a possibility, for a year at least. I beg you to say nothing to Hay unless you are sure he would not be displeased at the suggestion.

Very truly yours,

J. A. GARFIELD.

Reid was less hopeful this time than he had been when Evarts came to him to lure Hay into the State Department. He wrote to Hay, and with no encouraging results. "I am greatly pleased and complimented," came the reply, "but I do not see how I can do it. It will cost me about $10,000 a year, beyond the salary, and the work is terrific. I mean the bores. Not a dozen have even spoken to me this year outside of this Department.

I could not stand a million of them." When Garfield failed to advance the project through Reid he opened negotiations himself, but no more successfully. Hay's letter to Reid, describing the correspondence and its upshot, contains some passages of interest as explaining why his refusal of the private secretaryship meant for him a temporary retirement from public life. "This ends," he says, "any possibility of employment for me by this administration. For after declining so intimate a place with Garfield, I cannot accept what Blaine offers, with decency, even if I wanted to." And a few days later he continues: "I am very sorry this matter came up. Garfield will be good natured about it, of course, but he will be disappointed and it will make a little cloud on our relations which I shall greatly regret. But I could not, with my eyes open, go into such a false position, where the work he would expect me to do would be, so to speak, absolutely unconstitutional,—a sort of general meddling with all the other departments. In short, the place does not suit. As to my holding it a little while and then taking something else, it would be the worst possible taste. No matter who a man is, if a President appoints his Private Secretary to an important post, it is in the public view a glaring and indecent piece of favoritism." So on leaving the State Department he went back to the literary life—with a journalistic interlude to which we shall presently have occasion to refer. In the meantime he continued to discuss with Reid the all-engrossing topic of the period just before the inauguration—the building of the cabinet.

I have spoken of Garfield's political temperament as that of the good party man. It was manifested throughout his cabinet developments. It was certain, as The Tribune had announced, that the cabinet would be his own. But he was resolved to do everything in his power to bring it into harmony with the sentiments of the party leaders. His view of the matter comes out in a letter written at the height of the campaign, when there were disquieting stories floating about on the possibility of his taking over one of Hayes's men.

Mentor, Ohio,
October 7th, 1880.

My dear Reid:

In answer to the rumor that I have made some arrangement with Mr. Schurz which includes or implies a seat in the Cabinet for him, I have to say that there is no foundation whatever for the story. My idea of the construction of a cabinet requires such choices as will realize the prevailing wishes of the Republican party, and it is clear to me that his appointment would displease a large majority of the party. For this and for other reasons I have never entertained the thought of doing so—and shall not.

Very truly yours,
J. A. Garfield.

The one choice he was inclined to make, even though this had been against party sentiment—which was not the case—the choice of Blaine, was delayed, curiously, by the hesitations of that statesman himself. There is something almost comically ironical in the circumstance, as though the topsyturvydom of politics could not by any possibility be escaped. Here was Garfield beset by factional issues in the making of his cabinet, feeling sure that in picking the right man for the premiership he would not only please himself but the dominant wing of the party and an immense body of public opinion. Yet the right man balked! Indeed, his mood on the subject was so uncertain, even as his closest friends observed it, that the President-elect could not tell whether to make him an offer or not. Garfield sought light on the problem from Reid. They had a conference in Washington early in December, and on the way back to New York Reid and Blaine happened to share the same compartment. Garfield wanted to know "if he had any indications of the tone of his fellow traveller." Reid could only reply: "He left on my mind the impression that he could be induced to take it, although I don't think his mind is yet clearly made up." Hay, in frequent communications, revealed the same dubiety, but finally, on December 22d, wrote, saying: "I had a pretty full talk with Blaine yesterday. I think he will take the place if it is offered, and he evidently expects it to be offered—if it has not been. Nichol thinks it has not been, but will be. Some of us—who are 'steady and wise'—ought to be authorized by Garfield to go to Blaine and ascertain that the appointment will be accepted, before the formal offer is made. It would not do to have it formally made and declined. Give me all the wisdom you have got." Two days later Reid wrote to Walter Phelps that Blaine was "considering" whether to take the secretaryship of state in case it was offered to him. "My opinion is," he added, "that I can get it offered to him the day I can convey the assurance that he will certainly take it." And then, within twenty-four hours, he had a letter from Blaine, saying that he didn't relish the rumors flying around in regard to the secretaryship, and intimating that he might go off in March to join Phelps for six or eight months of European travel! Matters thereupon promptly came to a head, and before the new year Reid could write this letter:

New York,
December 31st, 1880.

My dear W. W. P.:

In the deepest confidence, the head of the Cabinet is fixed. Mr. Blaine has been offered the Secretaryship of State and has accepted, and it is mutually agreed that nobody but their wives shall know it for some weeks or months yet. I am told as having been consulted in the matter from the outset by both. About the 20th January Blaine and I are to go out to Mentor for a consultation, very secretly, in a private car already at our disposal for the trip. By that time the Cabinet will begin to take shape.

Next, as to you. It is agreed, and to do Blaine full justice he had thought of it just as quick as I, that you are to have the Italian mission. You are to take Italy because the climate suits you and because the classical surroundings will specially interest you.

Allison is much talked of for Secretary of the Treasury. There seems a chance for Depew on the Senatorship. Platt and Morton are both keen, but Conkling doesn't decide. I'm to go to Albany Sunday night, to tell our friends that they'll be defended if they defy Conkling and that they won't lose the good graces of Garfield. Over this last we've had a dinner here tonight, Blaine, Depew, Robertson and some others, and they've only just left me.

Faithfully yours,

W. R.

It is precisely as in a play. With action and counteraction the interests of the central personage, Garfield, are alternately advanced and threatened, the climax is postponed—and, in this case, Roscoe Conkling is always the villain of the piece. The premiership had been settled, yes, but now was to arise "the Senatorship." An observation of Hay's comes perfectly between the lowering of the curtain upon one act of the drama and its elevation upon another. "It would do you good to hear Sherman talk," he says. "He is just itching for the beginning of Conkling's fight against the administration —which he thinks inevitable." Sherman's itch was to be relieved without delay.

CHAPTER III

GARFIELD'S FAMOUS FIGHT

In the matter of the senatorship Conkling had the choicest of opportunities for the indulgence of his whim for political *sabotage*. The term of his Democratic colleague at Washington, Francis Kernan, was to expire on March 4th, 1881. In January, at Albany, the legislature was to designate his successor. Whether that successor went to the capital a Garfield or a Conkling Republican was to both men a question of signal importance, for reasons on which I have already made sufficient comment. And there were wheels within wheels to be considered in this affair. At the Chicago convention certain members of the New York delegation, led by Judge W. H. Robertson—a gentleman from whom we shall hear again, in the last and most exciting act of the drama—had made the bolt which brought about the rejection of Grant. Conkling, of course, had marked down their scalps for future lifting, and in this tussle over the senatorship he was, above all things, anxious so to control the decision that it would deprive them of any hope of recognition from the new President.

At the dinner-party at Reid's, mentioned at the close of our preceding chapter, plans were laid not only for the defeat of Conkling, which was desired in any case, but for the protection of the so-called "recalcitrant" legislators, the men at Albany who were, as a matter of fact, the flower of the flock. Reid thus described to Garfield what he and his guests had arranged:

New York,
January 1st, 1881.
1 o'clock A.M.

My dear General:

Blaine has written a strong "by authority" announcement which he wants me to print, double leaded, at the head of the editorial columns on Monday morning, to the effect that the Administration is not to be used as a make-weight in the Senatorial contest, and specially not against the [Chicago] seventeen. He is clear that it is best to put it in the most emphatic, semi-official way, and on his advice I shall do it—though I don't generally go very far in that way.

It really looks as if we had a chance to carry. At any rate we shall show that Mr. Conkling doesn't own the State. Half his strength at present consists in the belief, which his friends are everywhere inculcating, that he is to control your administration absolutely, and that all its patronage will be wielded against the men who dare to oppose him.

There is absolutely no change in his feeling or that of his people towards you. They mean to confront you with the two Senators from the State, and to demand the entire patronage of the State. In a word they mean to be your masters, and when you submit they will like you well enough. But they don't trust you; even their common mode of alluding to you shows their feeling. It is always "this man Garfield."

The happiest of New Years to you and yours,

Always faithfully yours,

Whitelaw Reid.

The "by authority" blast duly appeared, serving notice that the administration was to be for the whole Republican party, not for any faction of it, and thereby rousing the Conkling organs throughout the State to the highest pitch of wrath. They were furious because it "exploded the lie about the Treaty of Mentor," that ingeniously spread canard which in November John Hay had reported as causing all the "damfools" in his neighborhood to expect Conkling to name the cabinet and run the administration. With the political atmosphere rendered portentously electrical, the battle was joined.

Depew was Reid's candidate, which is to say the man upon whom the anti-Conkling forces pinned their hopes, and in a letter of Reid's to Walter Phelps there is a passage showing in what a disinterested spirit the railroad man went into the fight. "Depew," runs the letter, "has a fixed income now of about ten thousand dollars a year; and when he came to consult with me about it we agreed that with that amount sure he could afford to go into politics and neglect money-making for the future. For this neglect he deliberately throws away, as he says himself, the assurance of a great fortune which he can easily make in the next ten years. Vanderbilt dislikes to give him up, but will give him his moral backing." Alack and alas for Depew's unworldly hopes! A sacrifice other than that of fortune was soon put before him. The combat raged at Albany day after day. The friends of the half-dozen candidates in the field exhorted, canvassed, pulled wires, and raised, in short, one of the most fearsome rumpuses to which the State capital had ever echoed. And for their pains they got a maddening deadlock. It turned out truly enough that, as Reid had said, Conkling wasn't to decide the issue. In vain did General Arthur, flinging to the winds the discretion—to say the least—implied in his position as vice-president-elect, hurry to Albany to do what he could for Conkling's candidate and his own personal friend, Congressman Crowley. Though the anti-machine men could not have their way, they could, and did, impose the same deprivation upon their opponents. Reid was in Washington for a state dinner at the White House when the struggle approached its climax, and in the multitude of his papers there is nothing more pungently redolent of the smoke of political warfare, of the lightning-like mutations in the ancient game of campaigning, than the sheaf of despatches disclosing how the decision was made.

Since the anti-machine men couldn't rally sufficient

support for Depew, they were willing to take, rather than Crowley, whom they simply wouldn't take at all, ex-Congressman Thomas C. Platt. A machine man, unquestionably, was the only candidate with whom the deadlock could be broken. To that extent Conkling was a victor. But the choice of Platt was regarded at the time as robbing Conkling of any substantial laurels. In view of subsequent events the record of this circumstance reads to-day a little quaintly; yet it is nevertheless true that in January, 1881, Platt had not foreshadowed the peculiar eminence of his later career. The machine, indeed, so far from seeing in him one of its brightest lights, suspected him of a dangerous disposition to "set up for himself." The antis took the same view of him. Though nobody expected him to break with Conkling, he seemed the man—after Depew—most likely to deal with the senior senator on independent terms. He realized perfectly that he could not take over Depew's strength in the legislature and win the race without ratifying this impression, and he was ready to give guaranties. His offer of these was put before Reid, who forthwith set the wires humming. He received the proper assurances from Platt. He advised Depew to withdraw. The penultimate despatch in the collection I have mentioned is one from Depew, saying: "I saw him [Platt] last night and transferred the decisive strength." Amid the solemnities of the White House banquet aforesaid, which was given to the justices of the supreme court and had a particularly ceremonious tempo, came the last despatch of all, stating that Platt had been elected.

The first stiff engagement had terminated in something like a draw, but with the scales inclining toward Garfield. It seemed to have contributed toward the smoothing out of his path, and Reid wrote to Mentor in fairly cheerful vein:

New York,
January 16th, 1881.

My dear General:

The inside facts as to the Senatorial election are these.

Platt had the most alliances with us, and our people made excellent terms. He gave me personal pledges which insure not only fair but friendly general treatment. To Depew he pledged himself that—

1. He would countenance no effort at crushing or ignoring the Chicago bolters.

2. He would not oppose their getting either from State or Nation their fair share of patronage.

3. He would not oppose their confirmation, if any of them should come before the Senate, but on the contrary would do all in his power to help it.

4. He would help in the prompt confirmation of your Cabinet—even in so extreme a case as the possibility of its containing the name of Judge Robertson—though much opposed to such a nomination.

5. He would do all he could (not much, probably) to keep Conkling reasonable.

On these conditions Depew transferred to him twenty votes, and thus nominated him, on the first ballot, by one majority. He has since acknowledged his indebtedness to those votes, and to that agreement preceding, for his nomination.

Faithfully yours,

Whitelaw Reid.

There was exasperation as well as satisfaction in this settlement of the business. It irked Reid beyond measure that, while the serious problems of a presidential administration were toward, it should be obligatory upon anybody to "keep Conkling reasonable." Garfield was too big a man to be thus handicapped by a petty politician, and in any event the whole thing was offensive in principle to a man dealing on high grounds with public affairs. But I have referred before this to Reid's habit of facing facts. The ineffable Roscoe and the political conditions that had grown up around him were inexpugnable facts. The boss's following was as impermeable to reason as the boss himself. "The difficulty," said Reid to Garfield, "is that New York politicians have now been so long under the Conkling harrow that they do not have the courage of their convictions." But the new senator seemed bent upon rising above the status of a toad. His protestations of good faith were too ardent and explicit to be doubted and Reid was unfeignedly hopeful that the last had been heard of a troublesome possibility. "Platt has been in to renew allegiance," he wrote to Hay. "He means it. What we now look to is a broadening of the machine, with our fellows in and a united party, minus Conkling, who won't last forever! Platt's last words to me were, 'I am yours to command; draw on me at sight.'" Cabinet-making went on apace.

It enriched the correspondence that flowed between Mentor and New York with a multitude of suggestions and personalities. Hay often took part in the discussion, as Blaine did, and Reid transmitted to Garfield the result of numerous consultations with Thurlow Weed, whose long experience and ripe counsel gave his ideas great weight with everybody concerned. He had—the wise old politician—a keen sense of just what the situation required politically. Reid suggested that Joseph H. Choate would make a good cabinet officer. The sage praised the idea, said it was a good thing to turn over in the mind—but he feared Choate knew too little about politics. Levi P. Morton is a figure to be noted at this juncture. He had a startling way of suddenly posing Reid with a momentous question as to his own career. Thus, prior to the convention, he offered this paralyzing query: "As there appears to be a serious idea in certain quarters of using my name as a candidate for the Vice Presidency, I shall feel obliged if you will give me frankly and freely your advice as to my course of action in case it becomes necessary for me to assent or dissent from proposed action by others in that direction." Later, when the conflict at Albany was developing, his name was again in the field, but, as I have shown, the cabinet was being constructed, too, and that also had an interest for him. Once more he turned to Reid. "In case the choice of the Senatorship, or Secretaryship of the Treasury offers," he asks, "which would you advise me to take?" Reid had to do a lot of thinking for his friends in those days. Yet it is plain from his correspondence, as I may appropriately note here, that the only one for whose interests he really gave up his nights and days was Garfield. "I care precious little," he says, almost on the eve of inauguration, "about the men appointed, but am intensely anxious about men who should not be appointed." He thought well of Wayne MacVeagh for the attorney-generalship, as he did of Thomas L. James for postmaster-general, and said so, speaking as freely as he had naturally always spoken about Blaine, but his hardest work was done in threshing out all the pros and cons of specious candidacies.

A glint of humor is occasionally struck forth from these latter processes. There was a time when Garfield thought of asking Judge Charles J. Folger into his cabinet. He wanted Judge Robertson's views on the idea, which were expressed in this terse communication:

Albany,
January 25th, 1881.

MY DEAR REID:

With two stalwart Senators and Vice President from the State, the incoming Administration could in no other way so effectually put our Independent delegates to the Chicago Convention in a political metallic casket, hermetically sealed, as by placing in the Cabinet a stalwart from New York. It would surely give the delegation from the State to Grant, Conkling or Cornell in 1884.

Yours very truly,
W. H. ROBERTSON.

Exit, upon this, Judge Folger. He had to wait until Arthur came into power, when he was made secretary of the treasury.

There remains one other episode, illustrative of Garfield's perplexity and of the diplomatic excursions it prompted, which in its oddity is perhaps the most interesting of all. Talking the problem over with Reid, Blaine struck out the suggestion that the secretaryship of the treasury should be politely offered to Conkling himself! The chances were a hundred to one that he would decline. But suppose he accepted? Then he was fairly harnessed to Garfield's car. There was no chance for him to make a great reputation, for Sherman had reaped the laurels of the department, and for twenty years to come no man could do anything there which would not look feeble or small by the side of Sherman's success. On the other hand, if he declined, his mouth and the mouths of all his friends were forever sealed. Walter Phelps, writing from Nice, made the wittiest of comments upon this Machiavellian scheme. "The offer to Conkling would be genius," he says. "Just getting it, I have no time for an opinion—whether it would be sense." Garfield received the suggestion with the remark that he had for some weeks been thinking of the same thing himself, but as he and his counsellors deliberated they united on rejecting it. Weed strongly opposed, and Robertson frankly stigmatized the idea as nothing more nor less than an omen of certain disaster. When, about the middle of February, Conkling astonished the quidnuncs by paying a visit to Mentor, and there was a general feeling that olive-branches were waving in the air, the most hazardous of all devices for keeping them there had been definitively abandoned.

The cabinet was still inchoate, with inauguration day hardly more than a fortnight in the future. Nevertheless, Garfield awaited the ordeal at Washington with unruffled spirit, confident that even at the eleventh hour he would be able to reconcile the jarring elements in the situation. To do that he was resolved to stay both open-minded and firm. The frame of mind in which he approached the moment for decisive action is reflected down to the last shade, I think, in a sentence casually falling into one of his letters to Reid: "I ought to be ready for fight but should not begin it." On this diplomatic key-note the scene shifts from Mentor to the national capital.

In traversing what Garfield did there in the launching of his administration, the purpose of an historian would ordinarily be served by noting simply the names of the men finally chosen to assist him. But my own object, as I have said before, is to expose the human comedy hidden behind the official pageant, and in Reid's correspondence this is revealed in such wise as to convey more than ever the impression of swiftly moving drama. It appears especially in letters to Miss Mills, who was soon to become his wife. These constitute in some sort a daily, almost hourly, journal of the events in which Reid and Garfield's other friends shared, as they rallied around him in Washington, and I cite them in that form:

Washington,
March 1st, 1881.

The Cabinet is now made up as follows:

Secretary of State,	Jas. G. Blaine.
" " the Treasury,	Wm. Windom.
" " " Interior,	W. B. Allison.
" " War,	Robert Lincoln.
" " the Navy,	L. P. Morton.
Post Master General,	Judge Hunt.
Attorney General,	Wayne MacVeagh.

Morton has accepted the Navy. So we have carried our exact point there, and Conkling is at once utterly foiled and left without any cause of quarrel. The grave uncertainty is as to whether Allison can be persuaded to take the Interior, and on this point I am asked to do missionary work, if needful, tonight. Allison and I are, as perhaps you know, old friends. He would have taken the

Treasury, but both Garfield and Blaine are doubtful about the Interior. He is now with Garfield, having been sent for, to the Senate, an hour ago. I saw MacVeagh's invitation mailed before coming up to my room. Lincoln, Morton and Blaine have already accepted. Windom's letter has not been sent, and probably will not be till the Allison matter is decided.

Washington,
March 2nd, 1881.

The storm over the Cabinet is lively. Blaine is up in arms against Windom. At one o'clock last night the Conkling people got Morton out of bed and spent the night "bulldozing" him into a refusal to accept the Navy. Allison last night refused the Interior. Blaine an hour ago wanted to unite our forces on James as Post Master General, if that concession to New York would secure in turn an agreement to Allison in the Treasury. Garfield appealed to me to suggest some man from New York, if Morton refused, and declared that he was tempted to appoint Judge Robertson himself, the very head and front of the anti-Conkling people. But that will surely not be done.

Washington,
March 2nd, 1881.

The Cabinet has changed like a kaleidoscope. After finally agreeing again to accept the Navy Department, Morton has finally been worried out of it by the Conkling people, and has written a letter withdrawing his consent. This happened while I was at the White House. Blaine then patched up a new deal, thus:

Allison, Treasury.
Hunt, Interior.
Baldwin, Navy.
James, Post Master General.

Garfield assented to this if I would be responsible for James's loyalty to him rather than Conkling, and messengers were straightway sent after me. They hunted at the hotel, the office, the State Department, Hay's house, and pretty much everywhere excepting at the White House. But I went over soon, encountered Blaine at the door, was rushed into his carriage and driven up home;—then before the parlor fire, with the servant told nobody was at home, had the story told, and was urged to communicate with James. I went first to Garfield's, talked it all over with him, and then telegraphed James to come on, on the night train. I'm a little afraid of it yet, but it looks as if the plan would work. The policy is to detach James from Conkling and make him feel that he owes his appointment to that, and to his volunteered pledge to me last Monday.

Washington,
March 3rd, 1881.

Since eight o'clock, when I was waked by a tremendous knocking at the door by a passenger just off the New York train, I've had an embryo Post Master General on my hands,—with charges to keep him out of harm's way, and particularly to keep him away from his old political associates. So I took him first—after telling him why I had telegraphed for him, and just what the stage of the affair was—to Mr. Blaine's. The Maine statesman was still in bed but in time we got him out. He was delighted, and wanted the interview over with Garfield at once. So I took him over at once, caught Garfield's boy at the door, whisked James into a private room, and in three minutes had them together without the crowd's having discovered James's face. Garfield didn't even know him, and so I had to introduce the man to whom he was about to tender a Cabinet portfolio. Next I had to get Platt, and make him say that, while Conkling had nothing to do with this, and knew nothing of it, and had refused to recommend James or even mention him, he could not object with any reason, which he (Platt) fully approved. This I did,—taking Platt up and asking the questions myself in Garfield's presence. G. is greatly pleased. He does not make the absolute offer until he arranges the only unsettled place, the Navy, for which he is now thinking of Gresham of Indiana —having dropped Baldwin. Meantime he asked me to keep James as quiet as possible and to get him out of town on the afternoon train. It's done.

I'm not wildly enthusiastic, but it will be the most popular appointment that could be made from New York, and will placate all sensible Conkling people. James is profoundly grateful, and pledges loyalty in the strongest fashion, whether Conkling supports the administration or fights it, and you'll see that, while Conkling is as ignorant of it or of the intention of doing it as a baby, he and his friends will instantly claim it as his work.

Washington,
March 4th, 1881.
At Mr. Blaine's.

We are in a turmoil over Allison's action in refusing the Treasury. Today I was in the Reporters' Gallery of the Senate during the ceremonies there, and with the ladies of the Blaine household on the East portico during the delivery of the Inaugural—within three seats of the retiring and incoming Presidents. The procession I saw partly from James M. Varnum's room on the Avenue, and partly from Mrs. Gen. Sherman's at the Quarter Master General's office. And then Walker Blaine brought me the bad news about Allison and that I was wanted at the White House whither his Father had gone. But when I got up the Williams College people were making a speech at poor Garfield in the East Room and there was little chance for anything else.

The real secret of Allison's defection is the state of his wife's health. The Blaine people have now been urging Gresham for the Treasury, but not with much success;—nor do I think the scheme deserves it.

Here dinner was served. Since then we've sent Wm. E. Chandler to Allison, with messages. The James matter is all right, apparently, and our New York people are generally pleased.

Washington,
March 5th, 1881.

The long agony, I suppose, is over. At half past twelve, when I left the new President, he had decided to send in his Cabinet at three this afternoon.

Conkling, in his interview with G. on the night of the 3rd, complained of the interference of "the tall young man from New York" in the Cabinet, while he, Conkling, had not been consulted. G. told me of it with a chuckle.

As the cabinet emerged from under the hands of its manufacturers, with every strong factor recognized in its composition, Grant as well as anti-Grant, Reid felt that he could congratulate Garfield on having a united party behind him. The outlook certainly had its auspicious aspects. The Forty-sixth Congress, in making its unlamented exit, promised to carry divers unfortunate elements and conditions into everlasting oblivion, and in the forthcoming reorganization of both houses Republican control assured the new administration a fair field for its measures. At the moment there appeared to be only one untoward situation in Washington, that to which Reid makes joking allusion in a letter to Blaine—"I hope everything goes well with you, and that the enormous rush of office hunters is getting a little diked and dammed out of the Department—most probably the latter." The clamor for jobs was beyond all precedent. Hay heard it rumbling all day long in the marble corridors of the State Department, like the sound of beasts at feeding-time. He described the President and the secretary of state as living in a whirlwind, fighting like baited bulls against the mob, hounded down by politicians from morning till midnight. The frogs of Egypt weren't a circumstance to the crowd surging around them. "Heaven preserve you from being President," he said. "I could be Secretary of State easily enough, because I am not genial and magnetic, and have no friends, God be thanked." I have no occasion, however, for pausing here upon any of the routine business of the new administration, or upon any of the serious matters that claimed attention, such as plans for a new funding bill, or the problems of Civil Service reform, or the Star Route inquiry, or the ever-troublous question of Southern patronage. I pass over all these things in deference to the leading motive of this chapter, the duel with Conkling, which now rapidly approached its bitterest stage. The New York senator's complaint that he "had not been consulted" was renewed, and this time under circumstances moving Garfield to indulgence in something far grimmer than a chuckle. Their conflict was revived when on March 23d the President sent a batch of nominations to the Senate, among them one to the most important office, outside the cabinet, within his gift—the collectorship of the port of New York. He named Judge Robertson for the post, and Conkling forthwith declared war to the knife.

Judge W. H. Robertson, of Westchester County, member of the State Senate in New York, was a man of character and ability whose services to the party had been conspicuously marked in the convention of 1880. It was his leadership of the independent group in the New York delegation that had made the defeat of Grant possible. But for him the New York bolt would never have occurred. But for the New York bolt the Pennsylvania bolt would never have occurred. And but for these bolts Grant would have gone through roughshod. Obviously, that particular achievement in his record which confirmed Garfield's regard for him could only make him more than ever the object of Conkling's hatred. The issue at the outset, when the nominations were sent in, was clearly enough drawn. The New York senator was out at once to revenge himself, by blocking confirmation, upon a political opponent who had beaten him in the earlier fight. But much more was really involved. The issue, as a matter of fact, went deeper. It bore upon the whole question of appointment to federal office. Did such appointment rest in the hands of the President, subject to confirmation by the Senate as a body, or was it only nominally so placed? Was the power in question to be vested actually, and as a matter of practical usage, in the senators of a given State, authorized by an unwritten law to control the federal patronage within their commonwealth, as a kind of personal perquisite? The settlement of this issue could not but have, of course, the most far-reaching effects, involving as it did the very life principle of administrative independence, and as the reader will have already foreseen, in the struggle over Robertson's nomination it was not his individuality that, strictly speaking, was concerned. He figured rather as a symbol. It was not so much his fate as the fate of the administration that was to be determined. That is why I have been at pains to exhibit Conkling's inimical attitude toward Garfield from the beginning, and must follow the story to the end.

The same despatches which bore to The Tribune news

of Robertson's nomination brought echoes of the wrath it had instantly roused in the Conkling camp. Platt gave the paper's Washington correspondent the views prevailing amongst the Stalwarts, and Reid prepared for action, at first a little incredulous as to the power of the boss to carry out his obstructive plans. "I have had the new Collector of the Port and Chauncey Depew here all morning," he wrote to Miss Mills on the 26th, "deep in political talk. Mr. Conkling is very mad and vicious; but I don't see how he can prevent Robertson's confirmation." The fight, however, was to be a stiff one, as he learned when Depew hurried in the next day with news of "a flank movement on the Judge." This was on Sunday, but Reid contrived to get hold of the facts in the situation and telegraphed them to Hay, to be presented by the latter in person to Garfield the first thing Monday morning. With the facts there went these sentences of solemn exhortation:

> I wish to say to the President that in my judgment this is the turning point of his whole Administration—the crisis of his Fate. If he surrenders now, Conkling is President for the rest of the term and Garfield becomes a laughing stock. On the other hand, he has only to stand firm to succeed. With the unanimous action of the New York Legislature [in ratifying Robertson] Conkling cannot make an effective fight. That action came solely from the belief that Garfield, unlike Hayes, meant to defend his own administration. The Assembly is overwhelmingly Conkling, but they did not dare go on the record against Robertson, so long as they thought the Administration meant business. In one word, there is no safe or honorable way out now but to go straight on. Robertson should be held firm. Boldness and tenacity now insure victory not merely for this year but for the whole term. The least wavering would be fatal.

This trumpet-call was long afterward to have some sensational reverberations. The despatch, at the time it was sent, was stolen from the wires, and when Garfield was in his grave it was maliciously published with representations that he had been a "puppet," amenable to the wire-pulling of Whitelaw Reid and others. Its simple aim, of course, was—in answer to his repeated written requests—to let him know the precise posture of affairs in New York politics, and I may remark in passing that as the investigation of the theft of the telegram went on, ultimately nailing the thief, the general verdict was that Reid had done his friend high service in communicating to him what Reid called "a great deal of frozen truth." Garfield listened to it with the deepest attention when Hay came over to the White House on Monday and read him the long despatch. "Robertson may be carried out of the Senate head first or feet first," he then grimly observed. "I shall never withdraw him."

A little later in the day the President had another visitor in the person of his postmaster-general. Mr. James brought with him a written protest against the nomination for the collectorship, signed by himself, Conkling, Platt, and—of all men in the world—Vice-President Arthur. The recipient of this preposterous document remained disappointingly unmoved. He told James politely enough that the nomination was none of his business. He should run the post-office and not fash himself about the New York Custom House. Platt turned up, not very ferocious, as Hay said, but protesting that if the President had only consulted him trouble might have been avoided. Garfield told him that he had had the right to believe him friendly to Robertson. The resolution with which he proceeded to deal with the crisis is shown in this letter:

Executive Mansion,
Washington,
March 30th, 1881.

My dear Reid:

After giving the majority wing of the Republican party almost every place in New York so that no one failed to see they were generously treated, the President nominated a prominent Republican of unquestioned ability to a place now held by a man whose appointment was resisted by the New York Senator. He considers himself affronted because he was not consulted. It is a worrying struggle of two years or a decisive settlement of the question now. It better be known, in the outset, whether the President is the head of the Government, or the registering clerk of the Senate. That question shall be settled by the confirmation or rejection of Robertson. I understand that efforts are being made to induce Robertson to decline. I hope he will not yield. It is the crucial test of the Administration. Do you know whether Gov. Cornell has taken a position on the question? He ought to be with us.

The course of Platt is extraordinary. He bases it upon the ground that he was not consulted. Suppose he had been? Would he then have voted for Robertson? If yes, on what ground of reason can he now vote no? In either case he would vote, not on the merits of the nominee, but upon the wholly irrelevant question of his being consulted.

As ever yours,

J. A. Garfield.

The situation in the Senate, meanwhile, was such as to threaten an indefinite prolongation of the most fatuous of deadlocks. From the opening of its special session on March 4th that august body had marked its reorganization by squabbling over the distribution of its own offices, the Democrats holding up the public business while they strove to retain those priceless plums. Such an exacerbated state of affairs was, naturally, just what Conkling required for the exploitation of his own hand and he undoubtedly made the most of it. Hay was dumfounded at the pusillanimity of the men who thus permitted themselves to be made parties to an ignoble intrigue. "Conkling seems to have a magic influence over them," he said. "They talk as bold as lions to me, or anybody else—and then they go into caucus, or the Senate, and if he looks at them they are like Little Billee in the ballad. They are a strange race." Nor was Conkling content with intimidating the Senate, and trying to intimidate the President. Part of his plan, as was to be expected, was to see if the hateful nominee himself could not be worked upon, and presently stories were running about that the strongest efforts were being made to persuade Robertson to withdraw. He did not know the doughty judge any better than he knew Garfield. "Under no circumstances," wrote the judge to Reid, "will I ask President Garfield to withdraw my nomination as Collector of the Port of New York; nor will I consent to its withdrawal. And this would be my course were the President's interests alone involved, as the withdrawal of my name at his instance or upon my request would make him Conkling's abject slave for the residue of his term."

Thus the quarrel stood as April advanced, Garfield and his nominee holding firm, with the enemy leaving no stone unturned to shake their purpose. A letter of Reid's written at this time gives a withering exposure of the stratagems to which the conspirators had recourse as their plot grew desperate:

New York,
April 11th, 1881.

My dear General:

Mr. Platt was here over Sunday. He had some important business matters to attend to with me, but he was so engrossed in politics that instead of coming as usual he barely sent me a hurried note. He has not been either at my house or office since the Robertson nomination.

What he came for, however, was to set on foot another of his devices for compromise. He sent U. S. Marshal Payn to a gentleman who, as he thought, could reach and possibly control Judge Robertson with an earnest appeal for a secret meeting between Judge Robertson and Mr. Platt in which a final effort was to be made to persuade the Judge to withdraw and take the U. S. District Attorneyship on the pledge that Mr. Conkling would not oppose his confirmation for that office, and that Merritt should be left in the Custom House. In the course of the conversation Payn revealed more than has yet been known to us of the inside of the Conkling situation. He admits frankly that last summer and fall Conkling was from the outset in favor of having you defeated. He was only pulled into the campaign at all by main strength, and all the time he kept protesting that he believed it was a mistake, and that "this man would cheat us yet," meaning thereby that this man would really not make over everything to them. Now he admits that Conkling has thrown off all disguises, and cannot be kept from speaking with the utmost bitterness and violence against you everywhere, avowing his personal contempt and hatred and his resolute purpose to do everything he can from this to the end of his term to break you down.

He recognizes clearly that this means the division of the Republican party in the State and probable defeat, but this makes no difference to him, as he has already made up his mind that he must leave politics at the end of this term, and go to work to earn some money. Payn further represents that Conkling has utterly abandoned all idea of the Presidency, or of any future whatever in politics, that he would resign now but for the Robertson row, and that his present purpose is to spend the next four years simply in wreaking his revenges. Platt, Payn, and the rest, of course, do not like this prospect. Whether Mr. Conkling has any political future or not, they think they ought to have, and their appeal to us therefore, is to save them from the destruction their own leader is about to bring upon them.

Of course all this is utterly unimportant save in one regard. It shows how absolutely you are master of the situation. The one thing to be done with a firm hand is to adhere to your own programme, sustain your friends and teach those who fight against you that they can have no favors from you. This done, Robertson is soon confirmed and Conkling will every month become more and more powerless. I really believe you have him where there is a chance to make an end of him, and of the corrupt, insolent and bullying elements which he has carried into our politics.

Faithfully yours,

WHITELAW REID.

The consummation devoutly to be wished, indicated at the close of this letter, was even then nearer than anybody guessed. And it was being brought nearer every minute by Garfield's steadfast stand. He thus replied:

Executive Mansion,
Washington,
April 18th, 1881.

DEAR REID:

Yours of the 11th was read with interest. The facts you give are quite fully confirmed by others of similar import. If the person in question has resolved on suicide and murder, he may not be able to enlist a very large force of followers. The cry which is giving them some strength here is that the confirmation of Robertson will inevitably defeat the party in New York. Arthur says he knows it. I answer, Yes, if the leaders determine it shall. Summed up in a word, Mr. C. asks me to withdraw Robertson to keep the other leaders of the party from destroying themselves. Of course I deprecate war, but if it is brought to my door the bringer will find me at home.

As ever yours,

J. A. Garfield.

Against this serene defiance of his the pertinacious malcontents wore themselves out, and while they fretted in vain over retaliatory schemes the Senate slowly apprehended the egregious spectacle it was presenting before the country. Preparations at last were made to go into executive session, and in May the legislators were ready to vote on federal appointments. Garfield, in his turn, was ready for those members who had sought to cow him into submission. In order to let them know exactly where he stood he withdrew all his New York nominations—save that of Robertson. The thrust went home. Conkling was beaten, he knew that he was beaten, and ten days later he publicly gave the measure of his chagrin in one of the most amazing acts ever committed by an American statesman. Balked of his aim to put Garfield's administration in his waistcoat pocket he resigned from the Senate, and Platt resigned with him. It was on Tuesday, May 17th, that the bizarre news was made public. On Wednesday, May 18th, a purged Senate confirmed the nomination of Judge W. H. Robertson to be collector of the port of New York.

If in his relation to this controversy President Garfield had been actuated by any small motives, the discomfiture of the two senators from New York was of a nature to give him the fullest satisfaction. The measure they adopted to salve their pride served only to render them ridiculous. Their histrionic departure from the scene, a play to the gallery as indiscreet as it was insincere, provoked a shout of derision that rang through the country. But I would recall again what Reid had written of Garfield in "Ohio in the War," long before: "Personally he is generous, warm hearted and genial." The fight over the collectorship had inspired in him contempt as well as wrath, yet there came to him no emotion of gratified spite; it was not because *he* had won that he rejoiced. The victory as he saw it was purely a victory for good government. The question settled was not one between himself and Roscoe Conkling. It was the question which we have seen him stating to Reid, "whether the President is the head of the Government, or the registering clerk of the Senate." The vote ultimately secured was nothing if not a vindication of Republicanism. This was the object all along pursued by Garfield and his friends. In the correspondence I have traversed, covering the whole period of the feud with Conkling from the date of the convention onward—and my extracts constitute only a small fraction of the mass—the personal note is necessarily sounded again and again. Yet the purpose of these men is plainly directed at just one impersonal thing—the expulsion of what Reid called the corrupt, insolent, and bullying elements in our politics. There is a characteristic saying of Hay's, written during the long pull over the cabinet, which may serve as a tag to this story of a fight for political freedom. "I think several things are working out right—i. e., as you and I think right—which is right enough for all practical purposes." They could be thus sure of themselves—Hay and Reid, Garfield and Blaine—for all they had in view, if my story proves anything, was an untrammelled, honest administration. Garfield was to be denied the opportunity to show what he could do through four years in the White House. But he had not been in the White House four weeks before he showed that what he did would be "right for all practical purposes." That is why the narrative of his battle with Conkling has here been set down in full.

CHAPTER IV

MARRIAGE AND TRAVEL

Garfield's election added to Reid's hard summer a harder winter. The most strenuous passages in the campaign, indeed, had imposed upon him no such strain as that of the teasing factional war I have just outlined. He had never drunk so deeply of the political cup and never before had it contained a more potent brew. At the same time there were, for him, no bitter dregs to drain. On the contrary, he had every reason to feel exhilarated and refreshed. In the triumph of the President, for which he had done a good share of the fighting, he could take the pride of a stanch Republican, and with this there went, of course, the gratification a man derives from the ascendancy of his friends. Garfield was now dominant over his foes. Blaine and MacVeagh were in the cabinet, and the only diplomatic appointment in which he had any interest, that of Walter Phelps, was one of the earliest sent in to the Senate. The proposal of a Roman mission I have already indicated. Subsequently Blaine was eager to have his friend take the post from which Hay was retiring in the State Department, but that did not prove acceptable, and Phelps was nominated, instead, minister to Austria. These and other things were well calculated to sustain Reid's spirit far above the power of a Conkling to annoy, and, as a matter of fact, he had much else to think about, though seemingly he had no energy to spare for anything save politics. This ever-burdened winter, packed with work and anxiety, was nevertheless the happiest in his life.

He was not always at his desk, a circumstance which Evarts quaintly mourned one night when he sought him out for political talk at his office, and found he had gone to the theatre. "I stopped at ten o'clock on my way down town from dinner," wrote the statesman, "but alas! too early for a radiant editor who, studying the scenery and actors of public life, all day, flies to the mimic scene and paid performers for substance and sincerity." Reid was indeed radiant at this time, but not all his friends knew it, and it will lend, I think, a certain delightful force of contrast to the picture if I quote here part of a letter from Walter Phelps:

Naples,
January 13th, 1881.

My dear Warwick:

Your letter of Christmas Eve finds me seeing Naples and not dead; and calls me quickly back from the dreams of the Mediterranean to the activities of the Hudson. But before plunging into the cauldron, which boils near your library table and cooks now a little Attorneyship and now a great Premiership, as under your stirring it throws to the top the head of a Shepard or a Blaine, I had rather pause a moment over the young and melancholy wizard. Every now and then the comical irony of fate, perhaps never better illustrated than in your own case, of which we are both conscious all along the years, comes to a head and especially forces our notice and comment.

And this Christmas Eve you were writing me, as I you, and about the same thoughts were in both minds, the one tabernacled in Florence, the other in New York. The great contrasts. Money abundant. The Wabash preferred made its profits just right for Christmas. Power never greater. The very division of the New York Legislature making your influence the more valuable. Garfield more than grateful. The possibility that one of your best friends, Blaine, would be chief of the Administration; that Grow would be Senator; that Hay or Lloyd would be Private Secretary; that future judgeships were measurably at your nomination—and you sit, in the centre of your own library, with heat and light and comfort and beauty about you, at Christmas Eve—alone. You clear your table, and go slowly up to your lonesome chamber, the most enviable man in that great metropolis, not knowing whether you are happy or not. If that is not the irony of fate, what is?

I would like to be home. And you—don't you think that unless you get married, of which I now despair, you would want to see me and have me around?

W. W. P.

With a stroke Reid turned his friend's "despair" to rejoicing, and completely routed "the irony of fate." In February he announced his engagement to Miss Elisabeth Mills, the only daughter of Darius Ogden Mills, of California and the East. Things political fell into the background. From Washington, in place of cabinet difficulties, came a letter like this:

Washington,
February 13th, 1881.

My dear Mr. Reid:

I congratulate you!
I congratulate Miss Mills!
I congratulate all your friends!
I congratulate all her friends!
I congratulate the readers of The Tribune!
And last but not least I congratulate myself!

It has my fullest approval and my warmest sympathy, though good as you are I do not see what you ever did to merit such good luck. I was very greatly impressed by the young lady the only time I ever talked with her. Had I been in single blessedness and a youngster like you, why then! why then! Miss Mills would have had one more to make miserable!

I am glad you have it bad! It is the healthiest and most delightful of sensations! Be just as "spooney" as you please, despise those who laugh, and see only your own world that is filled with light and joy—as it may indeed I trust be to both of you forever!!

I write propped up with pillows, having been suffering horribly all the week with gout, which I preferred should go to the public as rheumatism. This is my only autograph for the whole time—and only a great occasion could have called it out. My sincere regards to the young lady. God bless and preserve you both.

Sincerely,

J. G. Blaine.

The wedding followed not long after the announcement of their engagement. They were married in New York on April 26th, and after a brief visit to Reid's mother in Ohio they sailed in May for Europe, to be gone several months. On the eve of his marriage he was once more given the opportunity to consider taking public office. Garfield asked him to accept the Berlin mission. But Mrs. Mills's health was not firm and her daughter was unwilling to take up her home too far away from her. Nor was diplomacy just then to Reid's mind. He preferred to adopt Blaine's advice on the advantage of "seeing only his own world." In a letter to the President he said: "Don't bother your head about offices for me, but make the best fight you can, and make those Senators understand that this Administration intends to take care of itself at any cost. For the rest, if you still hanker after pleasing me personally, come over with Mrs. Garfield on the Limited Express next Tuesday morning." That Tuesday morning marked the glad relinquishment to other hands, for a time, of the stirring of the political caldron, and all its cognate interests. For the ensuing summer the editorship of the paper was left to John Hay.

From England and Scotland, where they spent their first weeks abroad, the Reids went for a rambling trip on the Continent. They visited Paris, Amsterdam, and Brussels, travelled down the Rhine into Switzerland, and from there went on to Italy. They saw Rome and made an extended stay in Venice. Turning northward, through the Austrian Tyrol, they continued on to Vienna, where Walter Phelps was now established as minister, and afterward paused in Berlin on their way back to London. It was just as they were starting on their Continental wanderings that the news of Garfield's assassination reached them, and thenceforth they were in constant receipt of bulletins on the President's condition, telegraphed by Phelps as they came to him from Blaine. They were at Salzburg when the end came, in September, and proceeded to Vienna just in time to be at the memorial meeting organized there. Reid was asked to share in the ceremonies and embodied in his tribute to Garfield some reminiscences of the man as he had known him for so many years. From the beginning there had been between the two more than the sympathy and understanding of a common political aim, there had been the affection which springs from the bases of character, and there could not have been any of the dead man's intimates more moved than Reid was over the plans and aspirations now laid low. No one knew better than he their scope and their nobility. He could look back to the country school-teacher he had first known, just elected to the Ohio Senate; he could recall his friend as he had left him only a few weeks before, at the apex of political life, and in all that crowded career he could see but one motive force, a great-hearted ideal. Here, indeed, as he bade farewell to his comrade, there was something of the irony of fate upon which he was bound to reflect.

Yet the practical issues of the moment could not be postponed, and the mourner had to give way to the editor. On the day of Garfield's death there was need of communication with Hay, anxious in New York about the course to follow, and the realistic habit of Reid's mind comes out in the cable which he sent in the midst of his sorrow: "Arthur's antecedents do not inspire confidence. He is now, however, entitled to support, unless he forfeits it. No man can have either the support or the respect of the American people, who, succeeding Garfield, undoes Garfield's work." His reservations point to possibilities which were only too well fulfilled. Detached from public affairs, preoccupied utterly with other things, he yet sniffed the battle from afar off.

The European tour was crowded with interesting personalities and incidents, like a meeting in Paris with

Clemenceau, then characteristically active as editor of "La Justice"; but perhaps a livelier significance attaches to their experience of England, where they spent the greater part of their sojourn abroad. In London that spring and autumn old ties with Englishmen who had visited the United States were confirmed and new ones were developed, foreshadowing the sympathetic atmosphere in which Reid was long afterward to carry on his diplomatic missions. He dipped into the currents eddying through and around the House of Commons, and was carried by others through a wide range of London life. There were breakfasts and dinners at which to talk history with Kinglake and Lecky, science with Huxley, poetry with Lord Houghton, positivism with Frederic Harrison, Continental politics with Drummond Wolf, and everything under the sun with the diarist Grant Duff. Reid's old affiliations with certain leaders of the stage brought him, too, once more into their joyous company. This was the season of Edwin Booth's memorable venture at the Prince's Theatre and his subsequent joining of forces with Irving. John McCullough was on the scene, and one day in June he carried Reid off for a drive with a tremendous galaxy of stars, down through the parks to Richmond and a banquet at Hampton Court. Booth, Irving, J. L. Toole, "Billy" Florence, Edmund Yates, F. C. Burnand, George Augustus Sala, and the younger Dickens were of the party. But it was chiefly in the world of political society that the Reids lived on the occasion of this visit, and they had come to England at a fortunate moment.

Disraeli's six years of "spectacular adventure abroad and seemingly undimmed triumph at home" had been dramatically repudiated at the general election of 1880. The Liberals had come in on a huge tidal wave, and Gladstone had entered upon his most brilliant period.

Reid met the prime minister at The Durdans, Lord Rosebery's place near Epsom; he heard Gladstone make at Leeds one of his great speeches, and at dinner in London they had some talk. Years afterward Smalley set down what Gladstone had said to him at that earlier time: "Your countryman seemed to me a man so exceptional that I wished to know more about him. When you have men like that why do you not put them in positions of high public trust, where their abilities can be of most use to you?" Smalley replied that Reid used his influence in The Tribune. "Yes," Gladstone said, "but here we should not leave a man like that in private life. Mr. Reid talks to me like one who understands affairs of state and has dealt with them. He is of a type on which the state has a claim as the state." The American editor saw a good deal of members of Gladstone's circle. It was his luck to find in the London of 1881 much of the same sort of political sentiment for which he had himself been contending since the foundation of the Republican party, a circumstance giving a keener edge to the interest of his encounters with such people as Morley, Rosebery, Vernon Harcourt, Dilke, and the Lyulph Stanleys. He had left politics behind him when he had sailed away from New York, only to be pleasantly absorbed by them again in London. Nor could the theme as it was developing at home be altogether ignored. Evarts thought it could. He, too, had come abroad, and one day in London breakfasted with Reid, to meet the old friend whom he had transferred from the Spanish to the English mission, James Russell Lowell. There is a typically humorous allusion to the woes of the new administration in a note of his at this time. "It used to be thought safer in politics," he says, "to talk than to write, but in the present outbreak of perfidy in politics it is safe only—to be in England." For Reid not even distance and the sundering seas could abate the importunities of the "situation" at Washington. Walter Phelps could see how they were always pressing, and in his rôle of affectionate counsellor he writes at the end of the Reids' English spring to warn of the hard work ahead for the winter. "What a time you had in England, and what a series of *rencontres* with the great of every kind. And do you know, as I laid the record down, not a little puffed that friends of mine were easily and properly in such grand company, (I wonder if I shall ever cease to be, like Mrs. Gummidge, 'worritsome,') I felt my pride all merging into anxiety for a firm hold of The Tribune. Statesmen don't get such honor, nor do wits, nor savants, nor capitalists. You could go as Senator, author, rich man, gentleman, and get all evidences of honor and respect; but no such hurry-skurry on the part of all to exhibit it, if not the controller of the great organ, that can aid or retard the *sic itur ad astra* of the greatest of them." It would soon be time to think again of the workaday world and all the problems pouring in clouds athwart the horizon of The Tribune.

John Hay was a representative uniquely reassuring to have in the editorial chair. As Phelps wittily put it, he had been wound up for the period of Reid's absence and had kept perfect time. His letters reported no great difficulties, either, in the way of his maintaining the policy he had adopted from the start. "I am keeping the paper in such a position," he wrote in July, after the assassination of the President, "as to give you entire freedom of action when you come back—avoiding quarrels and commitments in any direction. Arthur and I have exchanged calls—both of us were out—so that we are on civil terms both personally and publicly." Nevertheless, he could not conceal the prospect of trouble. Conkling was always in the offing, even after his resignation from the Senate, and, in requital for his defeat at

Garfield's hands, was looking forward to a resumption of power under Garfield's successor. As the President's long struggle with death drew to a close Hay's messages centred more and more about the doubts enveloping the probable course of the new administration. "You will certainly have war with Arthur," he says, "but I will try to stave it off as long as I can, if possible until you come home." He had a talk with Arthur shortly before the latter took the oath of office. "He was very civil but nothing of consequence was said by either of us." Writing of the situation as it appeared to public view, he added: "Everything is at sea about Arthur. Perhaps the cable will tell you in a day or two what he is up to. But at present the Cabinet knows nothing whatever of his intentions. The facts are: 1. He is living with Jones. 2. Jones has gone to Utica to confer with Conkling. 3. The Grant crowd seems happy." This was early in October. Before Reid sailed for home, in the following month, he had made up his mind that he was going back, if not to war, at least to a condition of affairs in which his own wing of the Republican party would hardly be happy.

Of one thing he was in the meantime absolutely certain, and this was that the cabinet over which he and Garfield had labored with such earnestness would be unrecognizable in a few short months. The conviction is disclosed in a letter which shows, also, how he was prepared, as regarded himself and his friends, for a political interregnum, a period to be spent more or less detached from anything like intimacy with the administration:

London,
October 28th, 1881.

MY DEAR MR. BLAINE:

Today's news seems to make it clear that Grant is already exercising the power we all felt he must have in the new Administration. Let me tell you how it looks—as to you—at this distance.

To remain in the Cabinet (beyond a reasonable time, for the selection of a successor) unless to be the real head and controller of it, would be a mistake. But with Folger in, and Grant at the elbow, you can't control it. To take the mission to England would be to confess your fall, and accept a pension from your conqueror. It would be to become a dependent of Chester Arthur, instead of the greatest independent political force in the country. To go quietly to Augusta, take care of your health, have a good time and take your fair share in political campaigns, as they come along, is to garner and increase that force.

You are the popular representative of Garfield's Administration, the residuary legatee of his popularity. You ought to be and can be chosen at the next election, as his successor. To that end Augusta is worth a thousand Londons. The Panama letter is a great hit. So is the letter to Garfield. They're enough to retire on. No doubt all this has been better thought out by you, long ago. Still, I've fancied it might be of interest to know how the situation looked to friendly eyes, far outside the home hurly-burly.

Faithfully yours,

WHITELAW REID.

It was good to be back again in November, absorbed in a new life and surrounded by a multitude of friends. A rich aspect of his correspondence at this time is that which has no political implications whatever. Hay, returned to a life of law, literature, and leisure in Cleveland, kept up as always his running fire of sparkling notes. "You can't imagine," he says in one of them, "the pleasure I take in reading The Tribune now that another fellow is blowing the bellows. It *is* a good paper and no mistake." To cheer like this he added the solid aid of brilliant "copy." Henry James gave him one of his subjects, in the publication that winter of his "Portrait of a Lady." After writing an exhaustive and glowing review Hay throws in, privately, this characteristic saying: "It is a remarkable book—as unhappy as malaria itself—but *perfectly* done." In all the little gaieties and amenities of the letters there is a strain which I would willingly follow. Watterson, of course, like Hay, never fails in good cheer. "Welcome home, dear boy," he wrote when the ship came in. "Have you a red herring, *fleur de lis*, on your left ear? Did you run a Sicilian nobleman through the body on your travels?" It was the serenest of worlds to which the Reids had returned, and his correspondence reflects the well-being in it, which was perfectly rounded out when their son, Ogden Mills Reid, was born early that summer. But just when Watterson, a Southern Democrat, was welcoming him home with affectionate levity, an unconsciously comic contrast to their friendliness was supplied by a card left at The Tribune office by a Northern political leader of Reid's own party. It is his message that sets the key for my next few pages. He had called, said the secretary who received him in the editor's absence, "as a messenger from Grant, Arthur, Chaffee, John A. Logan and others, and the substance of it was that they wanted peace, and were anxious that The Tribune should not persecute them." The innocent little pasteboard is freighted with the presages of a long period of activity. Hay had warned him, "You will certainly have war," and though his visitor came to ingeminate peace it was not precisely peace that ensued.

The expected cabinet changes were swift enough in coming. Robert Lincoln, in the War Department, was the only one who remained throughout the administration. The secretary of state got out in December, as early as the exigencies permitted. From outside Blaine watched with growing vexation what his successor, Frelinghuysen, did with his foreign policies; but quite apart from any personal chagrin he knew well enough that Reid had been right in advising him to leave the cabinet. The atmosphere of that body was determined by an attitude on the part of the President which Blaine himself bluntly indicates. Candid students of this administration will admit that it was no private bitterness but a sound political judgment which he thus expressed —"I tell you Arthur means death and political destruction to every Garfield man." That was perhaps a savage but hardly an overwrought way of stating the fact that the star of the Stalwarts was steadily rising on the horizon. Everybody could see it, though Arthur himself fostered the illusion that he was proceeding with the discreetest impartiality. He was a well-meaning but not a strong executive. From certain confidential and authoritative reports made to Reid it appeared that he was sensitive and irritable, disgusted with the Star Route scandal in the postal service, investigation of which was one of the first features of his administration, and altogether out of humor with the trend of affairs. When his appointment of Folger as successor to Windom in the Treasury was criticized on political grounds, he querulously adopted the feeble explanation that that gentleman, and others he favored, were not, after all, "pronounced Stalwarts"; and when the charge was pressed he impatiently intimated that if he was to have the name he would have the game, meaning that if he was to be accused of putting nobody but Stalwarts in office none but Stalwarts should go in. The comedy is a little amusing, until it trails off into the minutiæ of petty political chip-chop. I note here the state of the Arthurian mind chiefly to point the effect which it had upon Reid's course. Arthur was by no means indifferent to newspaper criticism. As far back as the time when he had descended upon Albany to lend Conkling a hand, the editorials in The Tribune, temperate though they were, had driven him nearly frantic. Still, he was not ready to disarm criticism by eschewing factional interests, and the result, as I have hinted, if not war, was not unblemished peace. From Vienna Walter Phelps repeated with a chuckle the news he had received from home, that the Stalwart politicians were making merry over the fact that he and the editor of The Tribune would now "keep on the back benches for a season." The bench from which the editor of The Tribune observed the scene was not, just the same, an uncomfortable one. Neither, I may add, did it engender any acrimonious prejudice, hurtful to the point of view.

The course of the paper through this administration might be described as one faithful to the party and friendly enough to Arthur, but frankly critical. The Tribune wished nothing from the President but good government. It proposed to give the administration "a cordial though self-respecting support," and accepted Arthur's first message to Congress as a judicious, moderate, and, in most respects, satisfactory document. Naturally it spoke freely and to the point as the cabinet was made over, a fact on which Hay offers a significant comment. Alluding to a good appointment Arthur had made, and to the popular magnanimity giving the administration more credit for one wise choice than it withheld for twenty bad ones, he went on to say: "I don't mean that *you* are magnanimous—bet your neck. That notice of James and Howe [the retiring postmaster-general and his supplanter] was pure reason, untouched by charity."

It was very much in the light of pure reason that The Tribune approached the subject of the hour, tariff revision. Over Arthur's nomination of Conkling to be an associate justice of the supreme court it discoursed with a contempt which was in nowise placated by the nominee's declination, and there were other errors as roundly trounced. But the paper was eager to serve where the matter of the tariff was concerned. The appointment of a commission on the subject was heartily approved, and its labors received constant support. On this complex topic I may note, briefly, that The Tribune, stanchly protectionist, nevertheless preached as the sound Republican doctrine that the system had a liberal essence. Its object, ran the argument, was to adapt legislation to the actual and varying circumstances of different branches of industry, and not to subject all to the operations of a stupid cast-iron rule. The need for revision in certain schedules was freely admitted. But in the meeting of it, what was counselled was moderation and common sense, a solicitude for the welfare of American industries which would thwart the dangers of a free-trade policy. Against free trade the paper carried on relentless warfare. The Tariff Commission was protectionist in its personnel, a fact of favorable augury, and for a long time Reid's hopes ran high. But it is an old story that by the time the Forty-seventh Congress got through with the bill passed in its closing stages, only the seeds for further trouble had been planted. Blaine, who was to be brought to grips with the subject in the next presidential campaign, wrote these prophetic words just before the bill was approved:

Washington,
February 19th, 1883.

My dear Mr. Reid:

The attitude into which tariff legislation is drifting promises the most serious discomfiture to the Republicans and immense advantage to the Democrats. Practically it amounts to this, that the Republicans, being held responsible by the country for all that is done, are yet being driven to submit to such tariff adjustment as the Democrats dictate. The anomaly is presented of a total ignoring of the iron interest, every other petty fabric being taken care of, especially by our New England Senators and Representatives, and the iron and steel men—the largest of all—pushed mercilessly to the wall in a time of great and widespread depression among their leading men. See the failure of the Stone steel works, and now of the Ayres, and an impending calamity possible to all the big concerns in Ohio and elsewhere. If this bill is pushed through under whip and spur the Democrats have an easy road before them and the Republicans a very rough one. Look out for big breakers in Pennsylvania and

Ohio! We need one of your old fashioned bugle blasts in The Tribune, for the protection interest, strong, aggressive, cogent, such as you know how to write. Otherwise we are drifting, first to defense, then to destruction. The Democrats like Carlisle of Kentucky are in ecstasy over the situation and well they may be! You can issue the word of command. If it is not given there will be regret when too late. The bill as the Senate is perfecting it with Beck's leave should be mercilessly slaughtered by Republicans in the House—and will be if you say so boldly in The Tribune.

Very hastily,

J. G. BLAINE.

Better than any analysis of the bill itself is this urgent appeal as an index to the manner in which the tariff tinkering going on in Congress stirred not only the business thoughts of men but woke their emotions and made the whole question an intensely political issue. Reid shared his friend's forebodings. Writing to Hay, he declared that the things essential to success in the canvass of 1884 were the reduction of the tariff and the abolition of war taxes. To Demarest Lloyd, his Washington correspondent, who had conveyed messages to him from Blaine in the sense of the letter quoted above, he sent the appropriate instructions. "The people will not stop to inquire too curiously about these things," he wrote. "They will simply say: 'The Republicans had both branches of Congress and the President; they neither reduced the internal revenue nor the tariff; they did not even reduce so glaring a duty as that on Bessemer steel rails.' Nobody can successfully defend them before the people, and I don't think I shall try it." He felt very strongly that even an imperfect bill was better than no bill at all. On the very day that Blaine was writing to him he was writing to Blaine, expressing the hope that they might get, substantially, the Tariff Commission bill. "If, besides," he added, "we can go to the country on the record of having made an honest and united effort to readjust and, to some extent, lower the tariff without impairing its protective character, then we can doubtless make a good fight and have the benefit of having the tariff as an issue." The effort made had in itself, as he saw it, a value to serve as an offset to the extreme alarm Blaine had expressed. He recognized merits as well as defects in the bill as it was passed and, I repeat, was doubly appreciative of its being passed at all, considering that the Democrats were to be in control of the next House. But there were free-trade tendencies even then working in the Republican forces. The bill was the fruit of jangling and uninspired debate, and it ended by promoting more heated discussion than had accompanied its construction. As one party historian has candidly put it, the new law was unscientific in the extreme, and it did not take long to prove that the Tariff Commission was a failure. In the moment of the conflict, and when at least he had got his "effort," Reid saw that as the political complexion of the House was changed in March, 1883, the tariff issue would continue to be very much alive. It stayed alive and kicked more lustily as time went on. Democratic economic wisdom proved no more efficacious than Republican, developing a characteristic party split, and the Morrison bill died through the murder of its enacting clause in the house of its friends. There is a phrase which I must borrow here from one of Blaine's later campaign letters. "I wish you would agonize more and more on the tariff," he asks. Agonizing on the tariff was the order of the day all through Arthur's administration. It is late, now, to repeat the process, but if I have hastily sketched the earlier phases of the battle it has been not to recall controversies over rates but to bring into sharper relief a burning issue of 1884. The superstition dies hard in some quarters that Republican defeat was then due to the choice of a bad candidate, and The Tribune's defense of him has been interpreted as an instance of blind prejudice. The issue was framed long before Blaine was nominated, as I have shown, and The Tribune went into the fight for him not only with an open-eyed conviction of his sterling character as a man but with the belief that he was the most potent available champion of the protective system.

CHAPTER V

BLAINE AND CLEVELAND

The caldron bubbled fiercely, but Reid had many diversions. It was in the early eighties that he began the annual visits which he made to his wife's California home, in the San Mateo Valley. They meant rest and recuperation, and made him thenceforth almost a citizen of the Pacific slope. In later years some of his most important speeches were made there before university and other audiences. When, in 1908, as our ambassador to Great Britain, he told "the story of San Francisco for English ears," he recited the ravages of the earthquake as one who had in some sort made the Western city his own. I speak of his Californian associations here because they begin to run a new and delightful thread through his life in the eighties, supplying a respite that he peculiarly welcomed from the strain of political combat. It is from the early eighties, too, that there dates one of the undertakings in which he took a special satisfaction. I have already spoken of his work in sending boys West. In 1882 he assumed responsibility for the Fresh Air Fund, then in its infancy under the management of the "Evening Post," and gave it in The Tribune a new lease of life, bringing it to the vigorous state in which it thrives to this day. To this fund, through which many thousands of poor children have been sent to the country for a fortnight's vacation in the heated term, he gave in its formative years constant personal attention, and all his life he was watchful of its interests. In these years the steady excitement of political affairs was varied by far more of social relaxation than his bachelor routine had seemed to make possible. Looking over old souvenirs, I find echoes of his English sojourn perceptible in meetings with travellers from London—Matthew Arnold, Henry Irving, and Rosebery. Hay, now making a long holiday abroad, sent him lively budgets about himself; about Clarence King, "buying *bric-à-brac* with unerring judgment and unflinching extravagance"; about Howells, fleeing from the hospitalities of London for the quiet of Switzerland, where he might write in peace; and about a whole squadron of literary celebrities—James, Harte, Dudley Warner, and others. Returning to Cleveland in the summer of 1883, Hay suffered some illness, but was as resilient as ever, "because I scarcely ever die in these attacks."

That year, in the August number of the "Century," Hay began publication of "The Bread Winners," and, publishing it anonymously, gave his readers one of the most tantalizing of literary mysteries. Reid wrote him that the sleuths were on his track and, apropos of the first instalment, said: "Without being quite sure that you wrote it I spotted the story at once as relating to Cleveland and to you and as having some touches singularly like your work." Hay's reply throws interesting light on his demeanor in Sir Walter Scott's predicament:

Cleveland,
August 3rd, 1883.

DEAR REID:

I can't tell you, honorably, what I know about it, as yet. I may be released before long and then I will make a paragraph for you, if you want any, that will not hurt anybody. "Deal gently with the young book—even with the Bread Winners," for it was written by one who is a good friend of yours and mine. Meanwhile if anybody asks you about me, say I absolutely and teetotatiously repudiate it. I am very desirous the thing should not be attributed to me. My love to Mrs. Reid and the Boy.

Yours sincerely, J. H.

It was not long before Reid was put in possession of the secret. In fact, he received and cashed for Hay one or two checks from the publishers for copyright payments on account of the work. The author, in frank talk on the subject, spoke of some of the subjects discussed in "The Bread Winners" as extra-hazardous, and alluded humorously to the possible wrath of "the man who hadn't anything."

There is another semi-mysterious subject touched upon in correspondence with Hay, to which I refer in the interest of those readers who care for the more personal chapters in journalistic history. It is Reid's ancient feud with Dana. Its existence and what it added to editorial vivacities in New York are matters on which, first and last, there has been perhaps sufficient comment. How it was patched up is another story, not generally known, which Reid told to Hay, saying: "I can imagine the blank astonishment on your face when you read that I have been in a two hours' conference with Dana." It came about when the Associated Press, of which Reid and Dana were both members, got into a tangle with the Western Union Telegraph Company and the Western Associated Press. Dana's solicitude for his own service caused him to move at a meeting in Reid's absence that the question at issue be put in the hands of a special committee. Reid was one of those appointed, and thus he and his old foe met around the Associated Press table for the first time in ten years. They had not set eyes upon one another in five or six. The situation was droll. Without any greeting they solemnly and scrupulously transacted their business. Presently Reid had some odd experiences with contracts to tell. Dana let out a laugh. Before he knew it he was insisting that Reid was particularly fitted to serve on a sub-committee that was found necessary. "Neither of us grinned," Reid explained, but he revelled in the fun of it, and he refers with gusto to the climax to one of their meetings: "This brought Dana, Hurlbert [oh shades of Cipher Alley!], Stone and myself together—a happy family that Barnum in his prime would never have allowed to pass the old Museum corner in dispersing to our separate offices again. We would have been caged in a twinkling." As the meetings multiplied the ice was melted. Dana and Reid reached a point of friendly co-operation, in which, for the nonce, their historic enmity, the old soreness of the Greeley days, was submerged if not forgotten.

In politics, at about this time, friendly co-operation was hard to get. Reid made a brave fight against heavy odds in the fall campaign of 1882, but Stalwart influences in his own party proved his heaviest handicap. "The Tribune throughout was inspired," Blaine told him. "It was the battle axe of Cœur de Lion descending on the heads of the recreants with terrific, irresistible force." None the less the Democrats gave the administration a crushing defeat. They elected Grover Cleveland governor of New York. In Pennsylvania, Massachusetts, Connecticut, and Indiana as well they were ominously successful. Reid told his party without mincing words that the extent to which boss rule had overtaken the Republican organization was largely responsible. I have portrayed him all along as a loyal party man, but I have endeavored also to expose the unfailing independence allied with his partisanship. Nothing is more characteristic of The Tribune as "a Republican organ" than its way of telling the Republicans unpleasant truths. As the election aforesaid drew on, the paper protested that no candid person with ordinary powers of observation could deny that "the Republican party in many of the states—perhaps throughout the entire country—is rent with internal dissensions, disorganized and divided to an extent never before known in its history." It admitted the reasons, in detail, and when defeat came, as I have said, rubbed salt in the wound. Bad leadership had done it. The party still contained, in Reid's opinion, "the brains and the conscience of the country," and he was quite clear and outspoken as to those responsible for its setback. "The conduct of the men who have assumed to manage and have mainly represented the Republican party since Mr. Garfield died," he said, "has disgusted Republican voters, and deprived the party of public confidence; that is the precise difficulty."

He preached reorganization as essential in all the States, and moved heaven and earth to further it in his own. At the same time, of course, he went on animadverting upon Democratic shortcomings, fought Tammany misrule in New York tooth and nail, and in pouncing upon every one of Governor Cleveland's errors never for a moment lost sight of that official's growing prestige as a possible presidential candidate. A pleasant interlude is that which marks his helpful association with the earlier political life of Theodore Roosevelt. He was an old friend of the young assemblyman's father. He watched Roosevelt's developing career at Albany with a personal interest enhanced by his sense of the novice's courage and ability. The Tribune was of great influence in carrying the fight for municipal reform to the State capital, and when, early in 1884, Speaker Sheard engineered action on its exposures of New York frauds, Reid was quick to offer assistance to Roosevelt as chairman of the investigating committee. There could not have been a happier prelude to their many years of private and public intercourse than this letter, in which an "old political hand" places his experience at the service of a beginner:

New York,
January 17th, 1884.

DEAR MR. ROOSEVELT:

Your Committee seems an admirable one, and I am heartily glad that you have taken the chairmanship. As I am to some extent responsible for the interest you have taken, I feel on this account all the more anxious that you should make a great success, and venture, therefore, at this early stage, a suggestion or two which perhaps you may think it worth while to consider.

The subject you are to investigate is a large and complicated one with many details. The man to be attacked is able, adroit, fertile in expedients and thoroughly familiar with every point. We hear here that he has already engaged, for his purposes, probably the best counsel he could get in the city of New York.

Under the circumstances it is extremely desirable that your committee should familiarize itself pretty thoroughly with the business it has in hand; should decide upon the points first to be investigated; ascertain clearly what is likely to be found out and who are the best witnesses; provide itself with the very best counsel and experts, and, in a word, have its plan of campaign matured before it begins firing its guns.

You may be ready for a public session and the examination of witnesses on Saturday, but I should doubt it. At any rate, I am quite sure that thorough preparation is indispensable to prevent Thompson and his astute counsel from seeming to gain advantage at the outset.

We will gladly place whatever information or clues we have in your hands, and render any assistance in the way of suggesting witnesses or otherwise that we can.

With the heartiest congratulations and good wishes, I am,

Faithfully yours,

WHITELAW REID.

He was as good as his word. The Tribune backed the investigation with enthusiastic and constructive campaigning. In after years they sometimes had political differences, but a sentimental interest attaches to the fact that when Roosevelt was new to the conflict Reid did all that he could to uphold his hand.

With this attempt at housecleaning in New York, with the advancement of Republican reorganization there and elsewhere, the campaign for the presidency was ushered in. Half a dozen candidates were on the horizon—Arthur, Blaine, John Sherman, Senator Edmunds, Secretary Lincoln, and Senator Logan. The number was even increased, in the upshot, but not with serious implications. Reid is jocose about one addition made to the list, but, as usual, kept his eyes open for contingencies. "It is an uncertain quantity," he wrote to Walter Phelps, "a good deal like the Connecticut man's cow, which was brought to run against the famous blooded stock. They all backed out, you remember—they didn't know what the old thing might do." The Tribune held itself in reserve, waiting to see who promised most clearly to have the country with him, and reminding its readers late in the winter preceding the convention that "the man who begins to run very fast in February is likely to get out of breath before November." Meanwhile Blaine was moving to the front. While in his retirement at Augusta he was happily engaged in putting together his "Twenty Years of Congress," the first volume of which was to appear in good time for the campaign. He was receptive, but, as regarded the presidency, in no mood to force the fight. In November, 1882, he did not, as he wrote to Reid, "wish to pose for an hour as a Presidential candidate." He wanted to abstain from politics, anyway, for a time, and the only temptation that could lure him back was an odd one, suggested by himself in the following year, when Reid was giving a dinner to ex-President Hayes. Blaine couldn't come, but he wanted Hayes told that, having saved Ohio by running for governor in two crises of the past, he might have to do it a third time. "If I could be induced to make a political speech anywhere in the year of grace 1883," he said, "it would be in Ohio if the Ex-President should be the candidate for Governor." Hayes was agreeably affected over Blaine's letter, when Reid handed it to him after dinner. But he put it in his pocket, and when he got home returned it with the comment that though it made pleasant reading he was out of the category suggested. The only candidacy Blaine had to mull over was his own, for the highest office of all. Walter Phelps, out of diplomacy and back in Congress, kept watch of developments. The Third Term embers were not altogether cold, and in July, 1883, he asked G. W. Childs, who was very close to the general, what Grant really thought of the prospect. "Grant," he replied, "thinks Blaine will be nominated." A note of Depew's dating from this period is amusing:

West End Hotel,
July 22nd, 1883.

My dear Reid:

Cornell is here and fairly lifted me off my feet a few days since by following a question as to your whereabouts with an abrupt and utterly irrelevant declaration for Blaine. He acted like the young man who asked the girl if her Mother was fond of sardines and then popped the question. He had got the thing off his mind anyhow. Do you suppose the very shadowy spectre of Arthur as his own successor startled the Ex-Governor so that he plunged at once into Blaine's bath tub? This being Sunday, I may remark that like Paul I thanked God and took courage. At this distance from Sunday School days, and stranded in a summer hotel, I am unable to say whether the circumstances under which the Apostle made that observation were similar to mine.

Very faithfully yours,
Chauncey M. Depew.

The Arthur spectre was to stalk not altogether obscurely in the convention, but its potency to scare was pretty well discounted in advance of that event. "All in the world we want of him," wrote Reid to Phelps in February, 1884, "is to die with reasonable decency when the necessity of his political death at last dawns on his vision"; and the certainty of the obsequies is significantly supplied in a bit of news which Phelps had to communicate in the same month: "Blaine is at it—but slow." Reid did not mind the slowness. In March he wrote to Blaine: "I've been a little scared of late over what some of us persist in calling your boom. It began to look too booming for March." If Blaine was to come in he wanted him to do so at just the psychological moment, summoned by an unmistakable popular mandate and riding on a mighty wave. The hour impended. Not even a Democratic victory in Ohio in the preceding fall election could darken the signs of increasing Republican unity, which gained, of course, as the Morrison bill got into deeper waters, and in the spring, with its multiplying evidences of Blaine's popularity, the revival of the old Little Rock and Fort Smith charges only rallied his supporters closer around him. Walter Phelps traversed the tale of the so-called Mulligan letters, as it was retold in the "Evening Post," and in a long communication to that paper he tore it conclusively to shreds. The Tribune made that smashing argument its own. The popular verdict had dismissed the charges in 1876 and again in 1880 as "false, malignant and unsustained by the evidence." Reid believed profoundly that they remained nothing but "stale slanders" in 1884, and he went into the campaign on that belief. Since the facts supported this view of the matter, what, then, was "the nigger in the woodpile"? Why this virulent campaign of defamation? Why, for example, was Blaine so conspicuously hounded when, as was shown by Phelps in his point-by-point analysis, others went scot-free from similar aspersions, though the records bracketed them with Blaine as persons of the same innocent conduct? While Blaine's enemies were industriously painting him as so black that his personal turpitude could not but carry his party to defeat, The Tribune upheld his integrity and pointed out the real issue as lying in the tariff. The collapse of the Morrison bill only intensified the heat of this troublous question. Blaine was marked out for vilification on any grounds as the most formidable exponent of the protective system. Hence the Mugwump bolt. He was dreaded not only by the opposition but by the Free-Trade elements in the Republican camp. The Tribune did not hesitate repeatedly to charge that the bolt against Blaine was the result of a deliberate conspiracy of Free-Traders, who had been called Republicans, with the Democratic party. The legend of the Mulligan letters and of "the tattooed man" fostered by haters of the Maine statesman found its true status as a political dodge, a sort of "anything to beat Blaine" slogan. He himself put it in the proper light when he adjured Reid to "agonize more and more on the tariff." He said that not to divert attention from the Mulligan charges, which he had disproved, but to fasten it upon the essential issue of the campaign. And the rightness as well as the sagacity of his opinion is shown by his fortunes in the convention and in the canvass, though in the latter he met portentous hostility. He was willing, even anxious, to have the notorious correspondence republished, and welcomed the "new letters" brought forward as well as the old ones. When The Tribune analyzed the lot and found only vindication in them he was not surprised, and neither were his multitudinous partisans. The latter could see what was undoubtedly true, that much of the moral opposition to him was, though mistaken, sincere. They could see, also, that more of it was pure buncombe.

The influence of Blaine's friends in the country at large was unmistakable at Chicago. He led on the first ballot and kept his lead through the three that followed. A note of Reid's to him in April points to the part sure to be played by convention management. "Elkins tells me today," he says, "that Gen. Tom Ewing says he has assurances from John Sherman that at the proper time, if necessary, you will be sure to get his strength in Ohio." I have no wish to minimize the significance of political strategy in the convention. At the same time Blaine could say that he owed the nomination to the complaisance of no rival. The convention was fundamentally his when it was opened, and on the decisive ballot he had 130 more votes than those necessary for a choice. Throughout the campaign The Tribune supported him as beyond all peradventure a candidate of the people, and as such he marched rapidly to the very verge of triumph. His speaking tours over the country were merged into one tumultuous ovation. In the September elections a small Republican majority in Vermont was overshadowed by a tremendous victory for the party in Maine. Rousing receptions in New England, New Jersey, Pennsylvania, and the West were crowned by a superb Republican triumph in Ohio. The Tribune wanted a decisive election, to put an end to the recurring disturbance of American industry, to stop tariff blundering, to end control of the Southern oligarchy, and two weeks before the nation went to the polls there was every reason to believe that Blaine would win it. The war-cries of the Democrats, "The Republican Party Must Go," and "Turn the Rascals Out," fell upon ears too well qualified, in too many instances, to distinguish between war-cries and facts, and the tide continued to run in Republican favor. Nor was the opposition as strong as it had promised to be. Grover Cleveland had justified the withdrawal of Tilden in his favor, he gained in strength as a candidate, but it was not plain that he was irresistible, and as the campaign progressed there seemed brighter hopes of beating him in his own State, which from the beginning had been a knotty Republican problem. On the other hand, Reid's surmise before the convention that the nomination of

Blaine would heal factional strife in New York was answered by the pharisaical Mugwump movement and other untoward developments. New York had to be fought for tooth and nail.

Blaine, in the West, flushed with Republican victory in Ohio, was nevertheless mindful of the narrow margin trembling in the balance in New York, and telegraphed in October for Reid's views on the situation. The long letter he got in reply shows that by this time Reid was frankly anxious. The party organization, though improved, was not perfect. Around Utica, Conkling's stronghold, Stalwart dissatisfaction was rife, and it was not unknown in other sections of the State. Republican disgruntlement in New York City was still "alarmingly large." It had its principal source amongst the readers of the "Evening Post" and other journals resolute in their representation of Blaine as a man who would not do. In the clubs it was hard to find any one who was going to vote for him. All this was very discouraging. Republicans were saying that if they lost New York everything was lost, while if they gained it they could afford to lose Indiana and Wisconsin, too. On reading his letter over, Reid admitted in a postscript that it gave, seemingly, "a blue view of the situation." Yet he did not intend this, and closed on a cheerfuller note. The fight was not yet lost. Indeed, as the election approached, the prospect of winning grew very fair. On Blaine's return from his travels he paused in New York to receive a welcome which seemed the happiest of auguries, so spontaneous was it in its warmth, so impressive in its volume. But conditions in the State were nervous, unstable, ready to be swayed by almost any untoward trifle, and in an episode of this very welcome there lurked the compelling cause of his defeat.

It is one of the most familiar stories in American politics, the story of how Doctor Burchard, spokesman for a clerical delegation, hailed Blaine as the champion of the Republican electorate against "Rum, Romanism and Rebellion," and thereby injected into the campaign an element of prejudice and angry passion destined to have a decisive effect upon the Irish vote. For once the swift readiness which had so often been so brilliantly used in parliamentary debate abandoned the candidate. He heard the foolish inflammatory words without instantly taking in their full import, without seizing upon the need for summary repudiation, and when he offered that a day or two afterward it was too late to arrest the mischief. The religious issue, to which it had not been in his nature to give a moment's thought or hospitality, was now forced by his opponents, and it raised up the grotesquely minute majority which was nevertheless big enough to turn the scale against him in New York, the pivotal State. The vote was maddeningly close; so close that it remained for days in doubt. Until the official count was rendered, Blaine was steadfast in the fight, and urged upon Reid an aggressive policy. "It's the time for a word with the bark on it, as the children say," he wrote from Augusta. "I have a sort of instinctive faith that courage will win the day." Reid needed no urging. He, too, was fervid on seeing the battle through. But that tactless alliteration had lost the day, and courage could not retrieve it.

With rueful humor Reid told one of his friends that he wished Doctor Burchard had had a sore throat of the most aggravated type known to the profession. If some such visitation had only kept him mute, the promise of the campaign would have been fulfilled and Blaine would have brought about the first distinct and considerable break ever made in the solid Democratic Irish vote. But for the incredible folly of the clergyman's speech, as

Reid said, the Republicans should have carried the State of New York by ten thousand majority. There was no blinking the fact. Never was evidence clearer, or swifter in forthcoming. How the results of Burchard's error sprang to the eyes is shown in a letter to Hay, which I cite for the sake of the intimate reality with which it brings back the revelations of the moment:

New York,
December 1st, 1884.

My dear Colonel:

I am glad you liked the course of the paper. If it had only been a little more effective!

Don't deceive yourself about Burchard, however. He did defeat us. He did more than that. He took ten thousand votes away from us in this city and Brooklyn. I could give you dozens of instances. Take two: Mayor Wickham told me of a Catholic church in Brooklyn where a hundred men had signed their names to a pledge to vote for Blaine. By the Saturday before the election 92 of these men had gone to the parish priest and demanded that their names be erased from the pledge. In McDonald's livery stable on 41st St., where I used to keep my horse, there were forty men who were going to vote for Blaine. By Friday or Saturday McDonald sent for friends to try to get them right again, but without avail. Practically the whole force went against us. Rachel Sherman discovered that the very waiter at her room in the Fifth Avenue Hotel had decided to go against Blaine because of the Burchard speech. She argued and entreated and even her influence only extorted a reluctant promise, while he assured her that most of the others were hopelessly gone. Up to that speech we were sure of the unanimous vote of the whole lot. I could add to these instances indefinitely.

I was awfully blue for a while but have been helped to bear the party misfortune somewhat of late by contemplating The Tribune's advantages. We have come out of the fight in better shape than the paper has ever been in its history. You see how philosophy enables us to bear the misfortunes of our friends.

Seriously though, the calamity is appalling, and will be almost fatal if we don't contrive to pull together within the next year or two. I believe, however, that we can do it, and that we shall elect in '88 and quite possibly elect Blaine. The amount of talk for him now takes one's breath away.

Faithfully yours,

Whitelaw Reid.

Reid always scorned the Mugwump disposition to becloud the issue. He knew that the Republican candidate had won, morally, an extraordinary success. To Blaine, himself, he wrote in January that "next to being elected President, it seems to me, is the glory of having made such a canvass." In accepting the inevitable and citing some of its causes he said editorially: "Yet, of all these, only Doctor Burchard was fatal." He stated a fact which, with the tabled results of the canvass, is sufficient answer to all the "holier than thou" attacks upon Blaine's personal character. Whatever the Mugwump press made of the Mulligan letters, the immense popular vote cast for him showed that, as Reid had steadily maintained, he was the candidate of the people, and the American people have never yet stood in such force behind a bad man.

Of Reid's own share in the campaign, beyond what I have already indicated, I may leave Watterson to speak:

Louisville, Ky.
November 21st, 1884.

My dear Reid:

Well, the election is over, and, whatever may be its disappointments, in the general political sense, you, personally, and The Tribune, have no cause for regret. You have made a great and lasting mark, professionally. My sole gratulation relates to the change of parties for the sake of change, and the invigoration which the transfer of power peacefully from one party to another will give to our Republican system. Otherwise, that is personally, I am indifferent to the aspects of the case.

Your friend,
Henry Watterson.

What the party thought of his services may be inferred from the fact that from around the time of the convention there was a good deal of talk among the politicians about sending him to the United States Senate, when a successor to Elbridge G. Lapham had to be chosen by the legislature in January, 1885. Even in the camp of the opposition the idea had its supporters, as is shown by this note from Whitney:

2 West 57th Street,
January 13th, 1885.

My dear Reid:

The lookers on, you know, sometimes see more than the players. I want to say to you that if you care for it the senatorship is drifting into a place, as it seems to me, where you could have it without much trouble if you should choose. Now don't commit yourself to any third candidate. You may want it yourself. This may not be so, but it looks so to an outsider, and you will have it in your hands soon if you want it, I think. I thought I would warn you a little.

Yours,
W. C. W.

The contest for the office opened with a troop of personalities involved, some of them Reid's close friends. The names of Morton, Depew, Evarts, and Cornell were strongly urged, and Arthur's claims were assiduously pressed by a powerful faction. But from the start Reid was settled as to his course, too conscious of what was attached to his rôle as editor to contemplate any deviation into the field of political preferment. As early as June, 1884, ex-Governor Cornell called upon him, in a mood of indifference to any candidacy of his own, and said frankly that if Reid were to enter the race his resources and influence would be found in support. Reid thanked him, but did not succumb to the temptation, and before the campaign at Albany had gone very far he wrote for publication, to his friend and fellow regent, the editor of the Rochester "Democrat and Chronicle," this letter of formal withdrawal:

New York,
November 22nd, 1884.

The Hon. Charles E. Fitch.

Dear Sir:

Your favor of the 19th inst., asking if I am a candidate for United States senator, is at hand. I am not a candidate, have not been, and have not proposed to be. The mention of my name in connection with this or any other office has been entirely without any suggestion or approval from me, and whenever approached on the subject I have uniformly given the same answer. It cannot but be gratifying to be thought of in connection with an office worthy to fill the measure of any man's ambition; but my duties are already exacting, and I cannot seek new ones. It has not seemed becoming to rush into print to decline an office before it was offered, but under two administrations, as is known, I have declined office whenever it was offered.

I am very grateful to you and your friends for their good opinion, and trust that they will continue to think well of me in private life.

Very truly yours,
WHITELAW REID.

As the time for legislative action drew near, the subject was still urged upon him by leaders who believed both in his qualifications for the Senate and in his ability to carry off the prize. Yet those who knew him best were constrained to admit the wisdom of his choice. Blaine's words to him are typical of the feeling among his intimates:

Washington, D. C.
January 5th, 1885.

MY DEAR MR. REID:

When your name was originally mentioned for Senator I believe your New York friends thought the impending combinations unfavorable to your success. Hence you did not permit yourself to be considered a candidate. Don't you believe that in the complications which have since resulted a new candidate is likely to be chosen? If so, is there any one who could possibly compete with you? If you cherish any ambition for the place you should certainly have a trusted and discreet friend in Albany for the next few days.

At the same time I have never been able to comprehend how in any event you would be willing to take the place. I know all about the Senatorship in all its phases—and the editorship of The Tribune is inconceivably wider and larger and grander and more potential in every point of view. You remember the reply of the elder Rothschild when it was suggested that he might be the Sovereign of Palestine, established as a Jewish Kingdom. He thought it better to be Jew of the Kings than King of the Jews. So I say it is better to be Tribune of Senators than a Senator of the Tribune. There are no twenty Senators who combinedly influence public opinion to one twentieth the extent you do.

Are you coming to Washington soon? Or do you intend to wait until you can see the Capital under Democratic rule? With kind regards to Mrs. Reid believe me

Very sincerely yours,
JAMES G. BLAINE.

In the competition at Albany he welcomed with the most sympathy the drift to Evarts, "surely a senatorial figure," as he wrote to Fitch, and he did his best to strengthen the growing support for this candidate. When Evarts was chosen he was, personally, delighted, and from a purely political point of view he thought the decision about the happiest at which the legislature could have arrived. It was to be recognized not as a Blaine triumph or an anti-Blaine triumph, a Stalwart or Half Breed triumph, a Conkling, a Cornell, or an Arthur triumph, but simply as the deliberate choice of a conspicuous, able, and trusted Republican, by a majority of Republicans of all wings and shades, in the best interests of the whole Republican party. What made the result most satisfactory to him was, as he said, that it left few wounds and was full of promise for the future of the party in New York.

CHAPTER VI

NEW INTERESTS

The period of the eighties was one of new interests and decisive changes in the life of Whitelaw Reid, following upon his marriage. He was as busy as ever professionally, but with a difference. The demands of politics were necessarily less engrossing for a time, after the election of Cleveland, and in any case he was now realizing how wise was Blaine's advice on the occasion of his engagement, to "see only his own world." As I have noted before, it was for years a constant habit amongst his intimates to protest against his burning the candle at both ends, giving to The Tribune an often inhuman proportion out of the hours of the day and night. Family life was efficacious where mere good counsel in the interests of his health had been unavailing. His correspondence reflects a fuller measure of rest and relaxation, journeyings to California which took him completely out of the turmoil, and all the incidents which point to a man's home rather than to his office. It was a happy period. "The Boy," as Hay loved to call Ogden, throve lustily. In the summer of 1884, when the political fight was on, the Reids forgot all about it in an event in their own household, the birth of their daughter, Jean Templeton Reid. If the letters still contain echoes of public affairs, they have quite as many allusions to those of a private nature.

Conspicuous is the matter of building. Reid used to say with a laugh that from the day he laid the cornerstone of The Tribune's new home he had been occupied with architects and contractors for a little lifetime. It never bored him. On the contrary, his liking for such transactions was a marked trait. He was always keeping an eye on the homestead at Cedarville, making repairs, and finally giving it a thorough overhauling. I may mention here an enthusiasm which, like his love of horseback riding and of swimming, was in his blood—an enthusiasm for trees and tree-planting. He loved the very timbers that had gone to the building of his father's house in 1823, but he loved equally the surrounding woods, and each tree left upon the lawn, which had remained unbroken by the plough since the Indians roamed over it. To care for the trees already on the farm was not enough. Every year additions were made to them. The catalogues of booksellers were rivalled in his mail by those of the nurserymen. Orders were annually going forward for seedlings to be sent to Cedarville, and he was not more exacting in the typographical make-up of The Tribune than he was in the pages upon pages of instruction which he gave for the planting of his trees. In 1886 he was delighted to receive from the authorities in the town of South Charleston evidence that his fervor in these matters was appreciated. They planted a tree in his honor, giving it his name, in front of the old schoolhouse in which he had as a youth held sway.

When the Reids returned from their wedding journey in the fall of 1881 they settled in the house at Lexington Avenue and Thirty-seventh Street. For five years they lived there. Then, in 1886, they acquired a larger structure at Madison Avenue and Fiftieth Street, which was thenceforth to be their city home, and at about the same time began to look for a country place. This they found in the estate of about a thousand acres in Westchester County, lying some three miles east of White

Plains, which had been developed by Ben Halliday, of Overland Mail Express fame, and named by him Ophir Farm, for the mine in the West out of which he had taken much of his fortune. From his possession it had passed into the hands of John Roach, the ship-builder, from whom the Reids took it over. It was already provided with a large granite house, and this was so readily put in shape that the family was comfortably installed in the summer of 1887. But this life in the country had scarcely been begun when fire laid the building in ruins. Reid cabled news of the loss to his father-in-law, who was then in Europe. Mr. Mills, with his usual generosity, not only cabled back his sympathy but offered to help in the rebuilding, and in due course Ophir Farm, or Ophir Hall, as it came thereafter to be called, remained for the Reids a precious resource for relief from the pressure of city life.

As for The Tribune at this time, the sturdy condition of the paper at the end of the campaign of 1884 has already been shown in Reid's letter to Hay on the fatal intervention of Burchard. It had come out of the fight stronger than ever. This was consequently the period of an important step in the improvement of the plant, the introduction of the linotype machine into the composing-room. As a leading spirit in the syndicate formed to underwrite the Mergenthaler invention Reid was not only a preponderant stockholder but an extremely active official. He served for some years as treasurer, and from the beginning he was immersed in a prodigious correspondence looking now to the finances of the enterprise and now to the slow stages of manufacture. What was most like him in this affair was the patient, temperate view he took of the fortunes of the machine, never making large promises of prompt success, but never losing confidence in the final outcome. It took time, of course, to perfect the working of the linotype, even after its principles were clearly established. There had to be experiments without number, breakdowns, and crudities in the early results. The familiar tale of every mechanical revolution was re-enacted, and had its familiar stages of discouragement. But Reid's evenly held faith had its reward. Much of the experimental work was carried on in his own composing-room, and there the machine first functioned triumphantly as part and parcel of the process of getting out a great daily paper. There was, for him, a lasting satisfaction in his association with this progressive achievement. It had been a matter of pride to have seized with promptness upon every advantage that developments of the Hoe press had offered. There had been pride, too, in the erection of The Tribune's towered home. But in his support of the linotype, and especially in the backing he had given it in the composing-room, he had borne a part in a movement affecting an art he loved, the art of printing, all over the world.

In turning from the linotype, the great practical issue of Reid's life as an editor in this period, to the political aspects of his work, it is important to keep in mind the personal rather than the historical purpose of this narrative. From one point of view the election of Grover Cleveland would seem to give occasion here for a glance in retrospect. He brought the Democracy back into power for the first time since the administration of Buchanan, which is to say after a sojourn in the wilderness lasting for practically quarter of a century. The Republican party, as it withdrew from control, left a record upon which it could more than congratulate itself, and to a sketch of the campaign of 1884 such as has been given in the preceding chapter a brief outline of that record would seem a natural pendant in the biography of a Republican editor who had gone on the stump for the party's first candidate, and had been active in its interests ever since. More fitting in this place, however, than any comment on public events, is a note on what I might call Reid's private relation to them. Circumstances mark the period as one of far greater change for him than that from the status of the "ins" to the status of the "outs." He had been to a certain extent in opposition before, using the prerogatives of independent journalism, as we have seen, under Republican Presidents. But when he witnessed the retirement of his party he bade farewell, for a time, to any number of old habits and associations. Blaine's query in January, 1885, as to whether he intended to defer visiting Washington until he could see the capital under Democratic rule, stirs some curious reflections. For Reid to see the city thus transmogrified was like seeing his boyhood's home in the hands of strangers. He had lived with the Republican party since its earliest years. In his young manhood he had formed friendships with its leaders which had been strengthened and multiplied in succeeding campaigns, and as his own influence in journalism had waxed he had come to bear a more and more constructive part in their councils. It had been part of his life to be in fairly close personal touch with the seat of government. In 1884 the break of an order which by that time had taken on an air of permanence signified for him not only a political reverse but the interruption of a characteristic phase of his career. The political conflict went on. Its atmosphere was in a measure altered. Every one in public life felt this. The worst agitations of the reconstruction period had died down. A difficult chapter in American history which the war had left to be written was virtually closed. Though the tariff question was unsettled, statesmen were confronted with what was largely a clean slate. To both parties this very fact constituted a stimulating appeal. In sketching Reid's response to it I haven't the smallest reason for representing him as in any way cast down by the loss of the Republican ticket. His energies were not in the least abated by the cessation of personal intercourse with administration leaders. But it is impossible to ignore the change in sentiment which came at the parting of the ways. To a man like Reid, who had had such close contact with them since before the war, public developments were bound to have in them a tincture of private sadness around the inauguration of Cleveland, the sadness which always goes with the putting away of a host of ancient memories.

It would be a not unnatural assumption, I dare say, that he was prepared for little good in Cleveland's administration. He certainly had no love for the Democracy, and in this particular instance pretty close observation had failed to discover anything in the record of the governor of New York that promised a wonder-working President. Yet Reid had shown in his relations with Tilden, in the earlier years, before they had parted company over the weird proceedings in Cipher Alley, that his partisanship was not of the hidebound variety. He could render justice to Grover Cleveland. Partisanship was not going to stand in the way of his supporting whatever was good in the new administration. But there was small likelihood of his overlooking any of its sins.

This is apparent from his candor with the only member of the cabinet with whom he was on intimate terms, William C. Whitney. "We have seen so much of life as friends together," remarks that devoted Democrat in one of his letters, and their correspondence discloses mutual sympathy and understanding. Whitney was wont to turn to Reid for advice in old years. When in

1875 he began his brilliant career as corporation counsel in New York, their positions in rival political camps did not prevent their uniting on many a public issue. Reid advocated his resigning in 1880, but there was a fight on and Whitney stuck. The following year, when he was "weary of the drudgery and labor, tired of politicians and politics," he asked his friend once more to give judgment on the problem of resignation. Their alliance on questions of office was still intact when Cleveland came in, as may be seen from this announcement of Whitney's entry into the cabinet:

New York,
February 28th, 1885.

My dear Reid:

It may be weak but I have succumbed. I think *you* advised me to take something. I have at the urgent solicitation of both Cleveland and Manning consented to take the Navy Department. I refused yesterday at Albany but they asked me to consider and I have consented. "So goes the world."

Yours,

W. C. Whitney.

The episode is cited here because in the tone of Reid's reply, making the best of the outlook for the benefit of a friend, there is revealed not only the writer's point of view but the sentiment of many Republican observers.

New York,
March 2nd, 1885.

My dear Whitney:

I congratulate you very heartily. It is for you the best outcome of the situation. You know I don't look for a great success for the incoming Administration. But there ought to be a chance—if your Congressmen will only behave well—to make a decided success in the Navy Department. The President ought to be grateful to you —both for what you did before, and for the sacrifice you certainly make now. May he appreciate his mercies. With the heartiest good wishes for good luck and public favor for at least one of the Departments in the incoming Government, I am,

Faithfully yours,

Whitelaw Reid.

It is both friendly and candid. And what followed showed that when public questions arose not all the friendship in the world could lessen Reid's candor. Whitney himself, as a matter of fact, was one of the first men in the administration to encounter rough weather and to read in The Tribune the frankest possible animadversions upon the conduct of his department. They bore, like blisters, upon his treatment of John Roach in the famous affair of the *Dolphin*. But this was only one of the "sins" to which I have alluded. In the matter of Civil Service Reform the magnitude of the upheaval incident to Democratic assumption of control made it a little difficult to strike a just balance. Cleveland "removed, suspended and called for resignations of more public officials of admitted worth and fitness than any other President in American history." In a turnover so sweeping, some good as well as some evil was bound to be done. But the evil was serious. So, as it seemed to The Tribune, was Secretary Bayard's handling of the fishery question with Great Britain, and in the Department of Justice the conduct of Attorney-General Garland was attacked as nothing less than scandalous. There were other defects in the administration on which I need not linger. On the second anniversary of Cleveland's inauguration The Tribune minutely set forth an indictment under the title of "Half Way Through," a broadside which Blaine characterized as "without precedent or parallel."

To traverse the paper at this time is to conclude that it was never livelier or more powerful than when in opposition. "Half way through" it was pretty well convinced that Cleveland would have a Republican successor, and even before that crisis Reid and the men of his circle were full of talk as to who that successor would be. It leads up to the most interesting personal association of the period, his association with Blaine on the question of the latter's position in the field of candidates. Early in 1886, at a dinner of Democrats of Mugwump leanings, where quite another gospel was to have been expected, Hay heard it conceded that Blaine would again be the candidate and would be elected. At the same time Walter Phelps reported from Washington that the friends of the administration daily diminished in number, and that even that stanchest of Mugwumps, Henry Adams, was saying: "It's beyond words. If Blaine were nominated today he would go in without an opposition." Hay protested that he had never heard a President so riddled by his own party as was Cleveland. Nobody but the Mugwumps had a good word for him, and all they could do was to "shut their eyes and scream praises." But he believed that in spite of the current blasphemy the Democrats would renominate Cleveland for want of any one else. What, in that case, he wanted to know, was to be the Republican game? Reid's answer gives a good idea of the situation, as the Republicans began to see the probability of their coming back into power.

New York,
June 10th, 1886.

My dear Colonel:

I begin to think with you that the Democrats will renominate Cleveland. It seems clear that those of us who have been held by the public in the past as the special personal friends of Mr. Blaine ought not to be active in putting him forward again. It is too big a responsibility to take. If the Republican party wants him, it will make the fact known. If it does not want him, we must not undertake to force him upon voters.

My own impression, however, is that he is going to be nominated and that if he is we can probably elect him. I believe he would have a better chance in this state against Cleveland than he had four years ago, and we don't need to improve that record very much, you know, to win. Then it looks to me as if, with the friendship of some of the Southerners and the obvious necessity for a break-up there sooner or later, his nomination might be the signal for it.

Faithfully yours, Whitelaw Reid.

There remained the problem of obtaining a decision in the matter from Blaine himself, and the search after it makes diverting reading in the private records of the time. While he was making up his mind, the situation in which he was so important a factor kept all the leaders on tenter-hooks. In the summer of 1887 Reid had an interesting interview with John Sherman, who was to prove of substantial weight in the convention. The senator called to explain that the time was coming when it was more important than ever that nothing should be permitted to prevent the most cordial understanding and relation between his friends and Blaine's. He was not doing anything to encourage the movement in his own favor. He did not feel as eager for the office as he had felt in 1880 or in 1884. In 1880 particularly he had thought it would be a good thing for him, after having been senator and secretary of the treasury, to round out his career in the presidency. Now, he felt older, the office looked less attractive, he was elected senator for six years longer, and at the expiration of his term would be seventy years of age. He would be contented, if it so turned out, to make the senatorial term close his public life. On no account would there be any misunderstanding between his partisans and Blaine's, or any clashing between the latter and himself. He thought the thing to do was to make every effort for success in 1888, and to select the man who could best secure it. If Blaine desired to be a candidate, or if his friends decided to put him forward, Sherman would not be in the way.

All this, with cogent reflections on the probable status of the party in this or that region of the country, was expounded not only for Reid's edification but with the plain purpose of laying the speaker's cards before Blaine. *His* move in the game, however, was to turn his back upon it. He went off for a long holiday in Europe. Hay likewise went abroad, and meeting the supposedly potential candidate in London, observed simply that he seemed to be having a very good time, going about amongst English statesmen, and, for the nonce, apparently forgetting American politics. It was in a mood of detachment from them that Blaine had sailed. Writing to Reid from Paris he showed that this mood had only been confirmed by reflection at a distance.

Paris,
DEAR MR. REID: October 11th, 1887.

I have got on very well with my year of idleness thus far but I must say that considering the season and the climate the least agreeable place I have been in is Paris. It seems to be a dull and dispirited city. The contrast which I see with my recollections of a brilliant month in Paris when the Empire was at the height of its power is almost painful. That reverse of 1870 was a fearful humiliation to France.

Touching politics, I have been in a condition favorable to temperate conclusions. I have read much and said nothing. My judgment is that the Republican party has grown and is growing in strength, and that with ordinary good sense and good management we ought to win next year. But personally I feel very strongly disinclined to run. In the first place and *radically, I do not feel that I want the office—conceding the election.* In the next place I do not want the turmoil and burdensome exactions of a canvass. My health is good and above all things earthly I wish to keep it so. You of all men, certainly better than any other man, know how reluctant I was to run in 1884 and how I would have pulled out if I could have done so after the matter became serious. And then it is to be considered that a defeated candidate cannot be in the canvass gracefully except upon a general call of the party at least approaching unanimity.

Although I think it probable I could be nominated there will be a contest, serious with Sherman and incidental and irritating with Allison, Lincoln, possibly Harrison and some other favorite sons. Above all I abhor the idea of becoming a chronic candidate, a sort of "Tichborne" claimant for the Presidency. At the proper time if the friends entitled to be consulted—of whom you are chief—shall agree upon with me, I will pull out, and do it in a direct, open, aboveboard way.

Most sincerely, JAMES G. BLAINE.

It was not easy for him to withstand his friends. They sorely wanted him to run, becoming every month more convinced that he would win, and conviction deepened into certainty when he took up the famous challenge on tariff revision flung down by Cleveland in his annual message in December, 1887. It was printed in the papers here on the 7th, and an abstract was cabled abroad in time for it to appear in the European press on the same day. Blaine read it in Paris. Smalley was at hand and arranged for an interview. The result was three columns in The Tribune of the next day, in which the great champion of the protective system made one of his most crushing answers to the free-trade tendencies of Democratic policy. He spoke the right word at precisely the right moment. "That is a magnificent document you print today," wrote Hay to Reid. "What a tremendous contrast between the penny-cracker of the man inside, and the roar, as of great guns, from the man outside. If brains were votes, how easy our battle would be." The interview marked Blaine, of course, as the candidate wanted beyond all others by the Republicans. In a letter describing its effect and the "ocean of eulogy" it had undammed, Reid frankly revived the question of the presidency. "Nobody now considers the nomination of any other Republican candidate probable," he said, "and few doubt that the nomination will come to you with substantial unanimity." With such a nomination clearly foreshadowed, he deprecated above all things any statement definitely taking Blaine out of the race. "Your friends have the right to assume," he maintained, "without calling for any information, written or oral, from you, that you do not disown the obligations of citizenship and that if your party calls upon you conspicuously and by general consent for a public service, you will not refuse it." A few days later he wrote, saying:

"I have had interesting talks with Henry Cabot Lodge and Theodore Roosevelt—both, as you will remember, intensely hostile to you in 1884. Both now say, first, that they think the chances are that nothing can prevent your nomination, and, secondly, that at any rate they prefer your nomination to that of any other man, because they believe it would be the strongest nomination possible and because they are particularly eager to beat the Mugwumps with you."

For Blaine, however, the die was cast. Continuing on his travels, he wrote from Venice in January to reiterate what he had written from Paris in the fall. There was something like solemnity in his renunciation. "For your long strong friendship and sterling devotion to my personal and public interests," he said, "I will attempt no expression of my gratitude. God knows my heart overflows towards you." In that same month he wrote from Florence his formal letter of withdrawal to the chairman of the Republican National Committee, and it is a testimony to the rock-bed foundations of his popularity, unshaken by repeated slanders and the most malignant assaults, that even then the party hesitated to accept his refusal. There were those in the opposition who liked to pretend that he was only manœuvring, and that his followers were manœuvring with him. Reid knew the truth. "He is perfectly sincere, red-hot, in fact," he wrote to General Cassius M. Clay, "in insisting that his name shall not be used." The men who knew him best knew that he was in earnest, and they were terribly depressed. Walter Phelps, with political interests of his own afoot—he was being advocated both for the Senate and for the vice-presidency—nevertheless could not dwell on anything save his absent friend's grave resolution. "Just now I think more of Blaine than of Phelps," he wrote. "It's as if I went out of business."

Hay was similarly disheartened. "I want to see you," he wrote to Reid, "and if possible get some wisdom and courage from you, for the prospect seems excessively gloomy to me." Reid himself adhered to the idea that the demand for Blaine might yet be so overwhelming that there would be no course possible save acquiescence. A few weeks before the convention he wrote to Colonel Clapp, the editor of the Boston "Journal," a letter summing up the feeling of a multitude of Republicans.

New York,
May 2nd, 1888.

MY DEAR COLONEL:

Your view of the absolute sincerity of Mr. Blaine's letter has my full concurrence. Nobody could honestly question the perfect sincerity of his letter, and least of all those who, getting alarmed from hints about his state of mind, did their best to prevent its being written. But if you will look the letter over, you will agree with me, I am confident, in finding nothing in it absolutely inconsistent with his accepting a nomination. He withdraws his name as a candidate, which is his right. The Convention will then consider the names of other candidates who are volunteering. If, after full consideration they feel, as Mr. Lincoln did at the critical period, that the volunteer business is played out and that a draft must be ordered, then I see no reason why Mr. Blaine, more than any other citizen who has sought and received high honors from his party, could, or should, be exempt from the draft. In fact to refuse under such circumstances would seem to me much akin to desertion in the face of the enemy. There is a good deal of sense in the old maxim that the Presidency may not be an office to be sought, but is certainly not one to be refused. It does not seem to me that there is anybody in the United States so big that he can refuse the greatest office on earth without making himself ridiculous or worse. I certainly do not believe Mr. Blaine would.

Now, above all things we must nominate this time to win. If anybody can show a better prospect of winning with somebody else, I, for one, should be content. If they cannot, I shall feel it is our duty to draft Mr. Blaine into the service and his absolutely imperative duty to accept. His health is perfect, and there could be no other excuse.

Faithfully yours,

WHITELAW REID.

On the day he wrote this Reid had a letter from Andrew Carnegie, stating that Blaine had accepted an invitation to go with him on a coaching trip of seven hundred miles, and this ratified conclusions as to his health. "From all the signs," Carnegie added, "I judge he is to be nominated by acclamation. He will be elected." So went the Republican faith, in countless quarters, but from Paris, on May 17th, Blaine wrote the letter to Reid which was published in The Tribune on the 30th, placing his refusal on record with an emphasis that was meant to end discussion. And still it was not ended. At the convention in June, it is true, Blaine was not put in nomination, but so persistent were the hopes of his supporters that for a time they contributed to a deadlock. "The trouble is," said The Tribune humorously, "that the first choice of every candidate, after himself, is Blaine." He was never a stronger candidate than when he declined to accept nomination, a fact giving the handsomest of touches to the story of his presidential aspirations. The Tribune thus succinctly paid him tribute: "Mr. Blaine has done the most magnanimous thing in the history of American politics—intended it from the start, and could not be swerved from it by the most glittering temptations or the most persuasive appeals."

All through the strenuous debate leading up to Blaine's withdrawal Reid had been his friend and counsellor, handling the subject in The Tribune meanwhile with what the much-besought candidate called "consummate tact," letting both sides be heard and holding the scales even. A fitting epilogue to their consultations together is written in this letter:

Cluny Castle,
Kingussie, N. B.
July 6th, 1888.

My dear Mr. Reid:

I should do the gravest injustice to my own feelings—at the close of my personal aspirations for the Presidency—if I should fail to make sincere acknowledgment of the unfailing cordiality, the marked delicacy and the extraordinary efficiency with which for twelve years you have given me the influence of The Tribune, superadded to the personal weight of your own name. Pray be assured that if I have said little I have felt deeply and have now the profoundest gratification in recording in this simple, informal way my sense of gratitude.

You know, better in fact than anyone else, for you have seen my precise state of mind at each quadrennial struggle for the nomination, what a sense of relief it is to me to be out of the fight. The nomination never attracted me except in '76. In '80 I should have gone out if I had not seen, as you so cogently pointed out, that by doing so I could hand over all my friends to the Grant and Conkling axe—and in '84 in the same degree to an axe somewhat weaker but equally bent on the destruction of my friends.

I thought I saw clearly that no such danger could follow in '88. I therefore felt at liberty to act on my own conclusion and did it. I believe it has resulted well, and though I feel gratified in a high degree with the popular demonstration in my favor, I do rejoice with joy exceeding *in my liberty*. I notice that some of my "friends" are quick to announce that I have *retired from political life*. That travels somewhat beyond the record and there may be time and opportunity to correct it.

Faithfully yours always,

James G. Blaine.

He went on the stump for Harrison and Morton, and through his vigorous protectionist speeches contributed measurably to their election.

Reid faced the campaign with another personal disappointment besides that which Blaine's withdrawal had caused him. If Sherman, who had led on several ballots in the convention, had been nominated, it was on the cards that Walter Phelps would have gone on the ticket with him. Reid would have been peculiarly happy with that nomination. But the ticket once adopted, he worked for it with his characteristic thoroughness. There is an apposite passage in a letter of Theodore Roosevelt's in the summer stage of the fight. "I do not think," he says, "there has ever been a better piece of campaign work than your examination of Cleveland's appointment record." The Tribune was full of such things down to the last hour and its influence was heavy. Hay, as ever the first to recognize what his friend did for the party, sent him the morning after the triumph of that party at the polls these words of greeting:

Washington,
November 7th, 1888.

My dear Reid:

The merest justice—if friendship had nothing to say—compels me as an old Republican whose heart is with his party, to write and thank you for the splendid fight you have made in The Tribune, crowned by the glorious victory of yesterday. I have never seen a year when The Tribune has been stronger, firmer, more vitalized than this. And it has been so splendidly good-natured throughout—and good-nature is, after all, the great distinguishing American quality. "Well done, Tribune," is the signal the Republican flags should hang out today.

Yours faithfully,

John Hay.

Before the month was out Hay heard such rumors as he had heard before when a national election was closed, rumors that his friend would accept office under the government. There were always plenty of commentators on a Republican victory who recognized Reid's work in helping to bring it about and expected the new administration to offer him some tangible evidence of its appreciation. When these expectations had been fulfilled, Reid, for his part, had baffled the oracles by refusing all offers. Twice he had declined a foreign mission. Hay was confident, however, that when the third occasion arrived Reid would have to turn diplomat whether he liked it or not, and he amused himself by swearing that nevertheless he, Hay, would not again run The Tribune. He would content himself, instead, with crossing the sea in order to dine with the Reids abroad. He was a good prophet. The appointment was kept, in Paris. Before he went there as minister to France Reid made humorous acknowledgment of his surrender in replying to a telegram of congratulation from Murat Halstead. He said simply: "Do you remember Benedick in the play?"

CHAPTER VII

MINISTER TO FRANCE

Benjamin Harrison was of a deliberate habit of mind, and not only took his own time but kept his own counsel in settling the personnel of his administration. To a certain extent this seemed to have been settled for him by unmistakable circumstance. "It has been evident from the outset," Reid wrote in a private letter, shortly before the inauguration, "that General Harrison started his Cabinet-making with two points settled—1, that the Secretaryship of State should go to the man who was the last chosen Republican leader and came within 1200 votes of being the Republican President, and, 2, that the Treasury should go West." The points were, indeed, practically unavoidable, and in the upshot there was no surprise in the choice of Blaine and Windom. But it was long before the President-elect would put his imprimatur even upon that which had been "evident from the outset." An interesting explanation of his inaction and reticence is given in one of Reid's letters to Blaine. "A remark made to me by General Harrison last October," he says, "may shed a little light on the present situation. The talk had been running on some of Garfield's embarrassments about office. The General said he had often felt so strongly the embarrassments that must sometimes come from having promises of office out, that, like notes of hand, had to be paid or go to protest, that he thought he should never communicate a positive intention to make an appointment till he was actively ready to write the nomination." While the newspapers were taking him as conclusively "slated" for the State Department, Blaine himself, for weeks, was without any information on the subject.

His appointment, of course, was bound to excite some opposition. Hay took note of the grumblings amongst the politicians of Harrison's own State. As he tersely put it, they feared for the run of the kitchen if a first-class man were fixed in the leading cabinet position. They belabored Harrison with warnings as to his "holding second place," just as the small-minded gentry had belabored Garfield eight years before. At the beginning of the administration just enough capital was made out of this beggarly surmise to inspire prudence in both Harrison and Blaine and in all their friends. Against the malcontents who were persistently trying by underground methods to breed dissension between the President and his secretary of state, it became a matter of party loyalty to emphasize the harmony in the cabinet. The situation had its influence upon Whitelaw Reid's acceptance of the French mission.

He had not given a thought to public preferment for himself during the campaign, and he had nothing whatever to do with the talk about it that ran through the press after election day. "I want you to know," he wrote to one friend in March, "that this whole talk of office for me, foreign or at home, is entirely without any suggestion on my part. In no way whatever have I put myself forward or indicated a desire for anything; and the subject has never been even alluded to between the President and myself or between any of his family and myself. We are from the same college, and his wife's brother and I were class mates, so that there is a natural friendship; but that hasn't turned me into an office seeker." He was merely amused to come in the papers upon rumors, portentously circumstantial, to the effect that he was to enter Harrison's cabinet as secretary of the navy. Neither he nor the President knew anything about this supposedly certain appointment. They were equally in the dark as to any assignment to the English mission, but association of Reid's name with this nevertheless persisted, to such an extent that many of his friends regarded the thing as settled, taking Blaine's approval of the idea as a matter of course. Hay, for example, was sure of it. "I think there should be no question about your being offered the English mission or anything else," he wrote. "So I shall hope to meet you next May in London town." Later he said: "Have you made up your mind about England? I should judge it is yours if you want it." And in still another note on the current rumors he remarks: "I suppose you have got on your thinking cap about England. I take it for granted you will have to accept or refuse it." Walter Phelps was "morally sure" that his friend would be offered England, and represented Blaine as "hot for it." While the subject was in the air Reid was content to leave it to the ministrations of his friends. "I'm not indifferent to the distinction," he wrote to one of them. "Least of all would I like to be thought affected enough to pretend to be. But I am very busy, and, much as I might be flattered by the offer, I should be even more embarrassed in arranging to accept it. I haven't been in any sense a candidate. Offices generally don't come to those who don't seek; and if this one by any chance should—well, you remember the great comfort Lincoln got out of his decision not to cross Fox River till he got to it!" When the crossing was reached, and took an unexpected direction, it was John Hay's part to disclose some curious developments in the whole affair.

Blaine wrote to Hay asking him to call one evening in March and see the President. The latter began at once to talk about Reid. He said that the matter had drifted, without any fault on his part, into a position which was very disagreeable to him; that the press was representing Mr. Reid, or his friends for him, as applying for the English mission, and himself as refusing to give it to him; that both these ideas were false. There had not been a moment since the election in which he had not fully intended to offer Mr. Reid some distinguished mark of his regard and confidence; there were reasons why he could not invite him to a place in the cabinet, personally agreeable to him as this would be. He wanted now to appoint him minister to France, but was told by Mr. Reid's friends that he would not accept the place but that he would probably accept the mission to England. He went on at great length to enumerate the objections which lay, in his opinion, against this. Briefly they were as follows: The Tribune had taken up from the first and sustained with great energy and ability the cause of Home Rule in Ireland. It had thrown its whole influence in favor of Mr. Gladstone and against Lord Salisbury, the prime minister. This fact would of itself render Mr. Reid's relations with the British Government less easy and cordial than would be desirable. Hay replied that it was not customary among European governments to take umbrage at the political sentiments of envoys, whereupon the President rejoined that if Mr. Reid's relations with the British Government were friendly and agreeable, a no less regrettable result would follow. The Tribune would be hampered by that very friendliness. Every word telegraphed from London would be quoted to the disadvantage of the administration on one side or the other. The President then went on to compare the two missions, finding the French in many respects the more desirable. He finally said that he would regard Mr. Reid's acceptance of the French mission as a great personal favor to himself. He had been excessively annoyed by the newspaper statements that Mr. Blaine was pressing Mr. Reid for an office, and that he, the President, was reluctant to give him one. The question of cabinet harmony, as I have hinted, could not be ignored. As a personal favor to himself, the President asked Hay to go at once to New York and lay the whole matter before Reid. He did so, and Reid gave due weight to the consideration that if he declined the French mission—as he was inclined to do—it would be seized upon by the Democratic opposition as a proof of a break between him and the administration. He placed his acceptance in the hands of Hay, who returned to Washington and reported it to the President. "He seemed very much gratified and relieved," wrote Hay to Reid. "He said he was conscious that you were making a sacrifice and he appreciated it." Some months later, when Reid was established in Paris, Hay suggested that he imitate his predecessor, Benjamin Franklin, by writing his autobiography, and proposed that he incorporate therein the facts which I have summarized. I have set them forth in this place, believing that, in the absence of such a record, it is doubly fitting for me to show the disinterestedness of Whitelaw Reid's entrance into diplomacy.

He made it in the spring of 1889, sailing with his family for France early in May and arriving in Paris on the 12th. Two days later he was received by M. Spuller, the minister of foreign affairs in the Tirard cabinet, and on the 22d presented his credentials to President Carnot at the Elysée. The time was auspicious, both nations celebrating in 1889 historical anniversaries having unusually sympathetic points of contact, and Reid had a perfect cue for his first official address. "The United States," he said to M. Carnot, "have been celebrating the centennial of their constitution and of the inauguration of their first President, George Washington. It is my happy fortune to be charged with the duty of representing my Government here at a time when France is commemorating a centennial not less momentous. We never forget that you gave the support which helped to make our Revolution successful. It is a memory which quickens now our sympathetic interest in the magnificent display of the arts of peace with which you crown your anniversary. I am instructed that there is not a shadow of a question in dispute between the two great Republics to cloud the historic friendship which has endured for a century." The President in reply cordially recognized the coincidence establishing "one more link between the two peoples," and concluded: "Your task will therefore be an easy one, Monsieur le Ministre; and we bid you welcome." How welcome he was Reid was made to feel in an especially happy manner shortly afterward, when his speech at the Elysée was quoted in full in the Chamber of Deputies as an illustration of the extent to which the French Government had secured the sympathy and regard of other nations. "That speech goes straight to the point," declared M. Hebrard, and on every hand Reid met with the same warm appreciation. "Perhaps I ought to say," he wrote to Blaine, "that in the judgment of the Legation and of people who have spoken to me about it here, my reception has been unusually cordial. Certainly no imaginable element of prompt and polite attention has been missing. For the first time in the history of the Legation the Presidents of the Senate and Chamber of Deputies have made special appointments to receive me in person at their residences. The President sent to have me brought to his box in a place of public amusement before I had been formally presented, and there are everywhere the most friendly expressions."

The Reids made their home in the old mansion at 35 Avenue Hoche of the Comtesse de Grammont, whose father had formerly been French consul-general to Egypt. The house was full of his collection of antiquities, mummies in their cases, cabinets of bronzes and pottery, statues in black basalt of Isis and Osiris. These sombre objects were promptly placed in retirement, and there was little left visible of Egypt save a couple of marble sphinxes decorating the staircase. The whole interior took on a lighter aspect, which came to be widely known in Paris as it became the scene of constant hospitality. The offices of the Legation were in the Rue Galilée, where Reid found invaluable aid in his first and second secretaries, Henry Vignaud, whose name is so well established in the literature of Christopher Columbus, and Augustus Jay. There was a mass of work awaiting the new incumbent. John Bigelow, whose experience as minister to France under the Second Empire had made him a judge of the subject, had warned him of an arduous career. "You will find a little of that kind of business goes a long way," he said. "Going into diplomacy is much like experiencing a shipwreck or going into a battle—a very good thing when it is safely over." Reid encountered nothing to justify quite the disturbing forecast implicit in these words, but he admitted that there was enough to do. "The life here," he wrote to Bigelow, "is pleasant but busy. Americans have been swarming here as if Paris were a new Oklahoma, and the President's proclamation had just taken effect." To Walter Phelps, who had preceded him abroad, going to Berlin as commissioner to the Samoan Conference, he wrote in June in much the same vein. "It was all very nice," he said, "assuming that coming to Paris should be considered in the light of a vacation, but I have not yet found out where the vacation comes in." He had taken the French mission expecting to remain in Paris only about a year and a half. He stayed for three years, absorbed in treaty negotiations and other tasks that proved strenuously exacting.

From the beginning he was involved in a campaign to persuade the French Government to terminate its discrimination against the importation of American pork, and the story of his efforts in this direction runs intermittently through the record of his ministry. Its critical phases were slow in developing, however, and his earlier correspondence from Paris touches upon things in nowise burdensome. The city was *en fête* that summer, the great exposition being the all-absorbing topic. Apropos, he received highly interested inquiries from Americans concerned over the prospects of our own World's Fair, projected for 1893. It will be remembered that New York was intensely desirous of securing the fair. Charles Stewart Smith, president of the Chamber of Commerce, cabled the American minister for details of the French financial scheme. Reid sent them, but with an expression of the hope that if New York was successful in its plans it would not ruin Central Park in the process. To Mayor Grant, who also applied for information, he sent the significant warning that Chicago already had representatives in Paris, "hustling" to learn all that Paris could teach them about organizing an international show. Before the matter was closed he probably heard about as much as any one in the world concerning the opposing claims of Chicago and New York, some of which were calculated to make him gasp. Bigelow wrote that some members of the population were planning to build a tower on Manhattan Island "to which the Eiffel Tower would be only a walking stick." His own attitude was one of strict neutrality, but when Chicago won he specially gratified that city by obtaining from France the first agreement made by any of the European Powers to take part in the Columbian Exposition.

To the Paris fair he owed one of those delectable absurdities which fall to a diplomatic officer abroad as to no other individual. A visitor turned up who had heard that at the close of the exposition the Gobelins tapestries contributed by the French Government were to be given away to various institutions and countries. Reid was forthwith called upon to see to it that a good example was secured for an institution in northern New York. Another of the not infrequent "Legation humors" was the sad case of a certain American who owned some real estate in Paris. This confiding gentleman had the temerity to ask one of his tenants for the month's rent, whereupon the tenant soundly flogged him for his presumption. But the classical example of eccentricity was that which Reid thus describes in a letter to John Hay: "He wanted to know if I could present him to the President of the Republic, giving as his reason simply curiosity to see him, and finally asked me if I thought it would do for him to go up to the front door at Fontainebleau, where the President was then staying, and send in his card. I assured him there was no law against his trying, but he didn't seem to derive courage from my talk. Subsequently his real object in wishing to see the President appeared in a London paper, where in default of the conference he had hoped to get through my agency, he printed an open letter to the President, advising him that Napoleon Bonaparte is to be materialized within a few months for the space of an hour and a half, during which time he is to address an audience of 10,000 Frenchmen in the Place Vendôme."

In this same letter to Hay, by the way, there is an interesting backward glance, recalling historical days at Washington. A trifling controversy had arisen between

Hay and Dana over the question of Hay's presence at the War Department on the night of Lincoln's re-election. Reid had been there, and in his reply to Hay on the subject gave him these reminiscences:

> I recollect distinctly being shown immediately into a private room where Mr. Lincoln and one or two others were sitting about the fire. Among them was the Indiana Secretary—Usher, I think—who congratulated me on something I had recently written about Emerson Etheridge, whom the Republicans were then first suspecting of an intention to organize the House against them through his power of making up the roll.* Usher told me something more about Etheridge, and said I might make effective use of that also. Lincoln, turning to me, said: "No, Reid, I would not do it. Emerson ain't worth more than a squirrel load of powder anyway." I remember, also, being a little crestfallen in finding that some dispatch that I had brought in with what I supposed to be late news, had been anticipated by the War Department dispatches.
>
> Stanton asked me to come to see him in Washington not long before his death, read my sketch of Sherman, from "Ohio in the War," in proof, and told me, to my great surprise, that it was too hard on Sherman. When I expressed wonder at *his* saying that, he replied: "The longer I live, the more I am convinced that a great secret in life is the art of learning to forget."

Reid first made the acquaintance of the American colony in Paris within a few weeks of his arrival, when he called a meeting at the Legation to consider the suffering inflicted by the Johnstown floods, and to raise a fund toward its alleviation. A little later, on the Fourth of July, he acted as the spokesman of the Americans living in Paris who had united in giving to the municipality a reduced replica in bronze of Bartholdi's "Liberty Enlightening the World." The statue was unveiled on the Ile des Cygnes, in the middle of the Seine by the Pont de Grenelle. Reid delivered his speech in the presence of M. Carnot, M. Spuller, and many governmental and municipal notabilities. He had still another statue to deal with, presently. The final acceptance of

*See pages 108–111, vol. I.

the Lafayette monument, commissioned by Congress for Washington from Falguière and Mercié, was left to him to negotiate. He was requested to seek expert advice, and obtained it from the American sculptor Franklin Simmons, who came on from Rome for the purpose, and from M. Taine. He obtained also the warm approval of Senator Edmond de Lafayette and of the Marquis de Rochambeau, Lafayette's grandson, and wound up the affair at a dinner bringing them and the sculptors together at the Avenue Hoche, with Spuller and others. The Reids' relations with the descendants of Washington's comrade were amongst the pleasantest of their stay in Paris. They saw a good deal of his great-grandson, the Marquis de Lasteyrie. From him there came one day a souvenir in the shape of two gold studs, fashioned from buttons that had been worn by the revolutionary hero. Another of his descendants, Count Octave d'Assailly, sent through Reid to the United States a little gift of which probably not all students of Washington relics are aware. This is a pair of eyeglasses made for our first President and presented by him to Lafayette. Blaine placed the memento in the library of the State Department.

The episode of the Lafayette monument is typical of the terms on which Reid was established amongst the artists of Paris. He became familiar with many of the leaders of the Salon, and was soon recognized as the friend of his fellow countrymen in the studios. In the revision of our tariff policy he was unreservedly committed to free art, a fact which positively endeared him to both American and French artists. The most piquant of all his artistic experiences was connected, however, with a rather stormy affair, the publication of Whistler's "Gentle Art of Making Enemies." That inimitable anthology, it will be recalled, was first compiled by an

American journalist, Mr. Sheridan Ford. Before it could be definitively launched Whistler decided to bring the book out himself and had a tremendous time doing it, enjoining Ford in the courts, checkmating him in England and America, then pouncing upon an edition that had been printed in Antwerp, and finally stopping the publication of another in Paris. As Smalley put it in one of his notes from London, "nowhere was there rest for the sole of Mr. Ford's publishing foot." In the Parisian phase of the combat Whistler was substantially helped by the American minister, who introduced him to the *procureur de la république* and in divers ways furthered his campaign of suppression. The incident is commemorated in the inscription adorning the large paper copy of "The Gentle Art" which he received when the "true book" at last appeared—"To Whitelaw Reid, a souvenir of flattering courtesies, and most effective aid in pursuit of The Pirate." The signature is the famous butterfly. There are other names of artists sprinkling Reid's correspondence—Bonnat, Gérôme, Galland (from whom he commissioned a series of mural decorations, panels in the style of Watteau, for the house in New York), Cain, Dubois, and others. But perhaps even more characteristic are certain allusions which mark some of his earliest letters home. "De Freycinet and Clemenceau," he says in one of these, "are men with whom I am on the best of terms. The one is probably the most experienced and able man in the Cabinet; the other came within a vote of being the third man in rank in the Republic." His time was chiefly occupied, in the nature of things, in the observation of French public men and affairs.

He had come to France at a time when the country was nominally in a state of profound quietude, but when political unrest was still perceptible. Only two years previously M. Grévy had left the presidency pursued by the scandal of his son-in-law, M. Wilson's, traffic in the Légion d'Honneur and other decorations. Sadi-Carnot had been put in his place, not by any means under the pressure of a strong public demand, but through the good offices of politicians who thought him, as a respectable "outsider," the most judicious stop-gap they could find. His very respectability was, in some quarters, a matter for contempt. Rochefort scornfully said: "The fact that a man, if you ask him to dinner, will not put your spoons into his pocket, is not a sufficient reason for making him President of a republic." The famous editor of "L'Intransigeant" has cynically told in "Les Aventures de Ma Vie," a rather "yellow" but nevertheless significant epitome of political wire-pulling under the Third Republic, how on the fall of Grévy he was summoned to the offices of "La Justice" to hear the conclusions of Clemenceau, the oracle. Carnot, said the terror of administrations, was not a strong man, but he bore a Republican name. He was perfectly insignificant, but he was the grandson of the "Organizer of Victory." There was nobody better able to balk the return of Ferry, "le Tonkinois," whose expansionist tendencies were the bugbear of the Radicals. So Carnot was duly placed in the presidential chair. He proved, in the event, a more capable executive than had been expected, scrupulous and businesslike, uninspiring, no doubt, but safe.

Reid's acquaintance with the Carnot régime was made when the Boulangist movement was in its closing stages and the Panama affair was coming to a head. He understood the French psychology and the pitch of frenzy to which the country could be raised. I remember an expression of his to me apropos of a later crisis—"the mob, the lunatics and the army who seemed to comprise three-fifths of the French people during the Dreyfus excitement." But he witnessed none of those extremes while he was in Paris. Boulangism had practically spent itself only a few months before his arrival, when the vacillating general had marked time in Durand's café on the night of his election as deputy for the Department of the Seine, instead of seizing the chance which then offered for a ride to the dictatorship on his dark horse. By the time Reid presented his credentials the Boulanger drama, if not quite played out, was at all events limping to its inglorious conclusion. In his letters to Mrs. Reid, who returned to America for a brief visit in the fall, there are some passages on the elections which gave the general his quietus:

September 22nd, 1889.

This morning, after a long romp with the children, I took Mr. Ellis with me and drove about the city to see what Paris looked like on an election day. We went to the Boulangist headquarters in our own Arrondissement and to various polling places. I went through the lines, took my handful of tickets from the ticket distributors, went to the "urns" as they call their ballot boxes; and in fact did about everything but corrupt the French elections by smuggling a Yankee ballot into the box. The town seemed to me almost as quiet as on any ordinary day.

September 23rd, 1889.

Last night I spent driving about Paris and trying to find how it compared with New York on the evening of an exciting election. The scenes were very much the same excepting that they had less disorder and more soldiers. A line of cavalry blocked the way across the Boulevard de l'Opéra, out of the Place, and back of the cavalry was a strong line of infantry. I ran against similar obstructions in two or three similar places;—in fact near all the anti-Government newspaper offices of importance. But the crowds were in the main good-natured and very polite.

Once or twice, especially on Montmartre, the red, white and blue cockade* attracted attention and the crowd shouted "Constans!" Even then there was little rudeness, though they jeered the coachman and tried to find the monogram or arms on the door.

* The customary colors identifying the carriage of the American minister.

The result, as you may have seen from the papers, is, as yet, indecisive. Constans himself failed of a majority and is in *ballotage.* So, it is believed, is Clemenceau; and, oddly enough, so is Boulanger. As it looks now the Government seems likely to have a majority of the next Chamber, but a reduced one.

September 24th, 1889.

The election news will be generally considered a triumph for the Government. The Royalists have probably made slight gains; but the Boulangists have not, and it looks as if Boulanger were used up.

September 26th, 1889.

There seems to be no doubt now in the minds of any that the Government here has a substantial victory. Certainly the disappointment of the Monarchists, Imperialists and Boulangists is overwhelming. The "Figaro" is busy explaining what the Republicans ought now to do to consolidate their power and better the conditions of France.

CHAPTER VIII

POLITICS IN FRANCE

The American minister had more than a spectator's interest in the French elections. The results they produced had a definite bearing upon his principal diplomatic problem, the French policy in the matter of American pork. When this commodity was excluded from French ports in 1881 the prohibitory decree was based on sanitary grounds. Our pork was put under the ban —unjustly—as contributing to the spread of trichinosis. This fallacy persisted to some extent down into the period of Reid's dealings with the subject, but by that time the core of the controversy had come to be recognized for what it was—one essentially economic. Considered in that light the situation had grown somewhat serious. In the year before the passage of the decree just mentioned, the exports of American pork products into France had amounted to $3,900,000. In 1889 they amounted to but $5,000. Where the rehabilitation of this trade hinged upon political conditions in France, the trend of elections and the composition of cabinets, was in the mutations these things registered in French tariff policy. The tide was against Reid when he entered upon his task. Tirard was a premier of free-trade predilections, and he had sympathizers in his cabinet, but more of his colleagues were for a defensive policy, and the Chamber was thoroughly permeated with protectionist ideas. The events of September were not, on the whole, very encouraging to American interests. M. Spuller told Reid frankly that the question between them was generally considered one of protection, and that the new Chamber was more strongly protectionist than its predecessor. To that extent the American minister had a rather unfavorable report to make to Secretary Blaine and President Harrison. His letters to them, however, take a larger scope.

The year 1889 was a critical one for the republic. The exposition was a case of magnificent window-dressing, obscuring but not concealing a governmental instability which threatened every day to suffer complete disintegration amid the clash of parties. There were malcontents who laughed it to scorn as celebrating the principles of 1789. They appraised it rather as a move in the game of opportunist politics. Doubtless the enterprise had its ambiguous aspects, of which Reid was not unaware. Writing to the President of the friendly attitude on the pork question of nearly every member of Tirard's cabinet, he adds: "They all have a kindly feeling also because of our attitude towards their exposition while Europe was boycotting it;—and on their success with the exposition their official lives depend." Decidedly the fair was a political expedient as well as an index to the national prosperity which Reid's observations everywhere confirmed. But as a good Republican himself he rejoiced to mark in the September elections the triumph over party subversiveness which the exposition, when all was said, really symbolized. That the monarchical interests stayed away did, in fact, no harm. The principles of 1789 were, veritably, in the saddle. In a long letter to Mr. Harrison, which I append in condensed form, Reid sketched the leading tendencies in a notable moment of modern French history:

Paris,
January 24th, 1890.

My dear Mr. President:

The only really important piece of news I had to communicate was intrusted personally to Mr. Russell Harrison. That was the message from the Minister of Foreign Affairs given some months before the elections, to the effect that the Government was absolutely secure, and that the elections would show the utter collapse of Boulangism. Events, as we have seen, showed how thoroughly the Minister of Foreign Affairs knew what he was talking about. At the same time a candid onlooker must confess that he found also distinct signs that the Government knew how to use, and did use, its tremendous power in every quarter of France to secure its victory.

Its strength, of course, lay in the irreconcilable interests of the mongrel coalition formed against it. Imperialists, Monarchists, and the more reckless Radicals, who formed the bulk of the Boulangist party, could, of course, have no ideas in common as to the proper use of their victory, in case they should win one. An insidious effort was made to set up an issue. Instead of fighting the Republic, which, it would seem, was what they really meant, they insisted that their immediate aim was a revision of the constitution, with a view of securing greater stability and preventing the instant overthrow of the Cabinet at every fresh gust in the Chamber. No doubt many of the Government believe that such a revision is desirable; but now they hesitate to take any steps not compelled by the immediate necessities of the hour. Their policy now, as much as at any previous period, is best described by their own word, "Opportunist."

In a word, so far as I can see, the Tirard Cabinet, which is already noted as unusually long lived, has a fair show to live a good deal longer. The President has steadily grown in popularity and strength since last May. Even some of the Reactionary Monarchists now speak well of him as a respectable man, and express their satisfaction that France no longer needs to be ashamed of the Elysée.

The Foreign Minister yesterday confirmed what I have before reported to the State Department, that in his judgment there is very little hope of any speedy removal of the present prohibition on American pork, on account of the strong protection feeling in the Chamber. He is himself warmly in favor of the removal. So far as I can make out there is little, if any, positive unfriendliness to the removal in the Cabinet. But they removed it once only to have the Chamber immediately restore it. Naturally they do not wish another slip of that kind at present, and as far as any of them have been willing to express an opinion, it was to the effect that they have less chance with this Chamber than they had with the last.

If M. Spuller is correct in his opinion as to the probable course of the Chamber, then at present negotiation is not likely to do much good. They have heretofore, however, been a good deal afraid of retaliation. If there should be a strong movement in our Congress towards increasing the duty on wines, and if some of the speeches should advocate that on the same ground on which they base their exclusion of American pork, viz: the unhealthfulness of the product, it might have a good effect. Adulteration of French wines is, of course, notorious. Some documents already furnished Congress by the State Department contain a good deal of interesting evidence about it. Possibly a higher duty on silk might be judiciously proposed at the same time. The moment the French Chamber became convinced that there is a real probability of such legislation they would be deluged with protests and complaints from their constituents. If we could then approach the Government with a suggestion that the best way to avoid the threatened action of Congress would be to show a rational spirit on the subject of pork, and if we could add that prompt and friendly action on this subject might lead to a law admitting French pictures free, there might be a better chance for reaching a satisfactory result than at present.

The French commercial treaties with Germany and other countries expire by limitation in about two years. There is obviously a settled purpose not to renew these treaties but to adopt instead a strong, general, protective tariff.

Faithfully yours,

WHITELAW REID.

There was nothing to be done in Paris as regarded the tariff situation that winter save to wait with patience for a favorable opening, so it was in December that the Reids went south for a holiday on the Riviera and below. They drove in an open landau along the Corniche from Nice to Genoa, and then went straight on to Naples for a week of warm weather. They returned by way of Rome and Turin, getting back to Paris for the New Year's reception at the Elysée and a crowded season. Reid was planning then for a leave of absence of some weeks to be spent at home in the early spring. The Tribune was to celebrate its fiftieth anniversary on the 10th of April, and J. Q. A. Ward expected to finish in time for it the bronze statue of Horace Greeley which he had been commissioned to execute for a site under one of the arches of the paper's building. A letter of Reid's to Walter Phelps at Berlin contains some striking reflections on the speech he was meditating for the occasion. "I have long thought," he said, "of taking this, or some other suitable occasion, for a word on the real relations of Greeley, Chase and Seward to the anti-slavery movement, as compared with the status of the Boston sentimentalists, Garrison and Phillips. The latter confined themselves to denunciation, and to the work which was easiest, since all for which they could seem really to claim authorship was the arraying of the churches and of both political parties for a long time against their anti-slavery movement. The others confined themselves to practical work, and to political agencies. To the practical men who did the work, should go, in my opinion, the great honor. The brilliant talkers have already had more than they deserve, and will be less and less esteemed, while the fame of the workers will grow. To say this as tersely and bluntly as I would like would arouse a storm of dissent. Is it true in the broadest and justest sense, and, if true, is it wise to say it now?" He wanted to analyze Greeley's life as having been essentially summed up in a struggle for two classes, the poor negroes and the poor whites. For the latter Greeley had championed a homestead law, had urged railroads and all other means of developing the West, and by all the means in his power he had encouraged emigration to that region, "Go West, young man," being the slogan for a deeply constructive campaign. He had done his best, also, to assure living wages to these people by a lifelong advocacy of the protective tariff, and he had sought to insure safety and happiness for their families by popularizing temperance and education. Reid was sure, as he said, that the liberation of his "practical" ideas would create a storm, but he felt equally sure that the protestants would be chiefly Mugwumps or Democrats, "and it would be a solid satisfaction to show that class that the claims to consideration of the ancestors of some of them were as flimsy as their own. It would also be a satisfaction to pursue the thought and show the difference between practical politicians now, who do things, and the Mugwumps who merely denounce things." It was Ward's fault that the storm did not break. The statue was not finished in time. The provocative speech was not even drawn up. What Reid contemplated saying in it is of interest as illustrating the point of view of a man who had grown up during the anti-slavery movement and had witnessed the Civil War at first-hand.

It was one of the great pleasures of this European period of his that he could have a frequent exchange of thoughts with Walter Phelps, on the anti-slavery movement and innumerable other topics. Phelps was now in Berlin as minister, his letters suggesting that a winter in the German capital was "almost a cause of suicide," but giving along with this impression much piquant comment on people and things. He was ever a devoted "Tribune man," and matters journalistic as well as diplomatic engaged his attention. "I have got intimate with Bismarck and these tough old dignitaries," he said, "and discovered how even they are recognizing the insignificance of any individual, less than an Emperor, against the power of the press." In another glimpse of the Iron Chancellor he adds a rather unexpected characterization of him: "The Prince was simple and gentle and kind." This was in February, 1890, when the Samoan treaty was ratified in the United States Senate, and Bismarck had invited Mr. and Mrs. Phelps to a dinner to celebrate the event. A month later, when he broke with the Emperor and resigned his office, it is possible that his demeanor was less gentle and bland. Reid had many opportunities to talk German politics and affairs with one of the most intimate of his colleagues in the diplomatic corps in Paris, the German ambassador, Count Munster. Also they talked sport, having in common an enthusiasm for the horse. Munster was one of the great horse-breeders of Hanover, and a devoted rider. Long afterward Reid recited with feeling the picturesque experience he owed to this noted fancier. He had ridden horses all his life, he said, nearly everything, in fact, that goes on four legs, not forgetting a bucking Arizona bronco, but the animal that gave him something to do was a Hanoverian steed that he almost but not quite bought from Munster. He took the horse out to try it in Paris one morning, and after leaving the Arc de Triomphe it bolted three several times. Reid got the beast into the Bois finally, and rode for an hour or so, but then it bolted again, and this time went like a shot from the Bois to the Arc, straight through the crowd of fashionable equestrians who were out at eleven o'clock in the morning. The American minister had for a moment the hair-raising prospect of being held responsible for several deaths, including his own. He concluded that the Hanoverian horse had a mouth.

Riding was, on the whole, his sole open-air relaxation in Paris, but he had an amusing day's shooting in the presidential preserves at Rambouillet, in the description of which he gives a full picture of a characteristic French function:

Paris,
January 31st, 1890.

My dear Mr. Mills:

Perhaps it would amuse you to have a little account of my first experience in shooting. Arrayed in knickerbockers and leggings, but pretty well concealed in my big astrakhan coat, I presented myself at the Montparnasse station, and was cordially welcomed by Colonel Lichtenstein, of the military household of the Elysée, and by young Carnot, the President's eldest son. These two came to represent the President, who has not yet quite recovered his strength after his attack of the grippe. The party consisted of Count Munster, the German Ambassador; Count Moltke-Hatzfeldt, the Danish Minister; Ramon Fernandez, the Mexican Minister; Baron de Tucher, the Bavarian; Count Foucher de Careil, formerly ambassador in Italy, I think, and now senator, and a French deputy whose name escapes me.

It took an hour to run out to Rambouillet. Carriages met us there, and after a rapid drive through the town we entered the grounds of an old castle which dates from the fifteenth century and is still in a fine state of preservation. Instead of stopping at this as I expected, we drove on for about half a mile through the grounds until we reached what seemed to be barracks for the soldiers in charge of the national property, and a house which seemed to be the head-quarters of the commandant, and possibly, also, of the chief game-keeper. A young officer of Hussars in their exceedingly neat black-braided uniform, bordered with astrakhan fur, saluted us as we alighted, and the servants immediately grasped our overcoats and conducted us to our rooms. We were hardly given time to wash the dust from our faces when breakfast was announced. This was arranged as ceremoniously as if it was a dinner at the Elysée. Within a few minutes after breakfast the officer had us in our carriages again, driving rapidly toward the forest, followed by a big omnibus carrying the servants with the guns and ammunition.

Presently we were stopped at a point where the road ran for perhaps a hundred yards along the side of a thick wood; the wood, however, was only about a hundred yards deep. Beyond it were open fields with a quite thick growth of underbrush. Forty or fifty beaters, in long white blouses, each wearing his number on his cap and carrying a stout stick in his hand, were stationed on the further side of this open field. The officer stationed each of us at a particular point along the road facing the wood. When arranged we were in a line covering the whole of the front of the wood, and no one more than from ten to fifteen yards distant from his neighbor. Finally a bugle on our side sounded. A moment later an answering bugle was heard from the line of beaters, and then as far as we could see or hear, everything was silent for a few moments. Then through the openings in the woods we could see the pheasants beginning to run back and forth:—the line of beaters had begun to advance toward us. They came very slowly, using their sticks to make a noise in the bushes and occasionally to poke into the thick clumps. Within, say, four or five minutes after the first note of the bugle the first pheasants flew over us. In a moment or two there must have been half a dozen. The most went to my right down the line. Several were brought down immediately by Count Munster and Count Moltke. Presently one came my way, within rather long range. I thought the chance was against me, fired, and as luck would have it brought down my bird.

After the woods had been thoroughly beaten, we faced about and went over another common with the line of beaters behind us, keeping in the same respective positions in nearly all cases. The officer of Hussars accompanied us and put each man in his place. Then we took carriages again and drove for a mile or more, stopping at last in the midst of a thick forest, where the road seemed to cut it in two. At either end of the wood in the open fields beyond were men with bright colored flags. The officer stationed us along the road, but at much greater distance apart. The beaters also seemed to be a third of a mile away, or possibly more. We could scarcely hear their bugle in answer to ours. After waiting five or ten minutes, however, we could sight a deer stealing through the edge of the wood, and when startled by the bright flags there, turning and coming toward us with long high jumps. He brought a shot from the extreme end of the line but escaped into the woods behind. Two or three more came presently and before the beaters had reached us, something like twenty or thirty deer must have made the attempt to break past our line into the woods behind us. Two came within my range. I succeeded in getting one but had to empty both barrels for him. When he fell I found that I had struck him on the foreleg and in the chest. He was a young buck, and looked quite well, in my eyes at least, when he was brought out of the woods and laid at my stand. The German Ambassador got two deer during the same run, the Danish Minister also got two, and one or two others one apiece.

The German and Danish representatives shot about two to my one, the Bavarian a little more than myself, and some of the rest considerably less. Count Munster, who had stood near me at most of the stands and had been polite enough several times to express his approval of my shooting, confided to me on his way back that it had behooved me to make a fair record since the other representative of my continent had not. "In fact," said he in a good humored burst, "I don't believe the Mexican shot anything all day, except a beater."

Affectionately yours,

W. R.

The next note of interest in Reid's correspondence is, again, the political one. It was in this winter that there occurred a cabinet crisis of great importance to his negotiations. M. Tirard, who was slated to go out, was certain to take with him considerable free-trade influence, and on his exit the protectionist leanings of the Chamber would inevitably be strengthened. The situation promised greater difficulties in the solution of Reid's tariff problem. He was not to learn of the definitive phase of the crisis, as it happened, until he reached New York on a brief leave of absence—it developed three days after he had sailed from France—but he witnessed some of the preliminary developments. His account of them reflects the color and movement of life in the Chamber and discloses the typical political fluidity with which he had to reckon:

Paris,
March 7th, 1890.

My dear Mr. Mills:

For a week or two the air has been filled with stories of dissensions in the Cabinet, controversies between M. Tirard and M. Constans, hostility to M. Spuller, a general tendency inside the Cabinet to explode, and a general determination outside to break it down. Things came to a head inside in a controversy about the appointment of a judge to one of the highest courts. M. Tirard favored the appointment of a former Minister of Justice. M. Constans surprised some of his critics by insisting on the most rigorous Civil Service theory of promotion from among the highest officers already on the Bench. Some sort of a scene occurred, in the midst of which M. Constans tendered his resignation, rose, offered his hand to the President, and left the room, in spite of entreaties that he would remain. M. Tirard then tendered his resignation, which was refused. The Cabinet acted with promptness and as it would now appear with wisdom in selecting as successor M. Bourgeois, a strong Radical, whose appearance as Minister of the Interior somewhat consoled the ultra radicals for the disappearance of Constans.

From the outside came the inevitable interpellation in the Chamber. I went early but found the Diplomatic Gallery well filled, Count Munster, Count Hoyos and M. Leon y Castillo in the Ambassadors' seats and a number of Ministers in the others, besides a crowd of attachés. The speeches made on the interpellation were comparatively quiet. When M. Tirard took the tribune to reply he was received at first with solemn silence; when he said that the resignation of M. Constans was purely a personal course and that he himself regretted it, the Chamber burst into a storm of contemptuous laughter; and from that time on, every sentence M. Tirard uttered was greeted with shouts of derision and jeering replies, not only from the Royalists but from the very heart of the Radical camp. The scene was actually pitiable. When he left the tribune he did not seem to have a friend in the Chamber.

The new man to be in Constans' place, M. Bourgeois, then took the tribune. The contrast between his reception and that given to Tirard must have been galling to the last degree. Bourgeois spoke well and with absolute independence, apparently, of the rest of the Cabinet—announced *his* programme as if he had been a Minister for years instead of for hours, and played directly into the hands of the Extreme Radicals to whom he belongs. They received his speech with tumultuous applause and as he left the tribune he fairly had an ovation. The debate was continued chiefly by Republicans of various shades, all of whom united in attacking the Ministry, denouncing it for lack of policy, lack of courage, lack of leadership, and for allowing itself to be "decapitated" by the disappearance of its ablest member. M. Ribot and M. Clemenceau both made strong speeches which, though not quite so violent as some of the others, were distinctly and almost savagely hostile.

The climax was reached when M. Paul de Cassagnac, the fiery Bonapartist and hero of so many duels, took the tribune. He denounced the Ministry as the most worthless and impotent with which France had ever been cursed; sneered at M. Tirard as having already abdicated his position and yielded the real authority to speak for the Government to his colleague of twenty-four hours' standing, M. Bourgeois; declared that the new man was the real President of the Council, or rather that there were two Presidents of the Council, one of whom clung to the name, while the other one already enjoyed the power, asserted the authority and was recognized by the Chamber. He described the Ministry as having lost its head when Constans went out. The whole speech bristled with the most exasperating sneers of this sort, and strangely enough it was received with howls of delight.

At last came the vote, and then we had one of those bewildering surprises which make French politics such a fascinating uncertainty even to the close student of them. Count Munster had said to me half a dozen times during the debate, "the Cabinet will surely fall," "this will surely bring it down," "it must be defeated on this vote," etc., etc. Every experienced diplomat around me seemed to have the same view. Only just at the close we began to notice a change and it was whispered that perhaps the Radicals were going to save the Government after all for the sake of protecting their new man, M. Bourgeois. Sure enough, when the vote was counted, it was seen that the Extreme Radicals had not voted at all. The right had of course voted against the Government, and the Moderate

Republicans had voted for it. The Government thus had a majority of 49, and poor M. Tirard, after having been flouted and insulted by his own party in a way that would seem impossible in any other Government in the world, was actually kept in office by these same men.

Affectionately yours,

W. R.

The majority vote, though consoling to M. Tirard, was generally regarded as only postponing the crisis, and Reid went to the next meeting of the Chamber with expectations of tension which were not disappointed. M. Spuller, the foreign minister, was this time looked upon as the probable victim. With Count Munster he had been discussing the proposals of the French Government as to the forthcoming labor conference at Berlin, and he faced an interpellation concerning the sending of delegates. The Boulangist who opened the debate drew down upon himself the wrath of even his own allies by allusions having an interest to this day. He exposed the weakness of France in her supply of coal, the same weakness of which we heard so much in the late war. Germany was aware of it in 1890, as she was quarter of a century later. When the speaker explained that if the hours of labor were shortened in France the country could not get coal enough, Count Munster turned to the American minister and whispered: "That is true, and that is what makes them so mad at him for telling it." In the upshot Spuller won. He made a speech which swiftly obtained the respectful attention of the whole Chamber and wound up amid cheers. They were cheers for the solidarity of all parties in a matter being debated across the frontier. The irrepressible Paul de Cassagnac interrupted the calls for the *clôture* by rushing into the tribune and declaring that on an occasion involving a question of foreign policy they were all Frenchmen, and that the man did not comprehend the situation who imagined that in the face of the issue presented by M. Spuller there was any majority or any minority. Again the government was nominally secure. The Radicals, who were bent on overturning the ministry, saw that it would not do to attempt it on a question of foreign policy.

While Reid regarded the vote as strengthening Spuller, personally, he continued to look for the early overthrow of the government. His comments on the situation sketch the prospect, and his own concern in it. "Nobody believes," he wrote to Mr. Mills, "that the Ministry can last very long; and unless a great change comes, the next one will be overwhelmingly Protectionist. It will be friendly enough to us, no doubt, but will do little if anything for us, about pork,—will be less likely to than the present Cabinet. There were one or two curious things to note on the floor of the Chamber during the uproar. Poor Tirard sat on the front bench, beside Spuller, and witnessed every phase of his colleague's triumph on the very spot where he had been himself flouted and morally broken down. De Freycinet had been too ill—and people smile when they tell it—to attend the Cabinet meeting when Constans and Tirard quarrelled, or to appear in the Chamber when the matter was discussed. But he found his way to the Chamber today just after Spuller's speech, and sat down beside the man they credit him with the desire of supplanting. He does look feeble. Clemenceau watched everything like a hawk, but did not once rise or open his mouth. He had shared most actively in the demonstration against Tirard, and he has predicted the downfall of Spuller." The predictions of M. Clemenceau, touching the comings and goings of cabinets, were always weighty. In the middle of March the premiership passed from M. Tirard to M. de Freycinet, M. Constans formed part of the new ministry, and M. Spuller, as specifically forecast by "the Tiger," ceased to be foreign minister. He gave way to M. Ribot. The latter ranked as a moderate protectionist. Married to an American wife, and in warm sympathy with our people and institutions, he proved a by no means complaisant but still very friendly minister with whom to deal in what he was wont to call *l'affaire des petits cochons.*

The ramifications of that affair were numerous in the extreme and led through statistical and legislative tracts which would hardly repay exploration now. I may summarize briefly the campaign through which the American minister brought M. Ribot to his way of thinking. It was somewhat complicated, as he found on a flying visit home in the spring of 1890, by provisions in the McKinley administrative bill then pending, which were scarcely calculated to please the French. Reid took advantage of the opportunity to discuss the matter with his own people at close range, primed Blaine, and sought the good offices of John Sherman in the Senate. Returned to Paris, he had frequent conferences with M. Ribot in which the relation of French wines and of French works of art to the American tariff were not neglected. The going was not easy. "They are now all scolding about the McKinley bills," he wrote to Mr. Mills that summer, "and threatening retaliation." He brought up the question of retaliation himself, from the American point of view, making it serve as a delicate hint in a long letter to M. Ribot which was published shortly afterward through action of the United States Senate in calling for the correspondence on the subject. Satisfactory results from these negotiations began to take shape in the fall, when the struggle with the government was virtually over. By the summer of 1891 the cabinet was well committed to a tariff measure involving the prompt withdrawal of the prohibitory decree, and a favorable vote was obtained in the Chamber.

Action in the Senate was subject to some little delay, and in the interim an interesting effect ensued. Germany took the hint given by the demonstration in the lower house. All along she had been sending to the American minister and to others to find out what France was going to do, and when it would be done. She acted with alacrity on the vote in the Chamber, rushing in to get the credit of being the first to let down the bars against American pork. Reid seized the point to clinch matters with M. Ribot. "I have dwelt on the desirability of doing the thing handsomely," he wrote to President Harrison, "when they have made up their minds to do it; and I once told M. Ribot that their course was not French at all; that France was not accustomed to let Germany lead it, and that when the French did a thing it was a national characteristic to do it gracefully. I could see that this went home." His diplomacy went home not only with Ribot but with other members of the government and with numerous deputies. He made friends for the measure of Constans, Rouvier, Meline, Jules Ferry, Felix Faure, and scores of their colleagues. Jules Siegfried was especially helpful to him. Reid won over the opposition till an unusual friendliness prevailed. On December 5th, 1891, the lifting of the prohibitory decree marked a truly cordial reopening of the ports of France to an important American commodity. This success had, too, a more than local implication. The decisive vote in the Chamber, as I have noted, had accelerated German action, and it was not without influence upon similar legislation in Denmark and Italy. The secretary of state wrote thus:

Stanwood
Bar Harbor
August 4th, 1891.

MY DEAR MR. REID:

Accept my congratulations upon the successful conclusion of the pork question. It has been one of the most vexatious subjects that any minister has had to deal with and you have conducted it wisely from the beginning. You have shown patience, perseverance and great tact at every stage of the negotiation.

Very sincerely yours, JAMES G. BLAINE.

Along with his negotiations over the pork question in their later stages Reid also secured the adhesion of the French Government to a convention of commercial reciprocity involving certain other staples. In recognition of our giving free admission to two or three products of French or French-Colonial origin, a number of our own commodities were listed for admission into France under the minimum duties of a rather portentous tariff system. Reid was never inclined to overestimate the importance of this little treaty, to which he obtained M. Carnot's signature just before he returned to America in the spring of 1892, but neither did he regard as easy the long discussions through which he was able to further its interests with M. Jules Roche, the minister of commerce. When the French went in for protection they did so with a whole-heartedness staggering even to the advocate of a kindred principle in American policy. The definitive bill toward which the Chamber of Deputies was moving all through the American minister's term in Paris, and passed in his last year there, advanced the duties on some commodities as much as 400 per cent. With a spirit like that abroad in French tariff legislation, such a degree of reciprocity as he achieved required a disproportionate amount of hard work.

The other treaty with which he was concerned, that on extradition, was even more difficult to arrange. It was projected as early as May, 1890. In the preceding March President Harrison had proclaimed the new extradition convention between the United States and Great Britain supplementing the old Ashburton-Webster treaty of 1842. Our extradition treaty with France, dating from a year later, had twice been supplemented, in 1845 and in 1858, but the three documents contained altogether only ten specifications of crime, far fewer than existed in the treaties with Great Britain, Spain, Belgium, Japan, and other countries. President Harrison and Secretary Blaine desired to bring all the extradition treaties of the United States up to date, and as a contribution to this end a draft of a new treaty with France was sent to Reid, with instructions to forward its acceptance as quickly as possible. It took him nearly two years to put the matter through at the Quai d'Orsay. Not until December, 1891, did he begin to see light there. "The treaty negotiation has been kept back," he then wrote to Blaine, "because Ribot, years ago, prepared a bill covering extradition questions, which got through one house. He has now given up hope of its getting through the other, and so is willing to negotiate." Willingness aided, but was long in clarifying the task of arriving at a mutual understanding. Reid found that the French civil code and our American criminal law, based on the old English law, were very different institutions, and that with varying definitions of crime in the two it was a heavy task to harmonize them. Mere nomenclature made a formidable stumbling-block. The Legation's counsel had his hands full clearing out a dense thicket of technical terms. In Reid's various reports on the negotiations there is nowhere a more concisely expressive passage than this one—"The discussion for fixing the exact text of the instrument in both languages was elaborate and protracted." Protracted, indeed.

CHAPTER IX

SULTAN, KHEDIVE, AND EMPRESS

In a world subject to the gusty fluctuations of French politics the burdens of treaty-making were relieved by occasional absences from Paris. I have mentioned an excursion along the Riviera and into Italy, and a short visit home. In the winter of 1890 the Reids went to Constantinople and spent about two months in Turkey and Egypt. Dana had been at the Avenue Hoche not long before, and with him they had discussed their probable itinerary. To him, when the journey was over, Mr. Reid sent this account of it:

Paris,
February 18th, 1891.

Dear Mr. Dana:

We followed very largely the route you recommended when you were here. We missed Broussa, because the Sultan did me the honor to invite me to dinner at the palace, on a day which so exactly bisected the time we had left, that we could neither go to Broussa before the dinner, nor after it, without losing a week to catch the next steamer touching at the points we required on the coast of Asia Minor. The dinner at the palace was singularly interesting. The Sultan himself impressed me as an able, kindly man, much to be pitied in one way, because of the traditions of the place, and the constant suspicion of plots and intrigues all about him. He was most kind and courteous and his talk covered a wide range of subjects. It was a large dinner. The Grand Vizier, the Minister of Foreign Affairs, General Osman of Plevna, the Chief Admiral, and a lot of other Turkish officials of high rank were present. The palace was chiefly in the French style, although there were some rooms with a distinctively Oriental character.

From Constantinople we went to Smyrna, where we had a very pleasant day; and thence, with various stops at Rhodes and other islands, to Beyrout. Here the Governor of the Lebanon and others gave me all the attention I could dream of, and, in fact, rather more than I had time for. Thence we went on to Cyprus, Xaifa, and finally to Jaffa. We had a week in Palestine, with good weather, excepting when we were at the Dead Sea, where it rained as it must have done in the original storm that overwhelmed the cities of the plain.

In going to Cairo we went through the Suez Canal, which is an extremely interesting thing to do—once. Cairo was attractive, and there were more dinners and breakfasts than I found time for. The most charming portion of the trip in Egypt came afterwards, when I took a boat, and Mrs. Reid and myself started up to the First Cataract with our two servants, a Syrian dragoman, a French cook, and an Arab boat crew. It was assuredly one of the most satisfactory fortnights of sightseeing we have ever spent anywhere. We saw far more than the tourist ordinarily does, and did it in far less time. We immediately preceded the Khedive, and so had the advantage of the tremendous mending of roads, bridging of ditches, and whitewashing of Egyptian villages which had been done in his behalf. We went on to the island of Philæ from the First Cataract, and the depth of the impression it all made is perhaps best conveyed by my telling you that when, afterwards, we reached Athens, and I had driven the first afternoon up to the Acropolis, I could not help saying: "Why, after all, the Parthenon is modern, it is twenty five hundred years younger than the temples I was looking at last week, and not half so well preserved." We had only a week in Athens, and the weather had been so bad that we were advised not to attempt Olympia, but we saw Athens thoroughly. The hardest part of the whole trip was coming from Patras by way of Brindisi to Paris.

Very truly yours,

WHITELAW REID.

There were notable personalities all the way—the Sultan, the Khedive, and, in Athens, the King. There was the incomparable spectacle of the Greek monuments. Reid was deeply moved by the panorama of antiquity. "The part which will last longest," he wrote afterward to Walter Phelps, "is not the little glimpse of royalty in different countries, but the month in Palestine and Egypt." Nevertheless, it is a "little glimpse of royalty" which I would cite from his correspondence, an impression of Turkish court ceremonial which he set down to while away the time while storm-bound on the way to

Jaffa in his tour of the Holy Land. It amplifies with photographic accuracy of detail the passing note given in his letter to Dana, describing Abdul Hamid:

Haifa, Syria,
December 13th, 1890.

My dear Mr. Mills:

A day or two after we arrived at Constantinople I was told that the Sultan had expressed a willingness to our Minister to receive me immediately after his formal attendance at prayers at his private Mosque on the Turkish Sunday (Friday) which Lizzie and I were to attend. We were taken up in great state by the Minister, with a fine old Turk with curved scimitar at his side, pistols in his belt and a red fez on his head mounted as footman on the box. Our carriage halted exactly opposite the Mosque, where many troops were already drawn up, and, preceded by our *Cavasse*, we entered a house where, in the second story, two rooms with windows looking on the road and on the Mosque are set apart for the diplomatic corps. We waited nearly an hour. At last came carts, sprinkling sand over the road from the palace, and in a few moments came the first officers of the Sultan's suite, marching down the road and taking positions on either side the entrance to the Mosque. It was half past twelve by Infidel and Christian watches; but the Sultan regulates the time like everything else; and it was not till a little later still that the voice of the Muezzin from the balcony of the Minaret summoned the Faithful at high noon to prayer.

His summons began the moment the Sultan had passed the palace gates. It was a phenomenal, an amazing voice, and could be distinctly heard above the half score of military bands that were now playing their loudest, as the carriage of the Sultan passed slowly down under our eyes, between the files of his troops. The soldiers presented arms, and the high officers of state who lined the entrance stooped till their hands seemed to touch the ground, then touched rapidly their knees, their lips and their foreheads, with a quick and graceful motion still upwards. The Sultan saluted, right and left in reply, touching his lips and forehead. He sat alone, on the back seat of the landau, in military uniform, sword at side, fez on his head, and the uniform nearly concealed by an overcoat not unlike an ulster. Opposite him sat a great Turkish General, the hero of Plevna, in full uniform. As they passed under the diplomatic windows the Sultan looked up and saluted; a moment later his carriage had passed into the enclosure around the Mosque, had passed the carriages of the Harem where all the women sat, veiled, waiting to see their Lord and Master go by; and he had walked up the scarlet-carpeted steps into the Mosque. As he passed, going and coming, he impressed me as prematurely aged, and rather anxious-looking. But his bearing was one of great dignity, and his manner was very graceful. The people seemed almost to regard him as a god, and the troops evidently liked him.

On Monday evening we drove up the same road, passed the Mosque, and stopped at the palace gate. Here our old Turk dismounted from the box, red fez, curved sword, pistols and all, and an officer of the Sultan's guard mounted to the box in his place. When we entered the grounds I could only see in the darkness that they were extensive, and that we could look down on the Bosphorus and some vessels of the Turkish fleet. At last we stopped in a glare of light, officers saluted, servants took our wraps, and as we went upstairs soldiers presented arms. I was presented at once to the Grand Vizier. Next I was presented to the Minister of Foreign Affairs, a portly, fine looking and almost jolly official. He spoke French fluently, as nearly all of them do, and so I got on. I had some talk with Woods Pacha, the Englishman whom they have made Admiral; with General Osman Digna, who told me he knew General Gallifet, whose son I have been helping to get married to Miss Stevens, and with one or two others.

At last a splendid looking fellow, over six feet high, Musurus Bey, Grand Master of Ceremonies, came in, greeted me cordially, and led me off to be presented to the Sultan. The Grand Vizier, the Minister of Foreign Affairs, and our American Minister, with his Secretary and Chief Dragoman, also came. We went through three or four rooms. Then Musurus Bey left us, and entered an adjoining room. Presently he reappeared, walking backwards, and bowing to the ground and saluting at every step. A pace or two behind him came the Sultan. He advanced at once to Mr. Hirsch, bowed slightly, said a few words in Turkish and offered his hand. Then he asked after the health of Mr. Harrison, and the Dragoman translated Mr. Hirsch's reply. Then he addressed me in Turkish and held out his hand. I replied to his inquiries after my health. He bowed pleasantly, saluted his own Minister, and started for the dining room, preceded by the Grand Master of Ceremonies, who still walked backwards before him and bowed to the earth at every step.

The band played as the Sultan entered and took his seat at the head of the long table, nearest the door. Mr. Hirsch and I followed, he taking the Sultan's right and I his left. The two highest Turkish officers sat next, but near me was placed our Chief Dragoman, a man with the same rank as our first Secretaries, and highly accomplished. He was to interpret the Sultan's conversation. Part of the time, however, the Sultan called in the Grand Master of Ceremonies, who stood at the corner of the table throughout the dinner. He translated the Sultan's Turkish into French for me, and I replied, as best I could. They say the Sultan really understands French quite well, but he refuses to speak it, or to have any conversation save in Turkish. The Sultan of course led the conversation. In fact nobody spoke excepting the Americans, and, occasionally, a Turk, when the Sultan addressed some remark to him. The rest of the time they ate in silence and seemed to be furtively watching his every movement out of the corners of their eyes. Never before have I seen educated and intelligent men give such plain evidence of the effect the unlimited power of an arbitrary monarch over them may have upon their bearing and even their thoughts.

The Sultan spoke frequently and easily to Mr. Hirsch and myself—after the manner of a man of the world, not introducing many serious topics, and touching everything briefly. He seemed much pleased at the admiration I frankly expressed for the military display of Friday; and he assured me that the men were as soldierly as they looked, and that they were through and through devoted to their country and their Government. He spoke of the cholera in Syria, where he heard I was going, and said he could assure me it was decreasing rapidly and might even now be said to be almost at an end. He asked me about Lew Wallace; said he preserved a most agreeable recollection of him, and that he would like to have such men in his own service. He alluded to the electric light, with which the dining room was illuminated, as being the invention of a countryman of mine, and said he had also procured his phonograph, and wished to assure me that it worked very well. The talk ran on in this way, with intervals of silence, during the hour or hour and a quarter that the dinner lasted.

The company left the dining room as it had entered, the Grand Master walking backward before the Sultan and bowing to the ground at every step; Mr. Hirsch and I following the Sultan; and the Grand Vizier and the Minister of Foreign Affairs coming next. We passed immediately into the smoking room, only the three Turks named and our party accompanying the Sultan. Here the little company stood for two or three minutes in general conversation. Then the Sultan handed me a cigarette. He now took a seat behind a little table on which stood cigarettes and matches; and motioned the rest of us to seats about him. The talk here was light and general. Coffee was served and I was engaged in quietly looking at the curious furniture, all the legs and framework of which were made of gun stocks, gun barrels, lances and other kinds of arms, when the Foreign Minister advised me that the Sultan had just ordered that the highest decoration of his Government, for women, be sent to Mrs. Reid.

Affectionately yours, WHITELAW REID.

The allusion to Lew Wallace in the foregoing letter is enhanced in interest by remarks made elsewhere in Reid's correspondence. It would appear that the Sultan's appreciative remembrance of the American minister at his court during Arthur's administration was not altogether approved in his entourage. He wanted Wallace attached in a position of suitable dignity to his own person, because he felt that he could trust his honesty and friendship, as well as his judgment, but in asking Reid to convey this message he added: "I want to get an answer from him, and to get it through a safe channel." He gave careful explanations as to how the answer should be communicated. When it was procured Reid embodied it in a letter to the chief dragoman of the American Legation at Constantinople, who in turn delivered it to the Sultan, sealed, through the hands of a court chamberlain specially delegated to look after the incident. Prior to this Wallace had received more than one message from the Sultan and had always replied, but his own letters had regularly failed to get into the hands of his imperial correspondent, probably because of the intervention of some palace politician. If Reid had any doubts as to the existence of that traditional type in Eastern court life they were dispelled when he reached Cairo, and by a person who was surely qualified to speak with authority.

When he was presented to the Khedive, that potentate, speaking English with ease, made much light, pleasant conversation on harmless topics, like the little book in which the programme for his forthcoming voyage up the Nile was set forth day by day. He lingered with innocent pride over the beautiful map drawn for every stage of the journey. Then he suddenly asked his guest what he thought of Constantinople. Remembering that his interlocutor's father, the ex-Khedive Ismail, was held practically a prisoner there, though living at great ease in a magnificent palace, Reid was a little in doubt as to how much to say about Turkey. The Khedive promptly relieved his anxiety by saying: "You will find Cairo very different. There is no such net work of intrigues here as surrounds the Sultan. Things here are plain and above-board."

Sir Evelyn Baring, the future Lord Cromer, then in the earlier phase of his remarkable work for Egypt, struck his American visitor as already perhaps even more important than the Khedive himself. The Reids breakfasted with the Barings, and in one of his home letters there is a passage on the British agent's views. "He gave me the impression that the present Khedive is a great improvement on his Father, who had plunged the affairs of Egypt into dreadful confusion. He complains of the French and also of Turkish influences, but said the root of the difficulties lay in the religion, or rather in that phase of it affecting family life."

At Constantinople Reid had heard of the author of "Ben Hur." In the Holy Land he came upon the trail of John Hay. Returning from a rainy visit to the Dead Sea they rested in the hotel at Jericho, and there, hunting around for something to beguile a quiet day, Mrs. Reid found just one book in the place, an English edition of "The Bread Winners." Hay heard of this in due course, and when in the following summer he visited at the Avenue Hoche he added these lines to the souvenirs of his friends' recent travels:

"Through Jericho, through Jericho,
Brave Whitelaw and his bride did go,
Of literature they were in need,
For there was nothing there to Reid.

In Jericho, in Jericho
They sought good reading high and low,

But—here is where the joke occurs—
Found nothing but the Breadwinners.

In Jericho, in Jericho
From morning till the sun was low,
The Lady read, till dews 'gan fall,
The Breadwinners — by Mendenhall."

On their return the Reids were in time to witness a curious upheaval of French sentiment, provoked that winter by an unexpected visit paid to Paris by the Empress Frederick of Germany. She had left Berlin presumably to go straight to London, but she broke her journey at Paris, having business there in connection with the bequest of two millions left to her by the Duchesse Galliera. Her proceedings in the city were surely innocuous enough and even favorable to French interests, for much of her time was spent in the purchase of furniture and decorations for her castle of Königstein, near Hamburg. Otherwise she went to an exhibition of pictures at the Epatant, visited Bonnat, talked about the forthcoming international exhibition of the fine arts at Berlin, to which the leading painters of France had decided to contribute, and altogether dispensed olive-branches. Unhappily, these did not please the Boulangists, and though there were friendly hands to applaud Wagner and Mozart at the Lamoureux concert which was one of the episodes of her visit, there were firebrands, M. Déroulède and others, who tried their best by appeals to current chauvinism to revive the anti-German emotions of 1870. When the Empress chose this unlucky moment to look in upon Versailles, of all places in the world, something like a storm of public feeling arose. It subsided, however, with no worse effects than the withdrawal of the French artists aforementioned from the enterprise at Berlin. The Reids, who took luncheon with the Empress at the Bavarian Legation the day before she made her unpopular pilgrimage, and saw her on other occasions in Paris, had from her own lips the explanation of her innocent misstep. Writing to Dana about it, Reid said:

We have had a rather interesting time in Paris lately. The visit of the Empress was a case of skating on extremely thin ice, and for several days Paris was perilously near an ugly explosion. The Empress, herself, was serenely unconscious of the situation most of the time, and when she realized it, she met it with a courage and dignity worthy of her husband. She is altogether a remarkable woman;—I think you would call her almost as interesting as the Sultan. There seems to be no subject of "contemporaneous human interest," as Daly says, on which she has not information, as well as opinions, and these last are apt to be pretty positive. Her devotion to the memory of her husband is really touching, and it was a curious fact, which she mentioned to Mrs. Reid, that the famous visit to Versailles, which so excited Paris, was really due to her earnest craving to see again the spot where her husband had spent so many months, and from which he had written her so many scores, and even hundreds, of letters, which she still religiously preserves. Odd, isn't it, how often we find a bit of sentiment shaping the gravest international complications!

Dana's name frequently recurs in Reid's correspondence at this time. All the ancient irritabilities had fallen away and given place to a delightful friendship. In April, 1891, when The Tribune celebrated its fiftieth anniversary with a great meeting in the Metropolitan Opera House, at which McKinley, George William Curtis, and Chauncey M. Depew made speeches and Edmund Clarence Stedman read a poem, the editor of the "Sun" spoke on the traits of Horace Greeley. "The world has changed," he said, among other things, as he glanced at the old quarrelsome days in which he had first known The Tribune. "It is entirely changed now. It is wonderful how little personal controversy there is in our great newspapers." Whereat a ripple of laughter ran through the vast auditorium, for his hearers appreciated the private application of this public statement. He was more than once Reid's guest in Paris. It was to Dana that the American minister gave a dinner, just prior to the Eastern journey I have described, which in the list of those bidden to it reads truly like a dinner of all the talents. It embraced, of the principal guest's own profession, Clemenceau, Joseph Reinach, M. Magnard, and the inimitable De Blowitz. The painters Bonnat, Gérôme, Carolus-Duran, and Madrazo were balanced by the sculptors Dubois and Cain, and the composer Massenet.

These figures of the Parisian world are characteristic of the old records in which I have found their traces. It was natural that Whitelaw Reid should come to know in Clemenceau, for example, not only the statesman but the writer. At the balls, dinners, and receptions which made the hotel in the Avenue Hoche brilliant during the season, letters and the arts exchanged salutations with the *haut monde*. It is, of course, impossible to revive in this place the personalia of those scenes—the latter are too crowded—but it is interesting to recall a few of the high lights in the picture—Dumas *fils*, the Duc de Broglie, the Marechal Canrobert, Lord Lytton, from the British Embassy, Senor Leon y Castillo, from the Spanish, whom Reid was to meet again over the Peace Treaty of 1898, Essad Pacha, the Turkish ambassador, Jules Simon and Ernest Renan, John Sargent, and all the leading figures in French politics, Floquet, Tirard, Meline, Constans, Spuller, and so on. Amongst the Americans always present there were often old friends, men like Evarts and Hay, Speaker Reed, Wayne MacVeagh, W. E. Chandler, James Gordon Bennett, and Thomas Bailey Aldrich. Edison, who went over with his wife for the exhibition, came to know the hospitality of the Avenue Hoche, and in a farewell letter he touches on the secret of the welcome given by the American minister to his countrymen. He might be incapable of making a speech, says the great inventor of himself, and be obliged at times to seek protection beneath the official wing of the American eagle, but he was not incapable, he insisted, of anchoring his thoughts upon a sheet of paper. He thanked Reid "for having made me feel so much at home in a foreign country." At the Legation offices in the Rue Galilée and at his own house Reid received travelling Americans in an atmosphere which made the general verdict very like Edison's.

I may mention here, amongst his lighter occupations, a piece of literary work in which he took a strong interest. His friend the Duc de Broglie was editing for publication the long-suppressed memoirs of Talleyrand, and "in a moment of thoughtless confidence" Reid promised M. de Beaufort, who was making the translation for England and America, that he would write a brief introduction for the editions in those countries. "This," he wrote to Smalley, "was like letting one's little finger get caught in the cog wheels of running machinery; it presently drew the rest of me in." The brief introduction became a full-dress essay. Besides, he was soon obligated to make selections from the memoirs for three numbers of the "Century" in the winter of 1891, and as he had to struggle for the first French proofs off the press in order to get on with his own task, there were times when he wondered why in the world he had taken up the pen again. The resultant analysis of the famous statesman will be found prefixed to the memoirs, and in Reid's "American and English Studies." It is the most anecdotic and picturesque paper he ever wrote, a vivid, richly colored excursion into revolutionary history. As a portrait it is accurate, and, as an estimate, suavely pitiless. Talleyrand's prodigious ability is recognized and due weight is given to the strangely patriotic elements underlying his tortuous career. "The evil Talleyrand did was chiefly to individuals. The good he did was to France." But the broad conclusion is shaded by no diplomatic amenity. "The memoirs," he said, "will not change the world's verdict on the profligate Abbé of Perigord and Bishop of Autun. They will not lighten the censure of the Foreign Minister who made merchandise of his treaties, and became a millionaire on bribes. They will not make the world think it honorable in him to have deceived or betrayed in turn almost every man under whom he held office."

When Reid accepted the French mission his retirement from The Tribune for the period of his absence abroad was decisive, as explicitly announced on the editorial page. But he would have been more than human not to have been an intensely interested spectator of Tribune affairs. I have glanced at his notes for a speech to be made at the unveiling of the Greeley statue. It was a disappointment to him that the sculptor's work was delayed, and he was sorry again that he could not be in New York when the bronze was unveiled on September 20th, 1890. Hay presided over the ceremonies, in which Bishop Potter and Mr. Depew also took part. The jubilee I have mentioned was another event which it was hard for him to miss. "It is a solemn thought," Hay wrote to him, "that out of The Tribune's fifty years, nearly half of them are yours, and that you are still a young man. Before you pass over to the majority the history, as well as the prosperity, of that great organ will be principally your own." From Hay and from others he had much news on political developments. Elkins, writing after the fall elections in 1890, was perturbed over the shadow they threw upon the prospects of the party. Hay, in the following spring, reported comforting signs—the party, it was plain, had not lost its fighting qualities—but he thought the Republicans had come upon evil days, politically, and he was especially worried about breaks in the senatorial line. Ratting was in alarming vogue. There were about a dozen Republican senators who could not be relied upon for any distinctive party measure. He mentioned, also, indications of trouble in the cabinet; there were ugly rumors afloat about the relations of Blaine and Harrison. Hay expected to take ship before the end of April for a run over to London and Paris, and he would surely see Reid, but the measure of his distress over the situation is given in his inability to wait till he got abroad to disclose its bad aspects.

There was no end to the appeals to Reid to come back and take a hand in the fight. The fact was that his plans for retiring were made before any of these importunities reached him. This may be seen from the following letter:

Paris,
December 1st, 1891.

My dear Mr. President:

As you are aware, I was not able to accept the high mission with which you honored me on any understanding that it would be possible to absent myself from New York long enough to serve the full term. My private affairs have long required my attention and I should have been glad to retire months ago if I could properly have done so. But the negotiations for the admission of American pork and for an extradition treaty were still delayed and I did not feel that it would be just to the Government to leave my post in the midst of this unfinished business.

The pork question has now been fought through all its stages—at the Foreign Office, with the Cabinet, in the Chamber, in the Senate, and back again in the Chamber. So far as the Government was concerned, we had it settled over a year ago, and in the controlling branch of the French Parliament it was settled in principle last July, though the later contests in the Senate and Chamber have been sharp and difficult. Nothing now remains but the Executive decree, which is promised as soon as the Administrative details can be arranged.

For nearly two years I could get no satisfaction about the Extradition question. At last they have committed themselves to immediate negotiations which I have some reason to hope may be concluded within the next month or two. I deem it my duty therefore to advise you now that I hope to be able to tender my resignation at any time after the close of January next that may best suit your convenience—to take effect either on my leaving my post or after my report, with the treaty, at Washington, as may be thought best for the interests of the service.

Hoping that these plans, as well as my work here, may meet your approval, I am, with the highest respect,

Faithfully yours,

WHITELAW REID.

The President felt the force of this letter, and he, too, like the others I have cited, was well aware of the fact that the American minister's return would have its influence upon public affairs. He sent this reply:

Executive Mansion,
Washington,
December 14th, 1891.

MY DEAR MR. REID:

Your note of December 1st has been received. What you said to Mrs. McKee while she was at your house in Paris, prepared me for what you now say as to your desire to surrender your place. I assure you that, from a public standpoint, it is a matter of regret to me that you cannot finish your term at the French capital. The only mitigating circumstance is that you will be at home where your counsel and help may be needed by our party in a contest which is to determine whether the progressive and healthful American influences, which Republican administration gives, are to be perpetuated. You know I am not at all given to the use of indiscriminate praise; but I would not be just to you or myself if I did not say that your term at the Court of France has been very conspicuous and most eminently satisfactory. You have made the selection of a successor a work of very great difficulty. What a pity it is that diplomacy is not more a career with us! However, it is very complimentary to America and American society that our foreign representatives, even at the most attractive courts of Europe, get enough of foreign life inside of a four years' term.

With very kind regards to Mrs. Reid, I am,

Very sincerely your friend,

BENJ. HARRISON.

From the moment this letter was received the date to be fixed for the departure of the Reids from Paris was only a question of the extradition treaty. The negotiations for this were moving auspiciously, and, as we have seen, when Reid wrote to the President in December he expected only a month or two of further delay. He had established the best of relations with the government of Premier de Freycinet, and could count upon a confidence there which promised the speediest results. Then, in about the middle of February, the ministry fell, being defeated in the Chamber in a crisis developed between the Clericals and Radicals over the matter of the religious associations in France. With his staterooms on the *Bourgogne* already engaged, Reid had to swallow the fact that there existed in Paris no ministry to see his extradition treaty through. There was nothing to do but "reverse the engines." There was, however, comparatively little delay in setting them going again in the right direction. Ten days later the feverish efforts made by Rouvier, Constans, Ribot, and Bourgeois to form a new ministry seemed to have brought a deadlock; but just when the sky looked darkest there was a rift in the clouds, and M. Loubet proved successful. In his cabinet, fortunately for the American minister, M. Ribot, with whom he was accustomed to deal on sympathetic terms, took over the portfolio of foreign affairs. Carnot's signature to the treaty was thus secured, and Reid was able to make all his arrangements to sail with his family on March 25th. On the advice of a cable sent to him by Blaine he kept his resignation in his pocket, handing it to the President when he arrived in Washington.

Ribot, Tirard, and Spuller were among the speakers at the great banquet given the departing minister by the Americans resident in Paris. M. Ribot testified both to the popularity of Reid's mission and to its solid practical achievements. "Mr. Whitelaw Reid has won our friendship and our affection," he said. "He has paid us a compliment in so quickly learning to speak the French language fluently—and he has used this rapidly acquired knowledge, gentlemen, to become a most persuasive and most successful business orator!" He pointed out that Reid had made every one of his negotiations a success. Though the extradition treaty was destined to run against some snags in our Senate, Reid terminated his mission with the clear knowledge that it had won approval both at home and abroad.

As Mr. John Harjes, the chairman at the banquet aforesaid, had hinted, this mission had not been a sinecure. Reid sketched the interests which had occupied him. "With the Paris exposition at the beginning," he said, "and the Chicago exposition at the end; with the McKinley bill and the new French tariff; with copyright and the duty on works of art; with pork, reciprocity, and extradition, there has not been much leisure." He animadverted with a smile upon the idea that the President and Mr. Blaine had had in proposing his going to Paris—the idea that it would be good for him to take it as a vacation. For a vacation, indeed, he was returning to New York. But he did not find it there, either. On the contrary, he went back to the liveliest of political activities. The small chance that there was of his obtaining rest at home is thus suggested:

Washington,
February 11th, 1892.

My dear Reid:

I am glad to hear that you are definitely coming home; for although you and Mrs. Reid are representing us more splendidly than has ever been done before, or will be for many a long year to come, the place has done for you all it can do. If you stayed a year or two more you could do no more than repeat the successes of the past three years and that is clearly not worth your while. Over here, a great fight is beginning. You can come home with a very large addition of prestige, and can throw a greater personal influence into the scale than you have ever done before. The Tribune has been admirable in your absence and especially during the last few months. I fancy Bromley is back. But the imagination plays a considerable part, and the moment you appear on the ground and are seen in Printing House Square people will discover a new energy and force in everything the paper says.

Blaine tells me he has cabled you today not to hurry but to wait and bring your treaties over and resign after you get home. Blaine, after breaking all our hearts with his final letter of declination*—(for this, of course, *is* final, he will never more be a candidate) seems as gay as a boy. He looked positively well today, at a small concert at his house. His face had a good color, and the whole aspect of him was cheerful and serene. "The Great Renunciation" seems to agree with him, as with Prince Gautama. His position is henceforth unique in our history. The only man who ever refused two nominations for the Presidency, one of which at least was equivalent to an election. It makes me boil with impotent rage to see our Mugwumps blackguard this magnanimous statesman as the worst and vilest of politicians.

I think Harrison is sure of the nomination now and there is a fighting chance to elect him. It is going to be terribly hard work as the Democrats have the dice loaded almost everywhere. But I hope a great deal from the bitter animosity between Cleveland and Hill in New York—and the chapter of accidents. With the utter lack of conduct and leadership in their vast majority in the House, we ought to make a good deal of capital by June.

Mrs. Hay sends her love to Mrs. Reid and I am always

Faithfully yours,

JOHN HAY.

* Written on February 6th, 1892, to Hon. J. S. Clarkson, chairman of the Republican National Committee, saying that he was not a candidate for the presidency, and that his name would not go before the convention for the nomination.

CHAPTER X

THE CAMPAIGN OF 1892

For three years Whitelaw Reid had been out of American politics, observing them at a distance with the deepest interest, but scrupulously "keeping his hands off." Years afterward, in a public speech, he affirmed in some detail the principle by which he had been governed in all diplomatic matters from the moment that he went to Paris—"No ambassador has the right to carry his politics on the outward voyage beyond Sandy Hook." Fidelity to this axiom had undoubtedly contributed to the success of the French mission, and tact had added to the effect of his discretion. M. de Blowitz, paying tribute in the London "Times" to that success, cited one apt judgment: "He has added to the cleverness of the Americans the urbanity of the French." At home as well as abroad his record as minister was enveloped in an atmosphere of friendliness, and on his return he received a peculiarly cordial welcome. There were banquets given him by the Ohio Society, the Chamber of Commerce, and the Lotos Club. The press was appreciative and generous, as it had been, indeed, throughout the period of his stay in France. At the Chamber of Commerce dinner he specially thanked his colleagues in the profession for the support they had given him "without distinction of parties and without exception." When it came Dana's turn to speak, he, too, glanced at the point. "The honors which you are paying to our distinguished fellow-citizen, Mr. Reid," he said, "are not only well deserved, but, as has been remarked, they are paid in substance by all parties in this country. When you can get not merely a Republican like my friend Mr. Charles Stewart Smith, and a celebrated Mugwump like my friend Mr. Coudert, and modest and unpretentious Democrats like Senator Brice and myself, to come here and join in the honor; and when General Schurz, the worst Mugwump of them all, comes, and when they all combine in paying this well deserved tribute to a distinguished and successful public servant, we may be sure that the honor is perfectly deserved; and that greater services hereafter may be expected from the gentleman who has rendered them."

Dana's remarks were doubly to the point, for while they expressed the non-partisan character of the approval bestowed upon the French mission they also indicated a fact familiar to all those present, namely, that in partisan quarters there was every intention of calling upon Reid for "greater services." More than a year before this time he had been talked of at home for an elective office. He had been suggested for the vice-presidency and for the senatorship from New York. Through all this period of political gossip and newspaper speculation he preserved an attitude of detachment. He was not a candidate for any office and was, indeed, far more interested in the fortunes of the extradition treaty in the Senate. There were some minor matters from Paris that continued to occupy his correspondence down to the formal acceptance of his resignation on April 26th, and the mere process of settling down in New York after so long an absence was engrossing enough. Yet the battles of the party had always to be fought and he was drawn into them with the least possible delay.

The need of the hour was Republican harmony in New York. The Democrats had held the governorship for a comfortable period. After Cleveland's election to the presidency they kept D. B. Hill, his lieutenant-governor, in the chair at Albany to which he had automatically succeeded, and then, on the translation of that adroit politician to the United States Senate, they elected Roswell P. Flower in his place. In the ten years through which their own prestige had thus been blanketed, the Republicans had so sapped their party solidarity that factional restlessness within the State threatened a wider harmfulness in 1892. The "Big Four" responsible for management in this crisis—Chauncey Depew, T. C. Platt, Warner Miller, and Frank Hiscock—were unable to fuse the warring elements in the organization. Platt was himself a particularly incalculable factor. His retirement from the Senate with Conkling had not, after all, terminated his influence. Whatever ground he had lost had been regained and he was now a leader with whom it was necessary to reckon. Harrison didn't like reckoning with him, and the less he did so the more chance there was of Platt's failing to co-operate in the national campaign. Almost immediately upon his return Reid found that he was expected to do what he could to pour oil upon the troubled waters, and bring all the tonnage of the party into one orderly fleet. The very abstention from political entanglements to which I have referred marked him for the task. It was as a leader allied with no faction at all that he was made permanent chairman of the Republican State convention, held at Albany on April 28th.

The business of this assemblage was to elect delegates-at-large to the national convention and to provide New York with a sound Republican platform on which to make its stand at Minneapolis in June. The occasion was also one to blend with the enunciation of broad doctrine a little admonition to the local leaders. This was Reid's function, and in view of the fact that he was later to bear a heavy share in the presidential campaign I may cite some parts of his speech, those exposing the flaws in the Democratic record and those appealing for Republican unity against the foe. He said:

Having resigned office abroad, I hold it a privilege to resume at once the duties of citizenship at home. Thirty-six years ago, a boy fresh from college and not yet able to vote, I made my first political speech, for Fremont and Dayton. From that day to this I have never seen a time when the duty of Republican success seemed clearer or its possibility more evident than now.

We are often reminded by our friends who generally agree with us in principle more nearly than with any other party, but who as generally vote against us in practice, in order to chasten us for our good, that a past record is no title to present confidence. Perhaps not; certainly not, if the record is all there is. But if the record of the Republican party through the whole thirty-six years of its glorious history is not a sufficient reason for trust in it now, it is at least no controlling reason for distrust. Can any one say as much for the other party? Let us not be unkind enough to go back too far. Let me merely ask if its record last winter, either in Albany or in Washington, is a satisfactory guarantee for the future. Are the farmers of New York, even the Democratic farmers, anxious that another legislature like this should have another chance at their tax levy? Are even the Democratic business men of New York anxious that this Congress should have its way unopposed, about either free silver or the tariff? Is there one of them who did not secretly give thanks, last winter, that they had been beaten four years ago, and that there now sits on watch in the White House the safe, honest, sturdy, great big "man under his grandfather's hat"? Is there one who would not rejoice if this State of New York were fortunate enough to have some one like him now in our Governor's residence in Albany?

Our opponents may plan the capture of the next Legislature, as they organized the theft of this one. They may renew and multiply their devices for binding hand and foot the majority of the lawful voters of this State; but it is still the majority and it cannot be permanently bound. The spring elections have given but the first whisper of the coming storm. Nobody who knows our political history doubts that, on critical occasions and with a fair count, New York is now, as it has been from the beginning, essentially a Republican state. At the very outset it gave Fremont a plurality of 80,000 votes over James Buchanan. In the nine Presidential elections held since the organization of the Republican party, New York has never been carried by the Democrats excepting when their party had composed its internal dissensions and was absolutely united behind an exceptionally strong and popular New York candidate; just three times in thirty-six years.

Well, gentlemen, the stars in their courses have fought for us. We ask now but one thing, a right the denial of which means revolution; we demand a fair, non-partisan count. This secured, we can carry New York if we choose; and, with New York, we can carry the Nation. I do not say that we cannot do it without New York; but I do say that no prudent politician would make that sort of a calculation, or dream for an instant of taking that sort of risk. Well, shall we carry New York? Only one thing is needed to do it; simple, natural, and, as I believe at this time, very easy. We must "get together." As has so often been said, there are enough Republicans in the State of New York for one successful Republican party; but there are not enough for two. You cannot have one to win the victory this year, and count that the other can take the victory next year. One year the city would pull and the country wouldn't; another year the country would pull and the city wouldn't; and so it has sometimes happened that splendid popular leaders like Fassett have fallen by the wayside when they ought to have been elected. Whenever we both pulled the load was moved; and if ever, in the thirty-six years of our history we had an incentive to pull all together we certainly have one now. This then seems to me the short and simple road to victory—Get together!

It will be observed that while this is an administration speech it is not Harrisonian, in the sense of the speaker's tending to commit himself or the convention to the renomination of the President. The platform adopted disclosed the same reserve. It congratulated Harrison, gave him a vote of confidence, but that was all. Democratic comment was quick to interpret this as a case of giving the President less than his due, and waxed scornful of a convention that had neglected to "instruct" for him. The truth is that open-mindedness on the part of the people at Albany as to the choice to be made at Minneapolis was dictated by a common-sense view of the facts and was perfectly sincere, implying no undervaluation of Harrison. The all-important point was to pick the candidate who was most likely to win, and at that moment the problem was frankly insoluble. Blaine, in spite of himself, was an important source of dubiety. He had said that he wouldn't run, but his large following was still hopeful that he might be persuaded to do so. While Reid strove for the harmony in New York State essential to the effective support of a Republican candidate, whoever he might be, he was entirely willing to wait until June to see what June would bring forth. The completeness of his severance from the direction of The Tribune during his diplomatic service freed him from any embarrassment in the matter. For the readers who had any doubt on the subject an editorial published as he was returning from Paris contained these unequivocal words: "Just at this time it may with propriety be said that The Tribune has criticized the administration of President Harrison without hesitation where it has seemed to be in error. . . . The Tribune has never in any way urged the re-nomination of President Harrison, cordially as it admires the man and approves his course, for it has believed that the people were abundantly able to judge his Administration fairly, and that the Republican party had wisdom enough when the time should come to select the right candidate for the contest of 1892." Thenceforth, until the decision was made by the convention, the paper was only strengthened in its course of dispassionate neutrality by current talk of Reid's possible status as a running mate with Harrison.

The outstanding feature in the preliminary stages of the campaign of 1892 was the uncertainty with which Harrison's name was canvassed for a renomination, and nowhere was this uncertainty more diversely explained than in the inner circles of the Republican camp. Elkins, for example, now in the cabinet as secretary of war, was wont to attribute all opposition to machine politics.

"The opposition to Harrison," he wrote to Reid, "is based on no principle or sufficient ground—it is based on disappointment of a few leaders. He is strong with the people." Speaker Reed, on the other hand, thought the people were indifferent, that all the difficulty resided in arousing popular enthusiasm for Harrison. This question of personal magnetism was, indeed, impossible to ignore. It was out of the question, bluntly quoth the Speaker, to ask the Republican party to "live four years more in a dripping cave." He thought well of the idea of nominating Whitelaw Reid for the vice-presidency, averring that it would add immensely to the strength of the ticket, if the first place went to a Western man, but, he snorted, "Reid couldn't save Harrison." Blaine unquestionably had a monopoly of the warmth calculated to win multitudes of voters. If he remained proof against the blandishments of the convention it seemed to some observers as if the only thing to do would be to trot out a dark horse. All sorts of stories on this theme were rife, among them one which I detach from the rest because of its naïve gorgeousness. It ran to the effect that New York and Pennsylvania were to start the fun. Platt and Quay were to get the delegations of those States to nominate Blaine with a whoop and a hurrah. Blaine was expected—on the beautiful hypothesis that he would consent to be thus "used"—to telegraph a peremptory refusal to accept. Then the President was expected, in view of his aversion to being "served with warmed over victuals," as one of his closest advisers put it, to forbid the use of his name, and forthwith there would be a free-for-all scramble. Fearful and wonderful are some pre-convention plans, when the *quid nuncs* foregather!

Of course there were other aspirants in the field. Reed would have liked the nomination. He thought that his course on the tariff bill and on appropriations had been vindicated, that the bitterly opposed Czaristic "Reed rules" had been justified, and that if his name went to the polls he would win. There were still others, like Alger, Allison, and Sherman. But the dark horse never conclusively materialized. Blaine was Harrison's only possible rival, and he, as I have said before, could not be shaken from his resolve to stay out of the race. Less than a fortnight prior to the convention Platt tried to move him to reconsider, pleading with him to "let the thing take its course." He went over every point in the situation, every chance that was likely to be encountered down to the final election, fought against Blaine's doubt that his health could stand the summer months in Washington during the long term of each Congress, and harped on what the unwilling statesman owed to his friends. So ardent was this onslaught upon Blaine that in the heat of it Platt must have felt that success was possible. At all events, when, at the climax of his urging, Blaine silently looked at him, Platt thought he recognized "a significant and promising glance." On June 4th the secretary of state resigned from the cabinet. Never was there, as his advocates looked at it, a more welcome bombshell. They blessed the explosion. It lifted them to empyrean heights. Then they came to earth with the proverbial dull and sickening thud. There was no relation to be established between the resignation and the nomination. The true word was thus spoken in The Tribune:

Mr. Blaine, though often credited with mysterious plans and adroit wire pulling, is, in fact, one of the sincerest and most straightforward of men. He said four years ago that he was not a candidate for the Presidency, and could not take the nomination a struggle might bring him. At that moment he was absolutely sure of the nomination, and, as we think, of the election. But he meant exactly what he said; he stuck to it, and even sent an appeal by cable to his friends in the midst of the convention, to stop the successful struggle for him on which they had already entered. This time he has said exactly the same thing. To many friends within the past fortnight he has repeated that he does not wish the nomination and could not be a candidate for it. We see no warrant for the offensive assumption that he has not meant what he said now, just as he was proved to mean what he said in his withdrawal in 1888, which the whole world now recognizes as the greatest and most extraordinary act of magnanimous self-renunciation ever displayed by an American statesman.

The news columns of The Tribune that morning reported as cheerful the Harrison men assembling at Minneapolis. The next day they were confident, and with the formal opening of the convention progress toward a renomination of the President was speedily indicated. There was only one dramatic moment in the proceedings. That was when the anti-Harrison influences drifting in the direction of the chairman of the convention, Governor McKinley, of Ohio, caused the delegation from that State to flare up. Forty-four of its forty-six votes were polled for McKinley, the dissenting ballots being cast for Harrison by the chairman, and, at his request, his alternate in the delegation. This rousing challenge got everybody on tiptoe. It proved, in effect, hardly more than a flash in the pan, for while the opposition to the President, as it turned out, was almost equally divided between McKinley and Blaine, the renomination of Harrison was never seriously imperilled. There was only one ballot, and on that he obtained 535⅙ votes. The ticket went through with a rush. Whitelaw Reid's name was presented for the vice-presidency, first by State Senator O'Connor, and then, in a longer speech, by General Horace Porter, both orators describing him as the unanimous choice of the New York delegation. Speaker Reed's name was then offered but only to be withdrawn. Reid was then nominated by acclamation.

When a number of citizens of White Plains and other friends in Westchester County came over to Ophir the following evening to congratulate him, Reid said to them: "The speechmaker for this ticket is at the head of it." He hoped, and thought, that this would be the case. On being drafted to open the campaign in Illinois he thus acknowledged the congratulations of Major Halford, Harrison's private secretary, who had written to him at the President's suggestion about making the trip West: "As you say, you were pretty largely responsible for it. The truth is I went out against my own judgment—my personal belief being the old-fashioned one, that candidates on a national ticket ought not to be too prominent in a campaign." He did not in the least desire to go on the stump. Nevertheless, a good deal of the most arduous work of the campaign fell upon his shoulders. After the official notification brought to him at Ophir in June he made several informal speeches in Westchester County. Then, in August, came the important statement of party principles at Springfield, Illinois, just noted, with brief addresses to his old neighbors at Cedarville and Xenia, and a big Ohio rally at Woodside Island Park early in September. In that month he spoke at Buffalo, Brooklyn, and Tarrytown, and took part in a huge mass-meeting at Cooper Union. October took him to Boston and to Indianapolis. In the week before election he went with Depew for a political swing through the southern tier of counties in his own State, speaking at Ithaca, Hornellsville, and Jamestown. His last speech of the campaign was delivered on November 5th before a large meeting of working men at Albany. It was a busy summer.

He was encouraged in it by constant letters from a host of friends. Bigelow led them, the day the nomination was announced:

Highland Falls, N. Y.
June 11th, 1892.

My dear Reid:

I hope you are not so fanatical a friend of Mr. Blaine's as to reject the cordial congratulations of this household upon the nominations made last evening at Minneapolis. What a pity though that President Harrison—a staunch birth-right Presbyterian like ourselves—should have so early in his public career made himself famous for his Vices. I am sorry that you and Morton should be so much like two buckets in a well, one of which goes down empty when the other comes up full. Why the Republican party did not revive the fashion of promoting Ex-Ministers to France to the Vice-Presidency earlier, would be a good question for college debating societies.

My sympathies will be with you, all the same, when you take the V. P. seat as in an Aurist's chair, to have your ears bored by Senators. There is still one chance for you, however. The Convention which is to meet in a few days at Chicago may be wise and patriotic enough to say that the press of the country can no longer spare you. Do not however count too much upon this. The Democratic party in one respect resembles Apollo. It does not keep its bow always bent and like Jupiter is occasionally a Tom Noddie.

If Mrs. Reid is pleased with the prospect of a residence in Washington and being "the Second Lady in the land" I wish you would offer to her also our cordial congratulations. Please say to her also that in becoming the successor of Jefferson as a graduate from the French mission into the Vice Presidency, I hope you will be led to think better of his principles, that you may share his subsequent political fortunes. To be the wife of a P. or a V. P. is a distinction which Mrs. Reid did not need but if offered the opportunity she is sure to add to the value of both.

Always faithfully yours,
John Bigelow.

Evarts was as cordial, and as confident. "You and your friends," he wrote, "may well feel that you were able to take this Republican tide at the flood, but it is quite as fortunate for the Party that it could find you at its service." Hay came to Ophir fast on the heels of the nomination—he was there the next day—and through the campaign was ever ready with words of good cheer. He wrote from Cleveland, as soon as he had got back from his visit with the Reids: "I found Lodge and Roosevelt already quite energetic Harrison men—rather more so than myself. Every one I meet speaks well of the ticket, even those who are in favor of another. It is the general judgment that Harrison is a good, safe candidate, and you are universally regarded as giving the ticket a great reinforcement. The Blaine feeling is very strong here, but everybody will turn in and work for the ticket. The battle ground is New York. I think the Republican states are all safe enough." A few days later, when the Democrats held their convention, putting up Cleveland and Stevenson, Hay found only good auguries in the event. "I think Chicago did the best it could for you," he said. "The free trade plank is worth thousands of votes to us, and the nomination of Stevenson is 'butter on your sassige.' These two acts of Tammany are unexplainable except on the theory that they want Cleveland beaten. The tariff straddle in the original platform was just dull and cumbrous and wordy enough to have been written by Cleveland himself and its upsetting by Watterson and Tammany was a delicious piece of monkey mischief. Hurrah for Harrison and Reid!—I mean Harrison and REID!"

Reid's own optimism was tempered both by his habitual fear of overconfidence in a political campaign and by his clear sense of the stubborn difficulties in the Republican path. These were ominously increased when the troubles in the Carnegie works at Homestead, Pennsylvania, began early in July. The strike there fostered disorders which were destined to have a profound effect upon the labor vote in November. Besides this untoward development, there persisted the fret and worry of factional disaffection in New York. It came at the critical moment, too, when the attitude of the Hill Democracy made it extremely important for the Republicans to maintain a united front. The Hill people really wanted to defeat Cleveland. But they wanted to feel sure that the Republicans were solidly together and in a position to carry the State—for the obvious reason that they did not wish to begin steps looking to revenge without a reasonable certainty of success. There was a quaint element in the discontent jeopardizing the chance of the Republicans to take advantage of this posture of affairs. One reason why Platt was disposed to sulk in this campaign was that the few letters he had addressed to the President had never been answered save through the formal medium of a secretary! There is printed in his "Autobiography" the letter which, being signed in the President's own hand, assuaged this grievance. In that communication Harrison asked him to make one of the company of politicians to be assembled to meet him at the house of whichever one of two or three friends he found it convenient to visit in the course of his summer travels. He paused briefly at Ophir, and when Platt was there afforded an opportunity to "blow off steam," the oracles promptly began to vociferate. Platt wanted to dominate Harrison, they darkly hinted, and the President was weakly willing to yield; Whitelaw Reid was the Machiavellian manipulator of the two, impelled by solicitude for his own place on the ticket. The best comment on this moonshine is Reid's comment to John Hay: "There were absolutely no promises, direct or implied, and there is no dust on anybody's knees."

It is an historical fact, long since recognized, that the Republicans had been committed to a defensive campaign in 1892 by conditions traceable to the operations of the McKinley bill, a measure whose merits did not make it as a whole impeccable. Not all the criticisms that could be levelled against it, however, were sufficient to reduce its value as a bulwark against the changes prefigured in the Democratic platform. In Reid's opinion the dangers flowing from some of the McKinley schedules were as naught compared with these inherent in free trade. On the tariff, which was the issue of the campaign, the Democrats were unquestionably vulnerable, and his cue throughout was to force the fighting on that point. In all his public utterances it was as a combative exponent of protection that he made his chief appeal. The first exhaustive address which he made on this subject—that delivered at Springfield, Illinois, to sound the Republican key-note in the West—thus illustrates his quality as a campaigner:

We may well thank them for the clearness and candor with which they have for once stated their precise position on the tariff. They are opposed to the McKinley bill and demand its unconditional and immediate repeal. Ask the business world, which has adjusted itself to the McKinley bill and is getting on admirably under it, whether it wants that. They are opposed to any protective tariff. Ask the country, which has seen its greatest prosperity under protective tariffs, whether it wants such an absolute severance of National policy as that.

They demand a tariff for revenue only, declare any other unconstitutional, and proclaim this "the fundamental principle of the Democratic party." We are bound to take them at their word; but how that party has changed! They cite what they call "the long and illustrious line of Democratic leaders, from Madison to Cleveland." Well, Madison reported and George Washington signed the first Protective Tariff bill in our history, and it stated specifically in its title that it was "for the encouragement and protection of manufactures." But then the Democratic party of today knows that Washington and Madison didn't understand the Constitution they had just made! Andrew Jackson elaborately argued the constitutional right and duty to make a protective tariff, and cited his predecessors, Washington, Jefferson, Madison and Monroe, as his authorities. But the Democratic party of today knows that Andrew Jackson didn't understand the Constitution. Down to this day indeed there has been but one great representative body which did understand the Constitution, and in the long line of leaders the Democratic platform proudly refers to, "from Madison to Cleveland," there has heretofore been but one statesman vested with the power to enforce the present Democratic interpretation of it. The representative body was the Constitutional Convention of the Confederate States, and the authorized statesman was the Confederate President, Jefferson Davis. They embodied in their constitution and enforced in their practice the doctrine that no tariff should be levied, save for revenue only. Today the Democratic party, to use the current political slang, "turns down" Thomas Jefferson, Andrew Jackson and all its old leaders, repudiates alike their constitutional interpretation, their political belief and their acts, announces instead identically the same doctrine with Jefferson Davis and the Confederate States, and proposes that Grover Cleveland in your name shall execute it. Ask the people if they want that.

Citing official figures in support of his argument, the speaker traversed not only the tariff issue at large but brought out the claims of the reciprocity policy which he had himself helped to advance in his recent French experience, and passed thence to a warning against the Democratic plans for meddling with the currency. He concluded:

Our enemies have made our campaign for us. Hold them to their deliberately avowed principles. We go to the people claiming that the Republicans have given the country a clean, honorable, business-like and highly successful Administration, that a change without cause is a business injury to every citizen, and that there is no occasion for a change. The Democrats want this country to have an immediate and absolute change. They want to repeal the McKinley tariff at once. They denounce a protective tariff of any sort or description, refuse to let tariff legislation have the slightest reference to the defence of workingmen's wages, declare that Washington and Madison and even Andrew Jackson didn't understand the Constitution, and that nobody but themselves and Jefferson Davis ever did; denounce everything but a pure tariff for revenue only as unconstitutional, want to get rid of our Reciprocity, and demand a return to wildcat banking. Hold them to their doctrine.

I have before this touched upon Whitelaw Reid's distaste for personalities in political controversy. He brought none of them into the present campaign. But on one occasion, speaking in Boston shortly after Cleveland's letter of acceptance had been published, he thus paid his compliments to the Democratic candidate:

The letter of acceptance discloses a figure which our aboriginal friends of the far West would describe as "Big-Man-Afraid-of-His-

> Platform"; and the party gazes in perplexity and alarm on a candidate who accepts the nomination, but has not yet shown either the candor to accept or the courage to repudiate its principles. I mean to speak of Mr. Cleveland with that respect which all right thinking American people wish to show for one who has passed our supreme ordeal, and been once declared by a majority of American votes worthy to be the Chief Magistrate of this Nation. But it cannot be disrespectful, and it is obviously truthful, to say that Mr. Cleveland now acts toward the platform of his party as if he were afraid that if he should venture to step on it he would break through.

There was nothing in the least nebulous or evasive about Reid's own letter of acceptance, which appeared a fortnight after his demand in Boston for courage in such communications. He had been aggressive in his speeches and in the letter he was equally direct. In it he traversed in detail the issues which have already been pointed out, and as he analyzed them with the touch of a disputant who, after all, preferred the pen to oratory, he framed a trenchant statement of Republican doctrine. Its plea for the protective system and a sound administration of the currency is too long to be quoted here intact, and too closely knit to be profitably illustrated by fragments. Better than the latter is this message of Hay's: "I suppose you are overwhelmed with congratulations, but I must gratify my own feelings by adding mine, whether you have time to read them or not. Your letter of acceptance is remarkably fine and strong. It could not be improved in substance or in manner. It gives a perceptible lift to the campaign. How can any honest or rational man be against us this year?"

The answer to Hay's question as it was given in the November vote referred him and all other inquirers to but one explanation—the tariff. The Republicans had made out a seemingly convincing case for the McKinley bill. I have noted Whitelaw Reid's ceaseless hammering upon the preponderant merits of the measure. It was the confident belief of all the spokesmen of the party that they had a winning argument in the latest legislative affirmation of the protective system. One of the most interesting episodes of the campaign was Blaine's visit to Ophir in October, when he made his sole speech in support of the ticket. He in his turn challenged the Democratic statement that the tariff was a promoter of plutocratic government, and a handicap to the poor man. The poor man, feeling the pressure of an enhanced price on a single article of consumption, hadn't the inclination or the means to find out whether he was being victimized by "McKinleyism" or by the private profiteering which ingeniously turned to advantage his confusion of mind on the subject. In the upshot he swallowed whole the exaggerations employed in the Democratic attack. What was radical in the bill was exploited with telling shrewdness by Cleveland's managers. Writing to George Ticknor Curtis just after the election, Reid said: "The people have evidently made up their minds that the McKinley bill went too far." He was persuaded that in addition to their reaction against the bill the working classes had developed the belief that it was their own unions and not the tariff that secured high wages. Besides, to the prevailing vague feeling of discontent there was to be added the dislocating shock of the Homestead strikes. The influence of these, as I have previously remarked, counted heavily at the polls. The element of personal popularity may have figured to some extent before the Republican convention. The anti-Harrison feeling of such an outspoken extremist as T. B. Reed, for example, has been noted. He was convinced that the President was not going to be a vote-getter. But as things turned out it wasn't a question of anybody's personal popularity. It was a question of tariff schedules.

This fact undoubtedly deepened the calm with which both the Republican candidates received the result. "Personally I have little to regret in the outcome of the election," Reid wrote to Stedman. "I never believed in the effort to nominate me, and while saying that I should be a fool not to be gratified if it came, still advised against it." He had the satisfaction of knowing that he had made a stanch fight in the service of the party. There is no repining in the letter which he wrote to Harrison:

Ophir Farm,
November 28th, 1892.

Dear Mr. President:

I haven't written sooner, since the defeat, for the reason that in this, as in some other trials in life, there seemed to be at the instant no useful thing to say. Our opponents were as much surprised at their victory as we were; that, at least, is one point which the intervening period has made clear. Nothing that we did or left undone during the campaign caused it; that is another. Beyond getting the offices, they don't know what to do with their victory; that is another clear point. A success won by such incongruous allies cannot be maintained, and the Republicans must come in again.

I know you are at present naturally indifferent to the personal considerations that suggest; but your position will nevertheless, whether you like it or not, devolve an immense importance upon your every movement. You will be the first American private citizen; and will have a degree of esteem among the people of all parties such as no man, similarly placed, has enjoyed in our time.

I am most anxious that the closing months of the Administration should be fully up to the bold, conservative and yet initiative standard of the previous years. The Panama and kindred questions bring difficulties, but they may also bring opportunities. I hope the Behring Sea arbitration is in good shape; and that you may have your several agents and counsel for it so firmly placed that there is no danger of disturbance, when the new Administration comes in.

Faithfully yours,
Whitelaw Reid.

President Harrison was in as serene a mood and his comment on the cause of the rout, though sharp, had a humorous flavor. He replied as follows:

Executive Mansion,
Washington, D. C.
December 5th, 1892.

My dear Mr. Reid:

I have just let go of my message, which has for some days absorbed my attention. You will see it, before this reaches you, and will I hope judge it with a due regard to the distractions that have surrounded its preparation.

You take a just and philosophical view of the election result. If there were any faults of management I do not care to know of them. They cannot account for the result, which had more general causes. The workingman declined to walk under the protective umbrella because it sheltered his employer also. He has smashed it for the fun of seeing the silk stockings take the rain. If he finds that the employer has a waterproof coat, while he is undefended, he may help to rig up the umbrella.

I shall feel a great sense of relief when public affairs have for me only an interest and no responsibility. But there will be no letting down while I am here. With very kind regards for Mrs. Reid and Mr. Mills,

Sincerely yours,

Benj. Harrison.

Hay was off shooting ducks in an Ohio marsh when news of the election reached him. He was grieved and disgusted. But he wrote as he always did, with an inspiriting emotion: "At present my chief sorrow is that you and Mrs. Reid are not to be our neighbors in Washington for the next few years. Here, so far as you are concerned, my sorrow ends. It was a great honor to be nominated for the Vice Presidency. You have made a splendid canvass and grown constantly in standing and prestige before the country every hour since the nomination. You have got all the good, and most of the fun out of it, that was in it. The post would rather have wearied you—now you are your own man again, and are very much more of a political quantity than ever before."

A week after the election, at the annual banquet of the Chamber of Commerce, where Cleveland was this year the principal guest, Reid was called upon to speak.

He had no grievances to air as a defeated candidate, and alluded to his feelings in that rôle as akin to those of a gentleman of the African persuasion whose emotions on burying his fourth wife were tenderly inquired into by his sympathetic pastor. "All I can say," ran the resigned reply, "is that I am in the hands of an all-wise but perfectly unscrupulous Providence." He touched the subject lightly, in a sporting humor. The sole echo of the recent combat upon which he ventured was very warmly received. It came when he answered a query which Congressman Breckinridge, of Kentucky, had put as to the wishes of the business people of New York. "I venture to tell him one thing," said Reid. "There is nothing so injurious to business as uncertainty. He has told us that it is his purpose, and that of his party, to set their faces resolutely and conscientiously in directly the opposite course from that which the people of this country, through their Government, have been pursuing for thirty years past. I accept that statement with the frankness and candor with which it has been made, and I venture now to say to him as a business man that what the business men of New York and what the business men of the country desire is that whatever is to be done shall be done without unnecessary and harassing delays." The applause with which this passage was followed was evidence of the directness with which he had gone to the heart of the problem left for solution by the campaign of 1892. It was the wide-spread uncertainty as to just what was to flow from the Democratic programme which more than anything else engendered the panic of 1893.

But the anecdote with which Reid closed had no controversial implications. It described an incident which he had witnessed in the French Chamber of Deputies, when Paul de Cassagnac, as has been recounted in a preceding chapter, had proudly asserted the political unity of himself and his colleagues on any question of foreign politics. "I think we may say," Reid went on, "it has not always been said in the past, but I think I may speak for my associates in saying to the gentlemen who soon take the control—that whatever they may do to sustain the honor of the flag and promote the prosperity of the country will find no warmer applause than it finds from the opposition, and that on any question affecting the honor of the flag on foreign soil they will find in the United States no Republicans and no Democrats, but that we are Americans all!"

CHAPTER XI

IN EGYPT AND ARIZONA

The second administration of Grover Cleveland was well calculated to develop in him the traits which have marked him as one of the strong men in the succession of American Presidents. It embraced events calling not only for brains but for courage. Without force of character the panic of 1893, the railway strike at Chicago in 1894, the much-discussed bond contract with Morgan in 1895, might all have been mishandled. The Cleveland legend is rooted as much in his manhood as in his measures, perhaps even more. It is a point underlined in the story of Whitelaw Reid's relation to these years of politics. His place was amongst the leaders of the opposition, and he filled it with his usual fidelity to Republican doctrine; but it is appropriate to note here again the independence which has been indicated as tincturing the partisanship of The Tribune. On the homeward voyage from France his hard-hitting Republicanism had certainly suffered no sea change, yet experience abroad had, if anything, deepened his habit of detached thinking on public affairs. He formed a cool judgment on the great Democratic figure whose policies he had so often to combat. He thought the truth about Cleveland lay somewhere between the myth created by those zealots who exhausted the language in praise of his wisdom, and the patently grotesque portrait drawn by irreconcilable critics. Naturally he could never see eye to eye with Cleveland on the tariff, but he backed the President on the repeal of the silver coinage law, applauded his progress—

so far as it went—in Civil Service matters, and watched with increasing warmth of admiration the masterful settling of the railway strike. He read the challenging Venezuelan message with mixed feelings, of course, but then so did numbers of Cleveland's best friends. In all these affairs Reid was appreciative of the President's personal significance. "He has borne himself," he said editorially, when the end of the four years had come, "with a self-assertion and robust egotism that might almost be called magnificent." Shortly after the four years had begun Hay wrote to him: "You have been very mild and gentle on this administration so far." There were plenty of occasions on which he was neither gentle nor mild; but whatever there was at all "magnificent" about Cleveland was freely recognized in The Tribune.

Reid was a fairly constant participant in the political conflict under Democratic rule, but for various reasons I shall have to say as much in this chapter on his affairs as on the affairs of the republic. An echo of his service abroad belongs to this period. A gift from the French Government reached him in the shape of a piece of Sèvres, a large classic vase. The ministry had tactfully postponed sending it until, under our Constitution, his retirement from office had made it possible for him to accept it, and until the campaign of 1892 had been closed. It was transmitted with the following letter from the minister of foreign affairs:

MR. MINISTER:

At the moment when circumstances led to your voluntary resignation of the high diplomatic functions which you exercised for some three years at Paris, the President of the Republic was specially desirous of sending to you, in the name of the French Government, a souvenir of the mission which you have so worthily filled, and the premature close of which excites in us very sincere regrets.

Coming to Paris at the beginning of the year 1889, one of your first acts was to associate the Republic of the United States of America with the celebration of our grand centenary, and since then you have never failed, while defending the interests of your country, to think constantly of the friendship of over a century which unites it to France—a friendship which finds today, in the similarity of their political institutions, a reason for continuance and growth.

In accepting the object of art which I now have the pleasure of offering you in the name of the French Republic, you will please find in this testimonial a proof of the sentiments generally expressed on your account, and of the agreeable souvenirs of you which we cherish.

Accept, Mr. Minister, the assurance of my very high consideration and of my most sympathetic regards. RIBOT.

Meanwhile, as it happened, the French Government and our own were still considering Reid's extradition treaty. The affair moved slowly, owing to modifications proposed in the American Senate. When the treaty had first been laid before the latter body no minimum amount had been fixed for the embezzlement of which a criminal might be extradited. An amendment having been framed, and some slight verbal changes having been made, Minister Coolidge in Paris patiently sought the attention of a government distracted by the Panama scandals. Acquiescence was finally secured and the document was ratified by the American Senate on February 2d, 1893. All the modifications were departures from the instructions originally given to Reid. At the most they were unimportant and the treaty remained in essence his work, an appreciable contribution to the working out of a problem ultimately carried to a complete solution in the Taft administration. Elkins, congratulating Reid on his success, noted the especially gratifying vote by which it was secured. It stood forty to sixteen, eight more than the two-thirds majority required.

It was in the first month of this year that Reid lost two old friends in his political circle. Hayes died on

January 17th, at his home in Ohio. They had never been intimate, but neither had the stress of debate affected their cordial relations. Reid liked to recall their last meeting. It was in John Sherman's room at the old Fifth Avenue Hotel, during the campaign of 1892. The ex-President was just going out as Reid came in. He replied cheerfully to inquiries about his health, and then said, with a hearty hand-shake: "But whether well or ill, I want you to understand that I shall be able to go to the polls on election day to vote for you, even if I have to walk ten miles to do it." Blaine's death followed on January 27th, terminating a friendship more deeply rooted. I have already exhibited the closeness of their collaboration in politics and the mutual regard which went with it. Blaine had a way of engaging men's hearts as well as their heads. Walter Phelps was appointed that winter a judge of the New Jersey Court of Errors and Appeals, and in a letter of his from that sanctuary, months after Blaine had been laid in his grave, he expresses the profound sentiment which the New England statesman had inspired in his comrades. "I like it. Yes. Out of politics. I find poor Blaine and his fortunes were all those twenty-one years the mainspring of my love for them." The characterization of him in The Tribune as a statesman who was followed because he was loved and trusted, points to the affection which was one element in Reid's steadfast support of him. For Reid, however, the political life was bound in the nature of things to go on.

The Democratic party was there to be admonished, and there were always new issues in the air. In July, McKinley, who was campaigning for re-election as governor of Ohio, sent on an emissary to try to persuade Reid to come out and take the stump in his behalf. Hay, travelling abroad, picked up from a friend in a

London hotel the piquant information that Reid himself might presently be advocated as the Republican candidate for governor in New York. This speculation, though, was unusually wide of the mark. In the midst of the political talk that was always going on Reid paid heed to the signs that speechmaking in the recent campaign had confirmed him in an asthmatic tendency, and with prompt resolution to fight this from the start he made his plans to turn his back on politics and spend the winter on the Nile. He had another grief to suffer before he sailed. Walter Phelps died in the summer of 1894, on June 18th. It was the hardest wrench of all in the breaking up of an old group. Politics had made only an incident in their friendship, which had united them in some of Reid's earlier and more strenuous years in the editorship of The Tribune, and all the innumerable ties formed by sympathies held in common had been cemented in the atmosphere of home life. Their intellectual alliance was complete, they swam and rode together, they loved the same books and laughed over the same things. Phelps's death made an unfillable gap.

The Reids went abroad in the fall of 1894. Hay bade them Godspeed with no doubt at all that the trip to northern Africa would send Reid back in perfect fettle for every political eventuality, and, above all, for the "big fight of 1896." It was a pity, he thought, that the Republicans couldn't take advantage of the existing situation to elect their candidate at once. He was sure to go in, whether he was Roman or Scythian, bond or free. A Chinaman could be elected against Cleveland in 1894. There was sure to be a prodigious scramble when the fight for the presidential nomination was actually begun. Harrison would in all probability be in the field, McKinley would be there, too, as well as Tom Reed and Levi P. Morton, with Cameron of Pennsylvania making all manner of futile combinations in the background. Reid was to return well and strong, and ready to read the riot act to them all.

His idea, while the holiday lasted, was to live in an absolutely dry atmosphere, which would give his bronchial passages an opportunity to heal up and get over their irritability. In looking for the ideal climate he visited Morocco, Algiers and Tunis, Malta and Egypt. He went up to the edge of the Mahdi's dominions in the Soudan. He traversed the length and breadth of Arabia Petræa, and in Palestine travelled not merely from Dan to Beersheba, but from Gaza to Damascus. Often he rested in hotels and khans, but much of the time he camped out, especially by the oases of the Sahara. It was after a month on the Nile, during which he had a multitude of donkey rides and plenty of exercise wandering over old temples and ruins, that he started into the desert. The little caravan consisted of twenty camels, with as many Bedouins to look after them, a Syrian dragoman and several other servants. Half a dozen tents were necessary. The objective when they left Cairo was Mount Sinai. Thence their plan was to go back by way of Hebron to Jerusalem and Beirut, in time to go straight to Paris and London in the spring. A fragmental diary shows that this itinerary was smoothly followed, though they learned the discomforts of a sandstorm, and came across more than one sign of native unrest. In the Holy Land one quiet Sunday a French soldier, Count Henri des Moustiers-Merinville, arrived at the Reid camp exhausted, from Jericho, where he had been robbed. Reid's own worst mishap befell him on a ride up the hill above Nazareth, where the mount of one of his companions backed suddenly, and, lashing out, kicked him in the leg. It meant crutches for a little while, but that annoyance passed before they were on their way home. In Paris they found old friends in the Elysée, and at the head of the government, and Reid noted the popularity of Felix Faure. In London, where he received a cordial greeting from Rosebery, that statesman was just on the verge of a crisis in his political career. The Reids got there as May was drawing to a close. In the following month the Rosebery ministry, which had succeeded Gladstone's in March, 1894, was out. But all thought of politics was driven from Reid's mind when he landed in New York. The first news he had came to him in a telegram stating that his mother had died the day before. He and Mrs. Reid went almost directly from the ship to the homestead at Cedarville.

In a letter to Hay, Reid summed up the results of his travels for the establishment of his health. "I gained greatly in Northern Africa," he said, "especially in the Sahara; lost a little in Egypt; gained again in the deserts of Mount Sinai and the wanderings; lost from an infernal sandstorm, several rainstorms and the vicious kick of a horse bestrode by the good missionary, Dr. Post, of Beirut; gained again on the Mediterranean and was strong enough to enjoy a fortnight's dining and lunching and all manner of gossip and other hard work in Paris; lost a little in the abominable air of London; braced up again on the voyage, and arrived in New York as strong and well as I have been for a long time, barring the slight continuing bronchitis and the consequent consciousness that the wild beast asthma, which had been peremptorily kicked out, was nevertheless waiting around the corner for me. He has only got in once, since, in spite of a good deal to depress me; but then he gave me an uncommonly bad quarter of a day. The doctors pronounce me very much better, but insist on another winter's absence, and this time propose Tucson, Arizona. Meantime I have been doing more work on the paper than for a year or two past, and have been enjoying it." This was written in the summer. As autumn approached he carefully canvassed the Arizona proposal, and ultimately decided to go to Phoenix. In two winters there, with an open-air regimen he followed in the other seasons spent in California, at home, or in the Adirondacks, his refusal to drift into anything like invalidism was more than rewarded. The wild beast asthma was conclusively expelled. Moreover, even while subduing the bronchial tendency, he kept up his general health so well that he had a full measure of strength for all his interests. There is confident talk in his correspondence with Hay over the matter of editing a newspaper from across a continent. "The Tribune has been our only comfort throughout the winter," wrote Hay from Paris. "I presume you made a long arm from Arizona and kept it on the right track." Reid's reply intimates that he had made a long arm indeed. "In six years," he says, "I have not done as much regular work on The Tribune. In emergencies I telegraphed editorials from Phoenix or from Millbrae, and my typewriter has become so steeped in the politics she had to write that I am afraid she will be setting up presently as a strong-minded personage. Everything has worked the right way, and apparently the tide for protection and good money was taken at the flood. Since I came back, in spite of my resolute efforts to keep out of the whirlpool, I have been as busy as possible; but it is amazing how much work a man who is well again can stand under the stimulus of success." The success, of course, was the nomination of William McKinley at St. Louis in 1896. A great deal of the work Reid did for it was done in Arizona.

In this matter of the nomination Reid moved merely as an inquiring observer for a considerable time. As far back as November, 1893, when McKinley's re-election as governor was leading his friends to talk about the presidency, Reid added to his congratulations a word of caution against the premature development of ambitious plans. "A boom for '96 which starts in '93," he wrote, "is in danger of withering before harvest time," and McKinley took the reminder in good part. The interesting thing about Reid's interchanges with his political friends at this juncture is his judgmatic consideration of various booms, his endeavor to influence the party toward a really discreet handling of its unmistakable opportunity. The chances for any good Republican candidate were propitious. We have seen how confident Hay was. The President was at odds with his party. Far away in Egypt, Reid heard from another commentator on the scene that the feeling amongst the Democrats in Congress against Cleveland was bitter in the last degree. They blamed one another, but they all blamed him. On the rock of his personality his party seemed certain to go to smash. The problem of the Republicans was chiefly that of picking the right man to displace him. Reid's policy was to try out on public opinion every serious possibility, and there is a good specimen of it, showing "how the wheels go round," in his method of testing the eligibility of Senator Allison. A letter that he wrote to that statesman flings a revealing ray of light on the gentle art of President-making. It seemed to Reid that some of Allison's friends, or at any rate some of them in the East who had been talked of as his friends, were unduly modest, if not actually depreciatory, in the things they were saying about him as a presidential factor. Uncharitable people thought that perhaps this tone was being taken on intentionally, so as to belittle the senator's chances. Reid thought that it was about time for some candid representation of the views of Allison's supporters to reach the Eastern public. The Tribune had rather discouraged presidential discussions, but it had in hand some important letters from prominent people, to which it could not refuse publication, temperately setting forth and discussing the fitness, claims, and chances of McKinley, Robert Lincoln, Reed, and others. Therefore, on public grounds as well as out of a personal regard which had been developed through nearly a third of a century's acquaintance, Reid did not wish to see his friend's unquestioned position either ignored or belittled. Hence he wrote: "Is there not some capable friend of yours, now at home, sincerely devoted to your interests, and free from complications with our eastern managers, who would send to me (preferably though not necessarily over his own signature) a moderate, cautious and comprehensive statement of the attitude of Iowa Republicans with regard to yourself; their declared determination to present you as a candidate, their reasons for doing so, and their belief as to the prospect? It could be written so as to involve no awkward committals and so as to relieve you from all responsibility; and it could emphasize the fact that you have thus far remained absolutely quiet and refused to participate in any way in the struggle. But it would have the effect of counteracting impressions that the movement for you, in Iowa, is merely formal. It seems to me it would be a good thing therefore for you, and I am sure it would be a good thing for the party in broadening the personal discussions now in progress."

Thus is the way sometimes prepared for what is known as the crystallization of public sentiment. A thousand influences latent in the character and career of a public man lead up to the decisive moment; but on the power of the press the exposition of them at the proper time largely depends. A lot of this preliminary and essentially disinterested work went on in The Tribune as the convention drew nearer. It helped to clarify the situation. As the winter advanced Reid received in Phoenix divers interesting sidelights on the subject. Depew, after a long talk with Morton, then governor, related that that gentleman was in a curious state of anxiety and doubt about his own prospects. There was a general belief abroad, in the State and out of it, that his candidacy was to be used by the machine simply to keep the New York delegation together, so that it might have the strategic advantage of "creating the victor." But whether the laurel should be placed upon his brow was another question. He had, of course, received more than one assurance of loyalty from men who would be in the convention, and yet, ruefully, he had to admit the likelihood of their pleading, at a pinch, with Doctor Johnson's lapidary, that they were "not upon oath." He recalled an episode in the career of a former leader famous for millions of broken pledges. This potentate was once hauled over the coals by an irate, buncoed constituent. Thoughtfully and with emphasis he said: "Now that is a promise which I came damned near keeping." Morton never had anything much more comforting than this to go upon in the campaign. From first to last he was but a pawn in the game.

Depew, describing the situation for his friend in Arizona, also gave a humorous account of what happened in New York financial circles when Cleveland threw into them the bombshell of his Venezuelan message. "I see Mr. Mills nearly every day," he said. "He is about the only man not swept off his feet by the war scare. I dined on Saturday night with a lot of financiers, among them Morgan, Lanier and Sturgis, President of the Stock Exchange, and they all believed on Monday that the frightened English investor and European holders of our securities would be tumbling them across the Atlantic at a rate which would take out all the gold from the Treasury to pay for them; that they would find no market here capable of buying them, and so they would sell for nothing; that they would cramp the banks; that the loans would all be called in and no new ones made; that everybody owing money would fail in business, and that we were on the eve of a financial cataclysm the like of which had never been witnessed." It took some hours for this awful mood to spend itself. Reid had not anticipated any such effects, even momentarily, from the President's bellicosity; but he expected some trouble, for he felt that Cleveland had "played to the pit." Writing instructions to the office he said:

> The proposition to take the question of determining the boundary into our own hands, fix it by a Commission of our own appointing, and then declare that if Great Britain didn't accept it we would fight, struck me as presented in the brief abstract in the Phoenix papers as needlessly offensive. It seemed to be driving a very strong antagonist into a corner and then slapping his face. We disagree with them because they won't accept arbitration, which is right; but go further, and say that now we will arbitrate it ourselves and enforce our decision, which seems strong practice. A man who merely wanted to maintain the Monroe Doctrine, and the honor of the country, not also to further personal or political interests, and who also had the sincere desire every statesman ought to have for peace, if it can be had with honor, might, it strikes me, have found a less offensive way of convincing Great Britain that there was a point beyond which she could not go without breaking with us. And to convince her of that, it seems to me, was all that was really necessary. I presume the fact is that Chamberlain, who has never recovered from his chagrin at the rejection of his own treaty with us, was asked by Lord Salisbury to deal with this question; and, so far as one may judge of it from the abstract, he dealt with it with a club.

It was not long after this that in the course of his private correspondence Reid had conclusive news on a topic with which political circles were buzzing in vain, the question as to what Benjamin Harrison meant to do.

Writing in January the ex-President said: "As to further public honor, you know as do all of my friends, that there has never been an hour since I left the White House that I had any desire for further public service of any kind. With the majority in the Senate as it is now and as it is likely to be for some years, I do not see how anyone can make a successful administration and I do not feel that I could stand the worry of another term." Early in the following month he wrote to the chairman of the State Committee in Indiana formally announcing that his name was not to be used at St. Louis. All the leaders, and Reid among them, recognized in Harrison's withdrawal a distinct contribution to McKinley's strength; but neither this circumstance, nor the current estimation of Morton's candidacy as a mere trading factor, altogether made the future plain. On the contrary, there ensued a tremendous visitation of "favorite sons," through which managers inimical to McKinley sought to create a big enough field against him to insure some chance of his defeat. Even while his boom showed increasing vitality, the ultimate development of the campaign remained more than ever a puzzle.

Hay was completely mystified. He had seen some queer streaks of politics in his time, but nothing that could hold a candle to this welter of cross-purposes. He did not believe that anybody but Platt and the devil knew what he really wanted. Everybody watched with breathless interest to see if the spurt McKinley made in February could be kept up. Whitelaw Reid, who had been keeping The Tribune in an attitude of benevolent neutrality, tended toward the judgment that the Ohio man would prove the strongest available. Though he still maintained a free hand, that he presently allowed this view to be reflected in his paper is shown by the following note:

Canton, Ohio.
March 21st, 1896.

My dear Mr. Reid:

I want to express my very great appreciation of the work of The Tribune. All my friends are delighted. It is helping the cause to a degree that you may not realize at your distance. I thank you over and over again. Chairman Gowdy of Indiana reports that the 26 delegates from that state are solid for me.

With best wishes,
Your friend,
Wm. McKinley.

This is a personal souvenir of what was, as a matter of fact, an impersonal campaign. The business of laboring over presidential possibilities is always fraught with personalities, and considering all the factors—the play of friendship, the intrigues of group leaders, the pervasiveness of machine politics—it is no surprise that the layman sometimes thinks of the editor as nothing if not a cynical opportunist. Reid had occasion to make a concise exposition of his rôle when Elkins interpreted the methods of The Tribune as a sign that the paper was definitively committed to McKinley. "The explanation is," Reid told him, "that The Tribune is fully recognizing the facts, instead of trying to belittle them. A newspaper, to amount to anything, must keep its news columns honest and up to the times, and the paper which didn't tell its readers nowadays that McKinley was in the lead would be foolish as well as false. But in addition to this, there is certainly no concealment of The Tribune's intense hostility to any attempt, through a conspiracy of bosses, to control the nomination. You and I have co-operated in resistance to such conspiracies in the past, and during the quarter of a century through which you have watched the course of The Tribune you have never seen it acting otherwise. It would belie its whole history if it did." An appropriate foot-note to this is supplied in a page of instructions sent to the office:

I will not permit The Tribune to be put in the position of committing itself to the support of Mr. Morton. There is nothing whatever in his candidacy excepting a trick of the bosses to hold the seventy-two votes of New York together until they make a satisfactory bargain with the outside candidate, to whom, at the critical moment, they intend to deliver them. They haven't the remotest intention of nominating Morton; and if they have given the promise he is said to have required, to vote for him steadily up to and including the last ballot, and this even if they should stand alone in so doing, they will break the promise when the time comes; and justify it by saying that they couldn't control circumstances, and were not warranted in destroying the political influence of New York with the next Administration. I have only the kindest feelings for Mr. Morton personally, but I do not intend to be used, or permit The Tribune to be used to further this trading and treacherous game.

The "long arm" stretched from Arizona in 1896 knew perfectly well what it was about. Personal considerations were irrelevant. There sprang up, for example, rumors of his own eligibility for the second place on the ticket. Hay was delighted with the idea, and tried to find out if there was anything in the wind to prevent it. He could find nothing. But Reid never took it seriously. He was inclined, instead, to encourage the notion of nominating Thomas B. Reed for the vice-presidency.

As the pre-convention campaign continued, the most interesting phase of his work for McKinley bore upon the currency. That subject was every day forcing the tariff into the background. By the middle of May it was so far to the front that Reid telegraphed to The Tribune a leader on McKinley's record in the cause of sound money. On his return to New York he stopped off at Canton to have a talk with the governor. By this time hopes in that camp were confident and they plunged into discussion of the platform. He concentrated on the financial plank, and McKinley placed in his hands a memorandum for it to take home and turn over in his mind, with a view to suggesting any modifications that seemed to him advisable. The prospective nominee was even at that late hour strongly inclined to make his race as a protectionist. Reid helped to bring him to a sharper sense of the intense feeling that existed in the East on the currency. From New York he apprised McKinley of the prevailing sentiment. "The anxiety here," he wrote on June 13th, "on the whole subject of the money plank to be adopted next week, can hardly be exaggerated. There seems no doubt that the most conservative bankers are extremely apprehensive that any hesitation on our part to take the squarest sound money ground would bring on a great and probably sudden depression in values. On the other hand, there is no doubt that the enclosed plank—which practically says nothing we were not fully agreed upon at Canton—will be followed by an appreciation in values."

There is a rich suggestion in that phrase, "the enclosed plank." An immense amount of discussion has been held, some of it acrimonious enough, on the question as to who might claim the honor of having procured the explicit affirmation of the gold standard in the plank of 1896, and there have been plenty of claimants. The exact truth, if it could ever be determined, would probably assign the settlement of the policy to a discussion involving several men at different times and places, and the adoption of a form of words to similarly multiple action. The writing of the plank was, so to say, a cumulative achievement. Really of equal if not greater importance was the process of bringing McKinley to a proper sense of where the potency of the tariff as an issue left off and that of a great financial principle began. In this earlier constructive part of the debate Reid played an effective part. When he read the governor's plank at Canton and worked over it in New York his interlineations and pencilled drafts show with what solicitude he endeavored to safeguard the currency. The financiers he consulted differed as to the importance of the phrase "gold standard." One of them was frankly impatient with the many people he met who wanted it repeated over and over again in every conceivable form. Pierpont Morgan was keen about it. He wrote a plank himself, embodying the phrase "the existing gold standard," which Reid sent on with his own amended form of the memorandum he had received from McKinley. The allusion in that paper to "our present standard" he left unchanged, in obedience to a point of view thus editorially expressed in The Tribune on the eve of the convention:

> There is no occasion to maintain that the words "gold standard" must of necessity be used, because the present standard is that, and everybody knows it. There is not the least occasion to insist in form of words that silver monometallism would debase the currency, because everybody knows that also. But the Republican party ought to declare that the money in which wages of labor are paid shall not in any way be debased or lowered in purchasing power; that the pledges to pay money as good as the best that is known to the commercial world shall be sacredly observed, and that the Republican party is not going to run any risk of demonetizing gold, and therefore will not consent to the free coinage of silver, unless there can first be secured such international agreement as will fix the ratio between silver and gold, beyond risk of failure, in all the great commercial countries.

Reid sent a first revision of the money plank to McKinley on June 10th, with voluminous comment and the promise of further light on Eastern ideas. McKinley telegraphed for more counsel, and on Saturday Reid mailed a second revision, also sending, at the candidate's request, a copy to Hanna at St. Louis. It was just in time for the opening of the convention on the following Tuesday. He was not present at the deliberations there and his papers throw no light—beyond "the existing gold standard," the identical phrase in the platform adopted, in Morgan's plank—on the thorny question as to who wielded the thunderbolt in the committee-room. Hanna alone, probably, could have solved that riddle, and he left no decisive dictum on the subject. At the moment, in fact, nobody thought of grooming himself for the honors of the *deus ex machina.* The rush for those only set in when Bryan's speech at the Democratic convention in July, and his dramatic declaration, "You shall not crucify mankind on a cross of gold," sank into men's minds and the gravity of the currency issue was made doubly impressive. Then it was inevitable that the claimants should in the fulness of time arise. I would not presume to traverse their various pleas, yet it is, perhaps, permissible to remark that the excitement of this problem has been rather out of proportion to the intrinsic merits of the case. Is it not common sense to aver that the crux of the matter resides in the general urgency of a large number of men for what Reid called "the squarest sound-money ground"? He was well content to have taken and maintained that ground. In his editorial comment on the plank as adopted he said: "It is known to have been prepared by the immediate friends of Major McKinley, and, while he is in no sense responsible for it, it undoubtedly expresses his precise personal wishes." As one of the "immediate friends" he not only knew what those wishes were but had exerted an influence upon their formation.

In supporting the nomination made at St. Louis and entering the campaign, Reid figured as a known and powerful advocate of an honest currency. When Senator Teller and his fellow Silver Republicans bolted the convention, and a single ballot gave McKinley the prize, Reid's telegram of congratulation touched upon the candidate's favorite issue but remembered also the other.

"It is the greatest personal tribute our party has extended for a quarter of a century," he said. "And there has never been so good a chance for a square fight and a splendid victory for protection and honest money." McKinley replied:

Canton, Ohio.
June 24th, 1896.

MY DEAR MR. REID:

In making acknowledgment of your kind telegram, I wish also to thank you for all you have done, both personally and through the powerful influence of The Tribune. I also want you to feel perfectly free to communicate to me any suggestions that may occur to you as to the management of the campaign.

Very sincerely,
WM. MCKINLEY.

Hanna warned him that he would probably tax his friendship and aid to the fullest extent and he kept his word. They were often in consultation. The candidate asked him for suggestions as to his letter of acceptance, and in responding Reid urged him to make his argument against free silver specially strong and lucid, placing it before his discussion of the tariff. The Tribune was a leading force in the campaign, and though Reid made no speeches, he gave one effective contribution to the cause over his own signature. This was in the shape of a long letter to the Republican Editorial Association of Ohio, assembled at Canton on September 8th. McKinley's speech to the members from his porch was followed by this communication, in which Reid elaborated with fervor his financial faith. It made there and elsewhere a useful impression. Hay, reading it in New Hampshire, characterized the letter as "the condensed milk of the word, with the stuff in it of a two hours' speech."

The canvass that summer and fall is well remembered for its heat and the emotions of suspense it engendered. Conservative observers saw in the swift multiplication of the Silverites a deadly threat to the economic stability of the United States. Bryan's candidacy was an extraordinary one, extraordinary in the ardent and widespread support it received. He gained electoral votes only in the West and South, but even in States elsewhere, supposedly well buttressed against financial heresy, he made an amazingly respectable showing at the polls. Hay was outraged by the spectacle. In the multitude clamorous for Bryan he saw only the revolt of Caliban, an impulse of the unteachable horde. Reid called it "the awful fact of the election." It seemed to him that one whole section of our country voted for Bryan almost as solidly as it voted for disunion. As he said to Hay, "the strain of universal suffrage on the virtue of the country is tremendous." On the other hand, he never had any doubt of McKinley's success, once he had digested the results of the different State conventions, counted the delegates, and observed events following immediately upon the convention at St. Louis. And in contrast to the seemingly full-blown fruits of Bryan's far-flung oratory, he had an abiding confidence in the more lasting effects of the Republican candidate's famous "front porch campaign." McKinley lost nothing through his quiet, dignified course at Canton. Over and over again he addressed his countrymen as from beneath a great sounding-board, when he talked to men gathered under the shadow of his home, and Reid thought the speeches he made there the best he had ever known to come from a presidential candidate. They were apposite, they were fresh, they were skilful in condensed and epigrammatic statement, and they were exactly right in touch. Neither Harrison, Blaine, nor Greeley had in their respective campaigns materially influenced the situation as early as he had. When the victory Reid expected came in November, and, his own work done, he was preparing to go out for another winter in Arizona, he wrote to McKinley: "I think you have the greatest opportunity since Lincoln—as you have made the greatest campaign since his. and have had the greatest popular triumph."

CHAPTER XII

THE WAR WITH SPAIN

On his way West Reid paused at Canton and had a long conference with the President-elect. It bore upon the political outlook and the formation of the cabinet, both questions always dovetailing. In McKinley's meditations the great problem was how to adjust his administration aides to complete party harmony, and this was not by any means the simplest thing in the world to do. The New York machine was certain to prove a mischievous element. From the moment of the election it had planned to carry things with a rush, intimidating the major. Reid was against the smallest concession to such tactics. "They will make a mistake," he wrote to Hay, "if they imagine that friendly independence can be attained in this State by beginning with conciliation. That was Garfield's mistake. Conciliation at the outset will confirm these people in their estimate of the nerve and staying qualities of the man they have to deal with; and nothing thereafter but absolute surrender on every point will satisfy them." The reader will recall how candidly Reid preached this doctrine to Garfield. He renewed it at Canton, where he found that "everything was still fluid," and enforced the obvious truth that the only way to get on with Platt was to be independent at the outset, particularly when threatened. The major pondered these things in his heart. On one point he was explicit. He said that he shouldn't think of anybody from New York disagreeable to Reid, and as they parted at the train he added that he wanted to hear from him often, to get all his suggestions.

I will not revive here all the personalities that entered into the establishment of McKinley's administration. At this point I may cite instead that part of a voluminous letter in which Reid approaches the major's problem from the standpoint of large public policy:

Phoenix, Arizona.
December 5th, 1896.

DEAR MR. MCKINLEY:

The choice of a cabinet is absolutely your own personal affair—almost as much as the choice of a wife. It is the formation of your official family; its members are to bear to you a family relation. They should be peculiarly your personal selection; certainly not that of your enemies, nor even of friendly politicians, anxious to make the most out of you for themselves or for their respective states. Its members may properly be chosen by you, solely with reference to these questions:

1. Are they known to be absolutely competent?

2. Do you think them, in themselves, and with reference to their friends and backers, absolutely worthy of your unreserved confidence?

3. Have they staying power? Will they be absolutely in your interest two, three, or four years hence, not in that of the politicians who urge them? Will they be useful in storm as well as in fair weather? Would they have the means of bringing strength to an administration when it needs the powerful support of public opinion?

4. And finally, since you must judge of the future by the past; were they most in evidence when you needed *their* friendship, or only when they thought they could profit by *yours?*

I utterly reject the theory that Cabinet appointments can be wisely used for placating enemies or conciliating factions. Patronage may perhaps be so used, but a homogeneous and efficient administration, devoted solely to you and your purposes, is impossible if Cabinet places are not held above that level.

Another theory deserves more respect: that on which a President chooses his rivals in party leadership for his assistants in administration, as Lincoln did, or the elder Harrison; and then seeks to demonstrate his superiority as leader by leading and using them. Mr. Lincoln's experiences with Mr. Cameron, Mr. Chase, Mr. Seward and others were not altogether in favor of this theory; but at any rate it is doubtful if any one would now think it desirable, to attempt making up a working Cabinet of Gen. Harrison, Mr. Reed, Mr. Morton, Mr. Allison, Mr. Quay and the rest.

One more theory is apt to be presented by those who do not look below the surface—that a Cabinet ought to be so selected and distributed as to secure the widest and most varied applause from the politicians and the newspapers at the outset. But it is not the impression of the moment that concerns you; it is the capacity for four years' wear, and the impression *then* to be produced.

You will be much beset in the next few months. The best suggestion I can give is that you formulate in your own mind the principles on which you mean to begin your work, and then, in spite of interested pulling and hauling, stick to them; make up your mind as to what you want, and then have it.

Faithfully yours,
WHITELAW REID.

McKinley had thought, when Reid was at Canton, that Cleveland was likely to dump the Cuban question on the incoming administration. The outgivings had all looked that way at the time. Reid, on the other hand, had for some time entertained the suspicion that Cleveland was ruminating upon some sort of foreign *coup*, to recover lost prestige. Meanwhile the materials for forming a definite opinion on Cuba were locked up in the State Department. Pending their revelation Reid had certain well-settled ideas which prefigured the attitude he was to take in the greatest achievement of his diplomatic career. "Some day we will have Cuba, as well as the Sandwich Islands," he wrote to McKinley. "To that extent I believe in Manifest Destiny." A crisis, under existing conditions, was always imminent. If one supervened, and could be tided over for four months after the Republican President's inauguration, the next sickly season, suspending Spanish operations again, might bring them so near exhaustion as to promote a willingness to consider parting with the "ungrateful island" in payment of our claims or otherwise. He thought that a great source of alarm among many good people would be removed if it could be understood that, when either the Sandwich Islands or Cuba came into our possession, McKinley's plan would be to give them a suitable measure of local self-government, but to hold them as territories like Alaska—not threatening us with so large a half-breed citizenship, and with a further deluge of new States and senators.

Thenceforth events flowing from the unrest in Cuba rapidly develop an important series of documents in Reid's correspondence, culminating in those which recall his work as a member of the Spanish-American Peace Commission. The sequence is interrupted, however, by a brief diplomatic interlude which took him to London in the summer of 1897. Queen Victoria then celebrated the sixtieth anniversary of her accession to the throne. The subject had been brought to the attention of our State Department by the British ambassador at Washington shortly after McKinley's inauguration, and in May he asked Reid to accept a special mission to England for the jubilee. The Reids sailed on June 2d and remained abroad until late in July, taking part early in this period in an extraordinary programme of public observances. These began on a picturesque military note in the great quadrangle of Windsor Castle, where, with a massing of bands numbering more than two hundred instruments, a tremendous tattoo was beaten, as though to bring to the salute all the forces of an immense empire. On the following day, which was Sunday, June 20th, came the solemn commemorative service in St. Paul's, giving thanks for the fruitful reign begun in 1837. Monday the Queen made her formal progress from Windsor to Buckingham Palace, and the next day she rode in state through seven miles of London streets, packed with vociferous humanity, the central figure in probably the most imposing pageant that even London has ever seen. At the end of the week the naval might most expressive of her sway was demonstrated in the historic review of the fleet off Spithead, fit climax to crown a unique celebration. During the short period of the official ceremonies and for some weeks thereafter London was full of notabilities come from the ends of the earth, all marshalled in a social activity linked with one motive of national rejoicing.

On their arrival in London the Reids were welcomed by one of their closest intimates. John Hay had been established there as American ambassador since the preceding April. In their own house, leased from Lord Lonsdale in Carlton House Terrace, they renewed scores of old friendships, dined the Prince of Wales and a host of British and Continental figures, and were swept, in short, once more into the stream of European contacts they had known only a few years before in the Avenue Hoche. Beneath its surface ran now, as then, a current making for international good-will, and in communicating with the President, Reid noted the appreciation with which the American mission was received. Lord Salisbury was peculiarly cordial when Reid brought to the Foreign Office the President's letter to the Queen. She, herself, at Buckingham Palace, expressed the liveliest gratification over our participation in the jubilee. Reid rode with the other foreign envoys in the great procession of the 22d. The thing that most impressed him was "the tremendous depth of the devotion shown to the Queen," but after that the striking phenomenon was "the obvious and continuous cordiality towards America." The American mission was cheered at the beginning, and the same hearty friendliness was manifested at frequent intervals all the way along Constitution Hill, down Piccadilly, and almost to the Abbey. The American flags waved he assumed to be in the hands of countrymen, but there was no mistaking the fact that the majority of the cheers for America came from English throats in English accents. Twice Reid spoke in public on the prevailing theme—at the American Independence Day dinner and at the Cordwainers' dinner on July 8th. The speeches were applauded for their fusion of a candid Americanism with sympathy for an essentially British occasion. How far they and the whole mission succeeded in the furtherance of a good Anglo-American understanding is suggested in what Sir Francis Knollys, equerry to the Prince of Wales, wrote to Hay. "His Royal Highness directs me to assure you," he said, "that it would have been very difficult for the President to have sent to London, for the celebration of the Diamond Jubilee, a more acceptable representative of the United States than Mr. Whitelaw Reid, who has impressed the Prince of Wales, as well as all those who have been brought into contact with him, by the charm of his manner and by his agreeable qualities."

In Reid's letters from London there are a few scattered glimpses of the great Queen. She had a winning smile. Her defective eyesight caused her to need a little prompting in the course of presentation ceremonies, and at Windsor, when she entered, she leaned heavily on the arm of one of her Indian attendants, while she steadied herself on the other side with a stout cane. Age exacted its toll. But she carried herself, as she had for sixty years and more, with an incomparable queenliness, moving "with dignity and a certain grace in spite of the difficulty of walking." Her conversation with Reid he thus describes:

She began asking questions at once about my enjoyment of the Jubilee, and spoke of the great pressure of the successive "functions." She spoke very warmly of what she knew to be the cordial feeling entertained personally towards herself in the United States, and of the great kindness that had been shown to her from all quarters. She asked about the American Bishops who were here—mentioned one or two of them by name, and inquired as to the objects of the Lambeth Conference. Of course I took my opportunity in the various turns of the conversation to say some of the things personally to her which I had been saying in my Fourth of July speech and elsewhere, about the friendly interest of America, and our great pride in the achievements of her reign. Her face lit up constantly with smiles, and once or twice she laughed with great heartiness over something which I mentioned. She had referred to Bishop Whipple, whose interest in the Indians she seemed in some way familiar with, and she was greatly amused and showed cordial interest when I told her of his recent marriage and presence here now with his bride. She also spoke of the late Phillips Brooks with admiration. At the end of the talk she said quite earnestly that she hoped I would express to the President and to the people of my country her high appreciation of the good-will they had always shown her, and had especially been showing now, and her desire for perpetual peace and friendship. Altogether it was a conversation that showed thorough intellectual familiarity with what was going on, and exquisite courtesy, coupled with the greatest possible dignity. In the mingled dignity and simplicity of her bearing, she reminded me greatly of her daughter, the Empress Frederick.

This matter of simplicity Reid observed as a constant element even in some of the most splendid phases of British ceremonial. "They struck me," he said, "as somewhat more free and informal than I had seen such things in France. This, people generally tell me, is after all the characteristic of the English court circles. Outside they are hedged with tremendous forms; inside the characteristic English desire for simplicity and directness asserts itself."

Soon after his return from London Reid was immersed in a powerful though unsuccessful movement to purify local politics. The Citizens' Union was formed to put a good man in the mayor's office, if possible, and thereby not only smash Tammany but dethrone the bosses of the Republican machine. The latter were too firmly fixed, and, thanks to their selfish policy, Seth Low, the reform candidate, was defeated, and the upshot of the three-cornered fight was simply to put a Tammany man, Van Wyck, in power for four years. Tracy, the machine candidate, came in last. Platt's "leadership" was a costly handicap to the Republican party. The Tribune's opposition to it is noted here as an instance of the independence which we have seen Reid commending to McKinley. He certainly followed precept by example in this now well-nigh forgotten but then momentous campaign, and his arguments in the critical party councils which ensued were all along the same robust lines. They were needed. The political situation in the State was filling the national leaders with anxiety. But it yielded presently to a more engrossing topic. The Cuban question became paramount. Matters in the island had been going from bad to worse, and the publication of the famous Dupuy de Lome letter on February 9th, 1898, brought public emotion to a pitch at which almost anything was to be expected. Anything save the tragedy of February 15th, when the United States battleship *Maine* was blown up in Havana Harbor.

It is not my purpose to review the history of the war with Spain. I wish instead simply to exhibit Whitelaw Reid's relation to the subject and the growth in his mind of the policy which later had its influence upon the treaty of peace. McKinley had intimate discussions with him early in the development of these matters. At the time he sent Reid to the jubilee he was anticipating trouble over Cuba, and was wondering if we could avoid it by the purchase of the island. He proposed to appoint Reid ambassador to Madrid, with the idea that he should assume the post on the close of his duties in England, and carry on negotiations with a financial settlement held clearly in view. In London, however, Reid discovered that this would be impossible. He met there the members of the Spanish special mission, one of them the Duc de Sotomayor, whom he had known in Paris at the time of his ministry. He sounded them on the delicate point involved and received an unequivocal reply. "Spain would never sell the brightest jewel in her crown"—that was the substance of what the Spaniards had to say, and so Reid reported to the President on his return, abandoning the project of his going to Madrid, which he saw would be useless. Throughout the swift evolution of the unavoidable crisis he was one of McKinley's counsellors, and his letters contain characteristic judgments. The day of the loss of the *Maine* he was in the midst of preparations for a trip to California to escape the rigors of March in New York. He talked over Cuban affairs at the White House before leaving on this holiday, and out on the coast he wrote as follows:

Millbrae,
March 8th, 1898.

My dear Mr. President:

I have been giving a great deal of thought during the journey to this coast over various phases of the subject on which you did me the honor to ask my opinion at our last interview. It looks now a little more as if there were a possibility of Spain's forcing our hand. This would give still greater importance to your suggestion as to the immediate recognition of Cuban independence. Such a recognition would certainly be far better than the mischief-breeding recognition of belligerent rights. It ought, however, to be accomplished, if possible, by some signal Cuban success, of a kind different from anything which they have heretofore been claiming—for instance the opening of a port. Undoubtedly we could help them to this end even before making an attack on Havana. Our Navy Department has details as to the nature of the defences to be encountered at the different ports; but, other things being equal, the most desirable port for that purpose would be some one on the Northern coast, comparatively accessible from Key West without running too close to Havana—possibly Sagua la Grande, or even Cardenas.

Our recognition of the independence of Cuba would seem weightier if it should be accompanied or immediately followed by similar action on the part of as many as possible of the South American Republics, and our Ministers ought to be able to help greatly to this end. Brazil and Venezuela I should hope we might count on among the earliest.

The impression I got on crossing the Continent was that the more intelligent classes are not greatly affected by the sensational press;

but that, on a conviction that the *Maine* was blown up by Spanish agency, with or without the active connivance of the present Spanish authorities, there would be no restraining them. Meantime I have never seen a more profound or touching readiness to trust the President, and await his word. They really seem to feel, as every patriot must, in this crisis, a readiness to hold themselves subject to call when and where the country needs. Conservative public sentiment will sustain purchases of ammunition and even of war ships.

Very sincerely yours,
WHITELAW REID.

A week later he sent an interesting bit of news to Washington, received from a friend in Paris who had access to a person of authority in the Foreign Office. It was to the effect that the French Embassy in Madrid reported an inclination on the part of the Spanish Government to do everything in its power to maintain peace. If the *Maine* disaster should be shown to be an act of treachery, the Spanish Government would denounce the crime in such terms and offer such prompt reparation that, in the judgment of the French Foreign Office, war would be out of the question. Reid pointed out that of course the French Foreign Office and the French people, for financial and other reasons, were more in sympathy with Spain than was any other European nation. His own opinion at this time was that war could not be avoided and he had some definite ideas on the course to be adopted when it befell. The day that Congress adopted the resolutions on Cuban independence, directing the President to inaugurate American intervention in its behalf, he wrote to McKinley:

New York,
April 19th, 1898.

DEAR MR. PRESIDENT:

I have such a horror of "bothering the man at the wheel," to use Mr. Harrison's apt figure, that even after your flattering invitations to write, I thought it best not to interrupt you for an instant while the craft was in the rapids. Even now I venture only the barest outline of three or four suggestions—which in all probability have already occurred to you anyway.

Privateering is essentially the resort of the weaker power. As it has been abolished practically by the civilized world, with the exception only of the United States, Spain and Mexico, we should certainly gain a moral advantage by announcing at the outset that we did not intend to resort to it. There may (possibly—not probably) be something in our situation or plans that would make this inexpedient; but it ought to be carefully and immediately considered. With your commerce destroyers and fast cruisers, I doubt if privateers could be of much use to us now anyway.

Our position about capture of private goods at sea ought also to be made clear at the outset. Historically, we are committed for almost a century to the principle of "free ships, free goods"; and, when we refused to assent to the abolition of privateering, we took the strongest ground in favor of a general agreement for the exemption of all private goods at sea from seizure,—there being no exception even from the extreme case of enemy's goods on an enemy's ship. To the freedom of neutral goods on an enemy's ship Spain, herself, was committed by her assent to that part of the Declaration of Paris. Is not the way clear then for the distinct declaration that we shall recognize both (1) free ships as making free goods, and (2) enemy's goods on neutral ships as free, excepting, of course, in either case, contraband of war?

It seems to me these two declarations ought greatly to help us before the world.

I am sorry to see that the Spaniards have seriously begun fortifying the Canary Islands. Before this war is ended we may desperately need a coaling station there.

It is perhaps not a subject for much public discussion now; but, if volunteering should be slow, ought we not to determine at the outset that our policy is to be to call authoritatively on citizens to do their duty, not try to persuade them to it by bribing them with huge bounties? Volunteering, stimulated by the bounty system, was the colossal financial mistake of our Civil War. Nothing is so fair as a draft—or so economical.

Out next biggest financial mistake was in not trying to pay our way from the outset. Such a war-revenue as the papers have been talking about (beer, tea, coffee, stamp tax, etc.,) if passed within a week, would be highly popular.

I deeply regret the fourth paragraph in the resolutions as passed.* We are making ourselves morally responsible for decent government in Cuba, and we can't wash our hands of it after turning Spain out, by merely telling them to set up for themselves. I hope they may

* "That the United States hereby disclaims any disposition or intention to exercise sovereignty, jurisdiction or control over said island, except for the pacification thereof, and asserts its determination when that is accomplished to leave the government and control of the island to its people."

prove more orderly and less likely to plunge into civil strife and brigandage than has been expected. But if the result of our efforts is merely to establish a second Hayti nearer our own coast, it will be so pitiful an outcome from a great opportunity as to make Mr. Gladstone's pledge to "scuttle out of Egypt" respectable in comparison.

I've been very proud—as have been all your old friends—over your splendid management during this whole trying period. It has been a brilliant success in everything excepting in what was impossible—getting peace in Cuba without fighting for it. With all good wishes,

Very sincerely yours,

WHITELAW REID.

He wrote also in the same sense to Senator Elkins, who telegraphed his adhesion, promising to call at the White House, and then wrote: "I saw the President, and there is a disposition to follow the lines you have suggested." In the afternoon of the day on which McKinley received Reid's letter, the State Department made a semi-official statement as to the policy the government would pursue in regard to the question of privateering, and it thoroughly coincided with the views Reid had expressed. Elkins was impressed by his friend's usefulness. "Why not you in the State Department?" he asked, with one eye on John Sherman's impending retirement. Wherever he was, whether in or out of the cabinet, it was bound to be a helpful characteristic of Reid's advice that it would go straight to the point. All through the Cuban affair he knew precisely where he stood on details of policy, and drove unequivocally at what was to prove, indeed, the ultimate settlement. In June an interview with him, published in "Le Matin," gave to his old diplomatic friends in Paris a frank disclosure of his attitude. Sketching the inevitability of the war, our desire to avoid it but our unmistakable duty once it was forced upon us, he said: "We have interfered to give Cuba a better government, and we therefore stand morally responsible to the civilized world for the character of its government. The present insurgents may be able to establish one that we can afford to be responsible for; but, if not, our responsibility continues. Meantime, since war is serious business and not a mere dress-parade, we must strike and cripple Spain wherever we can. We have already struck her in the Philippines, and what we seize we shall certainly hold, so long as it serves our purpose, and so far as the responsibility in destroying the existing government may carry us. We have also struck her in Porto Rico, and the war will not end till we complete that conquest. If all this threatens other interests or disturbs our European friends, the only possible answer is that we regret it as deeply as anybody can, but that we did not seek the war, and it is not to us that appeals should now be addressed to stop it. The only rational interference for European nations is an interference with their feeble neighbor in its blind fight against Fate. The sooner Spain is stopped the less she will be damaged."

He was the more inclined to take an uncompromising tone in this interview because he knew the hostility of the French press toward the United States in the war. As Ambassador Porter wrote him, the government was behaving very well, but the Parisian journals were constantly printing articles inimical to our course. If these publications chose to call Reid an "Imperialist" they were welcome to do so and to make the most of it. At home he went on as cheerfully in the same path, indifferent to the plaints of the Mugwump. He advocated in The Tribune the same policy as that stated in the interview in "Le Matin," and set forth his views over his own signature in a paper on "The Territory with Which We Are Threatened."* Writing to Hay, in London, on August 11th, he says:

* See "Problems Flowing from the Spanish War," in "American and English Studies," pp. 107–124, vol. I.

Our truly good theorists have nearly all been "little Americans." In the "Century" for September Carl Schurz has a most pessimistic article deploring everything we have done, and everything we are likely to do as leading straight to the bottomless pit. I fancy Gilder must have hesitated about letting the magazine for that month appear with only that view; for he took the occasion of some frank expressions of mine at a committee meeting to ask me for an article on the subject, followed it up by telephone and letter, and finally came up to Ophir and sat up with me on the subject until in self-defence I consented to write the article. As the magazine was going to press there were barely two days for it; but I ground him out four or five thousand words which will be fatal forevermore to me among the people who are afraid that we may become too great. I haven't in the least undertaken to shut people's eyes to the difficulties and dangers of the Philippine business; but I don't see how we can honorably give them back to Spain, or do anything with them but try to make the best of what Dewey flung into our arms.

The little inside news I get on that subject is no doubt confirmed by your fuller information to the effect that the President's present idea is to get on with only holding Manila and perhaps the island of Luzon. Even so, I don't quite see how we can let Spain undertake to get control of the other islands again without giving them, in some way, a sort of right to appeal to us. It will be a big thing for the Pacific Coast, and not altogether bad for the country. But, if we don't insist strenuously that the territorial government is for all time, we shall be in worse danger than ever in our whole history from the demagogue who will want to make new states.

In strict confidence, the President did me the honor to send Charlie Smith over to talk this matter over before the Cabinet reached its decision, and I gave my views pretty much as you might infer from what I have written.

The conversation with Postmaster-General Smith, on July 28th, dealt with the issues raised two days before, when, through M. Cambon, the French minister at Washington, Spain had asked for the American terms of peace. McKinley stated these, through the same intermediary, on July 30th, they were accepted on August 9th, and on August 12th the peace protocol was signed, suspending hostilities and providing for an early start upon final negotiations. The crucial articles in the document ran thus:

1. Spain will relinquish all claims of sovereignty over and title to Cuba.

2. Spain will cede to the United States the island of Porto Rico and other islands now under Spanish sovereignty in the West Indies, and also an island in the Ladrones, to be selected by the United States.

3. The United States will occupy and hold the city, bay and harbor of Manila, pending the conclusion of a treaty of peace which shall determine the control, disposition and government of the Philippines.

It was also provided that the United States and Spain should each appoint not more than five commissioners to treat of peace, and that they should meet at Paris not later than October 1st, 1898. The correspondence between Reid's ideas, as he had all along made them known to McKinley, and those embodied in the peace protocol, had already foreshadowed the likelihood of his being appointed on the American side by a natural process of selection. On August 25th the President telegraphed, asking him to be a member of the commission, and he accepted on the same date. John Sherman had retired from the State Department toward the close of April, and Judge William R. Day, of Ohio, who had largely administered the office for some months, had then taken his place. In August McKinley invited John Hay to come back from London and serve in his cabinet as secretary of state. Day was appointed to the Peace Commission. He and Reid had for their colleagues Senator Cushman K. Davis, of Minnesota, Senator William P. Frye, of Maine, and Senator George Gray, of Delaware. McKinley, obviously, did not have the disposition, so unfortunately illustrated at a later date by Woodrow Wilson, to neglect senatorial aid. Three of his five commissioners were members of the Foreign Relations Committee of the Senate, two Republicans, and one, Senator Gray, a Cleveland Democrat. The secretary of the commission was Mr. John Bassett Moore. The Queen Regent of Spain sent to Paris Don Eugenio Montero Rios, who headed her commission, Don Buenaventura Abarzuza, Don Jose de Garnica, Don Wenceslao R. de Villa-Urrutia, and a military man, General Rafael Cerero.

CHAPTER XIII

THE PEACE TREATY

The choice of Paris as the scene of the Peace Conference had not at first commended itself to Reid. Environment, in his opinion, was always of importance in any negotiation, and Paris was overwhelmingly Spanish in its sentiment. There were half a dozen more eligible places, notably Berne or The Hague. But the Parisian environment turned out reasonably innocuous, despite the acerbities of the press, and so far as Reid personally was concerned it proved exceptionally favorable. He knew and he was known. His footing in government and diplomatic circles only gained from his former relations with both as American minister, and his possession of the language gave him another strong advantage. More than once during the negotiations his acquaintanceships and his knowledge of the ropes eased the labors of the commission. Besides experience and a command of French he had certain clearly marked diplomatic traits which proved conspicuously useful. Frequently I have touched upon Whitelaw Reid's independence, his firmness in pursuing a given course. There was great tenacity in him, strong will-power reinforced by persistence. At the same time he liked to look around a subject, he was open-minded, and his repute in Paris was that of a negotiator who drove with courtesy at the just and equitable solution of a problem.

He was scrupulously fair, even in disagreement. I may cite a pertinent episode from the summer of 1898. Abram S. Hewitt celebrated his seventy-sixth birthday in that year, and, thanking Reid for his congratulations, he said: "It has been one of the consolations of my life, as well as one of its chief pleasures, that I have enjoyed your friendship, and that even when you had occasion to censure any act of mine the criticism was always couched in language so kindly as not to afford ammunition to my opponents. Allow me to reciprocate the congratulations which you tender. Your own career is one not merely honorable to yourself, but most profitable to your country." That, from one of the stanchest Democrats of his time, with whom Reid had often energetically contended, is a fairly conclusive tribute to his polished skill in debate. It was profitable to his country at Paris.

By a curious turn of fate, one of the officials there most sympathetic in appreciation of Reid's diplomatic characteristics was the Spanish ambassador. It had so happened that on the occasion of his previous stay he had been rather more intimate with Señor Leon y Castillo than with most of his other colleagues. At the time of the signing of the peace protocol a mutual friend in Paris had seen the ambassador and transmitted cordial messages from him to Reid, adding: "He would highly prize any condensed statement of the real views and wishes of our people in regard to the Philippines, Cuba and the Cuban debt. He expressed great confidence in your judgment, and anything you say would have weight with him and also with the Queen." There was, of course, nothing that Reid could say to him at that juncture; but the note struck by Castillo is significant of the atmosphere in which Reid could meet his old Spanish acquaintance when he arrived in Paris. It was a very human atmosphere. That, indeed, is what I would emphasize in treating of the Peace Conference. Every one knows the conditions established in the treaty. Not so familiar are the spirit and movement of the meetings at the French Foreign Office. Before he left America Reid had been told by John Bigelow that we had a wolf by the ears, which we could not let go of with dignity, and that it would take a long time to bring the taming process to an end. The American commissioners sailed with a feeling of respect for the ability of the Spaniards they were to face, and every expectation of difficulty in making satisfactory negotiations. They were not disappointed.

They reached Paris on September 26th, and established themselves at the Hotel Continental, where all the private meetings of the commission were held. Their immediate problem was as to the language in which the proceedings should be conducted in the *salle* assigned to the conference at the Quai d'Orsay. None of the American commissioners spoke Spanish, only two or three of the Spanish commissioners were said to speak English, and only a minority of the commissioners on each side were known to speak French. Under the circumstances it seemed best that the proceedings should be conducted in English, having our interpreter present to repeat whatever might be necessary in Spanish, and leaving the Spanish commissioners to adopt their own course. The success of this plan owed much to the abilities and to the sympathetic address of the interpreter attached to the American commission, Mr. Arthur Ferguson. His command of Spanish was complete, extending to the subtlest nuances of the language, and his alert skill had a clarifying and most helpful effect at important moments. There was no formal organization of our side, though Judge Day was naturally accepted as its president. M. Delcassé, the minister of foreign affairs, formally received the American commissioners on the 28th, taking the opportunity to explain the disinterested position of his government, and on the following day he gave a luncheon at which the two groups met, M. Brisson, the premier, taking part in the occasion. Castillo was among the guests, and after the usual friendly greetings to Reid, plunged at once into business. He had been pleased to hear of Reid's appointment, because he was sure he would appreciate the situation of the Spaniards. They were poor and defeated. It became a great nation like ours, in the moment of its first great victory over a foreign power, to show itself as magnanimous as it had been successful. After the luncheon was over Castillo returned to the subject. Among the points he adjured Reid not to forget was the fact that, after all, it was Spain that had discovered America. This appeal to sentiment was succeeded by a very different mode of procedure in the meetings that presently ensued.

The Spaniards and Americans came together on October 1st with great courtesy, which soon thawed into almost an appearance of cordiality. It looked, however, as though they were to begin with endless arguments over unimportant details. Montero Rios was an heroically voluble disputant. He started off by expatiating at prodigious length over the question of the record to be kept of each day's proceedings. Reid cut the knot by jotting down a memorandum which he initialled and passed along to his colleagues, who all signed the document in the same way. "It is the sense of the American Commissioners," this paper read, "that the record should embrace only propositions presented in writing and action or failure to act thereon." This was adopted and the meeting went on, presumably with all decks cleared and with no likelihood of friction on the first and chiefly ceremonial day of the conference. But before adjournment Montero Rios justified the prediction Reid had made that the Spaniards would open the ball with something like a challenge, probably raising the question of the capture of Manila after the peace protocol had been signed. Precisely this thing was done. Montero Rios presented a paper asserting the Spanish claim that in view of the date, Manila had been wrongfully taken, and that we were consequently bound to restore the *status quo*. The demand was made in a fairly peremptory fashion, and as though it were intended to interpose an obstacle to any other negotiations until the point had been settled. When adjournment finally came the American commissioners knew beyond peradventure that the Spaniards meant to play a delaying game. Their reply was to propose that the order of business followed should be determined by the protocol, and to offer articles, accordingly, as to the surrender of sovereignty in Cuba and the cession of Porto Rico, other Spanish islands in the western hemisphere, and Guam in the Ladrones.

The scene, when the American rejoinder was read at the next meeting, was picturesque and in the highest degree dramatic. "Montero Rios," says Reid, in a note on the incident, "looked as if he was losing his last friend on earth, and the others obviously experienced considerable emotion also at being thus brought face to face with the results of the war." Later the Americans definitely refused to consider a demand for the restoration of the *status quo*, and then the conference proceeded to grapple with the Cuban problem. The Spanish idea assumed that the cession of the sovereignty of Cuba was made only in order that after a suitable time we should turn the island over to its people, and that the United States was to take over responsibility for the entire Cuban debt, including pensions and all sorts of Spanish obligations for running the government, even down to the very moment at which the proposed treaty should be signed. On this proposition the battle of wits was joined in deadly earnest. Rejoinder followed fast upon rejoinder, and, as the chances of agreement receded, the tension threatened to reach the snapping point. The emotional, purely human aspects of the situation come out more and more in Reid's souvenirs. Something of the electricity charging the air at the conference crept into the social atmosphere. Dining with the Munsters at the German Embassy, Reid found the Countess Marie rather quiet at table, but she made an opportunity to say that she had not sympathized with us during the war, and that she was in favor of the little dog. To the suggestion that the little dog ought not to have crowded the big dog into fighting, she replied: "Well, I wish he had taken a bite out of you anyway." The management of "Le Figaro" got up a "Five o'Clock" for both sides. The Coquelins took part, Renaud sang, there were Spanish songs and dances, and finally Miss Loie Fuller supplemented her share in the programme with an amazing stump speech in which she appealed for the sending of the questions before the conference to arbitration! Spanish sympathies in Paris were hugely tickled by this fantastic intrusion. And to the pin pricks accumulating day by day there succeeded the makings of a crisis. At the meeting of October 14th, in a roomful of taut nerves, Montero Rios fought over the Cuban quandary with a heat and a pertinacity suggesting that he was riding for a fall. Reid wrote to Hay on the 16th: "We may be on the eve of a Spanish *coup*. All of us thought, when we parted at the Affaires Etrangères long after dark, last Friday evening, after much the longest and most earnest session we have yet had, that the Spaniards were looking for an opportunity to break up the Conference, presumably with a view to an effort for European arbitration of some sort. We are now planning to let the break come, if it must, on a point that can readily be grasped by the general public, like the question of the Cuban debt, rather than on the more abstract question of whether or not we must accept the sovereignty which Spain relinquishes." Montero Rios admitted that the matter of the interpretation of the article on Cuban sovereignty was in some degree at least academical, but he and his colleagues hammered on this "abstract question," hoping against hope that they might thereby intertwine with it an admission on our part of responsibility for the debt. A few days after the hottest of the meetings on this subject Ambassador Porter gave a dinner to all the commissioners. Montero Rios talked with Reid about everything under the sun, including Velasquez, but he couldn't keep away from the condition of Spain, the necessity for peace, and, above all, the necessity for means of internal development. The whole tone of his talk indicated a readiness to be rid of the colonies, but a feeling that they ought to get money enough for them to be able to prosecute improvements at home. Castillo in his turn renewed his argument on the call for magnanimity to a fallen nation, pointing out that such magnanimity should take the form of recognition of the Cuban debt. He declared that a large part of this debt had been incurred for purposes of internal development in Cuba, railroads and the like, and repeated several times that, speaking unofficially, and as one old friend to another, on his word of honor, if he were in the place of the United States he would gladly take the Cuban debt—otherwise we should surely have trouble with the Cubans; on the other hand, if we assumed the debt, we had absolute control of Cuba in the eyes of the world. Reid told him there was not the remotest possibility of our doing it.

These personal encounters make an intensely interesting phase of the story of Reid's experience at this time in Paris. Castillo, especially in his own house, addressed him with the frankness of an old friend. "You are in danger of an *impasse*," he would exclaim. "You are the only diplomat there. It is the duty of a diplomat to find some middle way, to avoid the absolute failure of negotiations, to accomplish something." After dinner he plied Reid with his familiar arguments, and brought into the conversation the Marquis de Comillas, president of a Spanish bank. Mightily he labored, hoping, it would seem, that by impressing Reid he might in some sort impress the whole American commission. The wind-up of their talk Reid thus himself describes:

At the time I was convinced that Castillo had up his sleeve some trump card, which he wanted to play. Presently he led up to it by renewing his declaration that it was the duty of a diplomat to bring negotiations to a successful result, not to lead them into an *impasse*; that it was especially my duty to seek some middle way that gave Spain some opportunity and would not be offensive to the United States. "Were I in your place," he said at last, "let me tell you what I would do. I would agree upon a mixed commission of experts with reference to debts that might fairly be chargeable to the island, Spain choosing experts on her side, and the United States choosing experts on hers. It should be the duty of this commission to study the origin of these debts and report what portion of them is fairly chargeable to Spain, and what portion chargeable to Cuba." He did not renew his previous talk about their having debts incurred for building railroads, but did talk vaguely about permanent improvements and permanent betterments of the island. When I told him that the plan of such a commission would not be entertained by the United States, the countenances of both the Ambassador and the Marquis de Comillas could not conceal their feeling of disappointment and chagrin.

I said there was absolutely no considerable body of opinion in the United States that would sustain such a scheme and that we would scarcely dare to go home if we accepted it. I explained the view in the United States that these debts were incurred by Spain in its effort to hold the island in subjection, and that it would be monstrous after the island were freed to load it down with debts incurred for its enslavement. But, exclaimed Comillas, "The bonds pledge the revenues of the island; what are the bondholders to do?" I replied that the bondholders must reflect on the old common law maxim, *caveat emptor*. They knew perfectly what the object of the loan was. They knew that if that object were defeated, the so-called security was gone, and that Spain had no longer the power to pledge it. They gambled on Spain's success, and must pay the penalty of having gambled on the wrong side. Comillas looked as if he were being robbed of his last penny, while I made these explanations.

The conversation had by this time become almost dramatic in its intensity. All three of us were standing; Castillo was frequently touching my shoulder, or grasping my coat lapel in the earnestness of his gesticulations. Once or twice, when I hesitated for the French words, Comillas said, "Speak English, I can understand it, although I do not venture to speak it," and after I had spoken in English he rapidly translated in Spanish what I said to Castillo. In answer to Castillo's urgent appeals to do something, I finally assured him of my earnest desire to do everything for him personally that could be done; but assured him that, in this case, what he asked was quite impossible, and then warned him that at any rate the Cuban debt was not the chief difficulty. This seemed to surprise him still more. He said "You don't refer to the Philippines?" I replied "Yes, that, I fancy, will be a much more difficult question for you than the Cuban debt." He still insisted that he thought the big question was the Cuban debt.

The "trump card" that Castillo sought to play is a matter requiring comment by itself. It illustrated the Spanish hankering after arbitration as a recourse which might somehow extricate them from some, at least, of the consequences of the war. Reid found it perhaps the hardest contention of all to discuss with patience. The question of the Cuban debt was a thing which he couldn't consent to arbitrate under any circumstances, any more than he could consent to arbitrate a question whether we should or should not obey the moral law. To him the question of paying, or compelling the Cubans to pay the cost of the long, bloody, and finally unsuccessful efforts to enslave them, was primarily a question of morals, and he would not agree to say that such a question was a fit subject to be arbitrated or agree to be bound by an adverse decision on such a point if unfriendly arbitrators should find one. Also it was allied, for him, with a larger issue. There was arbitration and arbitration, desirable and indefensible. It was important in the conference, he felt, to keep the distinction beyond the shadow of a doubt, and a memorandum of his, written at the height of the debt wrangle, shows the clearly defined philosophy which he advocated throughout:

> The proposal to refer this to arbitration seems to overlook some fundamental considerations. When nations find it impossible to adjust their difficulties by negotiations, there are two remedies. They can resort to arbitration or to war. In many cases arbitration is much to be preferred. The tendencies of advancing civilization favor it, and the United States have employed it. But in the present case there was no suggestion or thought of arbitration. Spain chose war, and the war was continued up to the point when Spain asked for terms of peace, and agreed to and signed a protocol embodying the terms on which alone the United States were willing to suspend the war.
>
> At this stage arbitration has no place. Having failed with one remedy, the unsuccessful nation cannot then turn around and claim a resort to the other. Arbitration comes before war, to avert its evils; not after war, to escape its results. The so-called Cuban debt lay at the very heart of the war, now suspended; was one of the chief causes of the insurrection. After the war has settled them, to put them again at issue in an arbitration would seem to us unreasonable and unprecedented. Furthermore the United States has consistently declared for three quarters of a century that this is and must remain a question between the United States and Spain alone. It is one in which now we can neither invite nor permit the arbitration, mediation or interference of any other power. It was begun by and with Spain, and with Spain it must be settled.

Explicitly, on occasion, and even more often between the lines of their discussions, it was a prime function of the American commissioners to sustain the point of view which Reid, for himself, thus stated.

That was a period of perpetual strain in Paris. The American commissioners confronted an opposition of extraordinary resisting power. And all about them at the moment was the ferment of two French crises, those promoted by the Dreyfus case and Fashoda. The latter subject was not necessarily inflammable. Some Frenchmen found traces of humor in it. The Dreyfus case had some of the characteristics of dynamite. The Reids found that in any considerable company it had to be handled with the most meticulous care, and generally couldn't be touched upon at all. Even families were divided on this topic. Occasionally, however, circumstances permitted candid talk. That which they heard was apt to be anti-government. One leading Frenchman roundly asserted that "no good person out of the army could doubt that Dreyfus was horribly persecuted, and that the attitude of the government and the army was disgraceful." This was the period of a growing assertiveness of anarchistic ideas in French politics, and Reid had from Count Montsaulnin some light, not wholly unamusing, on their true nature. The most notorious of the anarchists and communists in the count's *departement* had come to him scores of times in the Chamber to borrow twenty francs to get dinner for himself or a friend or two, and had not scrupled to give receipts for such petty loans, of which Montsaulnin said he had numbers laid away in his safe. He had even offered to get an anarchist opponent in a campaign "removed" so as to give the count a clear electoral field—asking but five thousand francs for the job. Once Montsaulnin had given this fellow five hundred francs, and had required him to preside at one of his own meetings, which the anarchist had done with fairly good grace. There is a touch of comic opera in one scene which the count laughingly described. When crowds were howling in the streets "*A mort* Montsaulnin," the anarchist boss, at the head of the worst of the rioters, angrily shouted: "There is the Citizen Montsaulnin. I have a few words to say to him." He approached and said them—asking if there was anything he could do to help! Then he at once reassumed his defiant tone, crying: "Now, Citizen Montsaulnin, I hope you understand me once and for all, and know what you have to expect at the hands of myself and my friends." Nevertheless, the party of violence ultimately succeeded in defeating the count for the Chamber of Deputies.

Reid's colleagues listened with interest and approval to his report of the talk he had had with the Spanish ambassador, and they agreed that if negotiations were to be broken off it would have to be on Castillo's "big question." For the despatch to the State Department summarizing the situation Reid wrote a passage tersely stating the policy desired. "Our probable line of procedure, if you do not disapprove and if we think emergency has arisen, will be to repeat that our position on Cuban debt is final, and that, if now again rejected, nothing is left to us excepting to give notice of only one more meeting, to close the protocol." The reply was favorable, and the ensuing discussion at the Foreign Office, protracted and almost impassioned, brought the turning-point in the negotiations. When the meeting of the 24th broke up it was felt on the American side that the Spaniards would yield. Before they did so they made one more appeal to Reid. A letter from the Spanish Embassy, marked *Très Urgente*, proposed a call from Castillo that evening. He made it, with results which are best given in his host's own words:

> The conversation left me somewhat puzzled as to whether it was to be considered as an adroit and painstaking piece of Spanish diplomacy, or as an honest and sincere effort to avert a rupture. He began by telling me that he greatly dreaded the next meeting of the Joint Commission; that he feared a rupture; that Montero Rios

considered it inevitable; that he had spent a good part of the day talking with him and remonstrating against his views; that Montero Rios seemed ready to go back to Madrid at once; but that finally, in response to his (Castillo's) appeals to try to do something, he had said, "Very well, go and see Mr. Whitelaw Reid, and see whether it is possible to arrange anything to avoid a rupture." Castillo insisted that there ought to be some concession with regard to the debt in order to make it possible to continue negotiations. On this point I took very positive ground in reply, assuring him that there was absolutely no possibility of any concession; that the Commissioners were unanimous on the subject, and that the sentiment of the American people was equally unanimous, absolutely without distinction of party. I tried to explain to him our point of view,—that the debt was purely and simply a debt created by Spain for the purpose of maintaining a rule in Cuba which we found so bad and tyrannical that we had been at last compelled to intervene to upset it;—that it was not a Cuban debt at all since the Cubans had had no voice in the creation of it, and had derived no benefit from it. That now they had been freed from the rule this debt was created to maintain and perpetuate, it would be monstrous to saddle the debt upon them.

He insisted in return that the sovereignty was passing either to us or to Cuba, and that according to all rules of international law in cases of transfer of territory the power receiving the transfer assumed either the whole debts of the territory transferred or a portion of them, and he made some reference to the case of Great Britain in our Revolutionary War, and of Texas after the Mexican war. I pointed out to him how completely he was mistaken in both cases; that in the case of our Revolutionary War we never paid anything to Great Britain, and were never asked to, while in the case of Texas what we had paid was not a claim of Mexico, but a debt contracted by Texas in fighting against Mexico in the war in which she gained her independence. I pointed out also that not long before our Revolutionary War, France had been compelled to cede her enormous possessions in North America to England—colonies for which she had incurred large expenses in public works, public defence, maintenance of order, etc., and that in the transfer there had been no talk of transferring debts. He insisted that in that case there had been no debts to transfer. I asked him what then had become of the enormous national debt of France incurred in part in these colonial enterprises beginning with Louis XIV and continuing on down to this. He had no reply excepting to say that some errors had possibly been made in their statement; and then suggested that it might be wise, at any rate, to leave this whole question of a public debt in order to see whether they could not get concessions in the Philippines, which would justify them in abandoning it, otherwise, he said, it would be practically impossible for them to make a treaty and go home. Montero Rios would be hooted in the streets of Madrid if he secured no abatement whatever of our terms. To this I told him that we were in the same difficulty. We would hardly dare to show ourselves at home if we had made the slightest concession, on a point on which the American people were united, in favor of a demand which they considered not only unjust but monstrous.

Again and again he returned to the consideration that this left them powerless, that they must break off; that it was the ruin of Spain. I regretfully admitted that this might be so in part, but insisted that the consequence ought to have been considered before they forced us into war, and then told him I hardly thought he realized the American point of view with reference to the war. In trying to explain this I referred to the case of the *Maine*. He at once insisted that he had sought for full information on that subject, and was absolutely convinced that the *Maine* had not been blown up by any Spanish agency or connivance. I replied that our experts and whole people were morally convinced that it had been blown up by Government torpedo, not necessarily exploded by an officer of the Spanish Government, but in all probability by some one who had been under the command of Weyler; and tried to impress upon him the nature of the feeling such a barbarous crime had aroused in the United States, and the impossibility of pleading conditions growing out of their loss of Cuba as a means of softening the American demands, that they should absolutely leave the Western Hemisphere unburdened either with their government or their debts. All this I tried to put with civility but with extreme distinctness, and it evidently distressed him. In further justification of our attitude I said that he knew if there were debts incurred for public works as yet unpaid for, we were perfectly ready to assume these, and that all private debts, municipal obligations and the like would be safe. To this, however, I added that in my belief there were no public works of that character; at least none to speak of, and suggested that if there had been, they would have named them the other day when the subject was mentioned. In answer to his further incidents on the law of nations, and the sense of justice calling for a transfer of debts, I asked him to consider what such a doctrine led to—what there was to prevent a tyrannical government from piling debts on a discontented colony until it could never get its independence, or get any other nation to accept it.

Castillo kept returning to the point that we must find some way to avoid a rupture; that it was the duty of a diplomat; that it was absurd to have negotiations which merely consisted in laying down an unprecedented requirement; and said he thought never before had a vanquished nation been treated so cruelly. At last I said to him it seemed to me the best policy for Spain would be to accept the inevitable in the case of Cuba, in the hope that possibly there might be something to negotiate about in the greater question that was coming. He repeated what he had said to me at his own house, that he thought Cuba was the great question, and I repeated to him what I said there, that it seemed to me the Philippines prevented greater difficulties. At last I held out a vague hope to him that it was possible—repeating carefully "I say possible, not probable"—that there might be some concession there from the present American attitude either as to territory or as to debt. I explained that certainly the American people had not desired the Philippines, but that it was conceded on all hands that they must retain what they now occupy, and that now during the past few months there had been a rapid growth of a desire to hold the whole archipelago. At the same time I said, unlike the Cuban question, there is on this question of the Philippines a decided difference of opinion, there is a respectable and important minority holding different views. They are not sufficient to control the policy of the Government, but it might be that here would be Spain's best chance to negotiate. He repeated that he thought this doubtful, and that he feared the negotiations would have to be broken off. By this time he had reached the door, and was obviously greatly depressed. He said in saying good bye, "My dear friend, it is cruel, most cruel; pray God that you may never be likewise vanquished." In return I expressed the most earnest conviction that it would only be adding to their misfortunes to break off the negotiations; assured him that he could hardly conceive what an unhappiness they would be bringing down upon Spain, if they should persist in so unwise a course. Shaking hands again at the door, for perhaps a second or third time, I closed with the words—"Do not break off"; and with every expression of cordiality but obviously with great sadness the Ambassador disappeared in the corridors of the hotel.

The next day the Spaniards brought to the Foreign Office their latest contribution to the debate. Immediately it was plain that the danger of a rupture had been passed, and as the interpreter went on with his reading of the document, Senator Gray leaned over and pressed Reid's arm, whispering: "There is the result of your conversation with the Spanish Ambassador." The proposals of the American commissioners as to Cuba and Porto Rico were accepted, and while this acceptance was made "subject to the final decision on the whole treaty," the Spaniards must have realized that there was no longer the faintest chance of saddling the United States with the Cuban debt.

Considering the vast scope of Prussian ambition as it was definitively revealed in the World War, and considering especially the policy which culminated in the invasion of Belgium, a certain interest attaches to the question of Count Munster's attitude during the Peace Conference. The German ambassador was very much at home in Paris, in touch with all the currents and many of the undercurrents in diplomatic circles. In 1898 he had been there thirteen years, entertaining relations with nineteen governments. The tone of his household where our war with Spain was concerned may be inferred from the wish of his daughter which I have cited—that the little dog might have taken a bite out of the big one. It was rumored during the progress of negotiations at the Foreign Office that German holdings of Cuban securities had for weeks been steadily increasing. Whatever its source, German interest in the settlement was lively, and the Kaiser was desirous of being kept constantly informed as to the progress of negotiations. No unofficial news was to be gleaned from any member of the American commission, but he wished his representative to keep in touch with it, and telegraphed Munster to make a point of seeing Reid every day. The pleasantest of relations had existed between these two since the beginning of their official intercourse in 1889, and when their friendship was renewed they had frequent opportunities for talk. There was disclosed, on the old count's part, a point of view discreetly neutral, of course, tinged with an alert curiosity. He was always interested in details of the conference, wanted to know how discussions were conducted, how the remarks of the participants were translated, and so on, and from these harmless topics was wont to proceed to more specific questions. At the time of the crisis over the Cuban debt he was equally sure that the Spaniards wanted us to pay it, and that we wouldn't do it. He surmised that we wanted the Philippines, but all that he drew from Reid on that head was that when we had taken the capital, sunk the Spanish fleet, and captured the Spanish army, we had practically taken the Philippines. He asked many questions about the misconduct of the friars and other features of Spanish rule. The general impression he left was that while Germany was eagerly watchful she had no thought of interfering with us. Repeatedly when he and Reid met he confirmed this idea, sometimes being quite pointed on the question of the islands. On one occasion he said: "We certainly don't want them; at least I don't want them and I hope my Government does not."

His government was to be heard from later, and to show, ever so faintly, the cloven foot of Kaiserism as we have since come to understand it, when the Americans were negotiating for Kusaie, in the Carolines, as a cable station. Berlin got wind of it and interposed objections, hoping that nothing would be done in contravention of German rights and interests, on which the Colonial Office had more or less clearly formed convictions. Munster called on Reid more than once to talk about it, evidently not altogether in sympathy with his home authorities. Without taking the fidgetiness of the latter too seriously, and having no idea that the young Emperor wanted any trouble, Reid nevertheless believed that if there was the slightest chance to grab an island or a port anywhere, in a quasi-peaceful way, Germany didn't mean to miss it. To that extent at least he sensed in 1898 the proclivities which were unblushingly disclosed in 1914. He knew that all through the war it only needed the appearance of a fleet of ours in European waters to start the Kaiser upon a meddlesome policy, and if the Caroline episode did not precisely sound a danger-signal it was, on the other hand, one calling for a certain good-natured wariness. Reid was quite ready for the German ambassador, and with the necessary documents at his hand amiably showed him how insubstantial were the "ancient rights" that the Germans were disposed to press. He suspected that they were really avid of *all* the Carolines, to say nothing of a single member of the group, and remarked to Munster that he couldn't see why they wanted them. "My dear Reid," impetuously burst out the count, "no more can I. I agree with you precisely; and I tell you these Colonial Department people are all alike—all savages, who can't eat without gorging—not civilized sufficiently to know when they have had enough, and unable to resist the sight of raw meat! They are tiresome, these colonials!" Count Munster understood the psychology of his people even better than he knew.

The transition of arguments in the Peace Conference from the Cuban to the Philippine question was made in an atmosphere so charged with feeling that toward the close of October the outlook for a treaty was distinctly overclouded. Despite the secrecy of proceedings at the Foreign Office the question of our policy was everywhere in the air, and Reid's old view of what "environment" meant was amply confirmed. He had suggested earlier the possibility of an adjournment to Nice, and the American commissioners, amongst themselves, revived the idea. The French press continued unfeignedly hostile. In "Le Gaulois," in "Le Figaro," in "Le Matin," and in other powerful journals it was generally predicted that the Spaniards would refuse to sign a treaty surrendering the Philippines. That, none the less, remained the American position. Since my purpose in these pages is confined chiefly to a statement of Reid's personal relation to the subject I may here underline his views. He had stated them in Washington when he and his colleagues went into conference with the President. He spoke then of the difficulty, morally, of taking one part of the Philippines and abandoning the rest to Spain, and of the political difficulties flowing from the same policy, which would be merely organizing in a worse shape exactly the trouble we had been suffering from in the West Indies for three-quarters of a century. The islands which, on the hypothesis of making two bites of the cherry, would be abandoned to Spain, were much nearer to Luzon than Cuba or Porto Rico were to Key West, the necessities of constant intercourse were much greater, and it was obvious that the friction would be constant and the provocations to war far greater. The Philippines were ours by right of conquest, and gave us a commercial advantage in the Pacific which we had no right to throw away. He was not much concerned about the immediate nature of popular feeling in America on the subject, for of the ultimate popular tendency he had no doubt at all. Nor was he disturbed over the difficulty of our administering these distant possessions. What Great Britain had done successfully a kindred people did not need to be less skilful and successful in. He was for the retention of the Philippines *en bloc*.

In October, while the conference was still wrestling with the Cuban matter, he wrote to Hay adjuring him not to encourage the theory of dividing the Philippines. "All the expert testimony is against it," he said, "both because it tends to destroy the value of what we do take and because it is the sure way to organize further troubles first for ourselves and then for all the world beside. Have you considered that there is hardly one of these islands from which you cannot shoot across to another! The military and naval testimony here is clear and precise, to the effect that we can govern and defend the whole as easily as, if not more easily than, a part." To the theory of taking all the Philippines his arguments as a member of the commission were unremittingly addressed. That they were needed and that they played a decisive part in the formation of the final contention of the American side are facts no longer secret, so I may give in Reid's own words the gist of the matter, making clear how large was his share of responsibility for the great acquisition we made in the Pacific. Years afterward, when ambassador in London, he wrote to Smalley (who was then engaged upon his "Anglo-American Memories," in which he desired to tell something of the inner history of the Paris Conference) the following letter:

Dorchester House,
April 18th, 1911.

My dear Smalley:

The fact is, I was committed to the retention of the territory we had taken before my appointment, an article on that subject which Gilder fairly worried me into writing having been printed before we assembled in the Cabinet Room of the White House for our first official meeting with the President and ostensibly to receive his instructions. As a matter of fact he was not ready to give instructions but wanted our opinions. Day, who was then Secretary of State and who became our Chairman, was strongly against the retention of anything in the Philippines unless possibly a coaling station, and on even that he had some doubts. Gray was even stronger than Day. Senator Davis of Minnesota, to our surprise, declared himself in favor of retaining the northern part of the archipelago and giving away Mindanao and the whole southern part to Holland. Failing that he wanted to trade them to some other European power for something that would be of more use to us. Senator Frye did not express himself very distinctly against this proposal; in fact, seemed to think the northern part of the archipelago the essential part and was not even sure such a trade as Senator Davis recommended might not be desirable. He dwelt on the fact that some opposition to our holding the islands had developed in New England and promised to grow. I spoke after most of them and reiterated the position I had already taken in the "Century" article, dwelling particularly on my declaration that having broken down the power in control of them, we could not honorably desert them and should be extremely unwise to turn over the task of controlling them to any other power.

After we had been some time in Paris and the Spaniards had to some extent shown their hand, the President called on us for detailed expressions of our individual opinions, and Judge Day, who, by this time, had been made Chairman, asked each of us to reduce them to writing. I sat down at once and wrote my views. Day and Gray had brought theirs, which they read subsequently. I read mine. After a little oral discussion Davis came to me and asked me if I would not put mine in such a shape that he could sign it also, and Frye repeated the request. I turned it over accordingly to them, and so it happens that my despatch* went to the President signed first by Davis, next by Frye and last by myself. The union thus formed lasted throughout the remainder of the work.

Even if it had existed from the beginning it might still be said that it was my casting vote which took the Philippines; but, as you see, the circumstances are a little stronger. I think nobody would question the facts substantially as stated above.

Sincerely yours, WHITELAW REID.

The commission worked harder over this problem, Reid thought, than anybody at a distance would ever believe. In one of his letters to McKinley he says: "Every morning we meet in one of my rooms, which proves a more convenient and private place for consultations than the office on the floor below. By ten o'clock all five are apt to be gathered there together with Mr. Moore; and in a cloud of tobacco smoke the discussions, preparation of despatches, examination of authorities or of witnesses, etc., go on till one—often to be renewed again in the afternoon, on the days when we have no meeting with our friends, the enemy, at the Foreign Office. There have been days in succession when

* See "Foreign Relations of the United States" for 1898, pp. 932–933, where the despatch is printed in full.

not one of us got a breath of fresh air, unless in walking the eighth of a mile from the hotel to the Quai d'Orsay." For these morning sessions Reid had an experienced hand prepare a summary of the pertinent passages in the French, English, and Spanish newspapers. Thus the commissioners began their daily meetings with the censure of our critics for our unreasonableness, unwillingness to conciliate, and general brutality toward a gallant but unfortunate people, ringing in their ears.

The attitude of the Spaniards when the Americans presented their proposal on the Philippines, demanding the cession of the entire archipelago, is described by Reid as one of "despairing resignation." An adjournment of a few days was agreed upon, a period of anxious waiting. Ribot, at whose house the Reids were dining, expressed the hope that America would not alienate the sympathies of the world by pushing the Spaniards too far. That, it seemed, was to be the official tone, the tone of the "environment." The next day, when the Spaniards made their reply, it amounted to a rejection of the American proposal and an offer of other proposals in its place. The manœuvre had no serious weight, bringing no really cogent arguments to bear. The impression left upon Reid's mind was that the enemy was "sparring for time," in the hope that in the November elections McKinley's administration might suffer reverses weakening to the American attitude in the conference. Republican victories quenched that delusion. A little passing flurry was created at this juncture by communications from Belgium. They conveyed the curious information that the Spanish Government had offered to cede the Philippines to King Leopold. In the pauses of official discussion everything that Reid heard was to the effect that the Spanish commissioners were in an embittered state of mind, rebelling against a treaty which would ruin them at home. Munster assured him that they were resolved not to make martyrs of themselves—and in the same breath, by the way, he added that they deceived themselves if they counted on the slightest encouragement from his Emperor. Reid himself remained undismayed by Spanish obduracy and was only relieved when by the middle of November the policy he had advocated was so conclusively upheld in the despatches from Washington that there was nothing to do but present the enemy with an ultimatum. This, when it was brought forward, coupled with the maintenance of the original American demand an offer of twenty millions.

Montero Rios listened with a funeral face, puffing cigarette after cigarette in his perturbation. He permitted himself a single hot-tempered outburst, saying he was ready to answer at once, waiting only for the translation of the rest of the American paper. As a matter of fact, he had no power to answer at once, and indignant impulse gave way to nothing more than a request for further delay. Reid inclined to the belief that with all manner of protestations and outcries they would in the end accept. They did so on Monday, November 28th. In a profound and painful silence the Spanish reply was read, maintaining their conviction of the soundness of their own proposals, declaring an unwillingness to reopen the war and subject their country to greater calamities, and therefore submitting to the inevitable. During the reading the Spanish commissioners sat in their places with an air of mournful dignity. When it was finished, and just as the Americans were preparing to leave the room, the clouds that had been lowering over Paris all day cleared away for a moment, and a burst of sunlight illuminated the green table at which Ojeda, the Spanish secretary, was making his notes of the protocol. Reid happened to be standing at his side and expressed the hope that this meant good fortune for both countries. Ojeda replied: "No, everything is gloom around us."

There remained various details to be adjusted at future meetings. In the American deliberations Reid was strong for an early payment of the twenty millions, and suggested the term of three months, which was inserted in the treaty. He urged a similarly liberal policy in the offer of a price for Kusaie, and in the matter of the repatriation of prisoners. At the Foreign Office, too, when the question of the revival of old treaties came up, he was especially urgent in his pleas on extradition and copyright, suggesting a *modus vivendi* for a year or even for six months if nothing better could be arranged. The American side was not disposed to be grudging in its discussion of the "open door" in the Philippines and in the treatment of this topic and others steadily endeavored to expedite as much as possible the final negotiations. These were protracted, however, by the not unnatural desire of the Spaniards to grasp at any advantage conceivably remaining to them. They were exacting upon the return of certain pieces of their artillery in the islands, and, understandably enough, sought once more to secure the appointment of a mixed commission to investigate the cause of the explosion of the *Maine*. An odd question arose in that of the continuance of the pensions to the Duke of Veragua, the descendant of Columbus, paid prior to the war from the treasuries of Cuba, Porto Rico, and the Philippines. The Spanish article on this subject was ultimately rejected. In all these closing incidents Montero Rios did his gallant best to thwart the contentions of the American commissioners, to involve his antagonists in endless controversy, and, in short, at the eleventh hour, to put them in a hole. When the *Maine* issue was reintroduced he spoke with obviously suppressed passion and flashing eyes. As late as December 8th the old fear that there might be a sudden breaking off of negotiations, and no treaty, painfully recurred. But on that very day the Spaniards surrendered and the conference adjourned, with the understanding that the engrossing of the treaty should go forward at once. When on the evening of the 9th Munster called on Reid with congratulations he said that he knew directly from the German ambassador in Madrid that the Queen Regent and Sagasta had sent instructions to Montero Rios to sign the treaty as quickly as possible and get the matter ended. Seals were affixed to the document at the Foreign Office within twenty-four hours, on December 10th.

"*Enfin nous avons la paix, grace à Dieu,*" wrote Reid to Castillo, and there was good feeling in the Spanish ambassador's response. The closing scene at the Foreign Office was marked by a spirit immensely relieving the long strain. In the preparation of the last American paper the task had been assigned to Reid of composing a brief conciliatory and complimentary termination, and when the document was presented it expressed the sense of the American commissioners of "the thoroughness, learning, and devoted ability, no less than the uniform courtesy, with which the Spanish Commissioners have conducted the negotiations." When the two groups were assembled to sign, Montero Rios, in a perfect little speech, explained how he and his associates had been touched by these words. He desired to express the gratitude of his side for such appreciation, their agreeable recollection of the personal intercourse which had accompanied the deliberations, and the value which they should attach throughout their lives to the tribute I have just cited. Judge Day responded in the same key, and with bows and smiles the opposing commissioners came, as Reid observed, "nearer genuine cordiality than for months." Now that the grave task was ended it seemed as if the emotional springs of the conference had been dried up. Reid's last colloquy as they gathered around the table was with Abarzuza, on educational matters in America and Spain. The Don thought the tendency in his country was as strong as ever to depend on a thorough knowledge of the classics, as the basis for any liberal education, and he was glad to note a revival of the principle in the United States. He referred to his own experience at an English university, and talked with great good sense about the importance of laying a thorough foundation in the old-fashioned way in the classics and mathematics, not so much for the sake of the information actually acquired as for the training of the memory and for the acquisition of what he called educational tools. He showed considerable familiarity with English and American books, expressing high appreciation of Motley, and speaking with enthusiasm of Prescott. There is piquancy in this episode of an American and a Spaniard, met to ratify the cession of Spain's last possessions in the western hemisphere, and comparing laudatory notes on the historian of Ferdinand and Isabella.

The signing of the peace treaty was charged with a significance greater, if anything, for us than for Spain. Our territorial expansion carried with it responsibilities of a new order, on a great scale. Reid was to have much to say about them for some time following his return. But on the completion of the labors in Paris his thoughts on what we had gained and on the duties we had assumed were mixed with reflections on certain things achieved which were of moment to Europeans as well as to Americans. He stated them in print, soon after. Lady Randolph Churchill was then just starting her new quarterly, "The Anglo-Saxon Review," and for the first number, which appeared in the following June, Reid wrote a paper on "Some Consequences of the Treaty of Paris," in which he traced to the settlement some contributions toward the better regulation of international understanding. He noted first that "the distinct and prompt refusal by the American Commissioners to submit questions at issue between them and their colleagues to arbitration marks a limit to the application of that principle in international controversy which even its friends will be apt hereafter to welcome." The United States, he willingly admitted, was thoroughly committed to the policy of international arbitration, but, he insisted, the upshot of the conference had made it clear that "the rational place for arbitration is as a substitute for war, not as a second remedy, to which the contestant may still have a right to resort after having exhausted the first." Next the conference, in its disposition of the matter of the Cuban debt, had established the principle that "a national debt incurred in efforts to subdue a colony, even if called a colonial debt, or secured by a pledge of colonial revenues, cannot be attached in the nature of a mortgage to the territory of that colony, so that when the colony gains its independence it may still be held for the cost of the unsuccessful efforts to keep it in subjection." Furthermore, he cited the action of the United States, on the outbreak of the war with Spain, in repudiating any intention of a resort to privateering. The treaty contains no article on this subject, but on the signing of the document the status of private war at sea could hardly be said to have been left quite as it had been found. The very fact that the United States had not in 1856 given its adhesion to the abolition of privateering in the Declaration of Paris increased the weight of its acceptance of the principle in 1898. The effect, as Reid saw it, was about equivalent to completing that custom and assent of the civilized world which is the main thing. "Here then," he concluded, "are three great principles, important to the advancement of civilization, which, if not established in international law by the Peace of Paris and the war it closed, have at least been so powerfully reinforced that no nation is likely hereafter lightly or safely to violate them." Montero Rios, of course, saw the services of the American commissioners to civilization in a very different light. The last thing in the world of which he dreamed was that they had done anything to improve upon existing usage. Indeed, forgetful of the amicable note struck on the moment of parting at the Quai d'Orsay, he sent after them, as they left for home, a splenetic parting shot. In an interview given to Blowitz for the London "Times" he called them "*vainqueurs parvenus*," and their conception of international law "absolutely new." Reid's "Anglo-Saxon" paper gave him the answer which has ever since been confirmed by public opinion on the Treaty of Paris.

CHAPTER XIV

PROBLEMS OF EXPANSION

Even before his return from Paris Reid received from the closest of his friends intimations of the increased prestige which could be counted upon as resulting from his work on the treaty. They came from John Hay, established in the Department of State, and therefore in a position to add to personal feeling an exhaustive knowledge of the facts. "You have evidently had a most interesting experience," he wrote on November 13th, "and it is evident that your antecedent advantages have been of great value to the Commission. You call your place the 'tail end' but it is clearly 'where MacGregor sits.' Your talk with the Spanish Ambassador was to my mind the turning point of the negotiations. If you make a treaty, there will be credit enough to go around; but as it looks now, the treaty can only be made on your lines—and in this the Administration and, by a vast majority, the country, will be with you." In a brief note, written a few days later, he says: "It is comfortable to feel we have a man on deck who knows what to do and how to do it. I wish you were here—if you could be in two places 'loike a burd.'" Hay wanted him home to help combat the opposition to acquisition of the Philippines, an opposition which was not by any means inarticulate. Vociferous as it was, and much as Hay wanted his friend's assistance in stilling it, he nevertheless believed that it would ultimately die down, and in the meantime he assured Reid that the members of the commission would return as conquering heroes.

Reid resumed direction of the affairs of The Tribune immediately upon the termination of those formalities with which he and his colleagues turned over their functions to the President. For the next two years his editorial activities were carried on practically without interruption, absences in the Adirondacks or in California making no difference in the close attention which he gave to the management of the paper. It embraced as always a multitude of details, with those of a political nature well in the foreground. In New York State the party had been strengthened by the election of Theodore Roosevelt to the governorship in November, 1898, but the Platt machine was still powerful, with effects upon the course of affairs providing abundant food for comment by an editor of Reid's militant habit. It was not until Roosevelt took the vice-presidency in 1900 and his successor, Odell, improved conditions by taking over Platt's leadership himself, that the strain was relaxed. In the national field the task of renominating and re-electing McKinley was comparatively easy. The early enactment of the Dingley bill had settled, for a time, agitation over the tariff, and the establishment of the gold standard had exerted a similarly quieting influence upon discussion of the currency. So far as domestic questions were concerned there was little difficulty in preparing for the presidential campaign or in seeing it through. The international atmosphere was another matter, and it is his preoccupation with this that gives a special unity to Reid's labors at this period.

The transition from the nineteenth century to the twentieth was made under threatening auspices. It was in 1899 that England entered her long struggle in the Transvaal. This hardly touched us, but the Chinese crisis did, to the point of military participation, and in purely peaceful negotiations there were important episodes brought up for settlement, such as the Alaskan boundary and the Hay-Pauncefote Canal Treaty. Above all there was, for the United States, the consolidation of the fruits of the war with Spain to be secured. The times were terribly out of joint, and to some observers almost anything seemed possible. Reid's friendship with Senator Davis had been deepened by their association in Paris, and he was frequently in correspondence on these topics with the chairman of the Senate Committee on Foreign Relations. Writing on August 26th, 1900, after the relief of the legations at Pekin, Davis said to him: "The first act of the Chinese drama has been played, and well played on the whole. What will the others be, and what the catastrophe? I fear that a general war, an Armageddon, is imminent. The only chance I can see of averting it is by such wise action by Germany holding aloof as will make her feared by the other European powers in case they engage in a rough and tumble. The Kaiser never says a wise thing or does a foolish one—to reverse the lines of the ballad on Charles II." It is amusing here to glance at the Kaiser's attitude toward the Hague Peace Conference, held in the previous year. Reid received some indirect light on the subject in the following letter:

Paris,
April 7th, 1899.

DEAR MR. WHITELAW REID:

I was very much pleased to hear from you, and thank you sincerely for your kind letter. I agree completely with all you said about the Open Door, and all that you said about the Paris Conference. I was disappointed in one sense in reading your letter. The European papers had said that you were to be one of the American delegates at the, falsely so called, disarmament conference at the Hague. I would have been glad to meet you there and to work together with you.

The Emperor has appointed me to represent the German Empire at that conference, and so I am sorry to see that I do not find your name. I could not refuse and have to obey orders, although I think it a most difficult and ungrateful task. Beating empty straw is always a tiresome job, which may even be dangerous if it is, like in this case, Russian straw, that may conceal an apple of contention. As to disarmament, it is out of the question and it is ridiculous to have proposed it at this moment. The only important question to discuss would be arbitration and to come to an understanding on that point is, I fear, rather hopeless. We may agree about some points of international law and some new regulation of the Red Cross. We can, in regard to Russia, not allow the conference to end with an entire fiasco and must try to cover it with a peaceful-looking cloak.

I am glad to see that I know most of the delegates, and am very much pleased by the choice of Staal for the Russian, and Sir Julian Pauncefote. Both are very old friends of mine. The French send Bourgeois as first and d'Estournelles as second delegate. Both use the conference as a stepping stone leading to an embassy, which will make them prudent and amiable. We assemble on the 18th of May. I think that the conference will last six weeks, so that we shall have to pass all the month of June in Holland. Nineteen European and five foreign nations have been invited. It will be a regular parliament, difficult to manage, I fear. Is there no chance of your coming to Europe this summer?

Yours very sincerely,

MUNSTER.

Later, giving a friend an introduction to Reid, he added an epilogue, recurring to his figure of the futile flail: "The Peace Conference kept me for ten weeks at work. We did not do much. The thrashing of empty straw is hard work, particularly if it is Russian straw; but we thrashed peacefully and did not much good but *no harm*. You may have heard that the Emperor rewarded my services in giving me the higher rank of Prince." Reid's opinion of that famous conference was that its exercises, though academically impressive, necessarily lacked the weight of untrammelled and conclusive deliberations. The enterprise was theoretically attractive but not much confidence was to be placed in the schemes that were outlined on paper by the representatives of the Powers. The affair had its pathetic aspect. Preparations for the conference had been portentous, whereas the outcome was trifling. Incidentally, the immediate march of events under the chief nations participating indicated absolute obliviousness to the Hague proceedings. Every one was willing to listen with politeness to academic counsels of perfection. No one was ready to surrender the principle of national independence of judgment—and action—in matters touching a national interest. Whitelaw Reid saw this principle both as a factor rooted in human nature and as a fixed element in the political consciousness of his countrymen. It was one of the cardinal points in his campaign for a purely American interpretation of the responsibilities assumed on the making of our treaty with Spain.

I refer to a "campaign," for no other word so accurately describes the work which as a writer and public speaker he carried on after his return from Paris. "Imperialism," as an opprobrious epithet, was on the lips of Democrat and Mugwump, even while the peace negotiations were in progress, and ratification of the treaty was far from silencing the opposition, since the Philippine insurrection plunged us into hot water which promised to go on boiling indefinitely. In March, 1899, McKinley expressed the belief to a visitor at the White House that "Aguinaldo has had enough of it by this time." As a matter of fact, he was not captured until two years later. The long-drawn-out military operations in the archipelago only stoked the fires of criticism of the administration at home. On the first anniversary of the signing, Reid gave a dinner to his colleagues of the commission, and asked, among others who were to meet them, Andrew Carnegie. They shared Scotch sympathies, and the old ironmaster used gleefully to disagree with his editorial friend, playing on "the wee drap blude atween us." He couldn't come to the celebration. "Unfortunately I shall be in Pittsburg," he wrote, "the evening of your reception to the signers of the *War* Treaty with Spain, not the Peace. It is a matter of congratulation, however, that you seem to have about finished your work of civilizing the Filipinos. It is thought that about eight thousand of them have been completely civilized and sent to heaven. I hope you like it." That was one of the points of view Reid set himself to correct. The campaign of which I speak was one of education. It was his task to elucidate the treaty, to show its harmony with our Constitution, and to demonstrate the soundness, under that instrument, of the policy adopted in the administration of our new possessions. In the "Anglo-Saxon" paper referred to in the preceding chapter he had emphasized the broader implications of the treaty. Now he undertook to reassure the short-sighted, timorous folk at home who saw only disaster ahead, and groaned the more piteously over the prospect because, in their view, we had started with the immorality of "buying the inhabitants of the Philippines at two dollars a head." He could do much, and did it, in the columns of The Tribune. Personally, as one of the authors of the peace, standing up to be counted and bearing testimony on a subject which he knew from top to bottom, he did even more.

Public dinners and ceremonial occasions at universities gave him repeated opportunities to deal with the burning question. Were there Americans who thought that too good a treaty had been made at Paris? Traversing the document for their benefit he sought to allay their quaint fears. What precisely was the purport of the treaty? He went out to Chicago to give the members of the Marquette Club the light they needed. The making of the peace had imposed upon us new duties. Reid undertook to explain what they were and how they might be carried out. He pleaded at Princeton, at Miami, in Boston, in California, wherever he went, for a liberal but firm policy in our new possessions, answered constitutional criticisms, advocated the application of a pure Civil Service administration in the islands and altogether endeavored to clarify a problem which was, indeed, needlessly obscured. His various speeches, widely reported in the press, were circulated also in pamphlet form, and presently had piled up the material for a book, "Problems of Expansion," which the Century Company brought out in 1900.*

There was no apology in any of these utterances. Reid refused to admit that there was anything in the treaty that called for defense, and, as I have hinted before, the cry of "Imperialism" carried no worrying implications to his ears. The burden of all his discourses was simply the enforcement of what seemed to him irrevocable facts—that when the arbitrament of war turned the fortunes of Cuba, Porto Rico, and the Philippines over to our care we were in honor bound to assume responsibility for them; that there was nothing in our Constitution to conflict with the different measures for their protection devised, adopted, or contemplated by the Republican administration; and that despite a hundred Aguinaldos and a million "Little Americans," we could not, in decency, having put our hand to the plough, look back. Yet he was no blind advocate of a merely Republican policy. His arguments were not partisan at all, but examined the case in the light of a dispassionate Americanism, fortified by historical precedent and the sanctions of constitutional and international law. That the administration was slow in its preparations to restore order in the islands is an historical fact which it would be idle to deny. It was a Republican member of the

* Some of the more important papers in this collection are reproduced in his "American and English Studies."

Senate who said in a letter to Reid: "If McKinley would only take a big trumpet and blow upon it a blast in defense of his own policy, he would settle the entire business; but he will not do it, apparently. His horn is a good deal like that of Munchausen, the notes of which were frozen inside of it when blown in Arctic regions, and only gave out their music after the event." Reid's blasts were unimpeded, and there was one passage in his address at Miami, in fact, which was little less than startling to party observers of the hidebound order. He unequivocally recognized that conditions in Luzon were sadly awry, and noted the dilatory administration which was, in a measure, responsible for their growth. Such candor only strengthened the force of what he had to say. The party hack might squirm, but thoughtful commentators were grateful for the frank expression of the truth at the right moment. Davis, for example, laughed at the idea that the point made at Miami was to be construed as an attack upon the administration. "It did not strike me in that way," he wrote. "The fact is that sometimes affairs get in such a condition that a statement of facts is necessarily criticism, and sometimes implies censure. When that condition is presented, so much the better for the facts, and so much the worse for the Administration, which ought to be thankful and take warning. I thought your expressions were as temperate as they were true."

Some idea of what was thought at Washington about Reid's campaign is shown in what Hay wrote to him in February, 1900, when the Miami and Princeton addresses had both been published: "The other day, in Cabinet meeting, the Attorney General said the constitutional relations of our new possessions had nowhere been defined so clearly and ably as in your speeches and every man present agreed." His correspondence is full of appreciative expressions from public men of the day, and I may note that some of the most cordial of them come from the colleagues with whom he had worked over the treaty. "I am in accord with you as I was at Paris," said Frye. And Davis wrote him, at the end of the first year of proselytizing: "I do say most unfeignedly that your papers upon the questions which have arisen from the cession of the Philippines have done a great work in support of the convictions and forecasts which impelled the Commissioners to insist upon that cession." An apposite letter for me to quote here is one from Charles Dudley Warner, apposite because it shows Reid's success in what he had so largely sought to do, to persuade the thoughtful unbeliever:

Hartford,
July 19, 1899.

My dear Mr. Reid:

I am very much obliged to you for your excellent address at Miami. With a great deal of reluctance I am compelled to agree with most of it. I hate war, and hated this war and don't like the prospect of the burden it imposes; but I long ago gave up the notion that I am the best judge of what Providence ought to do; and looking back over the past I may frankly say that I should probably have taken the wrong side of a good many things that seem now to be a part of the inevitable plan of development. So my attitude is simply expressed by the fact that when I was in Mexico last spring, and interviewed, I talked freely for peace, and when on my return I reached New Orleans and found that war was declared, and was interviewed again, I said that I had nothing to say, that war was now on and that for an American there was only one side.

Your address is on the whole the strongest and most lucid word that has been said on that side, convincing in its historical array, and sensible because based on things as they actually are and not as many of us might wish them. We went into the war unprepared and we have a war department that is still unprepared and daily seems to me quite inadequate to conduct the military affairs of a great nation. From my point of view the President's responsibility for the war, before the country, is second to his responsibility for Alger.

Yours sincerely,

Charles Dudley Warner.

Joseph Pulitzer, another opponent in this field, was harder to convince, and, indeed, remained firm in his own position; yet he, too, when Reid sent him a copy of "Problems of Expansion," showed that he was not altogether insensitive to his friend's persuasiveness. "I quite disagree with your political philosophy on the subject of the Philippines," he said, "but I will confess to you that your speeches (and you know how from boyhood up I have had a passionate admiration for oratory and eloquence) struck me very much at the time they were delivered. If I were not afraid of encouraging you to even more radical violations of the Constitution I might tell you that it seemed to me you first made the point at Chicago which the majority of the Supreme Court accepted." If Reid could make only a slight impression on this particular Democratic editor he had the satisfaction of nevertheless seeing his missionary work bear fruit over a wide territory. Privately and through the press he received the evidences that he had rightly gauged the drift of public opinion. Little by little, as McKinley's first administration drew to a close, the Anti-Imperialists were pressed to the wall. "I am still firm in the faith," wrote Davis, in the summer of 1900, "that we did a great—a very great—thing for our country in Paris. This will be proved after the transient people who have never believed in or understood the 'swelling act of the imperial theme' which they are performing, have passed into the oblivion which, as to such impersonations, is called history." In so far as the vindication of a party at the polls may be taken as foreshadowing a verdict of the sort, the re-election of McKinley later that year gave Davis his proof.

A great deal of Reid's energy, as the foregoing pages have shown, was given at this time to the justification of a *fait accompli*. Much went also to the discussion of current issues. Salient amongst these, and closely related to his whole philosophy of the war with Spain, was that developed by the question of a Porto Rican tariff. Reid fought stoutly against the adoption of measures in which there lurked the possibility of a clamor for statehood. From the beginning of the war he had recognized the danger and his opposition to it is so characteristic, so bound up with his entire conception of our proper relation to alien possessions, that I must give intact this expression on the subject:

New York,
Hon. Wm. E. Chandler. January 22, 1900.

Dear Mr. Senator:

Seeing your familiar frank this morning on a copy of the Congressional Directory, leads me to inflict this letter upon you on a subject which seems to me very important to the Republican Party and to the country. The real danger in our sudden expansion lies in the cowardly tendency of so many of our public men to do nothing against admitting anybody and everybody to full partnership in the American union. It has been only a little while since one could get anybody in Congress to admit the possibility of dealing with the Sandwich Islands in any other way than by making them a state in the Union. Everybody seemed to consider it natural, as well as certain, that Cuba would come in some day as a state. But if Cuba and the Sandwich Islands, why not Hayti and San Domingo and the Philippines and Porto Rico? And yet everybody seems bent on taking the first step by treating Porto Rico exactly like a domestic territory in training for statehood, and stretching our grotesquely inapplicable Dingley tariff bodily over it.

It is all right to give Porto Rico a market and nothing is easier. An arrangement such as we had with Spain about Cuba would do it. Enacting the Dingley bill as a separate tariff for Porto Rico would do it, if we are bent on that—merely providing further, by separate resolutions, that the manufactures and products of Porto Rico shall be added to the free list on our own tariff. Anything is better than a precedent which even implies a sanction to the notion that such outlying territory is entitled to be treated as a part of the United States.

I am well aware that very few members of Congress, if any, are ready to agree with me in this. I am none the less confident that any other course threatens a large part of the danger which the Anti-Imperialists are now predicting. Only the other evening,

Andrew Carnegie said to me gloatingly "You will be driven off from your opposition to letting all these islands in as states. You'll have to swallow every last one of them. Already you are about making Porto Rico a territory." Again and again during the conversation he recurred to the idea that the Republican Party was sure to make states out of all our islands. Isn't it worth while to learn from an enemy? If I believed him I should hold it a duty of every patriot to oppose the Republican Party.

Please forgive this long screed. I know I have the advantage in part at least of sharing these views with you. With cordial regards,

Very sincerely yours,

WHITELAW REID.

All through the discussion of this subject in Washington he kept up a lively correspondence on it with Davis, Beveridge, Foraker, and every other possible source of sympathy in his opposition to what he considered a signal peril. To Hay, also, he uttered a word of warning against the plan of extending the United States tariff over Porto Rico in accordance with the contention that these new possessions were already an integral part of the United States with all that that might lead to. "It was not a grateful task to oppose this proposition," he said, "but I never felt clearer about a duty."

The problems of the time come constantly to the surface in his correspondence with Hay. Sometimes the secretary of state would ask his views on a question promoted by the war—the claims of American citizens against Spain originating prior to the outbreak of the Cuban insurrection, the precise interpretation to be given to a phrase in the treaty, the claim of the Madrid government to the island of Sibutu—but more often they were concerned with pending negotiations or with the crisis in China. In the Alaskan boundary matter Reid's support of the administration was energetic but tempered by caution, and though Hay could thank him for a "sound and generous" leader on the subject, he drew from him some shrewd counsels, especially on the political side of the situation. "This subject of our northwestern boundary," he reminded Hay, "is one on which our people have been touchy for more than half a century," and he deprecated the giving up of one of our Alaskan ports to Great Britain. In the upshot, when the Alaskan Boundary Commission rendered its decision in favor of the United States, in 1903, his judgment was confirmed.

Reid's backing throughout the painful Chinese crisis was very grateful to Hay; it was, he said, "so friendly and so helpful." The secretary's masterly handling of the "open door" policy rejoiced Reid's soul. Physically Hay was a little down at the time, with consequent depression, and Reid wrote to him: "Your successes ought to cure you. No man in our diplomatic history, so far as I have read it, has had so many of them in so short a time, with so little criticism and such an exemption from back-sets. You have been especially happy in hitting the bull's eye of the Chinese business and taking the lead of the civilized nations in marking at each critical point the path they had to follow. Cheer up, and get at it again as soon as you can!" In conversation with a mutual friend in Washington, Hay showed how much he valued the co-operation of his old comrade, expressing the wish that "we could have a man like Mr. Reid on the spot, to whom the Administration could give full authority." Meditatively, he added: "But I suppose Mr. Reid wouldn't think of such a thing." What Reid's policy would have been if he had "thought of such a thing" is indicated in a letter of his to Senator Davis. "The moment we have secured," he said, "the protection of Americans in China or withdrawn them, it is to our interest to disentangle ourselves from the European complications which seem sure to be coming. We must exert our proper influence for the open door, and exact proper reparation for the outrages to which our people have been subjected; but I fully agree with you that we can do this best playing from our own bat; *i. e.*, on our own soil in the Philippines, with troops, ships, military supplies and everything ready for an emergency." In his opinion there was no conceivable emergency which could legitimatize the suggestion then current for the conquest of the Chinese Empire and the partitioning of its territory among the allied forces of civilization. That seemed to him "simply the most gigantic military undertaking any madman has proposed in the last half dozen centuries."

On the war in South Africa Reid was an open-minded weigher of the facts. His attitude of detachment was criticised in some quarters, notably those of a Little American and Irish Home Rule cast of thought, but the general opinion is expressed by Captain Mahan in this letter:

New York,
October 20, 1899.

My dear Sir:

I had delayed, longer than I like to think, to thank you for the copy of your address, "Our New Duties," before the Miami University. I received it only upon my return from the Hague, in August, and the pressing necessity (as I felt) of preparing an article for the "North American," prevented my reading it for some weeks. Of my general accord with your position it is needless to speak; but I am greatly in your debt for enlarging and establishing my knowledge of the conformity of our action in the Philippines with the best interpretations of the Constitution.

I feel also indebted to you—through The Tribune—for keeping before our public that there is a British as well as a Boer side to the Transvaal controversy. This morning's leader—by whomsoever written—I read with great satisfaction. Let us by all means have truth, and as a nation stand by right, whomsoever it may array us against; but let it be truth, and all the truth, and in measuring censure let us weigh our words, and not mistake vituperation and prejudice for argument.

To the very great impending Eastern question—in China—I conceive that a cordial understanding, involving no alliance or pledges, but mutual trust, between Great Britain and ourselves, will be a most important factor. There will be a strong assault, made by those who would breed discord between the two nations, to use the Transvaal business as an opening therefor, and I cannot but think that a temperate and full presentment of the whole truth by a paper of The Tribune's influence most desirable. Abuse—such as Bryan's and Bourke Cockran's, of Great Britain—breaks no bones; but it does hinder good feeling.

Very faithfully yours,

A. T. MAHAN.

Politics, American and foreign, seemed fairly to have flooded Reid in the period I have been traversing, but there were other interests. On his return from Paris the staff of The Tribune had commissioned Eastman Johnson to paint his portrait, to be hung in the offices of the paper, and on the occasion of the presentation he was a little startled at being saluted as "the dean of the press of New York." It was in that capacity that he made, early in 1901, two addresses at Yale on the history, duties, and opportunities of the journalistic profession. The lectureship had been established by the widow of the late Isaac H. Bromley, so long one of Reid's most valued colleagues on The Tribune. Both Mrs. Bromley and the university committee having the matter in charge wished him to be its first incumbent. Amongst his literary activities there was also the recasting for the new edition of the "Encyclopedia Britannica" of the article on American newspapers which he had contributed years before to that work; and in contrast to this rather statistical task he undertook an altogether charming commission for the "Bibliophile Society." This was the annotation of one of the odes of Horace. The idea was that a volume in the society's edition of the poet should be prepared by fifteen members, each selecting the best English version of an ode assigned to him, to go with the text, and adding, with notes, such supplemental versions as commended themselves to him. Reid edited the third ode, "Quem tu, Melpomene," and chose Bishop Atterbury's version as the best in English:

> "He on whose birth the lyric Queen,
> Of numbers smiled, should never grace
> The Isthmian gauntlet, or be seen
> First in the famed Olympic race."

"To my amazement," he wrote to Hay, "I find that a little of my early knowledge of Horace still clings to me; and further that I am really enjoying the work, which is serious enough for me, though it would be trivial to a Professor." He was, by the way, much in contact with the world of professors. Intertwined with his diverse activities there runs through all these years his work as a member of the Board of Regents. Still another kind of duty was added to a busy life when early in 1901 he was elected a trustee of the Metropolitan Museum of Art. And in a reminiscence that he set down just as the old century was merging into the new he lingers over a scientific motive. It recalled to him a dinner in a London club, nearly thirty years before, with Kinglake, Rosebery, Huxley, and others. The fragment follows:

> The conversation happened to turn on the amazing progress of the civilized world, in all directions, during the century. At a lull in the talk I turned to Prof. Huxley and asked him what he would rate as the greatest single scientific discovery of the century. I expected—and some of the guests afterwards told me that they expected—to hear the telegraph mentioned, or the ocean cable, or possibly ocean navigation by steam, or rapid printing machines, or some of the other practical inventions, which have so enormously widened civilization, developed its activities and increased capacities of human life.
>
> But without an instant's hesitation, Prof. Huxley replied that he thought there could be no doubt of the proper answer to that question. He considered the discovery of antiseptic surgery the greatest and most beneficent scientific discovery of the century. He paid a proper compliment to the discoverers of anesthetics; but dwelt on

the actual addition to man's control over human life and the undeniable increase in its average duration which antiseptic surgery secured. He spoke of the possibility of curing multitudes of cases formerly helpless. He specified the relief on the battle-field, or at the scenes of those great catastrophes which occasionally spring from modern machinery or transportation, and from the daring with which man more and more turns, or defies the forces of nature; and concluded by reaffirming that, judged by any proper tests, antiseptic surgery was undeniably the greatest single scientific achievement of a century, marked by the most numerous and most important achievements of science in any century since history began. Whether he convinced everybody I cannot say. No one disputed his view.

The lines which most decisively emphasize themselves in a portrait of Whitelaw Reid are those drawn by the influences of public life. Yet that they are not absolutely paramount in the make-up of the man is shown by another passage taken from his correspondence with Hay. It is this souvenir of one of his stays in the Adirondacks:

Here my boy sails jib and main-sail boat races against Archie Rogers, Anson Stokes, Henry Hotchkiss and the rest, and occasionally wins a cup, to the delight of the rather doting pair who watch him from the piazza of the billiard room. My daughter gets up lawn tennis tournaments, and under our anxious eyes, stays in them—as far as the semi-finals. The camp is overrun with young people, boys from Yale and Harvard, and swarms of girls, very much at home in our squash court or billiard room or boats. I don't always know their parents, though they are apt to remind me of somebody I knew in New York or Boston or Washington, back in the sixties or seventies, who turns out to be a Grandfather. You see I have reached the age when I am apt not only to see young life from that venerable point of view but even to be amused by it.

I hear little from the great world, save by way of the office, and that I have learned to push off without conscience. They produce an occasional modern novel, which they say I must read, and when I do I generally regret it, though "Monsieur Beaucaire" was amusing for half an hour, and "They That Took the Sword" piqued my curiosity. But I've fallen back on McMaster and John Fiske, about the days before there was any Constitution to follow the flag, on "The Three Musketeers" and Foster's "Diplomacy."

He was near to his sixty-fourth birthday when he wrote these lines. Some of his best years were before him, but there is an understandable consciousness of the passage of time in his reflective mood. Every year an old friend departed. John Sherman died in 1900. Evarts followed in 1901, and, only ten days later, ex-President Harrison. It was in September of that year that the tragedy at Buffalo befell, and on the death of McKinley both Reid and Hay were disposed to dwell on the shocks which made it hard to "carry on." The event placed heavy burdens on the shoulders of the secretary of state, and they were the heavier because of the unceasing anguish inflicted by the loss of his son Adelbert. From his retreat in New Hampshire, in October, he wrote: "I shall be packing my *paperasses* next week, to go back to Washington after a summer of misery and disaster such as my life has never before experienced." Reid, too, had had to reckon with bereavements and glanced at them in writing to Hay, but then sought to recall him to fortitude, saying: "There is always a certain sad comfort when one can feel that fate has done its worst! Don't worry about the aches and pains. They come to all men! I 'haven't been old before,' either; and I don't feel so, very often, even now; but I know that the machinery is sure to keep getting out of order from this time on, and that every time it rights itself a little more slowly. That is no reason why it shouldn't keep going a long time yet, and shouldn't bring us a great deal of happiness, too. I never enjoyed a horse-back ride more than the one I had this very morning; and if you will only give yourself to it, it will set your blood to quick pulsation too."

He had great resilience. In the spring of this year he delivered in California an address on "University Tendencies in America," talking at large on educational ideas, but allying the humanities with the progress of the republic and pointing to the opportunities lying at home and in our new dependencies at the dawn of the twentieth century. Hay read it "with a renewal of the constant admiration and surprise which are excited in me by the freshness and the zest which you bring to the discussion of these subjects, always new and always old, by the very fact of their permanent importance." He went on with a comparison at once sorrowful and glad. "I sometimes think," he said, "I have as much sense, in a way, as I ever had. But I cannot blind my eyes to the consciousness that I am stale, that I cannot care enough about things to write entertainingly about them. You, on the contrary, hold the note of your sensitive and ambitious youth as clear as *am ersten Tag*. The strain of prophetic enthusiasm with which this address winds up, made my heart beat quicker and 'mine eyes dazzle.'" Hay underestimated his own elasticity. Neither for him nor for his comrade could the weight of events, no matter how tragic, persistently count in the balance against character and strength. "I do not know how long I can pull at my oar," he had exclaimed, overborne by public and private grief. But his dubiety passed. They had an inspiring leader with whom to work in Theodore Roosevelt, and under his administration both men pulled at their oars, in their finest form.

CHAPTER XV

RELATIONS WITH ROOSEVELT

In 1860, when Whitelaw Reid was a young journalist, he threw himself into the campaign for Abraham Lincoln, and saw the rise of Republican power under the greatest of our leaders since Washington. Forty years later, entering upon labors which were to close his editorial career and commit him to the diplomatic service in which he died, he was associated with the man now generally recognized as Lincoln's most remarkable successor. In 1860 he was an obscure worker in the ranks. In 1900 he was one of the leaders of his party. He had shared in the development of a great political organization, and was in a position to give aid and counsel to its dominant figures. There is a certain felicity about the turn of events which made him in his youth a friend of Lincoln's and in his prime a friend of Theodore Roosevelt's, supporting at the beginning and at the end of his newspaper work the highest types of political genius that the Republican faith has produced.

His relations with the younger man began early, as is disclosed in a letter written to Bishop Doane in February, 1900. "I knew Roosevelt's father, whom I considered one of the very best and most public-spirited citizens of New York in that day," he says, "and I have known the son since he was a college boy. His relations are all friends, and one of his sisters [Mrs. Cowles] and my wife have been peculiarly associated and attached." The reader will recall some allusions in an earlier chapter to the sympathy with which Reid gave advice to the young politician when he was a Republican assemblyman in the eighties. The Tribune backed him in his unsuccessful candidacy for the mayoralty in 1886, and was a friendly commentator on his later work as a United States civil service commissioner. It helped him, too, when he became president of the Board of Police Commissioners in New York. My own first impression of him is a vivid one of the rushing energy with which he plunged into the old editorial room, and, punctuating his talk with incisive gestures, explained his attitude toward some crisis in the proceedings of that body. He was seeking co-operation and he got it. Then came his brief term as assistant secretary of the navy, and the brilliant months of his service with the Rough Riders, crowned by his election to the governorship. Through all these stages of his progress he passed with plenty of encouragement from the paper, and, on the whole, very little criticism. He received that, on occasion, in generous enough measure. There was bound to be a rift in the lute of harmony during the period of the governorship, when Reid's antagonism to the machine inclined him to look with a dubious eye on Roosevelt's effort to make the best of its unquestionable influence; and for a time, even though they were on the cordialest terms in social meetings and in correspondence, there was next to no political consultation between them. It began, however, in the summer of 1900, when Roosevelt was nominated for the vice-presidency on the ticket with McKinley. He then sent a message from Oyster Bay, saying that he wanted to see Reid at the earliest opportunity, to have a long talk with him, and go over the whole situation. Thenceforth their contacts were frequent and their mutual understanding was perfect.

There are one or two characteristic indications in their correspondence at this time of Roosevelt's repugnance to the "shelving" that his candidacy was supposed to involve, and his resolution, nevertheless, to play his part as a faithful party man. Reid had cautioned him about trouble with his throat on the whirlwind tour of speech-making he had undertaken in the West. "I want it patched up," he replied, "so that it may go through until after election; then the deluge may come, provided we win. The Vice-Presidency is nothing, and the only point in my nomination is the chance of my helping the ticket, so I suppose I have got to be used as the committee desires." Again he writes: "The very fact that I do not like many features of the situation makes it all the more necessary that I should 'do or die.'" We all know how magnificently he put through the campaign, with flying colors, rousing tremendous enthusiasm, especially in the Northwest, and bringing balm to the hearts of the Republican managers. Whatever he thought of the vice-presidency, Roosevelt had made himself an indispensable factor in the success of the national ticket in November. Within less than a year fate had made him President.

At a White House dinner he and Reid talked over the first message that Roosevelt was to send to Congress, and later, from New York, Reid sent the comments and suggestions he was invited to contribute, especially on the subjects of tariff and reciprocity. He took the opportunity, also, to advocate, in this initial document of the new administration's, the citation of President Monroe's exact words in the pregnant message of December 2d, 1823: "The occasion has been judged proper for asserting as a principle in which the rights and interests of the United States are involved, that the American continents, by the free and independent condition which they have assumed and maintained, are henceforth not to be considered as subjects for future colonization by any European power." The President inserted the passage, thinking it would "immensely strengthen" what he had to say on the subject. A mutual friend who was at the White House at this time received a pleasant intimation of Roosevelt's feeling about his unofficial counsellor. He broke out with the declaration that of all the men he had ever met Reid had the most gracious manners and winning ways, that he was an accomplished diplomat, and that his advice with reference to certain passages of the forthcoming message had been of the utmost value. Their friendship from this time on only increased in warmth.

The principle on which Roosevelt took over the administration of his predecessor is well remembered. "It shall be my aim," he declared, "to continue absolutely unbroken the policy of President McKinley, which has given peace, prosperity, and honor to our beloved country." This included, of course, the settlement of the Cuban question according to the terms of the Orville H. Platt amendment. It was a happy augury for the new President that he could thus early in his administration proclaim our withdrawal from Cuba and the pacification of the Philippines. Equally gratifying was the ratification of the Hay-Pauncefote Treaty, which smoothed the way for that pushing of the isthmian canal project which was to make one of the high achievements of Roosevelt's career. His thorny problem in 1902 was the famous anthracite coal strike, which began in May, went rapidly through more and more ominous phases, and threatened to smite the East with something like a fireless winter. Its course was not arrested until the President's direct action and his call of John Mitchell, the leader of the miners, to the White House, challenged an intolerable menace. Reid recognized the benefit to the administration of the steps taken that fall. "The President and you," he wrote to Secretary of War Root, "have just come out of a difficult and dangerous situation with a howling success. Whatever Mitchell may do—and unless he is bent on destruction, there is only one thing he can do—the situation is saved for the seaboard this winter. It is also saved for the Republican party." But he was always insistent upon the point that the determining factor in this affair was Roosevelt's personal initiative. Two years later, after the nomination for the campaign of 1904, when at the President's request he was traversing the latter's letter of acceptance, he touched upon the paragraph in which the action in the coal strike and that against the Northern Securities Company were treated together as "acts of the *Administration.*" He said:

> But it is essential to the successful defense of your action in the coal strike that it should be kept distinctly on the ground on which you yourself originally placed it, as *not* an act of the Administration, *not* an act of the President, not an official discharge of any duty imposed by law or authorized by the Constitution. It was simply a volunteer interposition, unofficially, by the first citizen of the Republic, at a time when imminent disaster was threatened, when no other relief was in sight, and when his prestige was sufficient to induce the two parties to consent to an arbitration, and meantime start into activity again the industries without which the health and the very lives of many millions of people were in immediate peril. It will not be at all difficult to make the needful correction, but the paragraph will probably have to be rewritten, and the two acts should be treated separately and on different grounds.

Reid based his argument in this matter upon close observation of it at home, particularly during the crucial period of Roosevelt's intervention. But through two of the summer months which witnessed the first deadly growth of the strike he was out of the country. Queen Victoria had died on January 22d, 1901. The coronation of Edward VII was set for the following year, and the President appointed Reid to represent the United States at the ceremony, writing to him as follows:

White House,
Washington,
January 16, 1902.

MY DEAR MR. REID:

It is not always easy in making appointments to be sure one has the man best equipped to discharge the duties of the particular place sought; and hence it was a very real pleasure to be able to appoint to this particular place the man whom, after careful consideration, I felt was preeminently and peculiarly the very man who by training and aptitude was best fitted to represent our people and discharge his duties as their Ambassador on an occasion where I had to carefully consider how two nations would be affected by my choice. I am delighted that you are pleased with the other members of the embassy. I think that under the circumstances General Wilson and Captain Clark are the very men to send; and I was quite sure that you would be pleased with them also!

Give my regards to Mrs. Reid; and with many good wishes for yourself, I am,

Sincerely yours,

THEODORE ROOSEVELT.

The coronation was projected for June, so there was plenty of time for Reid's annual visit to California, where he tantalized Hay by drawing a picture of idle life in perfect weather, riding horseback in the morning, reading Dumas in the afternoon, playing bezique or billiards with Mr. Mills in the evening—and editing a newspaper by telegraph. Coming back to the East in the spring his thoughts were occupied with a proposal from the Houghtons having an unusual interest amongst the suggestions often made to him by publishers. They wanted him to write a biography of Blaine. There were many reasons why he would have delighted in the task, and he found it hard to put it from him. But the comparative leisure of Millbrae was brief enough, and, besides, the political controversies latent in the subject were very near in point of time. "The ashes over those heaps of national embers are yet too thin for comfortable walking," he said. Enterprises abandoned ordinarily invite no comment, but imagination lingers over this one. The incident wakes a real regret. A memoir of James G. Blaine by Whitelaw Reid would have made prodigiously interesting reading.

The mission to the coronation opened with what seemed only the fairest promise. The King had expressed himself to Ambassador Choate as much pleased with the President's appointment. By the leasing from Lord Tweedmouth of Brook House, in Park Lane, the Reids were assured appropriate headquarters. Just before sailing a letter received from Cambridge apprised Reid of the wish of that university to confer the degree of Doctor of Laws upon him on June 10th. He reached England on the 7th, and on the 9th went with Lord Lansdowne to Buckingham Palace. The King appeared in excellent health and spirits. When Reid went down on the morrow to stay with the Master of Trinity, there was no reason to suppose that the impending ceremonies in London would suffer any untoward interruption, and on his return, for several days, he observed that the plans for the coronation were beginning to take clear shape. How they were arrested and the postponement occurred, leading to the premature return of his mission, is explained in the official report to the secretary of state, which I cite in the following abbreviated form:

While the arrangements for the coronation were thus completed down to the minutest details, some anxiety began to be manifested as to the condition of the King's health. It was said that he had over-exerted himself in the review at Aldershot. The uneasiness was quieted for a time by the King's going from Aldershot back to Windsor and by newspaper statements that he was driving out there every day. On the Monday of coronation week the King came up to London and proceeded at once to Buckingham Palace in an open carriage, accompanied by the Queen. Some of those who saw him thought that he looked ill, though the spectators generally, as well as the newspapers, seemed to unite in declaring that he appeared much as usual.

The next morning I received at Brook House a telephone message from Buckingham Palace saying that the royal dinner for that evening would be postponed on account of His Majesty's health. A little later, as I was driving about with the royal equerry, Sir Fleetwood Edwards, completing the official calls upon the other special embassies, we were stopped on the street, near St. James's Palace, by an officer of the household under great excitement, who announced that the King was alarmingly ill, and that the coronation must be indefinitely postponed. We drove as soon as possible to Buckingham Palace to inscribe and make inquiries, and there learned that the situation had been found so grave that an operation had just been performed, for appendicitis the court officials thought, and that the King seemed to be rallying from the shock.

It was soon ascertained that the disease for which the operation had been found necessary was not appendicitis at all, but perityphlitis. One of the surgeons was credibly quoted as saying the next week, as he took a sheet of paper in his hand, "there was not the thickness of that between his Majesty and death when we operated." As late as Monday evening, however, the night before the operation, the King had still insisted that he would go through the ceremony on the following Thursday at whatever cost, and it was not till the peremptory declaration of the surgeon of greatest authority among those in attendance that without a prompt operation he would absolutely refuse to assume further responsibility or attend in the case, that his Majesty finally consented even on Tuesday morning to submit to this demand. Then instead of allowing himself to be carried to the operating table he walked there.

Reid was impressed by the admirable demeanor of the British public. It was sufficiently grave. The services of intercession at St. Paul's and other churches were attended by a people plainly under the stress of a great emotion. But there was no undue excitement, as there was no mawkish sentimentality. The early retirement of the American mission was soon decided upon. The Reids took leave of the foreign secretary at luncheon at Lansdowne House, and the next day were received by the Prince and Princess of Wales. The prince spoke with the greatest confidence as to his father's splendid physical condition and almost certain recovery, entering into many details as to the nature of the operation and the manner in which it had been borne. The following afternoon at Buckingham Palace the Queen received Mr. and Mrs. Reid in a farewell audience. She regarded the worst as over. "She spoke warmly," says Reid in his report, "of the way in which his Majesty had stood the shock of the operation, and of the keen interest he was already beginning to manifest again in public affairs, and mentioned particularly his pleasure at reading, himself, the cable dispatch in the newspapers reporting the President's sympathetic remarks at Harvard. She was confident that the coronation would take place this year, and probably sooner than had been expected." After a round of country-house visits the Reids returned to New York, sailing late in July. He made one speech on the eve of his departure, at the centenary celebration of the American Chamber of Commerce in Liverpool. John Hay, writing to him about the "maimed rites" in London, and congratulating him on his mission, which "had attracted more notice—altogether favorable—than that of any other Power," was warm in appreciation of this farewell episode. "The speech you made at Liverpool," he said, "and your academic honors at Cambridge, were well worth crossing the Atlantic for." The President congratulated him upon "the admirable manner in which you have handled the whole affair."

Before resuming the thread of Reid's activities at home I must touch upon an interesting incident of his brief stay abroad. At the time when his official calls upon the various special embassies were interrupted by news of the operation on the King, he had still to meet his Chinese colleague. His Imperial Highness, Prince Chen, presently called at Brook House, with cordial expressions of the particular friendliness felt by the Emperor and his country toward the United States on account of our action in the late disturbances. When Reid returned this visit the prince renewed the theme. He expressed high appreciation, for himself and for his government, of the conduct of the United States forces in China in upholding order and repressing outrages. He dwelt particularly on their great usefulness in preserving the palace, and remembered also with gratitude the behavior of our navy when the forts were bombarded. He said the Emperor had learned to look upon the United States as the true friend of himself and his countrymen. The prince explained that while he could not enter upon questions of domestic politics, he desired at any rate to say that undoubtedly his sovereign had not always been able to carry out his own policy or enforce his personal wishes. The Emperor had earnestly forbidden many of the regrettable acts that had occurred, and had once gone so far as to declare that if the armed forces continued to disobey him and fire on the legations, he would ask them rather to turn their fire upon himself. Throughout this interview the prince was clearly desirous of impressing his American listener with the special good-will of China. Reid's report of it offered a moment of pleasant relief to Hay in the usually vexatious atmosphere of his long struggle for the success of his Chinese policy.

The period following this mission to England was one of an increasing tendency on Reid's part to give himself to interests lying outside the routine of editorial work. He found a little time for literary diversions. He supplied Mr. Bodley, author of "The Coronation of Edward the Seventh," with some amusing notes on American participation in the coronations of Napoleon and Queen Victoria, notes based on researches that he caused to be made in the archives at Washington. He wrote a suggestive introduction to the posthumous work of his old friend William Henry Smith, "A Political History of Slavery." Another of his excursions was prompted by Mr. Francis Curtis, when that gentleman was writing his well-known work on the Republican party. Mr. Curtis wanted to know if that party owed its name to Horace Greeley, as was commonly believed. Reid told him that he couldn't recall Greeley's ever sanctioning the claim that he had done more than give an early approval to the selection of the name "Republican" and secure its general adoption; but the subject excited his interest and he went on with it, calling in the aid of a member of The Tribune's editorial staff, Mr. W. L. McPherson, who followed the trail as far as it could be traced. Hay was drawn into the discussion by his campaign speech in 1904 on "Fifty Years of the Republican Party." He believed in Greeley's invention of the name. When Curtis published his book he stated the conclusion that "the entire credit should not be given to one man." Reid accepted the decision as sound, but in an editorial he noted that an examination of the conflicting claims developed some facts of very general interest. For the reader of our political history that interest has not faded yet and it is, besides, peculiarly appropriate that I should quote in this narrative the salient passages in the summary to which I have referred:

It can be easily established that, whoever first suggested the party designation, Mr. Greeley through the columns of The Tribune and in private correspondence, did more than any one else to secure its general acceptance. The testimony on this point is incontrovertible. A. N. Cole, of Wellsville, Alleghany County, recognized as the "Father of the Republican Party in New York State," has put on record the fact that in April, 1854, when he was engaged in organizing a new anti-slavery party in Western New York, he wrote to Mr. Greeley, asking him to suggest an appropriate party name. Mr.

Greeley's reply was "Call it Republican, no prefix, no suffix, but plain Republican." This letter was published in Mr. Cole's newspaper, "The Genesee Valley Free Press." But neither the original letter nor a copy of the newspaper issue containing it had been preserved, both the letter and the files of the newspaper having been destroyed in a fire which occurred in Mr. Cole's office in 1857. In The Tribune Mr. Greeley did not use the title Republican until June 16th, 1854, when he published an editorial entitled "Party Names and Public Duty." In this he said:

"Accepting and upholding those ideas of public policy which used to characterize the Whig Party prior to 1852, and agreeing substantially with the Free Democratic party in all it affirms with regard to slavery, we could wish to see a union of all those members of the two parties who believe resistance to the extension of Slave Territory and Slave Power the most urgent public duty of our day. We should not much care whether those thus united were designated 'Whig,' 'Free Democratic,' or something else; though we think some simple name like Republican would more fitly designate those who have united to restore our union to its true mission of champion and promulgator of Liberty, rather than propagandist of Slavery."

This editorial appeared three weeks in advance of the "Under the Oaks" convention at Jackson, Michigan, which incorporated the title "Republican" into its platform. It also antedated all the other anti-Nebraska or "Republican" State Conventions of that year. Mr. Greeley had earlier written to leaders in Michigan urging the use of the new party designation.

Especially marking Reid's life at this time is his deepening interest in educational matters. At Mrs. Stanford's request he accepted membership on the board of trustees of the Californian university founded in memory of her son. Joseph Pulitzer asked him to serve on the advisory board charged with the framing of a plan of instruction to be embodied in the School of Journalism which he created at Columbia University. Reid gave unstinted aid in the organization of this project. On the Board of Regents his labors were increased by his election as vice-chancellor in December, 1902, and then as chancellor in the following June. To be thus honored gave him a satisfaction that nothing else could quite touch. I would, I fear, have overburdened these pages if I had recorded all the matters which had occupied him on the board since he was first elected to it in 1878. His influence upon it was both conservative and progressive. He was an unflinching foe of the "simplified spelling" which at one time tried to creep under the *ægis* of the Regents, and the principal reform to which he long gave his efforts was one which time has only confirmed. It was achieved, finally, in the year of his coming to the chancellorship, and, indeed, his elevation to the office might be regarded as in some sort a recognition of his constructive work on the board itself and with successive governors, confronted by legislative measures bearing on the subject. Calling to order the forty-second university convocation at Albany, the first as he saw it, in the whole history of the Regents' annual meetings, he said:

> This convocation follows immediately upon the unification of the State's educational system—the end of strife between wrangling departments and a controversy over divided powers. It assembles on the call of the constitutional body under whose supervising care the State has now placed the whole work; and signalizes the operation of the State's decree for the coordination of all efforts, public and private, tax supported or not, primary, secondary or collegiate, for the proper training of the young in the greatest community on this continent, one free commonwealth of eight million souls.

He exulted in the reorganization in which he had shared, as an officer exults over a successful battle. It may be doubted if he was any prouder of his transition from the editorship of the Xenia "News" to that of The Tribune than he was of that from the little schoolhouse at Charlestown to the chancellorship of a board governing the educational system of his adopted State.

On the Board of Regents he did his best to divorce the educational system of the State from politics. In numerous public addresses he gave himself to a kindred task, to that of clarifying political thinking. That education was incomplete, he incessantly argued, which did not embrace cool, dispassionate reflection on politics; and this reflection, in his opinion, could not begin too early. He advocated it, for example, before the students at Vassar, commending to them, above all, the steadying ideals which make for permanent results. President Woolsey wrote him from New Haven with approval of the stabilizing influence he was exerting. "The thought," he says, "that in the educated young woman one finds a genuine champion of conservatism, is true and valuable." It was the truer, as Reid enforced it, because it spelled no blind dependence on the lessons of the past, but implied a sane, well-balanced judgment on the present. The tendency, then current, to political fickleness and to the maddest of extremes, he castigated with a ruthless hand. In his commencement address before the Law School at Yale, in the summer of 1903, he examined certain old principles in order to advocate a more enlightened application of them. He traversed the Monroe Doctrine in the light of common sense, deprecating a pedantic interpretation which would ignore changed conditions. Speaking with special reference to the assassination of McKinley, he urged on this occasion a drastic treatment of the doctrine of anarchism. He wanted our extradition treaties overhauled and called for a tightening of the screws in international law which would help, in a measure at least, to throw an added protection around the lives of public men. Through all these speeches there runs as a familiar undercurrent Reid's refusal to accept the easy doctrine that everything is for the best in the best of all possible worlds.

A good illustration of his sociological criticism is provided by the address he made on Founder's Day at Carnegie Institute in Pittsburgh, in 1902. He spoke on

"Organization in American Life," and, speaking just as the great coal strike was nearing its end, he uttered an earnest warning against the dangers inherent in any trade-unionism that threatened to smother individual enterprise. He believed in organization and extolled its virtues. But citing the kind of organization that is embodied in our own form of government, he pointed out that its strength resided in the quality of man it developed. Describing our historic victory over the wilderness, he continued:

> To such a continental conquest of nature and of men have those two traits of the fathers brought us—their respect for authority and their widest freedom of individual initiative. These, with the original vigor of the stock, have made Americans what they are; and by consequence have made this blessed country of ours the joy and pride and hope of our lives. To harm either is criminal—whether to break down respect for authority by unlawful combinations, tricky evasions, and open defiance of order, or to cramp the widest freedom of the individual in any lawful enterprise or labor anywhere. Whoever or whatever now dares to interfere with the permanent union of these two traits and their continued development in the American life is an enemy to the Republic—whether known as Political Boss, or as Trust, or as Trades Union.

One of his most important speeches in this period was delivered at the dinner of the New England Society in New York, in the winter of 1903. He dwelt then upon a peril as great as that which is latent in an exaggeration of trades-unionism, the peril which lies in unrestricted immigration. I cite part of his protest against the menace which must always engage the consideration of those who give serious thought to the problems of American life:

> For seventeen years there has been a steady decline in immigration from the lands of our ancestors and of their kinsfolk—that is to say from England, Scotland, Ireland, Wales, Germany, Denmark, and Switzerland. During the same period there has been a steady and

progressive increase from Italy, Austria-Hungary, Russia, Spain, Portugal, Greece, Belgium, Roumania, etc. And, finally, to give an analysis by races rather than mere nationalities, 28 per cent of the whole immigration in 1902 was Italian, 11 per cent of it was Polish, 9 per cent was Hebrew, and 15 per cent was Slovak, Croatian, Slavonian, and Magyar—these races thus making practically two-thirds of the whole immigration.

We have emphatically and even vociferously made everybody else, from all over the world, at home in our Fathers' house. But as we look around at the variegated throng, do we always feel just as much at home ourselves? I will yield to none in reverence to our ancestors and pride in the work they did. But perhaps even these ancestors, viewing now from above, as we love to think, these scenes of their glorious achievements, might be better pleased with imitation than with praise, and might think it as important for us to preserve their work as to glorify it. And so I venture to take the past for granted. The men who made New England hold securely and forever a page resplendent as any in the world's history. The government they were perhaps the most potent factors in founding has developed into the greatest and most powerful agency in modern civilization. Let us leave it at that.

I ask, then, consideration of something different and more pressing. Are we, their sons, managing this heritage of our Fathers so as to further their ends? How are we likely to leave it to our sons? Will it still fulfil the purpose of those great men who, according to the eulogium of Mr. Gladstone, struck out at one blow the most perfect form of government yet devised by human intelligence?

A common notion seems to be that their real purpose in starting this government was a missionary one. They wanted, as our stump orators declaim, with unction, "to make America spell Opportunity." So interpreting the purpose of the Fathers, we have developed a continent in order that, first of all, it might bestow the benefit of their and our labors, in the shape of Opportunity, on the just and the unjust, on the fit and unfit, of every class and race and nativity under the sun.

The variety and number of engagements indicated in the last few pages suggests a rather narrow margin for Reid's usual political interests, and they became engrossing enough around the date of the Yale address to make him, thenceforth, somewhat chary of similar undertakings. In fact, Roosevelt's ante-convention campaign had begun even earlier. In June, 1902, Republican State conventions in Kansas and Pennsylvania passed resolutions in favor of his selection in 1904. Stanwood, in his "History of the Presidency," noting the fact, adds that "we should probably have to go as far back as the time of General Jackson to cite similar action, so early in an administration, in favor even of an elected President." The settlement of the coal strike widely confirmed the prestige developed by sheer force of personal character, and if his action in Panama provoked criticism in some quarters it did Roosevelt no harm with the country at large. Reid's interest in this matter was especially keen. In his address at Yale he had vigorously emphasized what he believed to be the real rights conferred by our strength and our leadership on this continent with regard to adjoining territory actually within our sphere of influence. He was not unwilling to relax the scope of the Monroe Doctrine in remoter regions, but at our doors he preached its fullest possible enforcement. The Gulf of Mexico, the Caribbean Sea, and the waters of both oceans about the Isthmus he held to be absolutely within our sphere of influence, and, he averred, "they must be forever dominated by the great Republic." Fresh from the enunciation of this belief as a private conviction he cordially welcomed the opportunity publicly to uphold the President's hands, and the hearty support he gave the administration is illustrated by his outline of editorial policy sent to the office on the recognition of the republic of Panama:

> The secession of Panama was the natural sequence to the barefaced hold-up of the United States by the Colombian Congress about the Canal. It is absolutely in the interest of Panama and seems to have originated in Panama. Panama has no close connection with Colombia, and really has as logical a reason for independence as any of the other Central American States. That independence, however, must necessarily be modified by the existing rights and obligations of the United States for the preservation of order

on the line of the Panama Railroad; as well as by existing obligations concerning the Panama Canal. It is also probable that the effort to maintain a national existence separate from Colombia would, in the long run, have a doubtful chance without the friendly regard of the United States. The statesmen at Washington should seize this situation. The recognition of the *de facto* government in Panama, which appears to be natural, if not inevitable (unless Colombia should soon show unexpected vigor) should recognize in distinct terms the actual suzerainty which the United States will be compelled to exercise. It is a suzerainty somewhat similar to that which the inevitable application of the Monroe Doctrine in the countries actually within our sphere of influence must ultimately compel us to assume with reference to the whole region of the Caribbean Sea and the Gulf of Mexico—as we have already assumed it with reference to Cuba. Let us have it now embodied in unmistakable terms in any recognition of the new Republic through whose territory we are expected to construct a canal.

The Tribune was thus ranged conclusively behind the President, and in a private letter sent a day or two later Reid restated his adhesion to Roosevelt's course. "It looks as if your Panama *coup* would be overwhelmingly successful," he said. "It is obviously the right thing for the country, which, according to my notion as you know, has the right to assert its paramount authority at any rate in any great emergency, anywhere in the region of the Caribbean Sea or the Gulf of Mexico. That, nowadays is the chief use of the Monroe Doctrine!" He had no fear of the consequences of the administration's policy, for that, he felt, was rooted in the essential bases of our government. Writing to Representative Gillett, of Massachusetts, in this crisis, he says: "I hope we may agree in the notion that the general policy of a Nation cannot be altruistic, but that its statesmen, at least, are bound to look first to its own interests; that far from there being anything discreditable in this, as so many of the sentimentalists assume, it is a statesman's chief duty. At this moment, for example, our first duty in the Isthmus is to protect the interests of the United

States to the fullest extent consistent with international law. That in the end this will result in a practical protectorate over the Isthmus I cannot doubt; and I believe, in the end, that is where our Monroe Doctrine is going to land us with reference to the whole region washed by the Caribbean Sea and the Gulf of Mexico."

In the first stages of preparation for the presidential contest, which began, as I have indicated, at an unusually early date, there were signs of opposition to Roosevelt within as well as without the party. Writing to a friend abroad in the spring of 1903, Reid mentioned the movement then in sight to bring forward Mark Hanna as the Republican nominee. "There is no doubt," he said, "that most of the politicians and some important financial interests, would like to trip Roosevelt up if they could; but they are confronted by the phenomenon of his unquestionable and apparently increasing popularity throughout the country, and particularly in the West. The very things which make the politicians hate him are the things which increase his popularity; and it may prove that the state machines will be as unable to resist the popular tendency in his case as they were in McKinley's." The "important financial interests" it was the particular function of The Tribune to combat, and it gave short shrift to "the small but determined body of people who think that a candidate whom the discomfited promoters in Wall Street choose to blame for their misfortunes must be defeated for renomination." The failure of Seth Low to win in the mayoralty campaign in New York was blindly seized upon by this cabal as a sign that the whole country was against Roosevelt. Reid exposed the true opposition behind such silliness, and the President thanked him for his editorial aid. It was needed aid. "One is lonely enough in the New York newspaper field at present," Reid had occasion to write in February, 1904, "in supporting the Administration." In his loneliness he preserved his confidence as to the outcome. In one of his letters there is an amused reference to "the angry politicians and capitalists who are vainly hunting around for escape from the inexorable and inevitable Roosevelt." He enjoyed their discomfiture, cheerfully adding to it to the best of his ability in the columns of his paper. I may pointedly cite here the tribute of a friend who was one of his strongest Democratic opponents, Joseph Pulitzer. "I am reading The Tribune here with pleasure," he wrote from Aix-les-Bains, shortly before the national conventions. "I prefer its political news to that of all other papers. I always like to see the other side."

The Democratic side, at this juncture, was headed, under the adroit management of Governor D. B. Hill, toward a repudiation of Bryan which was to produce, however, no more formidable a candidate in Judge Alton B. Parker. Reid pounced like a hawk upon the letter of acceptance framed by this eminently respectable but, on the whole, rather weak nominee. Parker, he declared, did not dare to say a word on the gold standard beyond the recognition of existing statutes he had allowed himself in a telegram sent to St. Louis during the convention. He did not dare to adopt the "Evening Post's" hostility to the tariff, commit himself to a revenue for tariff only, or even to a square demand for any basis of reduction. He did not dare to commit himself to giving up the Philippines, or, indeed, to go in that direction one iota beyond President Roosevelt's position. These were only a few of the multitude of awkward questions with which Reid found the letter bristling, and he marvelled at the Democratic policy which had put forward this candidate. "What a confidence game Hill played at St. Louis," he wrote to Hay, "and what a gold brick the bucolic southerners and hay-seed westerners bought!" It did not seem too hard a task to bring this edifying transaction to naught. Earlier in the year, before either of the conventions had been held, the "important financial interests" had been, as I have shown, trying to make trouble. "Some of these men," Reid wrote to Roosevelt, "find it hard to realize that money doesn't do everything, and that they can't always have their own way. It is still harder for some of them, even after intellectually convinced that they have at no time had any real grievance, to admit it to themselves. I think that to be the present mental attitude of a good many who were most angered some months ago about the coal strike, the Northern Securities, and certain trivialities like Negro appointments, etc." But even at this point he observed a marked change in the political tide, a change growing more decisive every week, and he could, for example, quote to his correspondent the heartfelt exclamation of one exalted member of the discontented Wall Street crowd: "Unless the President should be a darn fool now, he has everything his own way and will win hands down." It was a safe prophecy. The public temper everywhere was all the time making plainer the success of "the inexorable and inevitable Roosevelt." Neither Hanna nor Spooner nor anybody else could have kept the nomination from him in 1904. There was some manœuvring over the vice-presidency. In February Elkins wrote Reid that he was being pressed in many quarters to become a candidate and asked his advice. Reid counselled him to stay where he was, in the Senate. He himself favored the selection of Elihu Root and suggested it to the President. Roosevelt had a leaning toward "Uncle Joe" Cannon. There was general satisfaction, however, with the choice ultimately made, that of Charles W. Fairbanks, of Indiana.

The ticket was enthusiastically adopted at Chicago

in June, and the campaign was launched with every presage of victory. Reid had in June to make one more address, the chancellor's speech at Albany to which I have referred, but there were no further interruptions to his work in the political field. Following his practice of seeking the counsel of friends as to his public utterances, Roosevelt sent him copies of his speech to the notification committee and his letter of acceptance. Reid had a few suggestions to make on both documents, but rejoiced in their abounding vitality. He drew potent ammunition from them in the course of the campaign and his private letters breathe a stalwart faith in the upshot. "I can't persuade myself," he wrote to Hay, "that there can be any serious doubt about the final judgment of the American people in November upon the higgledy-piggledy nondescript array of Falstaffian soldiers attacking the Administration." It was always his way, to be sure, to commend the wisdom of waiting for any decision until the votes were counted, and not even his scorn of the Democratic ticket could keep him from reckoning on untoward possibilities. He didn't overlook the malcontents in his own party, nor was he indifferent to the mischief-making capacities of the Mugwumps. In New York State, too, he was nervous over the nature of the various candidacies discussed for the governorship. Since Root hadn't been chosen for the vice-presidency he wanted him to run for governor in his own State, and was worried over the fixity of the secretary of war's refusal. It was his habit to fight hardest, however, when the horizon was at all clouded, and The Tribune was never more gleefully aggressive, to Roosevelt's huge delight. "I think you have done up the 'World' and the 'Times' completely," he wrote apropos of one smashing blow, and their correspondence reveals no discouragement. Even as he noted the wave of despondency which touched the party in New York —and not there alone—in October, and watched with apprehension the struggle for the governorship, Reid remained convinced that Roosevelt would carry the State by a handsome majority. Discounting his own solicitude, he wrote to the President: "I am reminded of an old saying of Gen. Grant's. He admitted having been somewhat alarmed about the prospect on the evening before a certain battle, but said he afterwards discovered that the opposing general was worse scared at the same time and had more reason to be." Senator Chandler, writing the day before election, and assuming that the Republicans were to have an overwhelming victory, discreetly added: "There will be, of course, a few small-sized surprises." There were. One of them, over the size of which no one was disposed to waste any time with a measuring-stick, it was so peculiarly welcome on any terms, was the election of Governor Higgins, the Republican candidate. He won on his merits and he shared, besides, in the momentum of what Reid described, in his telegram of congratulations to Roosevelt, as "an unparalleled popular endorsement."

The President, in thanking Reid, expressed warm appreciation of all that he had done in this campaign. What he had done possessed, as I have pointed out at the opening of this chapter, a special significance. It marked the conclusion of a lifetime of editorial service to the Republican party, of long participation in the great game of President-making, of unremitting activity in national, State, and local politics. The record as I have endeavored to outline it, stretching from Lincoln to Roosevelt, is far richer, I think the reader will admit, in victory than defeat. It is a party record, and as such it has been unreservedly traversed in these pages. Whitelaw Reid himself never considered it in any other light.

The rôle of party man, if it needed any sanction at all, received it conclusively enough, in his opinion, from Abraham Lincoln, of whom he said in his address at the University of Birmingham: "He was an ardent partisan, and the most skilful master of men, and of all the intricacies of the game of politics, known in his state." But in any estimate of Reid's work for the political organization with which he was identified, just consideration of the independence which I have shown as his leading characteristic must tend to a certain discrimination in terminology. He remains an exponent of the Republican party. But in a larger sense he remains more significantly an exponent of Republican ideas.

CHAPTER XVI

AMBASSADOR TO ENGLAND

The expectation that Whitelaw Reid would be sent to England as the ambassador of the United States dated from a time prior to McKinley's first inauguration. If it was not immediately revived when Roosevelt entered the White House it was because, as has been noted in a previous chapter, the new President was resolved to disturb as little as possible the arrangements made by his predecessor. That the appointment was in his mind, however, he intimated some time before his own election, and following on that event Reid heard from several friends of Roosevelt's determination in the matter. By that time political conditions had ceased to exercise the obstructive influences operative in McKinley's administration. Hay, of course, knew all about it, and leaving Washington for a few days, just as the Reids were coming on to lunch with the President, he wrote these affectionate words:

Department of State,
Washington,
January 6, 1905.

My dear Reid:

I am afraid we shall pass each other on the train to-day and I will therefore not have the chance of seeing you before Tuesday. I have refrained from saying anything to you about a matter which, as you know, is very near to my heart, wishing to leave the President the pleasure of talking to you first, but I cannot help telling you with what long-looked-for delight I shall countersign your commission as Ambassador to England. When that is done I shall feel like intoning my *nunc dimittis*. It will be the crowning act of a friendship and close association of forty years. This for the personal side of it, without referring just now to the great and lasting advantage to our interests and to our honor and prestige abroad which will come from your Embassy. Mrs. Hay joins me in affectionate regards to Mrs. Reid, and I am always,

Faithfully yours,

JOHN HAY.

Among the first to congratulate him was Ambassador Choate, who wrote, indeed, before the official announcement was made. "So far as I have learned," he said, "no other man has even been thought of for the place, and that seems to be well understood here so that the English people will take to you at once, and in earnest. With your large and varied experience in public questions, your diplomatic record, and the important part you took in making the last great Treaty that changed the map of the world, your complete success may be foretold." The commission which Hay was so keen upon countersigning was dated March 8th, when Reid was in California, and he planned for an early sailing on his return to the East; but Mr. Choate received an extension of time, in order that he might personally dedicate his memorial window to John Harvard, in St. Saviour's Church, and his letter of recall was not presented until May 23d. In the interim Reid effected his formal retirement from the management of The Tribune, settled his business affairs, and attended more than one complimentary dinner. Apropos of his farewell to journalism, which was to prove even more conclusive than he knew at the time, there are some interesting passages in a letter of his to the President:

Here is the little paragraph which was printed at the head of the editorial columns on April 20th, 1889: "Mr. Whitelaw Reid, having taken office under the Government, retires herewith from the editorship and direction of The Tribune." Before printing this I consulted with Mr. Blaine and Gen. Harrison on the subject, and they both thought it correct and ample. I should think of doing something of the same sort now, and of so organizing the paper that it would run absolutely without direction or responsibility on my part during my absence. The question whether I ought at the same time to divest myself of the ownership was raised in my talk with Mr. Blaine and the President, and they laughed at the idea—saying, as I recall it, that I might as well be asked to part with bank stock or railway shares.

The publication of a paper like The Tribune in competition with copper miners, railway owners and others who think it an advantage to their business to run a newspaper and sell it below the cost of manufacture, is not in itself a very alluring business proposition while the one-cent craze continues to prevail. But I have long looked upon my ownership of The Tribune as a sort of trust, and should not feel at liberty to divest myself of it without trying to insure its continuing to stand for good morals, good citizenship and the public policies with which the country has learned to identify it. If in office I should not assume to direct it; but I should be sure its general course would not depart from these established lines during my absence.

There were rumors afloat, at the moment, of offers to purchase The Tribune. Discrediting these, Reid explained to the President that so far from thinking of selling, he was only waiting for his son to be graduated from the Law School at Yale to take up the question of ultimately putting the paper in his charge, the plan which was fulfilled when Ogden Reid, after a period on the staff, assumed the editorship in 1913.

At dinners given to him in May by the Lotos and Republican Clubs, Reid made the speeches which will be found in his "American and English Studies" outlining the diplomatic point of view which he carried with him on his mission. In speaking at the annual banquet of the St. George's Society he gave expression to the Anglo-American sympathy which it had become his function officially to promote, and London comments prefigured an appreciative welcome for him there. In a private letter to Professor Woolsey, at Yale, the mood underlying all his public remarks on the eve of his departure is concisely stated: "Your congratulations give a great pleasure, but inspire also a great sobriety. To attain worthily the aspirations we both cherish as to the relation of the two great English speaking countries is, as you say, well worth any man's ambition. Merely to help and never hinder in such attainment by others is an ambition high enough to make it sure that whoever takes up the work will naturally, if successful, lay it down again with a far lighter heart."

He sailed with his family on May 27th and reached London to be swept immediately into the thick of diplomatic activities. Their home was ready for them in Dorchester House, which through the intervention of friends had been secured on lease from Major Holford. Its status among the larger houses of London was not calculated to lessen its dignity as the residence of the American ambassador, but there are always some commentators impossible to satisfy, and in this case there were a number who feared that dignity might be carried too far. With this gratuitous assumption the Reids had naturally no concern, especially as their environment in London was in no essential an enlargement upon their environment in New York, and there would be ordinarily no occasion for reference to the matter here. But the housing of our diplomatic representatives abroad has always been a subject of public discussion, and it is not inapposite to show how the criticisms aforesaid struck persons vitally concerned with the government of the United States.

The secretary of state, at the outset, when Reid was negotiating for a house, confirmed his judgment that the best was good enough for us when devoted to the service of the American Government and people. John Hay strongly recommended Dorchester House. The President's views are too Rooseveltian in themselves and throw too refreshing a light on the whole problem to be omitted:

The White House,
Washington,
November 13, 1905.

My dear Mr. Ambassador:

As for those criticisms upon your method of life—all I hope is that they bother you as little as they bother me. I think a man should live in such a position as he has been accustomed to live. It is as it is with my Cabinet here. If I found just the right man for a given Cabinet position and he happened to be a poor man, I should not in the least object to his living in the hall bedroom of a boarding house. On the contrary, I should be rather pleased at it. On the other hand, as Root can afford a big house and can afford to entertain, I think it would be rather shabby, rather mean, if he lived in a way that would be quite proper for others—that would, for instance, be quite proper for me if I were in the Cabinet. I never feel in the least embarrassed because at Sagamore Hill, at my own house, we have a maid to wait on the table and open the door, instead of having a butler. I should feel nothing but scornful amusement for any man who felt that such method of living was improper for a President or a Cabinet officer; but I should have exactly the same feeling for the critic who objected to a rich man who was doing his full duty living as he had the right to live.

This is simply an application of the doctrine that I am trying to preach to my countrymen every day, and which is the direct reverse of the doctrine preached by fool revolutionists like Maxim Gorky. Ophir Hall is as different from Sagamore Hill as Sagamore Hill is different from the house of Captain Joe-Bill Underhill, the bayman, and a brother member of mine in Matinecock Lodge of Masons. My creed is that it would be quite as criminal for the owner of the big house to look down upon the owner of the middle-sized house as for the latter to look down upon the owner of the small house; and on the other hand exactly as criminal to feel jealousy on the ascending scale as arrogance on the descending scale; while it would be a piece of utter demagogic silliness for you to live as I live or for me to live as Captain Joe-Bill lived. And no man has the spirit of Americanism in him who would be guilty of such silliness.

Sincerely yours,
Theodore Roosevelt.

The first days in London coincided with the visit of Alfonso XIII to the court, and this meant the swiftest possible assumption of duties. The Reids arrived in time for dinner on Saturday night, only about a day before the functions for the Spanish King began—at every one of which it was peculiarly the obligation of the American ambassador to be present, in order that there should be no shadow of suspicion that he was not paying proper respect to the monarch against whom the United States had waged war at a comparatively recent date. Reid had immediate notice that the usual call at the Foreign Office would be waived and that, instead, Lord Lansdowne expected to see him informally at his own house on Sunday morning. When he went there the foreign minister at once told him that the King expected to have him present his credentials and introduce his staff at Buckingham Palace on Monday morning. When he got there the King said that Mrs. Reid and their daughter were up-stairs with the Queen, and that as soon as the formalities were over he was expected to join them. He left the palace just in time to start on a breakneck race around the different embassies to make the essential calls, and the following morning, only a little while after breakfast, he had to be in the line of ambassadors at Buckingham Palace for the reception given to them by the King of Spain. There was a state banquet that night at the palace, and the next night Lord Lansdowne gave a dinner to the King of Spain. Thus the royal festivities rushed on, coming to a climax on the 14th in a garden-party at Windsor. The new ambassador's letters described them as constituting a dizzy whirl. For a serious subject to be discussed as soon as the ceremonies began, Reid had been prepared by a cable handed to him as he had reached the Lizard: "Togo annihilated Russian fleet in Corea Straits, capturing six and sinking thirteen. Japanese losses trifling." His first diplomatic duty in London was to talk of peace. On the day that he was presenting his credentials to the King, President Roosevelt was writing him: "Togo's smashing of Rojestvensky was so complete that the

Russian case is absolutely hopeless. I should be sorry to see Russia driven out of East Asia, and driven out she surely will be if the war goes on. Accordingly I have urged her to let me propose to both combatants that they meet and negotiate for peace. Germany has supported and I think France will support this plea of mine." By cabling Reid to get from Lord Lansdowne the substance of a despatch sent by Sir Mortimer Durand from Washington, he put the American ambassador promptly in possession of the opening steps taken toward the Portsmouth Conference.

In the course of the evening at Lord Lansdowne's dinner Reid had a long conversation with the King, which the latter began by intimating that information would soon reach him through his own channels as to the disposition of the Czar to accept representations from the President concerning the importance of making peace. His Majesty thought the best mode of commencement had been adopted and expressed his gratification, with hopes for an early settlement. In this and in further meetings with both exalted and lesser personages Reid was impressed by the English good-will which was to persist throughout his long mission. "There is no mistaking," he wrote to the President, "the absolute determination of the Government and of the Royal Family to embrace every opportunity to show their marked friendship for the United States. I think, however, that they regard the whole European situation at the present moment as critical in the extreme and are exceedingly careful about every new move." The trouble in the East, for example, was rendered the more delicate by England's relations with Japan. Morocco, too, was a source of anxiety, threatening, as it was, every day in the summer of 1905, to develop into a positive storm centre, thanks to the Kaiser's ill-considered intervention.

An important task of Reid's, pending the assembling of the Portsmouth Conference, was the ascertainment of precisely what England's view was—whether, to put it bluntly, she really wished peace or not. Lord Lansdowne at once eased the tension on this point, explaining that of course the idea would be most abhorrent to them of doing anything that might tend to prolong bloodshed. At the same time they did not feel like exerting anything like pressure on Japan, especially at a moment when the Japanese terms had not been disclosed. Reid's despatch brought welcome light to the President, who was growing meanwhile "nearly mad" in the efforts to get Russia and Japan together. Japan had a right, he thought, to ask a good deal; he did not think her demands excessive; but Russia he found difficult, with a government that was such an amorphous affair that they really did not know *what* they wanted.

The Russian attitude was extraordinarily trying. For about two years, both in war and in peace, as Roosevelt expressed it, they had been acting in the spirit of the later Byzantine Empire. In conversation with Balfour on the subject, Reid found that statesman sympathizing most cordially with the views of the President of the United States, especially with his conviction that Russian policy was as unstable as water. Balfour was representative of the British disposition to go slow in the matter of interfering with Japan. Reid discussed with him a letter of the President's, citing especially Roosevelt's argument that since the Japanese did not want East Siberia, but would regard its acquisition as a disadvantage, it seemed to him that it would be wise for England to get them to abate any demand for an indemnity down to the point where it was obviously Russia's duty to give it. "Yes," said Balfour, "but still one would like to have that 'point' translated into pounds, shillings and pence." The choice for a Japanese statesman, Roosevelt indicated to Reid as, in his opinion, being between two courses. Should Japan endeavor to drive the Russians completely off the Pacific coast and out of East Siberia, west to Lake Baikal, or should they simply drive them out of Manchuria and Corea, take Saghalien from them, and leave them East Siberia? By adoption of the second course the Japanese would gain a certain security for Russia's good behavior in the future, inasmuch as they would thus leave them at the mercy of a forward movement by Japanese armies gathered in Manchuria. Reid's correspondence is a kind of mirror of all manner of interesting views on this whole matter of policy. At Ascot the King confidentially suggested to him that it might be a good idea for Japan to take Vladivostok, and restore it to Russia after the war with a magnanimous gesture. Roosevelt could hardly agree with this. He deprecated the idea, maintaining that it would be spending blood and treasure unnecessarily. What would really happen, too, he thought, was that if the Japanese took Vladivostok they would only give it back in exchange for something they wanted more, such as a big indemnity.

There is a sudden and bitter break in Reid's personal associations marked in his correspondence at this time, when the despatches he sends from London are no longer addressed to John Hay. One of them, bearing his name, is dated as late as June 16th, the day after Hay had reached New York at the end of a brief sojourn abroad for the benefit of his health. He died at his summer home in New Hampshire on July 1st. The blow was the more staggering to Reid because it had been undreamed of when they had met less than a month before in England. Hay was settled for a few days at Claridge's when Reid landed to take up his post. He sent to Dorchester House one of those characteristic greetings which told of the deep friendship between them. "There is not much left of me," he said, "but I shall be glad and proud to see you, where I have long desired to see you, in a place you will not only fill but adorn." Their happy talks together were marred by no presage of the end. On the contrary, all that Reid saw of Hay in those few days before the secretary's sailing for America gave him not only the liveliest hopes but every confidence in the recovery of his friend. It was the feeling of all the members of their circle in London. Hay's eldest daughter, Mrs. Payne Whitney, was on the ocean on the way to England when he died. She had left him well and in the highest spirits. When the news of the end came Reid read it with streaming eyes and a heart immeasurably stirred. The intimacy between them had begun in their young manhood and it had lasted, unclouded by a single shadow, for over forty-three years. In the course of this narrative I have given numerous instances of the perfect sympathy existing between them, of the instinctive impulse by which each was constantly moved to turn to the other in the handling and discussion of public affairs. From the days of their encounters at Washington, when Hay was Lincoln's private secretary and Reid was a correspondent, through their journalistic collaboration in New York, and afterward in campaigns and other political activities, their minds ran in perfect unison, moving as though by a common understanding through the same fields. Hay had spent far more of his life than Reid had in public office, but, looking back over their comradeship, Reid could not remember a year of it in which, in one way or another, they had not been allied in public service. Time had welded their abilities in the support of a cause, and it had welded their hearts in a happy affection.

Reid was moved by the evidences of English sympathy which poured into Dorchester House, the messages from the King, his foreign minister, and scores of others, and, finally, the touching memorial service at St. Paul's. I append Lord Lansdowne's letter:

Foreign Office,
July 3, 1905.

MY DEAR AMBASSADOR:

As you are aware, we did not lose a moment in instructing Sir Mortimer Durand to express in the proper quarter the deep sorrow with which His Majesty's Government had heard of Colonel Hay's sad death, but I am anxious that you, as one of his greatest friends, and the representative of the Government of which he was so distinguished a member, should know how sincerely my colleagues and I have felt for your country in that hour of sorrow common to both nations.

Colonel Hay was regarded with universal respect, and with something more than respect by the British people; he was no stranger to us, but he had endeared himself, not only by his personal qualities, so admirable, and so calculated to gain our affection, but because we knew that no public man in America had worked harder or more successfully than he did to keep the two nations together, and we feel that although our relations are happily of a kind which does not depend merely upon personal influences, his death is, for us all, an irreparable calamity.

We offer the respectful expression of our sympathy to the President who finds himself deprived of a devoted and trusted colleague, and to Colonel Hay's family in the great misfortune which has overtaken them.

Believe me to be
My dear Ambassador,
Yours sincerely,
LANSDOWNE.

Reid cancelled all his engagements for the week of Hay's funeral and the service at St. Paul's. Resuming the inexorable round, he wrote to Watterson, then passing through London: "Yes, we are getting lonely. Phelps and Hay are gone, and of the old comrades scarcely any but you and myself are left; but we must keep a stout heart, and, in the language of the Southwest, 'play the game to the finish.'"

It was part of the game, for the diplomatic corps, to keep constant watch on the political situation, and in Reid's letters, both to the President and to Hay's successor, Elihu Root, the developments of party conflict are clearly reflected. When he came to London, Balfour's ministry was tending slowly but surely to its fall. The rough setback it received over a question of the Irish estimates in July inclined Reid to the belief that it might be "tipped out any hot evening" by a repetition of the mishap. There was not the least question of the government's majority and of its intention to stand behind Balfour until the end of the session, maintaining Lansdowne at the Foreign Office until Parliament should meet again in February. There was, however, a great deal of discontent among the younger members of the party, who wanted more aggressive leadership in the pressing question of fiscal reform, and Reid thought that while they would not willingly bring on a dissolution at the moment, their zeal was not sufficient to make Balfour perfectly sure of a majority on any sudden issue. The opposition, meanwhile, perpetually clamoring for a test before the people of the government's fiscal policy, denounced the party in power as a party clinging to office, and after the prorogation of Parliament in August the Liberals inaugurated a campaign of discussion exceptional for its acrid tone. Lord Rosebery effectively reentered upon the scene. Mr. Asquith was heard from, as were Sir Edward Grey, Mr. Haldane, Mr. Morley, Mr. Herbert Gladstone, Mr. Winston Churchill, and, of course, Sir Henry Campbell-Bannerman, the Liberal leader in the House of Commons, to whom all signs pointed as the next prime minister. The debate went on to a well-foreseen conclusion. Mr. Balfour carried the resignations of himself and his colleagues to Buckingham Palace on December 4th, and "C.-B." being immediately sent for, "kissed hands" the next day as prime minister and first lord of the treasury, proceeded to form a ministry, and the Liberals came in.

The special interest of the American ambassador in all this resided, naturally, in the question of its ultimate effect upon the occupancy of the Foreign Office. Liberal criticism was slow to extend itself to that branch of the government. In fact, at a dinner one night, Campbell-Bannerman, alluding to the probable triumph of his party, remarked to Reid that such a triumph would be tinged with regret at the probable loss of Lord Lansdowne's services, which he considered as of extraordinary value. The question of his successor was rife in private conversation as well as in public quarters, sometimes with piquant turnings, as when "C.-B." indicated in a speech at Stirling, late in November, that his party, if successful, would probably take some steps in the direction of Irish Home Rule. Rosebery, who had all along been thought of as certain to take Lansdowne's place, promptly spoke up, saying that if this were to be the Liberal policy he wouldn't in any circumstances serve under that banner. While the supporters of the government were gleefully hailing this division in the opposition there were cynics who averred, first, that "C.-B.," doubting his ability to get a safe majority in the House without the Irish vote, had thrown out a tub to the Irish whale, and, secondly, that he had sought to do no more than make it impossible for Rosebery to serve in his cabinet. Sir Charles Dilke was much talked of for the Foreign Office, but his chances were slight before the exactions of the Non-Conformist element. Sir Edward Grey, on the whole, held the lead in all of the summer speculations as to the outcome, and Reid observed with special interest the drift of such pronouncements on foreign policy as he made in public. The three cardinal points he enunciated as fundamental to the Liberal programme were friendship and good feeling between England and the United States, an alliance with Japan, and the maintenance of cordial relations with France. With what peculiar sympathy he interpreted the American clause in this declaration Reid came appreciatively to know when Grey took over the Foreign Office.

The *enfant terrible* of the Liberal party, Winston Churchill, received a prodigious amount of attention in the political talk of 1905. Campbell-Bannerman, who expected to have him in the government, nevertheless spoke to Reid about him with complete frankness, deprecating his lack of judgment and his faculty for vituperation. "He told amusing stories," Reid wrote to the President, "about the extraordinary care with which Winston prepares his speeches, commits them to memory and even (as he was said to have told himself) practices them before the mirror in his room. The most curious point of all, perhaps, was that Winston had told him of his preparation for two or three possible turns interruptions from the other side might take, and of his having carefully written out the appropriate reply for each possibility." He was the subject of a hundred keen-edged anecdotes, of endless criticism and of a considerable amount of admiring comment. Lord Tweedmouth and others spoke in warm praise of his ability, and said that it would be well for the people who complained of his vituperation of opponents to look up some of the speeches of Disraeli. There was general acceptance, even in hostile quarters, of the view stated by Lord Spencer, that it would be impossible for any Liberal government to be made up which did not contain Winston Churchill.

In midsummer, before any of these changes in the British administration had been reached, Reid had the wonderful news from Portsmouth, the "colossal success," as he called it, of the President's plan for bringing about peace between Japan and Russia. It was, he wrote to Roosevelt, "easily the greatest thing in the diplomacy over European matters in the memory of this generation or the last," and the thing about it most pleasing was "that you did it off your own bat." Later he had some conversation with the King about it, and reported him as lost in admiration of the President of the United States and his work, convinced that nobody else could have done it.

The event befell in a time of comparative repose for the American ambassador, who was free, then, to make numerous visits promised for the summer and to take possession of his own house in the country. This was the old seat of the Cowpers at Wrest Park, in Bedfordshire, which he leased from Lord Lucas. Lenôtre had designed the gardens. In the house was a large library, apparently begun by Henry, Duke of Kent, and kept up by all his successors. There were many pictures, family portraits by Sir Joshua and other masters of the eighteenth-century school. Deer grazed in the park, sometimes coming to the very door-step. A brief glance at the estate is pertinent, for it made the background of a great deal of the life of the Reids during their English years. They were as often at Wrest as at Dorchester House. The serenity of the place made it an invaluable scene to which to turn from the busy life and the searching fogs of London. In a letter of Rudyard Kipling's, received not long after the establishment of the family in Bedfordshire, he says: "I see from your address that you have taken to the English country, which, I maintain, is in winter a hundred times better than anything town has to offer, and I hope you will find in it whatever of peace and rest is allowed to an Ambassador." The hope was well fulfilled.

Writing to Mrs. Cowles, Reid glanced at some of the incidents of their travels in the north that summer. On one day they lunched with Arthur Balfour. On another Lady Tweeddale drove them to Gosford, the superb place of the Earl of Wemyss, the sprightly peer who had celebrated his entry upon his eighty-first year by surprising his children with a brand new stepmother. There is a magnificent view from Gosford—Edinburgh in the distance and the Firth of Forth in the foreground. The old gentleman told Reid with some amusement of his pointing out this body of water to Mr. Herbert Gladstone on a recent occasion, when they had been discussing Irish Home Rule, and asking him how far he supposed it to be across to Kirkcaldy, on the other side of the Firth. Gladstone could not guess, whereupon Wemyss quietly remarked: "Several miles farther than the distance across the Irish Channel between England and Ireland, which you wished to have set up as an independent government." Lord Dartmouth, at his place at Wolverhampton, spread before his guest a marvellous collection of books, documents, and pictures relating to our Revolutionary period, fascinating souvenirs of George III, under whom Dartmouth's grandfather had served, of Lord North, and other salient figures in the old argument. He pointed out some droll marginal notes written by the Georgian Dartmouth in a folio edition of Bishop Burnet's "History of His Own Times." One in the second volume ran something like this: "I stated in the first volume that I did not think Bishop Burnet had written anything which he did not believe. I now feel bound to say, after reading that volume, that he certainly wrote many things which he knew to be untrue."

There was scarcely room in official despatches for impressions in the lighter vein which I have just illustrated, but these were received with keen interest at the White

House, and Reid sent them often to Mrs. Roosevelt. "I must send you a line myself," wrote the President, on one occasion, "to say how interested I was in your last letter to Mrs. Roosevelt, as likewise in all those that went before. Your letters make a kind of contemporary Greville's memoirs, but with even more interest and charm." He begged the ambassador to write to Mrs. Roosevelt whenever he got the chance. To her Reid sent detailed descriptions of visits at Buckingham Palace, Sandringham, and Windsor, or of ceremonies like the King's opening of Parliament, and interspersing these "set" pictures there are anecdotes and vignettes of the personalities of the hour. Some fragments from this correspondence follow:

July 10, 1905.

The next morning came the King of Spain's reception of the Diplomatic Corps in Buckingham Palace. This, like all similar receptions that I have ever seen, consisted in having the corps arranged around the two sides of the room in the order of their rank when the doors were thrown open and the King entered accompanied by his Cabinet officers and the Ambassador and began at the head of the line, the Spanish Ambassador presenting each Ambassador in turn. There followed a moment's conversation, and then the King requested to have the staff of the Embassy presented, shaking hands with each one. Then drawing his heels together until the spurs made a click which sounded almost like a pistol shot, he made his bow to that Embassy and passed on to the next. When my turn came you can guess at my surprise when the King began by saying in French, "You have served more than once in Paris," and then inquired as to my liking London. The next thing he said: "Your daughter is fond of horses and drives four. I have seen a newspaper picture of her on her coach with you by her side on the box seat. I would like you to have her send me that picture with her autograph and yours on it."

A day or two later I met the King again at the dinner given in his honor at Lansdowne House. I was seated nearly opposite him. His greeting across the table, when he glanced over and saw me there, was as frank and cordial as if he had been some college friend of my son's. That same night I saw for the second or third time an engaging bit of boyishness in the Spanish King. He had finished his cigar in the smoking room and was about leaving the room with

Lord Lansdowne when he suddenly discovered that he had forgotten his chapeau, which was lying on the table where he had been standing, and leaving Lord Lansdowne's side ran back to the table, seized the chapeau, and ran again to Lord Lansdowne at a sharp little dog trot, just as any boy of sixteen or seventeen would do who thought he ought not to keep his host waiting. On the night of the dinner given him at Buckingham Palace he did exactly the same thing with the King of England—forgetting his chapeau in the same way, deserting the King at the door and making a run for the lost article and back again to the King, who stood waiting with an amused smile and was evidently pleased.

The ladies all took a fancy to him. His face in repose is not handsome; in fact, he has the protruding lips and chin and general unattractive lower face of the Hapsburgs; but when he smiles the whole face changes in character and is very winning. At the review at Aldershot he led the regiment of which he had been elected Honorary Colonel in review past the King. As he approached, the blare of the band frightened his horse and he displayed some really handsome horsemanship in keeping it under control, giving the salute to King Edward at exactly the proper moment. Everybody decided that he hadn't admired horse flesh for nothing.

I went down on two of the four days at Ascot, having learned from former experience that at least this much attendance was expected from the Ambassador. Lord Churchill, who is now Master of the Hounds, made us his guests at luncheon the first day and told me that on the second the King and Queen would expect me at their lunch table. This was the day when the King had a rather remarkable talk with me which I have already reported to the President about affairs in the East. When we entered the enclosure from which the Royal party viewed the races one of the Lords-in-waiting told me that I was to take in the Princess Ena, daughter of the Princess Henry of Battenberg and niece of the King. She is the youngest of all the Royal Princesses, being barely eighteen, and is one of the most attractive, though I think the palm of beauty must be given to the Princess Patricia, daughter of the Duke of Connaught. When we started to go out I said to the young Princess, "I don't quite know when our turn comes," and said she, "I am the very last of everybody." To which I replied, "Well, you shall not be in this case, for now I'll claim my own rank." So I followed the Spanish Ambassador, and as I entered the lunch room was surprised to have the King, who was already seated, catch my eye and motion me to a place opposite him at the right of the Queen. It took me some little time to realize that the dumpy, fat, bald-headed person on the other side of the Queen was the Khedive of Egypt, who had been very civil to me years before in Cairo and up the Nile and whose father I had also known on the occasion of my first visit to Egypt. He hasn't grown in beauty as he has grown older, but the English say he has much more sense! At any rate, he has quit fretting about the fact that Lord Cromer is the real ruler of Egypt, and apparently gets on very comfortably now with the changed conditions which have transformed his country from poverty to great prosperity and general contentment.

During the visit of the Japanese Princes I had one or two experiences which reminded me of the President's struggles with the lady of the diplomatic corps, who, as he declared, spoke no known language excepting Aztec. At the dinner to the Japanese at Buckingham Palace I was told I had to take in the Duchess of Connaught and place her at the left hand of the King. So I thought I was sure of a good time, since she is at once one of the most gracious and one of the most intelligent of the Royalties. But alas! when I got seated I found a Japanese lady on my left with Lord Lansdowne next her. The King had, of course, taken out the leading Japanese Princess. The result was that after a few moments' struggle with her, he discovered enormous interest in his sister-in-law's conversation. So I had to leave the Duchess of Connaught alone and devote myself to the Japanese Princess on my left—whom Lord Lansdowne was quite willing to leave alone also. She did have a few words of English, but the struggles I had to find out for the Duchess of Connaught what was the name of the Japanese decoration they were wearing were such that I was exhausted for a day or two with the effort. The intense interest the King felt in his sister-in-law's talk throughout the dinner left me with this fair Japanese to talk to nearly all the time, and if my life depended on it I don't think I could now recall one intelligible idea evolved from the whole conversation.

Let me close with something a little less trivial than all this farrago of egotistical reminiscences. The other evening at the Duchess of Sutherland's ball fortune happened to seat me for a little while beside the Duchess of X., and the conversation somehow reached the German Emperor. "He is unbearable," she said. "The real trouble is that he is a tyrant by nature."

October 31, 1905.

Winston Churchill has been working very hard for a long time [on the then forthcoming life of his father] and he has plenty of ability in other directions besides that of merely making everybody angry who comes in contact with him. Someone quoted his mother to me the other day as having said: "The next Government will have to put Winston in the Cabinet. If it doesn't, God help them!" The only reason why I don't give full credence to this is that Lady Randolph, while quite capable of thinking it, is probably too clever to say it. The last time she was at Dorchester House was the morning after Winston had made his savage prepared invective in the House of Commons, on the occasion of Balfour's refusing to resign. You will remember that, in closing the debate, Balfour, who was Winston's father's great friend, gave the young man a tremendous dressing-down. In her call at Dorchester House Lady Randolph seemed worried about Winston's strong language and frankly said she had met that morning several friends who had told her her son had behaved abominably. I feel sure, however, that feeling did not go very deep or last very long. She is extremely proud of him and has a good deal of reason for it.

A week or two ago I had to go up to Scotland again to receive a degree at St. Andrews. Bishop Potter, Charlemagne Tower and the President of the Carnegie Institute at Pittsburgh were the other three Americans receiving the same degree. The scene was an extraordinary one. Mr. Carnegie was first installed as Lord Rector, and then attempted to deliver what they call the "Rectorial address." The boys, however, had some idea about that themselves. His speech was a violent denunciation of all war excepting a purely defensive war for your own land and home, which he said did not justify attacking anybody else's land and home. As he was speaking to a good many students who belonged to the volunteer regiments and was actually in the hall of the St. Andrews armory, you may imagine that his sentiments were not acceptable to everybody. The whole speech was punctuated with shouts of dissent, groans, cat-calls and the like. Carnegie took it very good humoredly, however; chaffed the boys a little at times, telling them that he had given them their turn and they ought now to give him his; and on the whole succeeded far better than many English speakers do in addressing these turbulent Scotch University audiences. I have never seen a speaker at home persevere in the midst of such interruptions and cannot imagine anyone delivering an address at an American college who would for a moment think of submitting to it. Once Mr. Carnegie was unlucky in giving the boys a tempting cue. In one of his violent outbursts against war he closed with the quotation, "Is thy servant a dog that he should do this thing?" He appealed to the boys to make such an answer when called upon to go to war. Instead, the whole crowd instantly began barking in every tone of canine expression from the bull-dog and the mastiff to the toy-terrier, and you may imagine the ludicrous nature of the scene for the next few moments.

Much to the astonishment of most of us, the boys took it into their heads that everyone who received a degree should address to them a speech of thanks. Luckily they were very amiable towards us, and interrupted, while we were all speaking, only with frequent and very generous applause. They were not so considerate, however, to the "public orator," who recited our alleged merits to the Vice-Chancellor in proposing our degrees; and I was particularly charmed by one fellow who, in the midst of some story of what I had done, whispered in a tone perfectly audible throughout the hall, "If you didn't say so, I could hardly believe it."

December 12, 1905.

Yesterday I took my leave of Lord Lansdowne at the Foreign Office a few minutes before he went to Buckingham Palace to surrender the seals. The papers announced that the new Foreign Minister would receive the diplomatic corps on Wednesday, but as I am sailing on Wednesday morning and as my relations with the new Foreign Minister, Sir Edward Grey, were pleasant, I telephoned to the Foreign Office, explaining the situation and asked if he could see me to-day. He immediately made an appointment, and I have just returned from paying my respects to the new Minister and presenting Mr. Carter as Chargé during my absence.

Sir Edward was, of course, most cordial, and he seemed gratified that the first diplomatic visit he received after entering upon his office was that from the American Ambassador. He says that as at present advised Parliament will be dissolved on the 8th of January, that a few elections will come off before the 20th, but that the more important will come then, and that they hope to have the elections finished before the end of the month. The new Parliament will then be convened in the second week in February.

I spoke to him briefly about the only question with Great Britain of the slightest importance which we have on the diplomatic slate at present. He seemed to concur heartily with me in the hope and belief that matters could be satisfactorily adjusted and spoke warmly of his earnest desire for permanent good relations. I mentioned the satisfaction with which I had heard of his appointment, particularly on account of his recent speech on foreign affairs in which he had dwelt on the necessity of continuing the present policy of the Government in three particulars and had named first of all among the points on which there ought to be no change the effort to cultivate constantly the most cordial relations with the United States. He seemed pleased when I told him that I had transmitted these remarks to our Government; and then went on to speak of his high esteem for the President and of the hope he had cherished that he would be able to go to the United States and make his acquaintance. He said that he heard so much of him from his intimate friend Ronald Munro-Ferguson as to feel almost as if he knew him.

With this altogether satisfactory interview the ambassador closed the first period of his stay in England. The Reids sailed on the *Oceanic* the next day to spend Christmas at home. They visited Washington, also, and the ambassador had some interesting talks with the President and Secretary Root. In January he returned to his post.

CHAPTER XVII

NEWFOUNDLAND AND MOROCCO

The question with Great Britain which Reid had mentioned as "on the diplomatic slate" was one over which negotiations were protracted far longer than had been expected when they began. A despatch from Washington to London, paraphrased in the "Foreign Relations of the United States," concisely indicates a problem in the solution of which the American ambassador was to be occupied over a considerable period: "Mr. Root informs Mr. Reid that the Newfoundland government has forbidden American fishing vessels already on the treaty coast to take fish within the treaty limits prescribed in Article I. of the treaty of 1818. They consider that their right is perfectly clear and in accordance with the construction of the treaty always followed, and never questioned by the British Government, and they have been so advised by the Department." Before he was through with the subject Reid might have qualified, academically at least, as an expert in the technic of life on the fishing-banks. The doings of those distant mariners reverberated in stately exchanges between two powerful governments. From the original broad question of fishing or no fishing, there sprang an infinity of ramifications. There was the distinction to be drawn between registered and licensed vessels. It carried implications as to fishing and trading, two very different things, and this collateral distinction affected the fishermen in the matter of obtaining their bait. A nice complication, all by itself, was involved in the designation of the precise coast on which it was legitimate for the American fishermen to construct platforms for the freezing of herring, and all that was needed still further to load discussion was the introduction of reports—duly provided—of wilful damage to nets and tackle or the illegal shipment of Newfoundland fishermen by American vessels.

Diplomatic proceedings over all this were accompanied by a good deal of comment in the press, not always helpful. Talking with Reid on the subject, the King shrewdly characterized these newspaper references as "tiresome" —the favorite English euphemism for things disagreeable or troublesome. The whole matter was "tiresome" but it was important, and, besides, very humanly interesting, as when, among the fishermen themselves, there were discovered Newfoundlanders keen against prohibitions which their governor and his council were desirous of enforcing. Our own men were equally ready to compose differences, their friendly disposition having been shown over the matter of "wilful damage" to their gear. Solemn declarations by masters or agents of some eighteen schooners made it appear that a large number of the fraternity were "well satisfied with the conduct of the local fishermen." The political powers in the island were not so accommodating. Reid thought them impetuous and disposed to make difficulties, a judgment which must sometimes have been shared by the Foreign Office itself. When Reid came back from his brief visit home he made a little gift of a diplomatic pouch to Lord Lansdowne, then retired from the government. Thanking him, Lansdowne humorously said: "Is there not something appropriate in the presentation of an empty despatch case to an extinct Foreign Secretary?" Since Reid couldn't fill that receptacle he filled Sir Edward Grey's—to overflowing. The literature of this subject is formidable.

It is marked in August, 1906, by a statement that divergence in the views of the two governments made an immediate settlement impossible. This conclusion, however, had its compensation for the American ambassador, who was able, thereupon, to negotiate a *modus vivendi* which for the moment poured salutary oil upon the troubled waters. The Newfoundlanders, to be sure, were left with what they thought a grievance. Reid's comment, in a letter to Nicholas Murray Butler, disposes of them with scant good-nature: "Boiled down, the case hasn't a look they ought to take much pride in. We have certain fishing rights guaranteed to us by the treaty of 1818 and absolutely undisputed. They wanted us to give them some privilege in our ports, which I personally (following Hay's lead) would have been glad to see them get, though the Senate thought differently. Because they don't get them, they turn around now and deliberately avow the purpose to avenge themselves by damaging and, as far as they can, destroying our rights under a treaty which has been respected for nearly a century. If they were not so little and so poor, one would be tempted to use strong language about such conduct." How the signing of the agreement was taken in London he tells in the following letter:

Dorchester House,
October 8, 1906.

My dear Mr. President:

We have had quite a lively stir this morning in London newspapers and among the newspaper men who have been coming to the Embassy about our innocent little *modus vivendi* with Newfoundland. As usual, the correspondent of the "Morning Post," in his Washington despatch, sees it through Newfoundland or Canadian spectacles and regards it as a "complete surrender on the part of the Imperial Government to the demands of the United States." Other despatches set forth that the Newfoundland Ministry feels so outraged that it threatens to resign, following the example set by the Natal Ministry immediately after Winston Churchill's speech. I don't believe they will resign, and I don't believe they have any just grievance.

At the same time we have, perhaps, a right to take their outcry as evidence that at least the *modus vivendi* doesn't wholly sacrifice the interests of the United States! The reporters who have been around the Embassy this morning say that the Colonial Office is indignant at the tone the Newfoundlanders have taken about it. At any rate, we have all we really asked for; and I think besides we have the feeling at the Foreign Office that we appreciated their difficulties with their cantankerous little colony and showed a friendly and conciliatory desire to help them out.

Your last letter reached me under an historic roof—"Camperdown," where I was the guest of the great-grandson of the big Admiral who was created Viscount of Camperdown immediately after the naval victory on the Texel. It made one feel quite naval to be surrounded by historic pictures by Copley and others relating to this victory over the Dutch, to see in the hall the sword Admiral Duncan had worn and the sword he received from the Dutch Admiral in surrender, and a hundred other souvenirs of his long service. Even the light walking stick, which he carried in his hand throughout the action, is preserved in the same case with the sword. It struck me as a queer collocation that on either side of this case stood a marble bust, the one of Charles James Fox, the other a laurel-crowned Napoleon!

They have an extraordinary mass of Camperdown correspondence. There must be fifteen or twenty volumes of it, I think. Among the curiosities in it which I looked at with special interest were the notes of the Admiral's speech to his sailors at the time of the mutinies on the Nore, which so shortly preceded the action off Camperdown. Another thing that struck me was a most enthusiastic letter from the wife of the First Lord of the Admiralty of the time, in which she wound up her rather ecstatic congratulations after the battle with the exclamation: "As an English woman, as an Irish woman, as Lord Spencer's wife, I cannot express to you my grateful feelings."

I am amused and ashamed to find that you know more in Washington about Oliver, who wrote the Hamilton book, than anybody I have seen in London has been able to tell me. I am going to get into communication, however, with his publishers here and with the Professor of History in Edinburgh University about him; and I shall pump Birrell dry on the subject the next time I meet him. I have been reading at the book as I had a chance but have not yet finished it. Some things in it seem to me surprisingly well done; on the other hand, now and then I strike on something which grates on all my preconceived ideas about Hamilton and leads me to think I must re-examine the other authorities. Such, for example, is his point about Hamilton's having made Washington impatient with his delay in answering a certain call only an excuse for a resignation of the private secretaryship, which he was bent on getting rid of any way.

But for your finding time in the midst of the worries over Cuba to write about this book, I shouldn't venture to think you could have time to give to another new book. As it is, however, I am going to send you in the first diplomatic bag a copy of Rosebery's new book just out last week on Randolph Churchill. You will read it in an evening—if you haven't already done so—and I am sure you will like some things in it, though I doubt if it will leave you with quite as high an opinion of Randolph as Lord Rosebery had. The truth is his son (who was on bad terms with him, as you know, in his life time) has already made good his ill-mannered boast that people would soon quit speaking of him as Lord Randolph's son and, on the other hand, would speak of Lord Randolph as the father of Winston Churchill! I think I mentioned to you once before that his biography of his father is an admirable piece of work. In fact, it is the best political biography they have had here for several years.

What you said about Bryan in your letter of Sept. 24th struck me as singularly acute and just. No man can consistently take the position he has taken about the Filipinos and yet fail to fight most vigorously against the conduct of his own party towards the negroes in the South. His wholesale denunciation of English rule in India was not only ignorant but curiously reckless. I believe with you that his fall after the Madison Square speech from the absurd height to which the European tour and the imaginations of the Democrats had lifted him was complete; but I don't believe we have heard the last of him. His party is dreadfully hard up for Presidential timber, and may come back to him again.

Sincerely yours,

WHITELAW REID.

Roosevelt's reply contains a terse statement of his satisfaction with Reid's handling of the fishery question. "I feel," he says, "the attitude you have taken is in every respect admirable." He was amused by Winston Churchill's book, which he found "a very bright and clever one," but, he added: "I should most mortally hate to have any son of mine write such a book about me!" There is a charming passage in this letter on two of his coadjutors: "Are not Root and Taft big men? I simply cannot say what a source of continual strength they are to me."

The Algeciras conference has taken its place in history as a superfluous vexation. Reid's relation to the subject well illustrates the power that it had to keep diplomats everywhere in a state of nervousness. He learned this early, too. The apprehensions over the Moroccan question which Kaiser Wilhelm raised in the chancelleries of the Powers was swiftly gathering when the American ambassador to England took leave of the President in May, 1905. Mr. Roosevelt touched then, in his last verbal instructions, on the attitudes of France and England, where the new problem was concerned. They were in process of establishment as Reid took up his service abroad, and wherever he went in London he found Morocco to the fore. It was a never-failing topic. In his conversations one seems to be assisting, behind the scenes, at the rise and fall of emotion in the development of a crisis to which the Kaiser was always striving to give a theatrical turn. His obvious influence in bringing about the resignation of Delcassé was the first startling episode in the drama as Reid saw it unrolled from the vantage-ground of the English scene. He gathered from the King that the latter deeply regretted the fall of the foreign minister. They talked about Rouvier, his successor, on whose traits Reid could speak with familiarity, having known him in Paris fifteen years before. His ministry was occupied at the moment of Reid's talk with the King in fending off the German proposals for a conference of the Powers. The French reply to these, while conciliatory in tone, indicated that so portentous a handling of the issues was unnecessary. Without distinctly refusing assent to a conference, it put Germany in a position where she could not insist without showing that her real purpose was not to reach a proper understanding about Morocco, but to force a difficulty. In the course of these opening parleys, when all sides were jockeying for position, Reid reported to the President that the English professed entire confidence in the good faith of France, that they were persuaded of Rouvier's skill in handling his negotiations with Germany, and that they were grateful for the assurance received from the United States that we should not come into a conference unless it was satisfactory to France. They meant themselves to stand by France in the matter to an equal or greater extent.

At Washington the President was obtaining light on the subject from Speck von Sternburg, the German ambassador, and his French colleague, M. Jusserand. Ultimately he sent to Reid the detailed survey of his Moroccan diplomacy, which closes the first volume of Mr. J. B. Bishop's recently published "Theodore Roosevelt and His Time." From this document and from Reid's own papers there is to be derived the picture of a grotesquely involved situation. The Kaiser started by seeking Roosevelt's co-operation in an intervention with the Sultan of Morocco, which, if nominally in the interest of internal reform and the "Open Door," was really aimed at the curtailment of French influence. Piously solicitous of the welfare of his own nationals and of other foreigners in the Sultan's territory, he was thinking all the time of possible eventualities between himself and France, with a sharp eye, too, on the chance of England's being drawn in. Under his malign manipulation, the question bristled increasingly with possibilities of war. He couldn't believe, or at all events pretended not to believe, that the Moroccan problem could be handled by itself; it was linked with too many other interests. Hence, the Powers must all take official cognizance of it. Especially was he uneasy about the English point of view, in which he suspected a sympathy for France inimical to himself. Our good-will toward his plan was certain, he thought, to dissipate British opposition. The truth was, of course, that American relation to the crisis was in the nature of things detached. Roosevelt did not feel that as a government there was any occasion for the United States to interfere. We had no real interests in Morocco. But as Germany's sabre-rattling became more pronounced he saw that he was in a position to avert catastrophe, and in an absolutely disinterested spirit, acting as the friend alike of France, England, and Germany, he made his decision. As he wrote to Reid, he "took active hold of the matter with both Speck and Jusserand, and after a series of communications with the French Government through Jusserand, got things temporarily straightened up." What he did was to overcome French reluctance to a conference, and thereby to pave the way for negotiations which at any rate discounted the nightmare of a continental conflagration. His powerful influence, as in the conflict between Russia and Japan, was on the side of peace. Through a constructive gesture at the right moment he did not pull Germany's chestnuts out of the fire—far from it—but he saved her face, and at the same time increased the friendliness between ourselves and the other Powers involved. We entered the Algeciras conference on a status making our participation really a benefit all around.

The preliminary passages at Algeciras, about the time of Reid's return from his holiday in the United States, were the occasion of some rather ominous comments. In the papers there were sensational despatches attributing to our representative in the deliberations an intention to intervene at the psychological moment with proposals for a compromise of the respective claims of France and Germany. The duty of policing and preserving order in the various cities in Morocco, on the hypothesis of this compromise, was to be so distributed that Germany would be assigned responsibility for the Atlantic port of Mogador. Reid had heard before of what was believed to be the Kaiser's desire for a coaling station which might be useful to the German navy and to German commerce on the voyage from Kiel to Buenos Ayres, and had mentioned it when in Washington. Now, in London, he found that this idea and others were renewing the tension in the public mind with reference to Morocco, and he divined that questions would be forthcoming at the Foreign Office regarding our own policy. Secretary Root promptly told him that that policy remained absolutely unchanged. "Our interests," he wrote, "are not sufficient to justify us in taking a leading part; and while, of course, we should be very glad to contribute towards keeping the peace, we do not wish to get into a position where we will be justly charged with intermeddling or to become a party to a controversy, and we have not yet considered that there was a situation in which any move by us would be practically useful." We were in, indeed, to keep the peace, but the conference seemed always to be simulating, nevertheless, the potentialities of a powder-magazine. In the course of a flying trip south that he made that winter, motoring along the Corniche, and visiting Rome before he returned, Reid had a letter from the President which reflects the tendency of the Moroccan imbroglio to bring back the shadow of war:

The White House,
Washington,
March 1, 1906.

My dear Mr. Ambassador:

Things do not look as well as they should in Algeciras. Last June the Kaiser, entirely of his own accord and without any need, promised me that if they had the conference and the French and German representatives differed, he would instruct the Germans to follow my directions. As my experience has always been that a promise needlessly entered into is rarely kept, I never expected the Kaiser to keep this one, and he has not. We may, however, get an agreement among them. The trouble is that with Russia out of the way as she now is, Germany firmly believes that she can whip both France and England. I have excellent reason for believing that the German Naval authorities are as confident as the German military authorities, and believe that England is relying still upon the memory of the Nelsonic triumphs and that they would have a first-class chance of temporarily crippling or driving off her fleet; while the military men firmly believe that an army of fifty thousand Germans landed in England would with but little difficulty take possession of the entire island.

Sincerely yours,

THEODORE ROOSEVELT.

The President never lost sight of the powder-magazine and the fuses lying so temptingly around. When he had counselled the French to agree to a conference he had spoken with the utmost frankness on the safeguard it would develop against a military clash. His moderating influence at Algeciras always took account of the one besetting danger, and that influence prevailed. As Reid wrote him on the emergence of the conference into innocuous waters, he had "for a second time rendered a great service to the cause of peace in Europe." English appreciation of the potency of his hand in the game was warm. Writing to him on the advisability of showing the King some of the more significant passages in his summary of what he had done, Reid made these observations:

Dorchester House,
June 19, 1906.

DEAR MR. PRESIDENT:

The King showed intense interest in the subject when I had my first long talk with him on his return from his Continental tour; and it was so obvious that the notion that Speck had been trying to get you to play the Emperor's game for him had been impressed upon the King that I was exceedingly eager to let him know how absolutely you had understood them, had drawn a line in the matter and refused to go to the lengths they desired.

The truth is that the Emperor's assiduous efforts to cultivate the most intimate relations with you have attracted the attention of all the chancelleries in Europe, and a common comment upon it is that the Emperor overdoes his love-making as he does his diplomacy, with a certain German confidence in the value of brute vigor in either pursuit! What I have sometimes feared was that this might affect the feeling here in a way which might not be beneficial in Mr. Root's coming negotiations on the questions still unsettled between us. The truth seems to me that our relations with England are of far greater importance to us than those with Germany—there being more points at issue, more chances of friction and greater difficulty in almost every question that arises on account of the irresponsibility and exacting temper of Canadian politicians. I cannot personally see anything to be gained from unusually good relations with Germany which would compensate us for the least jar in our relations with Great Britain, since I know of no serious question we have to settle with Germany, while there are certainly a good many with Great Britain still unsettled. Aside from that, Germany isn't planted all along our frontier, and our negotiations with her will ordinarily therefore be on subjects less acute and ticklish.

As of course you know, there has been at times great tension here between England and Germany. And I know (in a very confidential way) that the King has felt acutely some personal attacks which he thought might have been prevented. He spoke particularly of attacks made on him in the German papers during his late stay in Paris, and insinuations that he was staying there merely to intrigue against Germany. He intimated that his nephew knew better than this, and that such attacks could not appear in the German press without their Government winking at them. There had also been intimations that he was responsible for the resentment sometime expressed in English papers. "Yet the Emperor knows," he said, "as well as you or I that we cannot control the press here, just as you cannot control it in the United States, while he also knows perfectly that I know he can and does habitually control the German press."

Some of his talk, as well as that which I have heard elsewhere, leads me to think that at one moment they feared grave results from Algeciras; but were perfectly resolved to meet the issue. Their view, like that in France, is that the Emperor had no interests in Morocco worth mentioning, and that he recklessly stirred up a controversy, which might have resulted in a conflagration, merely to assert his importance and gratify his vanity. Whenever they discuss the question seriously they refer to the fact that the treaty which was the basis of his demand that the signatory Powers be called into conference, was merely a treaty as to the rights of Nationals; that it referred to nothing else; that the favored-nation clause, under which Germany claimed the same voice in Moroccan affairs as other of the signatory Powers, referred only to the same subject of Nationals; and that she really had no business in questions which belonged primarily, if not exclusively, to the Mediterranean Powers.

Another view commonly expressed among the Continental diplomatists, as well as the English, is that the Emperor's whole course towards France and Morocco, from the day when he caused the French to dismiss in a panic the best Foreign Minister they have had for many years, was pure bluff. They say it would have been ruinous for him, both at home and abroad, to go into a war on any pretext he had; and that, besides, it would have been madness for him to be engaged in stirring up hostilities at the West, when the chance seemed almost at hand for realizing the dream of his life at the East by completing the Pan-German Empire on the death or downfall of Francis Joseph.

On this point I had a curious talk the other night with Sir Frank Lascelles, the very capable British Ambassador in Berlin. He said he believed the Emperor too wise a man (no matter what his Pan-German dream may have been) to think of risking the annexation of South Germany, even if he could bring it about. The Ambassador's reason for this view was that the Emperor must know of the existing discontent in parts of his own domain and must realize that with the South Germans added the discontented elements would have an absolute majority in the Empire, with the certainty that sooner or later Prussian wings would be clipped. He had the same view as so many others have expressed, that the Emperor's Morocco course was pure bluff, but he did not believe that the Emperor was unwise enough to do anything actively at present towards the realization of the Pan-Germanic notions.

Very sincerely yours,

WHITELAW REID.

There are some delectable sayings of Roosevelt's in his reply, authorizing Reid to show to the King and to Sir Edward Grey all that he deemed it proper to show them in the long Moroccan letter to which I have referred. "In this Algeciras matter," he writes, "you will notice that while I was most suave and pleasant with the Emperor, yet when it became necessary at the end I stood him on his head with great decision. . . . As for the Germans, I really treat them much more cavalierly than I do the English, and I am immensely amused at the European theory (which cannot, however, be the theory of the French Government) that I am taken in by the Kaiser. I am very polite to him, but I am ready at an instant's notice to hold my own. In the same way my policy with Japan is to be scrupulously polite, to show a genuine good will toward her, but to keep our navy in such shape that the risk will be great for Japan if it undertakes any aggression upon us."

Various other diplomatic themes of importance were developed in this year of Reid's embassy, but for the moment I turn from them to glance at other activities. A deep shadow was cast upon the social side of these in the spring, when news came of the appalling disaster at San Francisco. The Reids were personally concerned on account of relatives and friends, they had practical interests both in the stricken city itself and at Millbrae, and there were besides, of course, other than family claims in the matter upon the American ambassador. The great railway wreck at Salisbury tragically deepened the gloom at the embassy. Reid was overwhelmed, privately and officially, in the business flowing from these two events, and the movements in promotion of aid and sympathy which were inaugurated by both. The annual American invasion of London was in full flood at the time. Conspicuous among his countrymen was Mr. W. J. Bryan. He didn't ask to be presented to the King. His Majesty saved him the trouble, proposing to Reid the interview at Buckingham Palace which was soon arranged. Bryan made a good impression there, as he did with most of his speech-making. Some English listeners found his style more demonstrative and rhetorical than that to which they were accustomed, but comment in general testified to his having vindicated his repute for "silver-tongued" oratory. Reid observed that the net result of Bryan's visit to London was that he rose decidedly in the estimation of the English and of the diplomatic corps.

The American ambassador himself had to do a good deal of public speaking. Before the presentation of his credentials he received a request from Lord Tennyson to preside at the next banquet of the Royal Literary Fund, and this invitation was the forerunner of a stream of communications of the same sort. He told the authors when he addressed them, on the problem of making provision for disabled members of their craft, what he had said to Mr. Gladstone on their first meeting, many years before. The great statesman asked, among a multiplicity of other things: "What does your Republic do to reward distinguished public services from private citizens?" After some cogitation Reid felt compelled to reply: "There are only three things we can do. If they live at the North, we can invite them to lecture; if they live at the South, we can call them Colonel or General; wherever they live, if they can get votes enough, we can send them to Congress and let them take the consequences." At University College, Bristol, where he went for a degree, he spoke on the development of scientific and technological education in the United States. The opening address which he delivered at the summer meeting of the University of Cambridge was devoted to an excursion into eighteenth-century history, "The Rise of the United States." Later, when the freedom of the city was conferred upon him at Dundee, he made the opening address in the series founded by Lord Armitstead and traversed the experience of his countrymen in facing and conquering their educational problem. The educational motive is always recurring in his speeches on English soil. It was as though he were carrying on abroad the discussion in which as a member of the Board of Regents he delighted at home. Alike at scholastic institutions and at dinners of all sorts he was called upon with a frequency which he sometimes found embarrassing. To an American friend he wrote: "As you know, I am never quite sure about these things myself, and I always approach the task of making a speech with a certain reluctance and a hope that it may be the last. At the same time, I am bound to say that the English audiences are extraordinarily amiable and cordial."

These speeches offer many an inducement to the biographer to stray off into a byway. For example, the one at the Royal Literary Fund contained a friendly allusion to Henry Adams, in the long line of American historians. When reported in the press it elicited this charming note from that writer:

Paris
MY DEAR AMBASSADOR: May 14, 1906.

Rarely have I been more bewildered than at catching sight of my name in the columns of the "Times," apropos to nothing, when I was thinking only to read about the Douma and the Education Bill. You do not know what it is to be dead, or to feel so, for twenty years, and suddenly to be called up for judgment. I like being dead; it offers great advantages to historians; it is also in good taste to be quiet and restful in society among the gentlemen of polished manners who lived in high philosophy with Plato and Confucius; but if I must be pulled up for judgment, I am beyond expression relieved to get so kind a judge as you.

Such a compliment merits rare acknowledgment, for I am not used to feeling flattery. I wish I could offer suitable recognition. I can offer no such return. The best I can do is to offer my latest work. It was meant only for girls, and you are certainly not a niece; but it will serve as proof of my appreciation. You need not read it, for it is meant only for the nursery, and contains only nursery lines. With profound thanks,

Your obliged HENRY ADAMS.

The work, written for his nieces, was the beautiful "Mont St. Michel and Chartres," the masterpiece in the study of mediævalism which since the death of Mr. Adams has happily been made more widely known than it was in the original privately printed edition. Reid had some talk about it with one of his most interesting literary friends in England, Sir George Otto Trevelyan.

A sequel to this, however, takes us straight from the Middle Ages to one of Reid's early achievements, his despatch from Pittsburg Landing. "I respectfully repeat," wrote Sir George, "what I told Mrs. Whitelaw Reid during our delightful talk at dinner, that I cherish the possibility of some day getting you to tell me of the battle of Shiloh as the most interesting to me of conceivable conversations." The ambassador told him, at Dorchester House, which was made doubly sympathetic to Trevelyan by the souvenirs which his friend gathered there, in prints, of the leading figures in the American Revolution. Periodically the subject of Shiloh used to come up in Reid's career. Another Adams, Henry's brother Charles Francis, revived it by quoting a passage from "Ohio in the War." Reid said that he read the extract with some apprehension, after thirty-seven years, and then went on: "But, barring a little youthful exuberance of style, I see nothing in it which I am not disposed to stand by today. I didn't remember having discharged my soul quite so completely on the excesses of that march, but am not sorry now that I did it! I was very fond of good old Sherman personally, and our relations grew very cordial; but there are at least three things in his career which nobody need attempt to defend. One was his persistent denial of his surprise at Pittsburg Landing or Shiloh, and the others were his licence to 'Sherman's bummers,' and his insubordinate attitude after the very proper disapproval of his treaty with Johnson. I remember once summing up, somewhere or another, one curious phase of his character by saying that he never acknowledged an error, and never repeated it." Adams replied:

Boston
January 6, 1906.

My dear Mr. Reid:

I entirely sympathize with your feelings when you learned that your book of thirty or forty years ago was to be quoted from. A cold shiver in such cases instinctively creeps down one's back. I have been there myself! Meanwhile, in the present case I had no hesitation in quoting from your "Ohio in the War," because it seemed to me that the sentiments expressed in the extract made reflected great credit upon you. That a young fellow should have then ventured so boldly to criticize the act of a man holding Sherman's position in the public eye was much to his credit. What you wrote was written in the flush and glamour following the triumphant close of the war. Everything was glorious; the record was immaculate! Under such conditions, for you to come forward and tell the disagreeable truth was to my mind, looking back through forty years, altogether commendable.

I, too, admire Sherman. I consider him as, on the whole, the most striking individuality I have ever met. The few conversations I had with him all left a vivid impression on my memory. He was instinct with a personality all his own. In this I think you will concur. As compared with Grant he was Hyperion to a Satyr. The one was a most interesting person to meet; the other impressed one as being thoroughly commonplace. There was a fine vein running through Sherman; a distinctly coarse fibre pervaded Grant.

As to Sherman's record, I concur in all your conclusions. I suppose you know how the disaster at Shiloh came about. It was all due to the old-fogy, West Point, regular-army theory that fieldworks made the men "cowardly." They should be required to "stand up and fight man-fashion." I cannot tell how often I heard that agreeable aphorism set forth in war days. It is the old, Brown-Bess, English theory which prevailed in Waterloo, and which they had to give up in South Africa. Incredible as it may seem, though the English halted at Mont St. Jean at four o'clock in the afternoon of a long day in June, and lay there, all night, until they were attacked the next morning, they never threw up any entrenchments; they never made the slightest effort to protect themselves. To do so would not have been according to regulation!

In this respect, Sherman got his lesson at Shiloh. Before that engagement he had maintained that the way to make men soldiers was to drill them; that any temporary earthworks or protection caused them to lose reliance on themselves. He there got his lesson and he never afterward forgot it. As you say, Sherman never confessed to a mistake, and never repeated it. Later, in North Carolina, he made a very wry face over Johnstone's "earthworks of the old kind."

I remain, etc. CHARLES F. ADAMS.

Reid confirmed the explanation of Sherman's slip at Shiloh, recalling a talk of the general's in which he had hinted at exactly the reason assigned by Mr. Adams for the misfortune he suffered. Apropos of this matter of military reputations, I may mention a country-house colloquy of Reid's with one of the strongest army officers he met in England. This personage did not think that Lord Roberts's strategy in South Africa amounted to much, although he spoke admiringly of the man. Nor was his opinion of Kitchener quite as high as that held by the general public. He was very positive in saying that far and away the best soldier in the British army, though then too old, was Lord Wolseley. It is in such intimate and unconventional glimpses as these of Englishmen and their point of view that Reid's correspondence with Mrs. Roosevelt is especially rich and I may here return to some further extracts from it:

February 27, 1906.

You must have noticed that there is a great crop of new peers—some promoted by the late Government when it went out of power, some by the new Government when it came in. One of the best earned was that of the late permanent Under Secretary for Foreign Affairs, Sir Thomas Sanderson. After his advancement to the peerage was announced; there was quite a little interval before it was determined under what style he should be known. Meantime, his brother in New York, Sir Percy, was naturally desirous to send congratulations on the event, but didn't know how to address the new peer. So he put his letter inside another to his sister and requested her to see that it reached its destination. When the new peer received it he found it thus addressed: "To my brother, the Lord."

June 1, 1906.

Alma Tadema, the artist, told me the other evening a little story about Winston Churchill's encounter with one of his brother artists which may interest you. As Tadema told it, the artist was making a little sketch of a group of noted people gathered at some social occasion. The sketch was intended for publication and Winston was not one of those to be included. He thought it a good group to be in, however, and kept hovering about it and putting himself under the artist's eye until the latter rather in self defence sketched him in slightly in profile in the outer line. When the sketch was finished they were all crowding around to look at it and expressing, as is apt to be the case at such times, favorable opinions of the artist's work. Winston, having got into the picture in this fashion, came up to give his opinion and in his characteristic way said: "I don't agree with you. I don't think the likenesses are good at all. Look at that thing of me. Surely that isn't like me." The artist, whom Tadema described as one of the most patient and gentle-spoken of his race, turned at this like the proverbial worm. "Yes," he said, "I think you are right, Mr. Churchill. It doesn't do you full justice, but then you see it is in profile, so that I could only get in half your cheek."

Any little story like this against Winston is received with delight in London. There is nobody at the moment more thoroughly unpopular, in fact, detested in the more important social circles. They don't like him as a Liberal, and they don't respect him as a "turn coat"; but for his bad manners, his recklessness and the row he has stirred up in South Africa, they hate him. At the moment, this boy is one of the most prominent people in the House of Commons, and scarcely one of the older members shows much more ability in catching the ear of the House or in making what might be called distinctly "smart" speeches. His fertility, too, is wonderful.

We are just sending out the invitations for the first big dinner after the expected arrival of your daughter and her husband. With a fair voyage they ought to reach here Saturday night—possibly in time to let me take them out in the motor car to Wrest Park for a quiet Sunday. The dinner comes on Tuesday. The King will come, probably accompanied by Major Holford as his Equerry. After dinner there are to be about fifty or sixty people invited to come in for some music. Eames is to come over from Paris to sing, and there will be music by Caruso and others. When I was in Rome I happened to see a fine spread eagle, carved in marble, which took my fancy; and I bought it really for the grounds at Ophir Hall. After getting it here, however, it suddenly struck me that I could mount it over the porte-cochere of Dorchester House, so that our noble bird would seem to be just poising his wings for a flight down Park Lane and across Hyde Park. So I have set the masons to work to put a proper pedestal for it on the balcony above the porte-cochere, and trust to have the fellow spreading his wings, six feet or more from tip to tip, over Mrs. Longworth when she arrives.

There was an Indian prince in London early this summer, the Gaekwar of Baroda, who wanted to observe the American eagle in his native element. He was a very up-to-date prince, extremely keen about public institutions, governmental methods, inventions, and so on. He was bent upon visiting, among other things, the electrical works at Niagara Falls. Reid talked over his itinerary with him and gave him a sheaf of introductions. When he got back the Gaekwar offered in return a glimpse of the West as seen through Eastern eyes. "For a long time," he wrote, "I have been thinking of sending you a letter with a short account of my trip to your fine country. Not only the wealthy people but even the poorer classes struck me as being both well informed and patriotic and their whole tone is at once manly and sympathetic—their sympathy with the down-trodden being very great. The women are well educated and of fine physique. Altogether the people and institutions of the United States have created in me a very favorable impression, and I heartily wish them every success. With her vast extent, resources and active civilization, I am quite convinced that America has an even greater future before her and is bound to play a large part in the moulding of the destinies of the world. No one could grudge her this position should she continue to maintain her present high ideals of liberty. I was much impressed with her great Ministers from the President downward —all of them men of great ability and scholarship."

The Gaekwar was bland and amiable, if not precisely original. If he had travelled to Dundee when the American ambassador delivered his Armitstead lecture there he might have noted in the speech a veiled intimation that the "great Ministers" to whom he alluded were just then interesting themselves in one of the crucial problems of the East. On accepting the freedom of the city, Reid had occasion to touch upon this question. They were lectured a good deal, he said, about the tyranny of habit, the whiskey habit, the tobacco habit, and the opium habit; and this reminded him that they were copartners in the opium habit. Britain had a corner in her Eastern possessions where they grew opium, and the United States had an Eastern corner where they consumed opium. Some fine day they might, let them hope, put their heads together and somehow mitigate that habit. In this guarded way he referred to negotiations which he had already begun at the Foreign Office. Our government was supplied with impressive data on the opium traffic when the committee on the subject appointed by the Philippine Commission made its report. In September, 1906, a Chinese imperial decree had denounced opium as responsible for "the poverty and weakness that for the past few decades have been daily increasing amongst us," and the United States was resolved to take drastic measures for the correction of its own relation to an indefensible trade. Reid saw Sir Edward Grey about a suggestion from Secretary Root of the issuance of an invitation by the United States to China to join it, together with Great Britain, France, Holland, and Japan, in a common investigation of the opium question. It was important to ascertain the British view on this project in advance of any general overture to the other Powers. The American ambassador explained that we were "much concerned" in this question, and that "it was desired to come to a decision as to whether the consequences of the opium habit were not such that civilized powers should do what they could to put a stop to them." He energetically urged all the points that could be brought to bear. Sir Edward was sympathetic and promised to consult his colleagues. On a later occasion he stated the attitude of the ministry as one of ready concurrence in the proposed conference, on the understanding that the other countries named also agreed to it, and that the growth of, and trade in, Chinese as well as India opium should be considered. The path was thus broken for the organization of the international meeting held at Shanghai in February, 1909.

In the preparations for the second Peace Conference at The Hague, it fell to the American ambassador to obtain the co-operation of the British Foreign Office in changing the date first fixed by the Czar. That potentate had contemplated the opening of the meeting in July. With the Geneva Red Cross Convention on hand, and the Pan-American conferences scheduled to assemble at Rio de Janeiro, Secretary Root advised delay. England acquiesced and so did Russia, and though the disorders and massacres in that country threw a kind of ironic light on all these humane negotiations, they went forward without remission. Reid's conversations at the Foreign Office brought out the difficulties always hedging a pacific enterprise. Sir Edward could assure him that the British delegates would be instructed cordially to support the proposal for the reduction or limitation of armaments in which Secretary Root was then ready to take the initiative. He was aware, though, that there would be two Powers which would be difficult on the question, France and Germany. He thought France would wish to follow the line taken by her historic enemy. Germany, in his opinion, held the key of the situation. Secretary Root was well aware of the obstacles in the way, but there is a noble statesmanship expressed in a comment of his to Reid on one of the subjects mooted, that of limiting the collection of public debts to private persons. "If we are right," he said, "it is better to press the subject and endure many defeats in the hope of ultimate success rather than remain silent."

The President, of course, was intensely interested. That he was also, in his characteristic way, profoundly practical in his view of the matter, this letter shows:

Oyster Bay,
New York
August 7, 1906.

My dear Reid:

I have received your letter of July 27th. I am glad that the British Government seems likely to take the same ground that we do in the Hague Conference. I enclose you copy of a letter to Carnegie. As he speaks very freely to Grey, I think it just as well for you to see this letter and to tell Grey you have seen it. I do not want this new Liberal Government, with which in many matters I have such hearty sympathy, to go to any maudlin extremes at the Hague Conference. It is eminently wise and proper that we should take real steps in advance toward the policy of minimizing the chances of war amongst civilized people, of multiplying the methods and chances of honorably avoiding war in the event of controversy; but we must not grow sentimental and commit some Jefferson-Bryan-like piece of idiotic folly such as would be entailed if the free people that have free governments put themselves at a hopeless disadvantage compared with military despotisms and military barbarisms. I should like to see the British Navy kept at its present size but only on condition that the Continental and Japanese Navies are not built up. I do not wish to see it relatively weaker to them than is now the case. As regards our own Navy, I believe in number of units it is now as large as it need be, and I should advocate merely the substitution of efficient for inefficient units. This would mean allowing for about one new battleship a year, and of course now and then for a cruiser, collier, or a few torpedo-boat destroyers.

Sincerely yours, Theodore Roosevelt.

Early in December Reid sailed home for Christmas, as he had done the holiday season before, and this time even in greater need of rest. In referring to matters like the fisheries dispute, Algeciras, and the Hague conference, I have touched only upon salient incidents in his official year. A multitude of interests made that extremely arduous. Colonel Watterson once printed some reflections on ambassadorial life, cordial and considerate where our representative in London was concerned—he was never anything else in their association of thirty odd years—but not altogether favorable on the subject at large. With Reid's remarks to him, in rejoinder, I may appropriately close this chapter:

I think your view of the diplomatic service would be more accurate and useful if you had reflected more on the inside view of it, and if, besides, you hadn't lost sight of our history in your impatience with some jack-in-office, who may naturally enough have disgusted you, and had not, when in that mood, written with your eye on an audience always ready to respond to the sort of slashing attack you make.

If you sat in my office for half an hour and ran your eye over the files showing the questions that suddenly come up and can be dealt with, not by special commissions and not by cabled despatches, but only by telling your representative to find out how the land lies on certain subjects, and then to move according to his judgment of the local conditions with reference to the end you desire—after looking over even a brief record of this sort of thing you would realize how impracticable is this notion of dispensing with diplomatic representatives to which you have lent the great influence of your name and brilliant work.

People say the cable has done away with the necessity for them—that mere despatches between our State Department and the various Foreign Offices can do everything. But a despatch can't carry any more than a letter used to, in the days when letters were our quickest mode of communication. If, then, the interests of a Government of eighty millions of people can be properly and entirely managed from the Home Office by cable despatches, why couldn't the interests of the three millions in 1776 have been managed just as well by letters? What was the use of sending Benjamin Franklin over and Thomas Jefferson, and the rest of our early diplomats? The cable merely gives us the quickest transmission at the present day; the letter gave us the quickest transmission at that day, and if need be, that could be sent by a special post-bag as well as by Benjamin Franklin. If the diplomatic service is useless now it was equally useless then, and we have persisted in a costly folly for a century and a third. If, on the other hand, the system has had a public service to do, how can it be thought patriotic to bring it into ridicule and contempt?

CHAPTER XVIII

A DIPLOMAT'S CIRCLE

In the letter to Colonel Watterson which terminates the preceding chapter cable communication is put clearly in its right place, as a means, merely, of accelerating international negotiations. These are benefited, obviously, by any convenience which increases their pace. Yet the *tempo* of diplomacy remains what it has always been, the *tempo* of conversation. I have turned over innumerable state documents as I have followed the activities of the American ambassador in London, but their dry official phrases yield only part of the history of his work. Quite as rich a part, if not indeed a richer one, is to be found in the record of personal contacts, of that interplay of friendly discussion without which the solution of a given problem is, to tell the truth, impossible. The point involved is not as trite as it might seem. Even John Bigelow, who had been a minister of the United States himself, was disposed to think that the telegraph minimized a diplomat's labors, overlooking the fact that the reduction of time in the transmission of instructions made no difference at all in the responsibility involved in carrying them out. "At this moment," Reid wrote him, "I have instructions requiring the use of all arguments and influence I can bring to bear on matters ranging from Canada to China, Russia and Japan, and in fact pretty much over the habitable globe." In the stout volumes of "The Foreign Relations of the United States" one may trace the results of our diplomatic service throughout the world—and still miss the atmosphere in which those results were achieved.

Of the springs of "argument and influence" significant to Reid at the period of which I write there was one transcending all the rest in freshness and force. President Roosevelt was an incomparable chief. He had a gift for the initiative if ever a man had it and I remember a conversation with him in which he told me with the utmost frankness how he had been, upon occasion, his own State Department. But, "instructions" having been once given, through the usual official channels, he delighted in the conversation which I have noted as so important in diplomatic exchanges and liked it only the more when it took an unconventional turn. His letters to Reid are true talk, so spontaneous, so free, that they seemed to annihilate the distance between him and the ambassador. He hated circumlocution. When he wished to appraise the mentality of a certain functionary who had crossed his path he wasn't in the least mealy-mouthed about it. He described the unfortunate man as having a mind of "eight guinea-pig power." And the directness which filled his correspondence with arresting characterizations of men and things told even more heavily in the enunciation of high policies. In all international matters, dealing with Roosevelt, the American ambassador knew in a very full, inspiriting sense just where the United States stood, and the circumstance was reflected in his diplomatic surroundings. The President's name and the Kaiser's were sometimes associated in London, because of the ebullient personality characteristic of both men; but Reid noted the difference between the two observed by his colleagues: "They both talk unconventionally, but your President always makes good." All England recognized this difference. When Roosevelt's administration was drawing to a close and his African hunting plans were taking shape, Reid happened to fall into conversation with the foreign minister over the visit of M. Fallières, which was good-naturedly but not enthusiastically received. "Now if your President would come," said Sir Edward Grey, "London would grow wild. There is no man anywhere in the world who has such a hold on the imagination and admiration of our people."

It was with Sir Edward Grey, of course, that the American ambassador came most in contact over diplomatic questions, but I may appropriately touch here upon his relations with King Edward VII. Their acquaintance dated from the time of the great Queen's jubilee, and when it was renewed in 1905 it developed into a warm friendship. They met frequently on ceremonial occasions, and on country-house visits where there were more opportunities for informal talk. Reid's impressions, scattered through his letters, uniformly illustrate the King's devotion to business and his sound statesmanship. He saw how rigidly the line was drawn between royal and governmental action. When the King, on one of his sojourns at Marienbad, gave interviews to Clemenceau and Izvolski, without the participation of his foreign minister or the permanent undersecretary usually assigned to duty on such occasions, there were immediately critical whisperings in London. But this jealousy for parliamentary prerogative left the King plenty of margin for effective service. In a letter of Reid's to the President, written on his return from his Christmas at home in 1906, he speaks of the importance of our being as cordial with the King as with the Kaiser, and adds: "The more you know of him the better I am sure you will like him, and the more you will come to the prevalent English and in fact European belief that he is the greatest mainstay of peace in Europe." If his influence upon public and especially political opinion could be exercised only indirectly it nevertheless had its force. Alluding to some criticism the King had passed upon a recent speech by one of the leading men in the House of Lords, Reid wrote to the President: "Nobody ever ventures to repeat remarks like this in London, but, nevertheless, the spirit of them oozes out imperceptibly and has an extraordinary effect on the opinion of society."

There was an interesting case of this "oozing" in 1908, when the Kaiser's weakness for seeing his notions in print resulted in the famous interview in the London "Telegraph" and a consequent tempest. Reid observed to the President that if Wilhelm had sat up nights for a month to devise the best way of discrediting himself at home and abroad, he could not have hit upon a more successful method. "Doubtless it will blow over, like the Kruger telegram, the Tweedmouth letter and all the rest. In the language of the southern negro, commenting on his son's experience with the hind legs of a mule: 'Bill'll never be so handsome again but he'll know a heap sight more.'" Meanwhile Reid expected that English opinion on the subject would be formed more or less in exalted quarters, and when these promptly began to "ooze" he wrote to the President as follows from Wrest:

Among my guests down here this week were several who had been passing a good deal of time in various house parties for or by the King during the previous fortnight. Their whispers about his attitude confirmed the opinions I formed during the two or three days I spent with him in a house party three weeks ago. He was not then mourning particularly over the fact that his head-strong nephew was beginning to be entangled in the results from his own indiscretions. But the retention of Bülow and the subsequent incidents have occurred since I saw him. From the talk of my guests, it was plain that he views the explanations in the Reichstag with utter incredulity. He regarded the alleged English gentlemen who put together their recollections of the Emperor's talk and so made up the famous interview as utterly mythical. And the elaborate story about how the interview passed from Chancellor to Foreign Minister, and from Foreign Minister to *Locum Tenens*, and thence, duly countersigned, to the office of the "Daily Telegraph," as equally mythical. In short, the Court belief at least, whether the King avows it or not, is obviously that the Emperor wrote the interview himself, sent it "off his own bat," and then, when the hubbub arose, compelled Bülow and the rest to invent such an explanation as they thought would be accepted by the Reichstag! They may be all wrong in this; but after all they know the Emperor pretty well, these English.

Of earlier origin, but forming a suitable match for this episode, is another "scrap of paper," what purported to be an extremely free-spoken interview with the German Emperor, printed in a Manchester journal at a time when the restless monarch was actually visiting on English soil. Reid thus recorded the occurrence:

> The interview was promptly repudiated and thereupon the paper denounced the repudiation and declared the interview in question had actually been revised by the German Ambassador at Highcliffe —where, as you know, the Emperor is staying. There came a second Reuter contradiction from the German Embassy, admitting the revision, but denying that the interview was with the Emperor. Thereupon the Manchester paper came back again with a facsimile of portions of the interview, with the interlineations and corrections made by the Ambassador, apparently in his own handwriting, and with statements of what the Councillor of the Embassy, Herr von Stumm, had said to the correspondent about it. Von Stumm happened to be staying down here over the week-end with a small shooting party. Out in the woods in the middle of the afternoon he was pursued by a messenger boy on a bicycle with a telegram on receipt of which his countenance fell, while he seemed to take little further interest in the pheasants. Soon after we got back in the evening he was enquiring about trains up to London, and presently he explained to me that he had been summoned back on account of this mess, and that evidently it was a situation in which he had to go as promptly as possible. I was sorry for the poor fellow—especially as I am afraid he will be made a scape-goat. The "Times" comments on it as an illustration of the German methods of managing their press bureau; and it does remind one of Bismarck's old talk about the reptile press.

The predicament of the hapless Von Stumm brings him a little more tangibly into the picture than is usually the case with the American ambassador's colleagues. They figure rather impersonally in his correspondence as "the Italian," or "the German," in the idiom of the diplomatic corps. But the circle embraced many warm friends. Conspicuous among them was "the Spaniard," Villa-Urriuta, well met again in London after their encounters over the peace table at Paris in 1898. Metternich was Germany's representative and Benckendorf Russia's. The dean of the ambassadors was the Frenchman, Paul Cambon, and his rank among the ministers was held by M. de Bille, of Denmark, who, as coming from Queen Alexandra's native country, enjoyed a peculiarly prominent position. Reid glances at the solidarity of the diplomats in a letter to the President on a dinner given by the Chinese ambassador. The corps had accepted invitations to this when the government sent out cards for a dinner to be given on the same evening for the athletes and committees at the Olympic Games. The ambassadors were in a quandary, but only for a moment. "The conflict between the previous engagement with the Chinaman and this invitation in behalf of the Government was submitted to Cambon, who ruled that if it had been an invitation from the King, we would have been obliged to throw the Chinaman over, but as it was only an invitation from one Minister, in behalf of the Government, the previous acceptance of our colleague's invitation in the name of the Emperor could not be thrown over without offense." Apropos of these mysteries of etiquette, I may allude to a phase of them which the President brought up when he was planning his hunting trip and the travels through the European capitals which he soon saw were bound to follow. "I want to avoid," he wrote to the American ambassador, "the frightful nuisance of big banquets or other formal entertainments. My idea, if it meets with your approval, is that I should take with me the dress uniform of a colonel of United States cavalry (which I am entitled to wear as an ex-Colonel of the Spanish War—not a paper colonel either, but one who saw service). Then if I have to appear at some function I could wear this, and if it was felt that in a military country like Germany or Italy they would like to see me in uniform when I called on the sovereign I could wear it. But I should hope to avoid wearing it and that I could go in civilian costume."

Reid reassured him. There wouldn't be the least harm in bringing the uniform, but Roosevelt would probably have no occasion for taking it out of his trunk. At Buckingham Palace, "you would go dressed exactly as you would be in the afternoon in Washington." Winding up the subject, he said: "Even if you should want to go to a Levee or a Court, you would wear exactly the same evening dress already described; but there also you would find yourself made the most conspicuous person in the room, since everybody else would be in uniform. As Choate once remarked to me, when we were standing together in the line of Ambassadors formed upon the left of the King and supporting him, 'At a Court this republican simplicity dodge of ours about "plain clothes" is the most impertinent piece of swagger in the world. Under pretense of making our Ambassadors modest and inconspicuous we single them out from everybody else in a room with a thousand people, and not one human being in the room fails to notice the conspicuous character of their dress or to know that they are the modest and retiring American Ambassadors!' Personally, I don't dislike it in the least; but there never was a case where demagogues so thoroughly defeated their own desires."

At the American Embassy, where republicanism functioned in its own atmosphere, untrammelled by considerations of court formulas, I have hitherto stressed the transaction of government business. Reid made it also a stronghold for the interests of his countrymen travelling abroad. He was fortunate in his staff. His first secretary, when he came to London, Mr. John Ridgeley Carter, was one of the most distinguished and efficient of the younger men in the service, and from a succession of accomplished private secretaries and other figures in the embassy personnel Reid received indispensable help in endless matters of detail. Of detail, infinite detail, the business of an American ambassador is all compact, and without the tactful, sympathetic, and really devoted work of Delancey Jay, Sheldon Whitehouse, Elliot Bacon, Craig Wadsworth, Lydig Hoyt, Grant Smith, and others, Reid would have been overwhelmed. He was deeply appreciative of all that was done for him by the members of his "official family," a fact to which he was wont to make warm allusion. The offices were the scene of much hard work for everybody, lightened not infrequently by amusing episodes. There is no place in the world like an American embassy for the accumulation of things incredible. Reid chuckled over some of the "curios," as he called them, that came his way. When a certain minor European throne was the subject of discussion in the chancelleries one American visitor turned up having at hand an excellent occupant for it, and seeking advice as to approaching the King of England on the subject. Another incident is thus described in a letter to the President:

You may be interested in knowing that I have warded off—as far as I could—the offer of some brand new territory and responsibilities for the United States. Some years ago Great Britain found her authority on the Mosquito Coast of Nicaragua chiefly a nuisance and contrived to land her control over the Mosquito Indians in the lap of Nicaragua. Since then the Indians think they have been badly treated by the Nicaraguans and have been appealing to Great

Britain for protection or intervention, and have, I believe, got a little money out of them, at least for the expense of delegations here. They were definitely "turned down" however a few weeks ago. Whereupon they appeared solemnly at our Embassy offices and sought an interview with me to tender the sovereignty of their country through me to the United States! I avoided seeing them at the time, but this only brought on me a formal letter from their agent, offering absolute sovereignty over the Mosquito Territory to the United States in return for protection by us and asking for an interview in which the chiefs of the tribes wished to make the tender in person and give any further evidence that might be required of their authority. They enclosed various documents with their letter to substantiate their right to represent the tribe and their good faith. It seemed to me best to decline any interview with them at all, and to say that if they were bent on making such a proposition it should be presented directly to the Government through the Secretary of State at Washington. I sent, therefore, the enclosed letter signed by my private secretary. To this the agent replies that he proposes forthwith to carry out my suggestion! So there you are.

If only some of the other visitors at the embassy could have been as easily placated! It sometimes seemed to the secretaries that the universal American desire was to listen to debates in the House of Commons. A man would calmly send in a note stating that he had just arrived, was leaving for the Continent in two days, and meantime would like to spend that afternoon or the following one at the House. He would therefore want tickets for himself, his wife, his son and daughter, and for John Jones, whose acquaintance he had made on the steamer, and whose wife, son, and daughter also wished to join the party. It then became necessary to explain to him, first, that the House of Commons furnished the embassy with no tickets at all for ladies; next, that it furnished the embassy only two tickets per day (just double what it furnished any other embassy), and next, that previous applicants, taking time by the forelock, had already asked for and been promised tickets for every day when the House would be in session for the ensuing fortnight or three weeks! By the time all this was made plain the disappointed applicant would want to know what a United States ambassador was sent over to London for, anyway. The requests of women for presentation at court and for invitations to the royal enclosure at Ascot or to court balls were always greatly in excess of the number of such privileges to which every embassy is limited, and sometimes it was next to impossible to convince a resolute lady that denial of her wishes had nothing personal about it. Nor did presentation at court always suffice to satisfy ambition. Regardless of the fact that it carried no right to subsequent invitations, one embodiment of offended majesty addressed to the secretary who had taken special charge of her interests this concise note: "I am at a loss to understand why no invitation was sent for the Court Ball of next Tuesday. Having been presented, one is eligible. I am not pleased."

But first and last the American Embassy succeeded in pleasing a myriad of Americans, and always when the Fourth of July came round they flocked to the reception at Dorchester House in thousands. On innumerable occasions through the year the ambassador's countrymen lunched and dined there or at Wrest, a broad stream of Americans, his own old private friends and a larger host of others. Through their hospitality, as well as through the routine processes of the embassy, the Reids made the latter truly a rallying-ground for travellers from home. At the offices, as I have said, the ambassador had a staff which greatly aided him, and there were matters, too, in which he received invaluable co-operation from the American Society in London, headed by Mr. A. T. Van Duser. It was one of Reid's pleasantest duties to speak at the Fourth of July and Thanksgiving Day dinners organized by this body. But just in tasks of this sort his burdens were heavy. Anthony Hope Hawkins, in proposing his health at a public banquet, once said that the American ambassador was the hardest worked man in England, and Reid was fain to believe that the novelist wasn't so far wrong. Certainly the American ambassador was immeasurably the hardest worked man in the diplomatic corps. In July, 1907, he gives the President this sketch of some of his lighter obligations:

Within a week I have unveiled a tablet to the memory of the second President of Harvard at Ware (where John Gilpin dined, you will remember, while his wife dined at Edmonton), and made a serious little speech to a large congregation in the course of the religious exercises which accompanied the unveiling; have attended the dedication of a tablet to the memory of John Davenport, founder of New Haven, Connecticut, an early benefactor of both Yale and Harvard, and progenitor of all the Davenports in America; have made a little speech in the midst of the religious service at Southwark Cathedral, and turned over in behalf of Harvard graduates the Harvard Memorial Chapel to the Cathedral authorities; have spoken very briefly in response to a toast in your honor at the luncheon given by Sir George Chubb for the Duke of Connaught's Soldiers' and Sailors' Home, and have acted on a committee of reception for the Duke and Duchess themselves at the opening of an extension to the Home. Meanwhile, I have made the proposal for arbitration in the Newfoundland business and discussed it on two occasions with the Minister of Foreign Affairs, have had revived their proposal for reciprocity, giving the reductions on art authorized by Section 3 of the Tariff Act in return for free commercial samples, and have discovered two or three things in the form which they wanted signed that we have never agreed to and were obviously to our disadvantage, and have had the document sent back to the Board of Trade in accordance with our agreement.

He deprecated what he called "this perpetual speaking," but found it hard to escape from "the bondage of the fatal precedents." And there were some occasions which he found not unwelcome. One of them, for example, was that offered by the opening of the John Bright Memorial School at Llandudno in the fall of

1907. He remembered Bright's services to us in the Civil War and the shabby incident in Congress which was one of our returns to him for it. He was glad to pay the great Englishman his tribute. He enjoyed, too, the dinner of the Titmarsh Club, at which he was asked to speak on Thackeray in America. He spoke with a gusto which led the editor of "Everyman's Library" to extract from him a version of his address to use as a preface in the edition of "Vanity Fair" printed in that series. It was with peculiar interest that he spoke before the Luton Chamber of Commerce, describing the destruction of San Francisco by earthquake and fire and the rapid restoration of the city. But the episode of this period which most strongly appealed to him, I think, came when he went to Bath in the autumn of 1908 for the unveiling of a tablet on Edmund Burke's old residence there, and delivered an address on Burke as America's foremost friend in Great Britain. The paper may be found in the second volume of his "American and English Studies," a brief but searching essay in historical analysis and portraiture. A sentence in his reply to a letter about it from the Reverend Edward Everett Hale indicates how early his acquaintance with the subject had begun. "Like you," he said, "I was brought up on extracts from Burke, which we had to declaim, and I have been rather surprised to find how apparently slight is the acquaintance of the present generation with his work." I may cite a passage on that work especially illustrative of Reid's appreciation of the Englishman's service to ourselves:

No other man in England, hardly one even in America, saw quite so clearly as Edmund Burke that after an unwise ministry had forced the colonists into a long war in defence of the English principle of no taxation without representation, the only possible outcome of the war by which the real England could succeed was an

American victory. Yet no other deprecated the struggle so much; no other at the outset more sincerely desired to preserve the authority of Parliament and the just rights of the crown. He even admitted the precedents, both in Great Britain and in the colonies, for taxation without representation. But when once the right was determinedly challenged, he frankly recognized that, as he put it in lawyer-like phrase, "the assertion of the title would be the loss of the suit." While there was still a chance to draw back he pleaded with the ministry and with Parliament: "It is our business to rule, not to wrangle. It is poor compensation to triumph in a dispute whilst we lose an empire." "Your ancestors," he exclaimed, "did at length open their eyes to the ill-husbandry of injustice. They found that the tyranny of a free people could of all tyrannies the least be endured." And then he reminded the ministry that, while reciting the entire and perfect authority of the crown, its predecessors had nevertheless, with the approval of the crown, given successively to various English communities and also to the Welsh all the rights and privileges of English subjects. "Are not the colonists," he demanded, "as much Englishmen as the Welsh?" By such steps he came to regard the struggle as not a rebellion, but a civil war, in which Englishmen in the colonies fought for old English rights, and in gaining these rights for themselves made them henceforth forever secure for England, too.

In this speech the American ambassador was very frank and he says, in a letter to Senator Lodge, "the thing which most struck and interested me there—as it has struck me several times before—is the singular amiability and tolerance with which the British public of to-day receives sweeping condemnation of the general course of their Government and people before and during the Revolutionary War. I have always shrunk a little from treating such questions; but when specifically invited to do so, have always felt that it was better not to 'shy' at them." The subject is pursued in another letter to Mr. Root, from which I must quote at greater length:

As to your question whether Burke is really appreciated in Great Britain as fully as in the United States, I think I should answer, first, that I have some doubt as to the vivid nature of his appreciation in either country, excepting among literary men, and, secondly, that when his merits are recalled, I believe there is a much quicker response in America than here.

I doubt if even after this lapse of time the English mind generally has forgiven Burke for being an Irishman, or, in spite of his own Protestantism, for his frank efforts in a legislative way to befriend the Roman Catholic religion of his mother and of his native land. In addition to that he was what they were accustomed in those days to consider an Irish adventurer; and they did not quite forgive him for his obvious intellectual superiority to the representatives of Great English houses, who then controlled English politics. Besides, they refused to see how he could afford such a place as Beaconsfield, even after his inheritance and the gifts from Lord Rockingham were explained; and, while they could shut their eyes against Pitt's and Fox's extravagances and debts, they could never forgive the Irish adventurer for the presumption of having similar, though smaller, debts. Of course this is mainly true as to the attitude of his contemporaries and of the generation that immediately succeeded them. But I have fancied that the same note could be felt in the discussions about him which sprang up after the Bath ceremonial, as well as in the frequent remarks made to me on the subject by various Englishmen.

The life of a diplomat as constantly occupied as Whitelaw Reid was must have proved arduous for even a younger man. It was arduous for him. But the systematic regimen he followed, and his always buoyant will, kept him abreast of his work. In October, 1907, he had an invitation from his old friend Colonel A. K. McClure to the celebration of that gentleman's eighty-first birthday. In the course of his reply he said: "I shall be turning the seventieth mile stone on next Sunday. There was a time when I thought this was about the limit of old age; now it seems to me just about the beginning of some little real fitness for the duties of active life. The curious thing about it is that, while I can't shut my eyes to the fact that I trace in myself some signs of advancing years, I never did my work easier or seemed to myself to be more capable of doing it than at present." A great source of rest and recuperation was his home in the country. The library at Wrest was by itself a well-spring of repose, full of rare old editions, steeped, as the whole estate was, in memories of an historic past. A modern souvenir of the place came to him from Trevelyan. "I should like immensely some day," he writes, "to see you and Mrs. Whitelaw Reid at Wrest, and to renew my recollections of 1864–5. I shot a woodcock across the nose of William the Third in the ornamental garden; and there is a little room—I think on the opposite side of the hall from the dining room or breakfast room—where I had the most curious talk, almost a dramatic scene, with Mr. Disraeli." But most of the Wrest stories go further back. Rosebery, after one of his visits, writes to the ambassador, saying: "You had either forgotten, or concealed from me, at Wrest, that Henry Duke of Kent, to whose honor everything at Wrest seems to tend, was known in his life time as 'the Bug,' from his extreme dirtiness, as you will see in Pope's Imitations of Horace! I must break this gently to Lucas." The allusion follows:

"Barnard in spirit, sense and truth abounds;
Pray then, what wants he? Fourscore thousand pounds;
A pension, or such harness for a slave
As Bug now has, and Dorimant would have."

They had some diverting colloquies on this quaint subject. Reid looked it up in the only edition of Pope, that of 1806, which was on the shelves at Wrest. In this, by good luck for any reader favorable to the house of Kent, a note by Warton confessed ignorance of the person aimed at in the poet's satire. "Lucas is armed in his own library, you see," wrote Reid to Rosebery, "and if you break it to him, I am afraid you'll have to do it more than gently, to make him lose faith in his ducal ancestor." Rosebery responded by sending him the latest edition of Pope, containing all the evidence that he really meant to castigate the Duke of Kent for his uncleanliness and other disagreeable qualities and that the name of "the Bug" had been applied to him by Swift, in the correspondence of the Duke of Marlborough, and in Lord Dartmouth's notes on Bishop Burnet. Swift's lines were particularly bitter. The Duke of Kent died on the 5th of June, 1740, and in 1741 Swift wrote some verses on the new Knights of the Garter, in which these lines appear:

> "That short bit of riband, for men never meant,
> May serve little Portland that served little Kent.
> Though stained . . . by nasty old Bug,
> What tied an old monkey may hold a young pug."

Reid cheerfully acknowledged the evidence. "No; you didn't disturb my enjoyment of the Duke of Kent a particle," he said. "To me, he is the man who had the wit to employ Lenôtre, and the luck to have heirs who didn't spoil the work. The note is most interesting, and I suppose conclusive as to Pope's meaning. Whether the decent looking old Duke deserved it is another question. I wouldn't condemn a skunk on Marlborough's testimony, or on that of Her Grace's correspondence; nor would one accept Swift as final. But Dartmouth's manuscript notes in Burnet's History I suppose to be another sort of thing. I spent a whole Sunday once poring over them, and found many curious stories—about the youth of William of Orange for example—which haven't got into print, but didn't stumble on this."

It was on the occasion of this visit, which started their researches into the history of "the Bug," that Reid describes Rosebery as in great form, in fine health and spirits, and very sanguine over the labors of his committee on the changes which the House of Lords was preparing to work in its own body. He wouldn't go out with the guns. He said that he had reached that time of life when he felt that his shooting was better done at home and with few witnesses. In Reid's letters to Roosevelt, who was always interested in matters of sport, the shooting-parties at Wrest, and their bags, are often mentioned. One story I reproduce as unique. It relates to a party in November, 1907, when Prince Arthur of Connaught was among the guests:

The total of pheasants should have been 1294. It was not, for a reason which the old gamekeeper pronounced to be absolutely unprecedented. There were eight guns in the line, and advancing upon them were forty beaters driving up the game. Just as the beaters had nearly reached the guns, the Prince shot a pheasant which dropped almost at his feet. At that instant and in full view of the forty-eight pairs of eyes, a splendid, well-fed fox dashed up, caught the still fluttering pheasant in his jaws, and was off like an arrow. The Prince's exclamation was: "What infernal cheek!" The amused remark among several of those about him was: "That's lèse majesté! If we were in Germany, the fox would have a hard time of it." Even in America, I fancy that some of us would have been tempted to give him the benefit of an undischarged barrel. But not a gun was lifted, and evidently every Englishman thought that the fox was within his rights.

The French ambassador, M. Cambon, was among the witnesses of this curious occurrence, a sportsman, like the rest. His presence, however, recalls us for a moment to diplomacy, to the commingling of political and social threads characteristic of English country-house life. These gatherings at Wrest, from which one catches the whir of pheasants and the sound of guns, constantly echo, also, with the conversation of public men on matters of moment—the fate of measures pending in the House, the rise and fall of party reputations, the affairs of the world everywhere. On one occasion the prevailing informality was interrupted by a ceremonious observance through which the King charmingly signalized his good-will for the United States by a courtesy which established a new precedent. The 27th of October, Whitelaw Reid's birthday, was likewise the birthday of the President. In 1907 the King intimated in advance a desire that his congratulations to Mr. Roosevelt should be personally presented to the American ambassador by the master of ceremonies, a thing which had never been done before. Accordingly, the private celebration at Wrest was transformed into something like a diplomatic function. There was a very formal call paid by the Honorable Arthur Walsh, in the morning, with a little speech and a reply, both of which were duly cabled to the White House. The German ambassador was there, and in view of what we have seen of the Kaiser's attitude toward the United States, maintained with a jealous eye on England, one can extract a little humor from speculation on Count Metternich's thoughts. In the course of his toast Reid took account of them, and by a friendly allusion sought to allay the possible emotions of his German friend, judiciously ignoring Germany's rôle in the Hague conference, then recently concluded.

Before adverting to The Hague and similar subjects I must add to this chapter on the more intimate side of the life of the Reids in England some reference to the marriage of their daughter to John Ward, son of the late Earl of Dudley. He had served in South Africa on the staff of Lord Roberts, and that famous soldier spoke highly of him as an officer and as a man. He was occupied there in the supervision at headquarters of the despatches sent by army correspondents from the field, and the ambassador was charmed by the tribute paid him by the most distinguished member of that corps. Soon after the engagement was announced he met Rudyard Kipling, and the author said: "Your future son-in-law isn't half a bad sort, in spite of his having censored my despatches." Soldiers and civilians spoke well of Ward when he returned to England. He entered, then, the War Department, but during his stay there was sent for by King Edward to be his equerry. The King and Queen were present when the wedding took place in the Chapel Royal on June 23d, 1908. It was difficult for the Reids to contemplate a future with their daughter separated from them by the sea; but there was too much of genuine happiness in the event, too sure a conviction of its lasting significance, for this thought to weigh heavily.

It was in 1908 that Ogden Reid gave them another cause for congratulation in beginning the service on the staff of The Tribune which was to end in his establishment in the editorship. The ambassador watched this launching of his son's fortunes with an interest that is often disclosed in letters to his friends. It was always in his mind, hoped for, planned for, and encouraged with delight. His friends in turn gave him pleasure when they touched upon a subject so dear to his heart. I may cite one of these communications:

New York
November 18, 1908.

DEAR MR. REID:

When I was talking to Mr. Mills last evening he seemed so gratified at my observations on your son that I feel there can be no harm in writing and telling you my impressions of the young man's work here. At my first encounter with him neither my secretary nor I had any notion that he was your son and we were much pleased with the very conscientious way in which he set about interviewing me. Afterwards we found out by accident who he was and I naturally observed him at public meetings and other places to which I went.

I must say that I think you have in young Mr. Reid the material for a very good journalist and a conscientious one. I was only sorry that I could not see more of him. I am so fond of my profession that it delighted me to see his keenness.

Yours sincerely, NORTHCLIFFE.

Reid rejoiced as he saw his son following the advice which he had himself received from an old hand at the outset of his own journalistic career: "If anybody wants to succeed he must do whatever work he can get to do, and do it better than it has been done. Report anything they set you at and do your very best every time." In the glimpse into Ogden Reid's apprenticeship that the English editor gave him he read one more augury of the continuance, after he had gone, of that policy for the paper to which he had alluded in writing to Roosevelt on the eve of taking up his embassy. "I have long looked upon my ownership of The Tribune as a sort of trust," he had then said. His son's thoroughness pointed to the same spirit.

CHAPTER XIX

A TROUBLE-MAKING KAISER

When the American ambassador got back to London after the Christmas of 1906, in time for the opening of Parliament, he found elements in the air heightening his zest for diplomatic business. Mrs. Reid was extending her visit at home and he wrote to her: "I am afraid we are in for a period of rather more fault-finding in the English press than heretofore. The Conservatives are likely to find it suit their political interests to find fault with the Government about the *modus vivendi* (which has just come up in the Newfoundland Parliament and is likely to here) and in general to accuse the Government of such a desire to keep on good terms with the United States as to be ready to submit to anything. 'Man never is but always to be blest.'" Nor was the *modus vivendi* the only subject productive of atmospheric mutations. In January occurred the earthquake in Jamaica and Governor Swettenham's curious behavior over the American aid promptly rendered by Admiral Davis. When Reid, on the steamer, first heard of the disaster, the news was accompanied by the intimation that our men had only been landed at the request of the authorities, and his natural expectation was of words of appreciation in the English press. Instead, he discovered that in the opinion of a good many commentators we had "butted in" without adequate warrant, unable to conceal our unholy hankering for possession of Jamaica or at least for paramountcy in those waters! Even among the public men he met, whose feeling of surprise and disgust at their own governor was manifest, there was a certain nervousness. They hated to accept the fact that the Swettenham incident had been, in fact, merely ridiculous. It made a queer little flurry, in which the English were as sore as if they had burnt their fingers. "I have never seen them so thoroughly ashamed of anything," said Reid, in one of his letters home. "It isn't an altogether satisfactory mood, however, for it naturally leaves them on the look-out for some occurrence of the same kind on our side which would enable them to let themselves down a little easier. I am afraid they are going to be pretty captious about fisheries and other questions we have on our Northern frontier."

Whatever effect irresponsible agents might have upon public opinion, the American ambassador was sure of a thoroughly open-minded and judicial attitude at the Foreign Office. The Liberals inspired a confidence in that branch of the government which was as wide-spread as in Lansdowne's time. "Sir Edward Grey," said Reid, "is perhaps a little less of the traditional official, but, on the other hand, he has a singularly fresh, strong intellect, and he makes the speech of a broad-minded and thoughtful statesman. Nobody in either party has a word to say against him." He made short work of the Swettenham business on the occasion of Reid's first visit after his return, introducing the subject himself and expressing warm appreciation of the whole attitude of the United States in the matter. With the withdrawal of the governor's unfortunate letter to Admiral Davis a trifling but unpleasant episode easily gave place to more important questions. In Sir Edward Grey's hands these could never be the sport of party politics. At the same time there were bound to be certain links between them and the Liberal programme, and some of the most striking passages in Reid's correspondence with the President carry on the survey of political conditions which was a constant part of his work. It was a congenial diversion. Secretary Root makes this reference to the passages in question: "I have been much interested in your recent letters both to me and to the President, and I took occasion to say to the President that they showed the good results of editorial training in enabling a man to select the matters which really constitute interesting news to write about." I quote some fragments:

May 24th, 1907.

Last autumn it was my impression that nobody in public life had gained more in the British estimation since the opening of this Parliament than Campbell-Bannerman. People generally had not been accustomed to think of him as a personage of first rate or perhaps even of second rate political importance; and everybody was astonished at finding that he was leading with an unexpected authority and vigor. They had all been standing ready to guffaw at his blunders, and were feeling a little cheap at the fact that he kept using his majority relentlessly, and enforcing his purposes with a vigor they hadn't in the least anticipated. It was not possible to sneer at him or to undervalue him.

But since then I fancy we have all been conscious of a relaxation. It would be a little hard to tell why the change, but I don't think I can be mistaken in the belief that there *is* a considerable change in the general public feeling concerning "C.-B." and his government. It certainly has not gained by Mr. Birrell's new Irish bill, by Mr. Asquith's budget, or even by Mr. Haldane's army bill; while the first impression at the close of the Colonial conference is one of a distinct disadvantage to the Government. Some of the Premiers themselves have been almost defiant in the tone they have adopted. It probably does not mean much; but it certainly does not indicate any great substance in any British hold on the Colonies the moment the Colonies fail to get the chief profit from it.

The outburst most noticeable to us is, of course, that of Sir Robert Bond [Premier of Newfoundland]. He has contrived to get a great deal of sympathy for himself and for the colonies. There has been little unfriendly talk toward us and not much that we could complain of concerning the *modus vivendi* of last autumn. But the tone now certainly indicates that we cannot get such a *modus vivendi* again, and that Sir Robert Bond has secured a large amount of sympathy for his little colony on the ground that it was not permitted to regulate its domestic affairs as a self-governing colony should. From one point of view this is quite right; from another it is absurd. It is grotesque to suppose that a long-standing right, which seems unquestionable under an independent treaty between two great powers, can be nullified by a spit-fire little colony of one of them, barely two hundred thousand in number. When, in the course of negotiating the *modus vivendi*, I had occasion to point out that this little colony was deliberately telling the United States it meant to put its local law against our treaty right and call on Great Britain to back it up, the Foreign Office recognized the absurdity of that situation, and we had little difficulty in inducing them to say that for the present at least they would have to suspend such colonial legislation.

July 25th, 1907.

Sir Henry Campbell-Bannerman was asked the other night whether it was true that he was going to be cruel enough to keep Parliament in session until the middle or end of September—in spite of the grouse shooting opening on the 12th of August. "Oh, that is entirely a meteorological question," said the canny Scot. "If the weather clears up, we should probably find it difficult to hold them. If it remains as damp and dismal as it has been, they'll think they might just as well stay here in London and serve their country, since there is not much fun to be had elsewhere."

August 28th, 1907.

Parliament was prorogued to-day, and we shall see nothing of them again until next winter. It has been a session bringing disappointments to nearly everybody. The Liberals are disappointed in having succeeded with but a very small part of the programme they set forth in the King's speech. Mr. Birrell is particularly disappointed in seeing the failure of his Irish bill added to his previous failure on an education bill. The Conservatives are disappointed in finding that after all the session has been productive of a good deal of legislation—rather more than an ordinary session—and that much of what has been done is likely to be fairly well received by the country. But I don't believe that it will be felt that the net result of the session gives the Liberals any considerable gain throughout the country. They are still somewhat under the influence of a natural reaction; and have besides stirred up a great deal of hostility by land measures, disagreements with the Irish, with the Labor leaders, and with the suffragettes. If the other party were better united, this situation might be somewhat threatening. As it is, I don't believe there is much to interfere with their holding power considerably longer.

Few men, either in the Government or in the opposition, have made any great personal gains this season. In the Government it may fairly be said that Sir Edward Grey, John Morley, Mr. Haldane and "Lulu" Harcourt are all stronger than they were; and Winston Churchill has by sheer dint of pertinacity and speaking power conquered a degree of toleration which at the outset was not expected; in fact he has made himself much too important in his party to be quarrelled with. On the other side, both Arthur Balfour and Lord Lansdowne have gained in authority and in the public estimation of them as capable party leaders. Balfour, at any rate, seems stronger in opposition than he did as leader of the House. To have Lansdowne as leader of the House of Lords was thought an experiment, but the experiment has worked so admirably that certainly nobody would dream now of proposing to put anybody else in his place. The other great discovery of the session was the continued personal power of Lord Rosebery. His single speech defeated the Scotch small landholders' bill and was universally talked of, whether by his Liberal associates, on whom he turned so effectively, or by the Conservatives, whom he helped, as a beautiful and telling intellectual display.

Early in 1908 the Liberals were possessed of an overwhelming majority against which the tide nevertheless seemed to be running strongly. "C.-B." was in a critical state of health, and the prospects were that Asquith would soon be coming in in his place. In March the parliamentary waters were tremendously stirred by the famous letter from the Kaiser to Tweedmouth. There was a bad slump in Anglo-German feeling, and it looked for a little while as if the first lord of the admiralty would be driven into retirement. The American ambassador's notes on the subject yield a good picture of British solidarity in the face of an awkward episode. "Nothing but the patriotic feeling of the Opposition," he writes, "and their determined purpose to minimize the incident in Parliament, saved an extremely embarrassing situation. On Saturday night I happened to sit near Lord Lansdowne at dinner. After the ladies had retired he talked with some freedom about the trouble; spoke of it as a patriot would; deplored the tone the 'Times' had adopted; and said that unless something came out in the statement on Monday to make a different course necessary, he should do nothing to embarrass the Government. Later on in the evening I had a similar talk with another member of the late Ministry, Lord Midleton (better known still as St. John Brodrick, late Minister of War), who said he had not talked with Lord Lansdowne, but on his own account expressed with a good deal of emphasis very much the same opinion. Evidently these men and their associates gave the tone to the Parliamentary temper as well as that of the press generally, for before the two Houses met yesterday it was well understood that the Opposition would help the Government out of its situation." There was, nevertheless, a little salt sprinkled over poor Tweedmouth's wounds. When the opposition learned that he had immediately carried the Kaiser's letter to the Foreign Office it saw that there was nothing to do but laugh at him for not having followed Sir Edward Grey's advice and treated it as a private communication. In a grave and even tone Lansdowne remarked that if such letters were not public they should be private, and that this one appeared to have been kept about as private as the "private view" of the pictures at the Royal Academy. In the key of that bland *mot* the incident was closed, not, however, without the development of a feeling that it might have its force in the determination of the next naval estimates.

The American ambassador was struck by the personal misfortune which pursued this Liberal government. It seemed to him enough to attract the attention of the superstitious. Sir Edward Grey tragically lost his wife just as he was entering upon his career at the Foreign Office. Lady Campbell-Bannerman's invalidism became more pronounced almost in the moment of her husband's rise to the premiership. As Lloyd George was taking the first steps in his phenomenal capture of British confidence, the death of his eldest daughter occurred. "Lulu" Harcourt's activities were for a time checked by an alarming illness in his family. "C.-B." himself collapsed at the zenith of his ministerial success. He made a brave struggle for recovery, put in a few rather perfunctory appearances in the House, went off to Biarritz to recuperate, and came back for another attempt at his duties, only beginning thereupon a last gallant fight for life—while his elder brother was lying in similar case across the border. As for the man who was marked to be his successor, Reid makes this note:

> Next comes poor Asquith—a man they speak of as having fewer friends than "C.-B.," who nevertheless one can't help admiring for his ability, and in whom I have also found a very agreeable personality. He has never made an appearance in an important speech in the House in which he has not strengthened his position, till at last it became perfectly clear that in spite of the number of other strong men in the Government, he was overwhelmingly indicated as the new Prime Minister. Finally he was summoned to Biarritz and "kissed hands." On his return and before he had had a chance to appear in the House as Premier, his brother-in-law, whose guest he was to have been over Easter, was burned to death by an over-turned lamp. Poor Asquith was down there only to be called in for the inquest and now for the funeral.

It was under the administration of "C.-B." that the American ambassador recorded progress made in what had become "a perennial question," *i. e.*, the question of the Newfoundland fisheries. I have glanced at the slight perturbation with which he took it up again, early in 1907, when, as he wrote to Mrs. Cowles, "Parliament opens next week, and the prospects are that in the language of our southern friends, there'll be razors in the air." In his talk at the Foreign Office he found soon enough that the demands of Sir Robert Bond were an inescapable factor. Our government steadily maintained its position, and with very little delay the American ambassador was authorized to propose a reference of the pending questions under the treaty of 1818 to arbitration before the Hague Tribunal. In carrying out this policy of Secretary Root's he executed a delicate task, involving serious issues, but there was a fund of amusement supplied in the movement developed in the press as the discussions reached the critical point. It had for its object the laudation of Sir Robert Bond, no less, as the man to come first into the field with the idea of arbitration on the subject! The honor was really our own and Washington was gratified at the outcome. "I want to congratulate you," wrote the President, "on the admirable way you have handled the Newfoundland business. I think it has come out pretty satisfactorily." Meanwhile, of course, a *modus vivendi* had to be fixed again, since the fishing fleet could not hold up its regular August sailing while awaiting the Hague decision, and these subsidiary negotiations ran on for weeks. It was not until September that Reid could thus describe, in a letter to Mrs. Roosevelt, the clinching of the matter:

> The King came back on Saturday afternoon and left on Monday for Balmoral. I met him at luncheon on Sunday and found him in extraordinary health—I should say looking better than I have seen him for years. He was in excellent spirits over his last European trip. I had the opportunity to tell him that between the Embassy and the Foreign Office we had succeeded in celebrating the day of his return by settling a *modus vivendi* for the Newfoundland fisheries pending the arbitration of the whole question at the Hague Tribunal, and had thus, as it was to be hoped, taken forever out of diplomacy this century-old source of irritation between Great Britain and her colonies on the one hand and the United States on the other. He seemed much pleased and expressed decided gratification at the end of the business.

The argument was not to be dealt with at The Hague until 1910, and so the American ambassador went on, knowing that in one way or another he had the fisheries question always with him. But it was there, now, with a difference.

In the matter of the second Peace Conference, discussion of which went forward side by side with the Newfoundland negotiations, he came to very close quarters with that tangle of unappeasable national interests which so pathetically invalidates pacifist gestures in international affairs—when those happen to embrace more than academic elements of controversy. When I touched upon the conference in a preceding chapter Reid was occupied with the simple matter of sharing in conversations to change the date. Secretary Root was meditating a move regarding the limitation of armaments and Sir Edward Grey thought his government could readily second such a proposal. However, the difficulties even then perceived rapidly took on more tangible aspects. Reid looked at them all from a cool, common-sense point of view. Least of all was he impressed by the counsels of fanatics. "The amateur diplomatists," he wrote the President, "have never yet learned that human nature when swept by elemental passions can't be controlled by the resolutions of dilettante reformers. Some European nations, I am sure, will not consent to a reduction, and probably not to a limitation of armament, especially on land." He received abundant evidence that he was right on this point. Professor Martens, the Russian representative, after a visit to Berlin, paid a visit to London, to learn, if he could, the position of Great Britain and to give that government the lead by some candid intimations at the Foreign Office that Russia, Germany, and France would all be opposed to discussion of the armament problem. He was also extremely anxious to find out where the United States stood on the question. Sir Edward couldn't be drawn. Neither could Reid, when a telephone call from the German Embassy preceded the visit of a secretary of Metternich's. This emissary had been peremptorily instructed to get out of the American Embassy what Russia had been trying to get, to find out whether the United States was going to insist on bringing up the question of disarmament which the trio of Powers designated by Martens thought inexpedient and likely to do harm. Where these indirect methods failed, Prussian bluntness succeeded. Followed Prince Bülow's forthright speech, in which the German attitude was explicitly declared. Secretary Root was loth to abandon the point. With the high philosophy to which I have already alluded, he felt that it would be perhaps the better to make the effort and fail than not to make it at all. But in the circumstances to press the matter was, for England, to winnow the wind, and our own view was inevitably adjusted to the stubborn facts. The scope of the conference was narrowed as the opening approached. On his way to The Hague, as a delegate, Choate saw Reid in London and told him that we were not to propose discussion of armaments, but only to second a proposal if it were made by some other government. The results of the meeting were not impressive. Reid had a weakness for steps that really counted, and with pardonable frankness he wrote to Andrew Carnegie: "I don't believe the whole Conference this year has done as much for the course of peace as our single success in getting the Newfoundland fishery, which we have been wrangling over for a century and a quarter, referred to the Hague Court." Carnegie, of course, though grateful for the small graces he could extract from the affair, was a good deal disappointed. So, in a measure, was Reid. But then he had never shared the ironmaster's sentimental hopes. Clipping from the "Times" for Roosevelt what he trenchantly called "the obituary of the Hague Conference," he added these brief observations: "As I didn't expect much else from the beginning, I cannot myself profess any surprise. In fact, I feel about it a good deal as you will remember the New England farmer did about the pig he had taken to market. 'That hog didn't weigh as much as I expected he would, and I always knew he wouldn't.'" Prince Munster's reflection on the futility of threshing old straw at The Hague, especially Russian straw, came back to him with renewed force. Only it brought with it, far more than in 1899, a sense of the Kaiser's reactionary influence.

We have already observed more than one instance of the German Emperor's capacity for giving the diplomats of Europe something unsettling to talk about. Allusions to it increase in number in the ambassador's letters as the months pass. When the Kaiser made his visit to London in 1907, and Reid met him at the state banquet at Windsor, he looked well fed, perfectly well, extremely alert, and in the highest good-humor. But that good-humor, no matter how earnestly manifested on a ceremonious occasion, was never any insurance against some vexatious outbreak. English nervousness over the possibilities latent in his temperament comes out comically in the colloquy that Reid had at Wrest in the fall of 1908 with a distinguished guest. "There's bad news this morning," remarked this personage at breakfast, after glancing through the papers. "It will surely give us an unsettled state of affairs in Europe for weeks." As the Balkan business, the trouble over the German deserters in Morocco, and other things were at the moment acute, the American ambassador started a little and asked what was the matter. "The German Emperor," was the reply, "lost his box containing all his uniforms the other evening on his Austrian visit, and had to come to dinner in his shooting clothes. I tell you there must be great unrest in Europe for at least a month to come." Prince Arthur of Connaught once asked Reid what he had thought of the Kaiser when he met him; if he seemed as agreeable and as fascinating as he was to most of those who met him for the first time. Even remembering the cousinly relation existing between his interlocutor and the Kaiser, Reid had to reply that while the latter had seemed agreeable and desirous of showing cordiality, somehow he did not inspire confidence. The American ambassador recognized a similar feeling in England, and apprehension that the Emperor's restless plunging from one extravagance to another, in the hope of making people forget the last mistake by shocking them with a new one, would ultimately embroil the countries and bring on war. In fact, the feeling seemed to creep out that since it was inevitable, the sooner it came on and was got through with the better for both countries. Continuing on this subject in a letter to Mrs. Roosevelt, Reid says, in November, 1908:

His last performance, demanding an expression of regret from France on a question in which he had already agreed to refer to arbitration the point as to which country was to blame, outrages the general feeling of fair play here as much as in France. If he should be so ill advised as to push it to extremities, France is sure to resist; and so far as the present temper of the press and the people gives any clue, it would seem that Great Britain would be sure to help France in the struggle. But I cannot conceive that he is unwise enough to force a war on this issue. No Emperor is powerful enough, no matter what the size of his army or what the population of his country, to go to war in flagrant defiance of the judgment and conscience of the civilized world.

But meantime the Emperor is in the very position most trying to his nerves and most humiliating to his pride—he is being laughed at by everybody. The excuses for the "Telegraph" interview were ludicrous; the attempt to divert attention by picking a quarrel with France outrages the conscience of his own people as well as the rest of the world; and the news that they have had to purchase the suppression of an interview already printed in the "Century Magazine" caps the climax.

And now comes, just as the previous dictation has been written out, the further news that poor Prince Bülow, after having been forced to take upon himself the blame for the "Telegraph" interview, has also been compelled by the threatening attitude of the Reichstag to give a notice, which is half pledge, half warning, that his versatile Imperial master will hereafter practise greater reserve in discussing foreign affairs, under penalty not only of losing his present Chancellor, but future ones! At the same time they have crawled down on the Casablanca incident. One doesn't know whether to be amused or sorrowful over the whole business, and yet it is the most incredible recklessness in playing with fire. From France to Constantinople, and from the Dalmatian coast to St. Petersburg, Europe is at this moment like a powder magazine; and through this magazine goes the short-sighted potentate, striking sparks at almost every movement he makes. He means so well in many ways, and is such a terror!

How, in the midst of such an atmosphere of mingled mirth and alarm, could the American ambassador, incredulous of any such tragedy as was actually to come, yet conscious all the time of European peril, get any satisfaction out of the flutterings of the dove of peace at The Hague, "beating in the void his luminous wings in vain"? He turned with relief to other matters, negotiation over which at least yielded concrete results. The organization of the opium conference was still further advanced, and it gave the American ambassador a special pleasure when in an informal discussion of the subject Sir Edward Grey stated that the filling of the chairmanship would naturally fall to us. The path was thus opened for the choice of Bishop Brent, the senior member of the American commission, and Reid's personal friend. In seeking British co-operation where disorders at Harbin woke Secretary Root's solicitude for the open door, the Foreign Office found it was not directly enough concerned at that particular geographical point to render any great services; but at any rate it did what it could to meet our wishes half-way. The same sympathetic spirit was manifested when topics like the fate of the Congo and the boundaries of Liberia came up. In the sphere of every-day practicality Reid was drawn into a channel somewhat outside his province, expediting the adoption of penny postage between Great Britain and the United States. His convention securing a lower tariff on British works of art in return for the free entry of our commercial samples was nominally of trifling import, but it had its uses, and, humble instrument that it was, nevertheless gave the American ambassador more satisfaction than was to be got out of "threshing old straw." The day it was signed at the Foreign Office, Sir Edward Grey remarked: "That is about the smallest commercial convention I fancy ever negotiated between two nations, and it is curious that it should be between two of the biggest nations. But it is in the right direction, and perhaps something more may come of it." Reid's belief that it would encourage the pushing of our trade in Great Britain was confirmed by several of the London papers, in which Sir Edward Grey was asserted to have suffered a lapse in astuteness. They rapped him over the knuckles on the score of having signed a convention which was a great concession to the United States, intimating that we gained at both ends of it. Reid thought it was certainly an advantage to those Americans who regarded the whole tariff on art as discreditable to see it reduced one-fourth. If we could wipe it out altogether, he thought, it would be still better for the country.

His interest in art is frequently reflected in his correspondence—apropos of the great collection of paintings at Dorchester House, the work of Alfred Stevens also there, his own gathering of historical portraits, begun as a Christmas surprise for him by Mrs. Reid and steadily enlarged by them both, and the masterpieces in the many town and country houses they frequented. The "Modernists" were just coming into view, and he amusedly observed their performances. He sent me a copy of the manifesto issued by the Futurist painters in 1910, and on the margin made this appreciative comment: "See how little *nous autres* know! The Pope's bull against the comet was nothing to this." In matters of art he clung to the classics. I have alluded in the pages on his ministry in France to his sympathetic relations with Whistler. In London he knew the leading American artists living in England, especially Sargent and Abbey. He was deeply interested in the President's effort to improve our coinage, and was so enthusiastic over the double-eagle design by Saint-Gaudens that he had some correspondence with the secretary of the treasury about it. There is a piquant reminiscence in his letter to Mr. Cortelyou, referring to his old friendship with the sculptor. "I was concerned," he says, "in persuading General Sherman to give him the sittings which resulted in the magnificent statue at the entrance to Central Park, after the old veteran had profanely refused to be pestered any more with 'd—d sculptors.' Stanford White came to me in despair about it, and I tackled the old gentleman first through his daughter Rachel and afterwards in person the next time he came to my house. He swore a little, but finally consented to give Saint-Gaudens the sittings. In memory of the incident, Saint-Gaudens and all the Shermans who were able to attend the unveiling of the statue, met afterwards at dinner at my house, and that happened to be the last time I ever saw poor Saint-Gaudens alive."

Cambridge University had conferred a degree upon

Whitelaw Reid in 1902, when he had come to England as special ambassador to the King's coronation. Five years later a similar honor was thus offered him by Oxford:

Munden,
Watford.
May 2, 1907.

DEAR MR. WHITELAW REID:

As the newly elected Chancellor of Oxford University it is my privilege to select a number of distinguished names for the grant of an Honorary Degree at the ceremony of my installation which will take place at Oxford on June 26th. I should like to be allowed the honor of conferring the degree of D.C.L. upon yourself in recognition of your distinguished career and services and because of the illustrious position that you occupy with so much satisfaction to both great countries. Will you do me the favor of accepting it?

On the same occasion it is my desire to confer the Hon. Degrees of Doctor of Letters and Doctor of Science upon two others of your countrymen, the former upon S. L. Clemens (Mark Twain) whose influence upon public life seems to me to have been uniformly healthy and pure and who is one of the conspicuous literary figures of our time; the latter upon Thomas Edison, who enjoys a world-wide scientific reputation. But these degrees can only be conferred if the recipients are present in person to receive them at my hands. It occurs to me as the time is so short that you may perhaps be willing to telegraph my invitation to them with such explanations as you may think fit. I would either accompany or follow this with a personal letter. It would I think be a novel and certainly an intentional feature in my list that it should contain the names of as many as three of the most eminent of Americans.

I am, dear Mr. Reid,
Yours sincerely,
CURZON.

Edison couldn't leave his experimenting. "So many new things coming along," he cabled, with his thanks. Clemens accepted and followed his despatch with a note in which he added: "The dates are exactly right; they couldn't possibly be righter. I wanted two engagements, and only two; and these two are the choicest that could be imagined. [The other was to dine with the Pilgrims.] They and Oxford leave me seven days for private dissipation and last good-byeing with old friends whom I shan't meet again without their haloes. And there's one or two whom I shan't ever meet *with* them. I am sorry for that, for they are among the best of the flock." A few days before the ceremony at Oxford there was a dinner for Mark Twain at Dorchester House, at which the American ambassador assembled about twoscore authors and artists to meet him, the president of the Royal Academy, the Poet Laureate, Sidney Lee, Edmund Gosse, Conan Doyle, and others. On the Queen's request he presented him at Windsor. Describing the great humorist's visit in a letter to Mrs. Roosevelt and alluding to Mark's various speeches, some of which, as it happened, did not show him at his best, Reid said:

> There was one good sentence (which I have taken great pleasure in repeating several times to his harsh critics) in a speech at the dinner in the great Hall of Christ Church at Oxford which was not reported—these dinners being always held strictly private. His speech was rather longer than was expected, rambling, and, as the English said, thin in straining for humor to which he did not attain. But the closing sentence redeemed it. He wished them to understand, in spite of the light tone in which he might seem to have spoken, that he fully appreciated and was profoundly grateful for the great honor they had done him—perhaps the greatest he should ever receive. It impressed him all the more when he realized that in receiving it he had been bracketed between a Prince of the Blood (here he turned and bowed to Prince Arthur of Connaught) and a Prince of the Republic of Letters, whose fame enveloped the world like an atmosphere, Rudyard Kipling. And with that he sat down. It struck me as really fine.

One of the earliest of the American ambassador's contacts with the world of British authors was with Kipling. In 1905, at the request of the New England Society, he asked him to write the centennial poem for that organization. Kipling replied that there was no honor in America's gift appealing to him more closely, but said that he felt himself "unequal to doing this worthily." Reid had an interesting meeting with him in the summer of 1908. Two years previously the Royal Literary Fund had drafted Reid to preside at the annual banquet. This time, in recognition of the service, they made him immune from speech-making, and he had only to enjoy himself. Writing to Roosevelt about Kipling, beside whom he sat, he says:

He was full of talk through the evening about his late experiences. He seemed delighted with the abuse he had received from the labor unions on account of his candid statements as to the mischief they were doing in Canada. He regards the hostility to the open shop as an absolute warfare upon freedom, and thinks the despotism of the trades unions more dangerous than any other despotisms, because more ignorant and irresponsible. He was full of the most sanguine hopes as to the future of Canada, and he reserves his special admiration for the western part of it.

From Canada he went on, as you know, to South Africa, and his account of the condition of things there was curious and discouraging. He considered it the most conspicuous case in modern times in which a highly advanced and civilized race had deliberately turned over the Government of a country to the half-castes. He regarded the future of South Africa as most discouraging, and by way of emphasizing his opinion, said, "You might just as well turn over the Government of the Philippines to the Filipinos."

It was pretty, after he had finished his speech, to see him ignoring the applause and leaning eagerly forward to catch the glance and smile from his wife. He is singularly devoted to her and she worships him.

On one literary occasion, which he described in a letter to me, Reid had an amusing passage with the Poet Laureate. There was a meeting of the Dante Society at Dorchester House. The exercises were really over when, in the course of the speeches of ceremony, Alfred Austin made the usual polite remarks and then surprised everybody by saying: "And yet in the candor which I am sure my host and his countrymen appreciate, we must frankly say that greatly as we admire their magnificent country's progress and the wonderful material things they have done, we cannot yet admit that they have produced poetry or a great poet." To this charming deliverance the American ambassador had to make his acknowledgments. He made them:

I waited until I had said several other things which occurred to me as suitable for the occasion. Then referring to the Poet Laureate's remark, I said that I understood he objected that our young country had not yet produced, for example, a Dante. I was not disposed for the moment to dispute it, though perhaps I might take the liberty of finding some encouragement in the fact that even his old country had not for the past three hundred years produced either a Shakespeare or a Milton. With that I turned off to speak of translators, paid a little compliment to that wonderful old nonagenarian, Sir Theodore Martin (ninety two years old and making a ten minute speech to defend the moral character of Francesca), and then went on to speak of later translators from my own country, including Longfellow, Charles Eliot Norton and James Russell Lowell. But I wasn't quick enough to stop the instant outburst of laughter, and glancing out of the corner of my eye felt really a little uncomfortable at seeing how squarely the shot had gone home. But they all told me he could not possibly complain, and the English seemed to be particularly pleased. I don't think Austin meant anything discourteous; he is simply built that way. Withal, he is a very agreeable fellow, and I think means to be sincerely friendly. But if Heaven had only taught him that he was a good prose writer and not a good poet, he would have fitted into the scheme of the English world very much better.

The American ambassador has always ex-officio relations to certain English boards. He shares in the meetings of the Peabody trustees. He is concerned with the house that is preserved as a memorial to Carlyle. The latter was peculiarly interesting to Reid from his life-long admiration for the great Scotchman. Unexpectedly, in a purely artistic quarter, he stumbled upon a notable story of Carlyle and Froude. He had it from Sir George Reid, when that artist was painting his portrait, and passed it on to Mrs. Roosevelt in this form:

The hullabaloo about Froude's treachery to Carlyle in the volumes about him published by Froude when he had become Carlyle's literary executor, but quite shortly after the Chelsea philosopher's death, was curiously recalled the other day. Sir George Reid, the eminent Scotch artist and for many years President of the Royal Scottish Academy, was telling me that he had painted Froude's portrait at the time of this disturbance. Froude talked a great deal during the sittings, but didn't happen for a long time to refer to the racket in the newspapers and magazines at all. Finally, one day he asked Sir George if he had seen the attacks and what impression they had made on his mind. Sir George replied that he felt sure they were based on imperfect knowledge of the facts. To this Froude replied by the question, "What would you think if you knew that every line for which I am being censured was revised by Carlyle himself?" He then proceeded to tell how Carlyle had turned over to him a great bunch of his wife's letters, which he wished Froude to examine with reference to their possible publication, or, at any rate, to some use of them. One long letter particularly struck Froude. It was lively and witty, but brimmed over with dangerous personalities. He took it to Carlyle and said, "I would like to print this, but I am afraid it is too dangerous, and, as you see, it ridicules an important man and a friend of yours, who is still living." Carlyle read it over, chuckled over it, and handed it back to Froude, saying, "Print it if you like. If he ever sees it, it will do him good."

The incident led Froude to thinking it would be well to let Carlyle see what he was then writing about him. Carlyle readily assented to looking over the pages before they were sent to press. "Now," said Froude, in concluding his narrative, "every word that I am being censured for writing about Carlyle in the first volume was revised by himself. He read also a large part of the second volume, but by that time, as he was growing feeble, he began to feel it a burden, and told me I must finish the rest on my own responsibility." Somebody may have made this defense for Froude at the time; but if so I can't remember it.

I haven't had access to the book since Sir George told me this story, to see where the things which were most severely criticized occurred, but Sir George's recollection was that most of them were in the first volume, and he says he got distinctly the impression from Froude that nearly all that Carlyle's friends assailed him for had been read and approved by Carlyle.

Reid had numerous delightful meetings in England with members of the writing craft, with novelists like Mrs. Craigie, Rider Haggard, and Conan Doyle. At his acquaintance with Kipling I have already glanced. With

Trevelyan he had much good talk about that historian's work on our Revolution. One bookish episode that especially occupied him was of purely American significance. It developed when Mrs. Hay decided to collect her husband's letters in a privately printed edition and placed the task of preparing them for the press in the hands of Henry Adams. Quantities of the best of Hay's letters had been written to Whitelaw Reid. They were in correspondence practically all their lives. Reid ransacked his files from early journalistic days down to their last period of comradeship in diplomatic matters, and entered into exhaustive consultation over the souvenirs of their alliance to be scattered through the three volumes ultimately printed. Rereading the thick sheaves, he had a deepened sense of his friend's brilliancy. "I have just been going through Hay's letters with Henry Adams," he wrote to Stedman. "They are far better than Horace Walpole's—better literature, and with more of a man behind them." Adams came over from Paris and they spent nearly a week at Wrest on these papers. It was a delicate enterprise. As Reid wrote to Mrs. Hay, her husband had a fad, almost a craze, for imagining that every particularly good letter he wrote contained something that might some time make trouble, therefore marking it "burn when read," "destroy," "*delenda*," etc. Many of these, nevertheless, were letters which at the time could not be destroyed and ought not to have been, since they related to things in progress and often concerned others as well as the writer and his correspondent. Adams proceeded with mingled prudence and courage, disclosing his point of view early in his labors:

You have to settle the same difficulties that fret me. I feel no great hesitation in ignoring the order to "burn when read," because I believe it was meant only as a safe-guard during his life-time.

And if I wrote it on letters of my own I should regard it as equivalent to "personal" or "private"; but I feel more hesitation about allusions to persons, dead or living, public or private. Therefore I think Mrs. Hay would probably prefer that you should edit the letters yourself, and send only what you pass.

As editor I have always strained liberality of assent. No editor ever spared any one of my family that I know of, and, in return, we have commonly printed all that concerned other people. Whether this state of war ever injured anyone I do not know; but it lasts to this day, and makes me rather indifferent to conventional restraints. On the other hand we have never willingly hurt anyone's feelings, and yet have sometimes been compelled to do it.

To Adams and to Mrs. Hay Reid gave counsel, looking to every nuance of the correspondence. It was a labor of love thus to aid in a tribute to Hay's memory. Incidentally the episode brings into the present narrative one of the most fascinating personalities in Reid's circle. It was only after his death, when his privately printed "Education" was made public, that the world at large was permitted to know more about Henry Adams than had previously been inferred from his historical writings. One of the finest talkers of his time, the beloved comrade of John Hay, Clarence King, and John La Farge, all masters of conversation, the gifts which enabled him to hold his own with them were obscured for some observers because he was curiously shy. Only with those whom he really knew did he show his true self. Reid had known him for many years and they foregathered in perfect harmony over the Hay letters. "Adams talked with great freedom about everything under the sun," Reid wrote to his wife from Wrest, and was loth to let him go when the time came for him to travel on to Tillypronie. "Tonight I am to eat the dinner at Ampthill Park that was meant for both of us," he writes to the departed guest. "Did you realize when at Ampthill Park that you were not only where Katherine of Aragon fretted out her soul, and where the inconsiderate Henry had deer driven that she might see Anne Boleyn shoot them with arrows; but that it was where Horace Walpole sent all those interminable letters to Lady Ossory and where Lord Holland reigned, what time he escaped from the urban charms of Holland House!"

Adams at this time was disposed to recall Reid from excursions into the remote past, and for a very definite purpose. "I think it altogether necessary," he argued, "that you should lose no time writing your own life, and printing in it—very freely—all the letters that illustrate our contemporaries. They will not be the worse for it, even if none the better." Over and over again he returned to the charge. He pointed out the importance of fragments in the correspondence with Hay as *pièces justificatives,* and impressed upon him the duty of writing out a record which he alone could frame. "No one else survives of our time," he said, "who has enough literary skill to tell his own story—much less that of his enemies. The innings of us damn literary fellers comes last, and best." Presently the correspondence took a wider sweep, as was always the way with Adams. I reproduce a few of his characteristic sayings:

Paris,
September 27, 1907.

This morning I read your Welsh address in the "Times," and congratulate you on your achievement. You have put into it a quantity of information quite new to me, and that gives me matter for reflection. The next generation needs more mind than it can get out of any schools I can yet see in the future. What it wants is more brain. How can we give it that? Some day I shall send you my own volume of lucubration on the subject. At present you are too busy to invent a new man; but I am clear that the physical substratum of grey matter has got to be supplied, and we must supply it—or bust. This world is too much for us. It was too much for me from the first. I never could master logarithms.

I fear that your colleagues at The Hague are examples of my point. Society cannot march abreast; it must be dragged by leaders. Progress is piecemeal. But the crowd need not be helped to pull apart.

Paris,
October 7, 1907.

I am bored out of my life, as Hay used to say; and if I don't discover some galley-slave work to do I shall take to composing Mark-Twainisms and funny paragraphs for the N. Y.-Paris "Herald." Yet I see nothing much to be funny about. Our chief magistrate does not make me laugh much. Poor Taft! I rage when I think of the soup into which he is pitched and left. Not but that we are all of us in the soup more or less.

Paris,
September 9, 1908.

I did tell you, in our talks about education, etc., that I have set forth views of my own on the subject, which I meant to offer for your suggestion and correction when you should recover leisure for such matters, and I was earnest for you to set down yours. The value of such studies is at least quadrupled by being doubled. You have a direct right to the volume as one with whose name I have taken liberties. At the same time, I ought to add that in theory the volume is still only a proof sent out for correction. Nothing in it is supposed to be final. As yet no one has objected, not even the President or Cabot Lodge—still less their wives—but, what troubles me most is that no one has as yet corrected. My views on education are radically revolutionary but no one cares.

So I have always found my American audience. No one ever cares. Nothing diverts the American mind from its ruts. Harvard College itself is outside of its own education. Not only it doesn't fret but it really doesn't care. Even when I belonged to it, I could never make it fight. Theodore Roosevelt himself never could do it, though he does little but try.

I will send you the volume promptly since you wish it, instead of waiting till you have time to think about it; but pray do not forget that it is what it avows;—a story of how an average American education, in spite of the most favorable conditions, ran down hill, for twenty years, into the bog labelled Failure; and how it had to be started again, under every disadvantage, and the blindest fumblings to crawl up hill a little way in order at least to get a little view ahead of the field it should have begun by occupying. Of course the path is sugar-coated in order to induce anyone to follow it. The nearer we can come to romance, the more chance that somebody will read—and misunderstand. But not one reader in a thousand ever understands.

Paris
September 13, 1908.

I trust the "Education" will arrive all right, and, as for dissent, if you will kindly draw a pen through all you can, without too much fatigue, you will save me much trouble. An experiment, like this volume, is hazardous, not as history, but as art. To write a heavy dissertation on modern education, and fill up the background with moving figures that will carry the load, is a literary *tour de force* that cannot wholly succeed even in the hands of St. Augustine or Rousseau. The only doubt is whether it wholly fails, and I want my extra two years to decide whether or not I will pass the pen through it all. The volume on Chartres is involved in the same doubt, for both go together, the three last chapters of the "Education" being the Q. E. D. of the last three chapters of Chartres. Two years hence, if I can keep my balance, I shall decide whether to put both in the fire—or what.

I must be back in Washington, not so much to elect Taft as to bury my friends. Lafayette Square is a grave-yard. Even the Roosevelts will be packing up to go.

It was apropos of the "packing up" at the White House that Reid enjoyed some of the most entertaining passages in his correspondence with the President. The famous hunting trip in Africa, and Roosevelt's subsequent meteoric travels in Europe, involved numberless preliminary inquiries and arrangements concerning which he turned to our representative in London, partly as an ambassador but even more as a friend. Responding to requests for both information and advice, Reid found himself once again in the rôle of presidential mentor.

CHAPTER XX

THE ASQUITH MINISTRY

Going back to the changes in the political atmosphere which always ensue at Washington with the coming of a new administration, even when the party in power remains intrenched, Adams expressed to Reid his anxiety to know what to expect there, "and in what of my manners I had best hold my tongue." Without being in a position to throw any light upon his first problem, the American ambassador was, on the other hand, qualified to give him expert advice upon the second. On our domestic politics he had himself been holding his tongue for four years. But not the most rigorous detachment from activity in their field, however, could dim his interest in the subject, and this was served not only by the despatches in the press but by numerous private letters during the campaign of 1908. "It looks like Taft on the first ballot," one well-informed friend wrote him before the convention, and Secretary Root confirmed this prognostication. Of the certainty that Roosevelt would not run again he had similarly early news, Admiral Cowles writing to him: "There are still plenty of Third Termers, or Second Elective Termers, but they get cold comfort from the President, who is working for a political victory in a hard times year, which is not so easy." Public men in England were, of course, full of curiosity on this point, and Reid explained to Roosevelt how he answered their queries. He thought nothing could prevent the nomination of Taft. "On the other hand," he wrote, "I have said that if there should be delay for several ballots there was of course the possibility of somebody protesting against further delay by saying that the country had a president now with whom it was satisfied, and insisting on his re-nomination; and this I have always said, if it occurred, would probably be like a spark in a powder magazine." The President's reply is good to read:

The White House
Washington,
June 13, 1908.

My dear Mr. Ambassador:

Your letter of the 1st, as usual, is most interesting. I am happy to say that it now looks as if Taft would surely be nominated on the first ballot, by a three to one vote. There are still a great many people bound to try to force a third term. As I have tried to explain to them, and as I have succeeded in convincing most of them, my value as an asset to the American people consists chiefly in a belief in my disinterestedness and trustworthiness, in the belief that I mean what I say, and that my concern is for the good of the country; and if they should now nominate me, even under the circumstances that would force me to take the nomination, I could only take it as the least of two evils, and with the bitter knowledge that many good people would have their faith in me shaken, and that therefore my influence for good would be measurably, and perhaps greatly, diminished.

Faithfully yours,
Theodore Roosevelt.

He wrote rejoicingly when the election was won. "I feel like saying *nunc dimittis*," he added, and after the inauguration he wrote again of his satisfaction in having put a quietus to the Third Term movement. "Looking back," he said, "I am convinced that the part I took was the wise part, for inasmuch as I was to an especial degree acting as a crusader for decency and honesty, I could not afford to have my action tainted with self-interest; and it would have ruined the effect of what I was trying to accomplish if I had put myself in a position where it would have been possible to make out a plausible case that I was simply acting in the old familiar rôle of the demagogue who, as man on horseback, desires to continue himself in office under the plea of being savior of society." Reid congratulated him on his "triumphant exit from the most conspicuous success in our modern times, in the greatest executive office in the world."

Their correspondence continued from this time on, and I shall have occasion to draw upon it again, especially apropos of Roosevelt's travels, but I must make an extract here from another of Reid's letters to him during the campaign. Englishmen, as I have said, were greatly interested, and the American ambassador had an amusing instance of this at Wrest:

> Just before dinner the other evening I happened to show Lord Rosebery the Taft button. He looked at it critically, and inquired if I was perfectly sure that this was Taft and not Hughes, and on receiving my assurance to that effect immediately put it on. If it had been Hughes, he declared, he would have been tempted to throw it in the fire—perhaps not an unnatural feeling for a Derby winner.* To the amusement of the company he continued to wear the Taft button during his stay, transferring it in the morning from his dress coat to his morning suit, and finally going off Sunday afternoon to his Committee work in London still wearing it. I fancy that's as curious a tribute as Taft has received—having a former Prime Minister of England wearing his campaign button.

Secretary Root went from the cabinet to the Senate. He was anxious to close up certain matters before he left the State Department, and Reid did everything he could to expedite his wishes so far as the Foreign Office in London was concerned. He was especially gratified at being able to head off the British protest which threatened to come over our exemption of Colombian war-ships from Panama Canal tolls. He was also effective in clearing up the last approaches to the Newfoundland arbitration, in which Root was to play an important part at

* The reference, of course, is to the policy of Governor Hughes in pressing legislative action, which, through the reformation of abuses developed around the race-track in New York, incidentally discouraged racing as a sport in that State.

The Hague in the summer of 1910. In these and all other matters the team-work between the secretary and the ambassador had long since been singularly satisfying to them both, and as a souvenir of Reid's service under the outgoing administration I may cite this fragment from a letter of Root's written in May, 1909, from the Senate:

> I have appreciated very highly the admirable tact and good judgment and wisdom with which you have managed the many delicate and important matters which have arisen and have had to be disposed of in whole or in part in London while you have been Ambassador. The country probably never will know how important some of these things have been or how easy it would have been to go wrong or what unfortunate results would have followed if the Representative of the United States in London had not been competent and able. I have appreciated, too, something which the people of the country have a much better opportunity to judge than they have to judge your diplomatic work, and that is the high character, dignity, and merit of your public address. Taken all in all I am sure that you ought to look back over your period of service in the distinguished list of American Ambassadors to Great Britain with the greatest satisfaction.

Whether that period of service was to continue or not rested, of course, with Mr. Taft, at whose disposal the American ambassador, following established precedent, placed his office soon after election. The activities of continuance and the repose of retirement were about equally attractive. There was much to be said on both sides. The work in London was interesting, in the course of it many delightful friendships had been formed, and through their daughter's marriage the Reids naturally found in English life an added appeal. On the other hand, there were family ties at home, to say nothing of the claims of rest, which made the possibility of a return look a little more than beguiling. The decision was left on the knees of the gods. Meanwhile it was pleasant to receive from friends both in England and in the United States evidence that the work of the American ambassador was estimated at such a value that the idea of its termination was considered with regret. In London rumors of his retirement were roundly scouted. Nothing could have been more obvious than that in that part of the world Reid was *persona gratissima*. At home the respect for his ability and his record which Roosevelt had was shared by his successor. No action was taken while the new administration was getting under way, but the matter was then canvassed, and in December, 1909, Secretary Knox cabled for the President that there was no thought of a change at that time in the embassy at London, and that his tenure was therefore indefinite. The news elicited this letter from the King:

Milton Abbey,
December 10, 1909.

DEAR MR. WHITELAW REID:

I rejoice to learn that your tenure of office as Ambassador of the United States to the Court of St. James' is likely to continue. There is no one who could fill such a post with greater distinction than yourself, and I personally rejoice that one who I have learned to know as a friend will not now leave my country.

Believe me,
Very sincerely yours,
EDWARD R.

The Kaiser was, for once, quiescent at the time that Roosevelt was retiring and Taft was taking his place. Reid had no imbroglios of his making to report at this juncture. But the scene on which his influence was ultimately to be so disastrously felt was even then attracting attention. If war-clouds were visible anywhere, they hovered above the Balkans. What the diplomatic corps thought of the outlook there is reflected in one of the American ambassador's last letters to Roosevelt, in the winter of 1908:

I haven't troubled you or Mr. Root with the war rumors with which the papers here have been flooded. From the first I had no belief that a war was likely to come out of the Bulgarian and Austrian complications, at least immediately. My view was confirmed by all the talk I had with my brother Ambassadors and with leading Englishmen.

Events thus far fully sustain us. There is no immediate prospect of war, at least until after a Conference. Nothing would be likely to bring it on but a popular outbreak in Servia; and if this should come, there would be a general European desire to see Servia well spanked and sat down on hard. It is difficult to express the contempt which most European politicians feel toward the Servians, anyway. Circumstances connected with the assassination of the late King which have never got into print, but are perfectly known in every capital, are of so incredibly revolting and bestial a nature, that most of them feel it is a pity to recognize Servia at all at present as having a civilized Government.

I have reason to know from high sources that the King and the Ministry here were very much exasperated at Austria's action; but they attribute it entirely to the ambition of Baron Aehrenthal. There will be no breach, however, with Francis Joseph, whom all respect and admire. On the other hand they would be quite willing to see him put to some trouble to furnish the spanking aforesaid to Servia in case of need.

That was the inside view. Over in Paris, Clemenceau and his minister of foreign affairs, Pichon, were very uneasy about Austrian methods in the Balkans, fearing that diplomacy might fail to prevent hostilities between Austria and Servia in the spring, when large armies could be easily fed and moved. But in London recognition of the fact that the Balkan pot was boiling was accompanied by the belief that the lid would stay on for some time longer. There was no international nervousness of a military nature tingeing the American ambassador's contacts with the Foreign Office as he proceeded to carry out the purposes of the new Republican administration at home. In the first year of that administration he suffered a certain dislocation in his staff. Mr. Carter was appointed minister to Bucharest, and though Reid rejoiced in his promotion, he mourned the departure of a first secretary for whom he had a peculiarly warm regard. Happily, a man likewise of great ability took his place, Mr. William Phillips. In one of his letters to Mrs. Reid, then on a brief visit to California, the ambassador sketches the variety of subjects pressing upon him. "It never rains but it pours upon this Embassy," he says. "Curiously they keep stirring up more business of all sorts than we have had for a long time. One day it is a fresh turn on the Chinese railways, the next day is an arbitration with Chili, the next a desire to settle something about the government of Spitzbergen, the next a trouble in Newfoundland over the landing of the Commercial Cable, the next a new demand for examination of the originals of a tremendous lot of documents in connection with the approaching Hague arbitration!" It was like dipping every day into Pandora's box.

Of all these subjects, the one on which Reid was most solicitous, of course, was that of the Newfoundland fisheries. Though there were tedious passages in the work of preparing for the debate at The Hague, it was always inspiriting to realize that that consummation for which he had so devotedly labored would finally dispose of an age-long controversy, and his confidence in the upshot was doubly fortified since Senator Root had undertaken to act as senior counsel for the United States. He had interesting news from his friend, in July, 1910, when the court of arbitration was in session. "We are having a long, hard, close fight," wrote Root, "and it is quite impossible for any judgment to be made, of any value, as to how it is coming out. However it comes out, one thing is certain, that we shall be better off than we were before the submission to arbitration, because our fishermen were then entirely at the mercy of the Newfoundland Legislature." The Gloucester fishermen were among the first to cable their congratulations to the American agent at The Hague when the verdict was rendered in September, and, as Reid observed, they were the people most affected and most likely to find fault. There was, indeed, no fault to be found. Senator Root's great closing argument summed up a singularly strong case, recognition of which was manifested in the most gratifying measure in the award. There remained to be carried out the reorganization of existing regulations by the commission of experts agreed upon at The Hague, and pending the completion of this work it was necessary to provide for the usual programme of the fishing fleet. The American ambassador had anticipated this in visits at the Foreign Office, obtaining assurances that affairs might rest, in the interim, on the last agreement. When Secretary Knox brought up the point he could promptly reply: "I have just received a note from the Foreign Office saying, 'With reference to our conversation we agree that it is not necessary to raise the question of the *modus vivendi.*'" To Reid the brief message was in the nature of a benediction.

At the same time it left him with quite enough of complications on hand. The fisheries dispute, vexatious as it was, possessed, after all, a certain simplicity. For one thing it was, in a sense, almost a family affair. As a matter for negotiation the American ambassador would willingly have had it back, I think, in exchange for the subject of Chinese railways, which lingered on and on with a far greater entanglement of interests. The origin of this problem dated as far back as 1903, when our minister at Pekin, Mr. Conger, happened to read in the London "Times" that British companies had applied for a concession to build a railway from Sinyang, Honan, to Chengtu, Szechuen, and that the government in reply had declared that the line would be built by the Chinese themselves. The answer of the British Government reported in the "Times" was that if ultimately foreign funds were required, the British should have the preference. Minister Conger forthwith reminded the Chinese Foreign Office that Americans had long before applied for a similar concession, and that he had in a personal interview called the attention of the Chinese Government to this fact, and specially asked that, if foreign capital were needed, application should be first made to Americans, as they were the first in the field. He then entered a formal protest "against any arrangement with others which may deprive my countrymen of their just claims to consideration in this matter." Three days later the Foreign Office replied to Mr. Conger's note, repeating the statement that China expected to build the railway herself, but adding that if in the future foreign capital was needed, since American and British companies had successively applied for concessions to build the road, application would be made to American and British companies, and that the British Legation had been told the same thing. A detailed analysis of the developments ensuing from this posture of circumstances might be carried to lengths hardly necessary in these pages. In due course the French and the Germans came in, and by Secretary Knox's time the Chinese railways embodied one of the most complex topics in diplomacy. He gave sturdy backing to the bankers comprising what came to be known simply as "the American group," recognizing that the problem involved, while nominally financial, had a collateral significance essentially political. There was more than a menace to trade in the possibility of any lack of sympathy "between the Powers most vitally interested in the preservation of the principle of equality of commercial opportunity." He pointed out in his instructions to Reid that the United States regarded "full and frank cooperation as best calculated to maintain the Open Door and the integrity of China."

The American ambassador's duty at the Foreign Office was to urge the hypothesis that "the formation of a powerful American, British, French and German financial group would further that end." Easier said than done. The American ambassador soon had all the facts at his finger-tips, thanks to voluminous exchanges with the State Department and frequent conversations with Sir Edward Grey. At a dinner at Dorchester House he brought together members of all the banking groups, American and foreign. The talk was luminous and of happy augury. Secretary Knox meanwhile was from Washington carrying on a vigorous campaign in every direction, and the desired settlement appeared to be certain. Reid's optimistic view is disclosed in the following letter:

Dorchester House,
August 31, 1909.

Dear Mr. Secretary:

I congratulate you heartily on the reported happy results of the negotiations at Pekin. I am sure the outcome both in business and in national prestige will be far greater than any mere profits on the present loan and railway construction would indicate. It has always seemed to me that with our long coast line and absolute predominance on the western side of the Pacific Ocean, and our splendid foothold on its eastern side looking out from the Philippines on the China Sea, we ought to be at least the equal of any other power in the world in the Chinese trade and in influence with the Chinese Government. In fact I think we ought to be far ahead of any other power. I have long believed also that before the close of this century the Pacific Ocean will carry a more important commerce than that of the Atlantic and that our geographical and political positions ought to enable us to control the larger part of it. You can judge therefore how thoroughly I am delighted with your opening success in this field.

When you were good enough to grant my application for a brief leave of absence, I understood perfectly the suggestion that it might be better to await the result at Pekin, and abandoned my plan of accompanying my family home; renewing the application the next week when the Pekin business seemed to be closed. If it had been necessary I believe we could have secured any further support that seemed proper and necessary from the British Foreign Office. I think I telegraphed you the substance of Sir Edward Grey's very frank private conversation on the subject while negotiations were pending. He repeatedly expressed his regret that we had not told him of our desire to act under the old concession of 1903 before he had got complicated with other nations. Of course it was perfectly natural that, if they were to have associates at all in the Chinese business, they would prefer us to the Germans or even to the French; and I hope we can count upon this feeling as a constant factor in future questions of that kind.

Yours sincerely, WHITELAW REID.

The letter unconsciously throws an ironical light upon the Chinese railway negotiations. Once more was the American ambassador moved to repeat to himself the old axiom that man never is, but always to be, blest. When a personal telegram from President Taft to Prince Chen, Regent of the Chinese Empire, apparently removed all the obstacles that Oriental inertia had placed in the way of American participation in the loan, new difficulties supervened, and at one point, in October, 1909, since none of the mundane powers was exerting any untoward pressure on the situation, the Fates themselves took a hand. "I have the honor to report," cabled the American chargé at Pekin, "that the negotiations, which had practically resulted in an agreement, have been brought to an abrupt pause by the death of the aged grand councillor, Chang Chihtung, the director general of these railways." The diplomats could hardly have been blamed if they had irreverently suspected the old gentleman of dying with malice aforethought, his taking off was an episode so completely and so exasperatingly "in the picture." But I need say no more now of the Chinese business, only noting its incredible vitality, hardy enough to defeat the shrewdest and most industrious of statesmen. "To sign or not to sign" came to be one of the most familiar queries caught up in the world-wide negotiations in which Reid was always playing his part. Other topics—the Congo, Liberia, the fur-seal question involving Great Britain and the United States, Russia and Japan, the opium conference and its aftermath—might come and go. The Chinese railways, multiplying their ramifications, went on forever.

The American ambassador's communications to the State Department all through the first half of the Taft administration are heavily freighted with pure business, but in his private correspondence with Secretary Knox there is one subject outside the routine of diplomatic negotiations which constantly recurs. It appears also in those discursive letters which he wrote to Mrs. Taft, as he had written them to Mrs. Roosevelt. This is the subject of English political life as it affected the fortunes of the Asquith ministry. Measures and personalities alike figure in the chronicle. When Reid first began to write to the new secretary of state he had dissensions in the British cabinet to report, signs that the prime minister was finding it hard to maintain discipline in his own house against the pronounced temperaments of such colleagues as Winston Churchill and Lloyd George, and the debates over the budget seemed to him to land the Liberals fairly in the breakers. He thought even then that their government was likely to hold on for pretty nearly the full average life of a Parliament, and in stating that opinion in a letter to Senator Root, he observed also that the personal weight of Asquith, Grey, and Morley, in particular, remained unimpaired. But the attacks of the opposition were ceaseless, and Reid's sketches of the political scene reflect a tension steadily unrelieved. He did not neglect the touches of comedy, when at rare intervals they enlivened the prevailing grimness. Thus in the course of a letter to Secretary Knox he throws in this anecdote:

One more bit of the never ending gossip which permeates all London political society. The other night Mrs. Asquith had a dinner at which Maud Allan (the dancer) was one of the guests, and she seated this lady beside Mr. Winston Churchill, H. M.'s President of the Board of Trade. Winston did not seem to think well of his neighbor, and absolutely paid no attention to her during the dinner. When the ladies rose she got even with him. As she turned away, she said, "Well, Mr. Churchill, we don't seem to have had much in common to-night. In fact, I think there is in the whole world but one thing we do have in common. We were both kicked out of Manchester." You will remember that Winston was overwhelmingly defeated at Manchester when he came up for re-election after his change in the Cabinet, and also that the authorities made a great sensation by refusing permission to Maud Allan to dance there.

Another anecdote of Mr. Churchill recounted in Reid's lighter correspondence relates to the time when he went to John Morley, secretary for India, and asked his influence to get him (Winston) made viceroy at Calcutta. Morley leaned back in his chair with a gasp, and, bracing himself on the arms of it, finally ejaculated: "Winston, rather than recommend you for Viceroy of India, I would commit suicide myself on this spot." In the fall of 1909, when the American ambassador went down to the University of Manchester, of which Morley was lord chancellor, to receive a degree, he witnessed an extraordinary heckling of the statesman by several suffragette militants, and described to Mrs. Taft his serene demeanor in a dramatic moment. The unexpected challenge had brought about a tremendous uproar. In the midst of it Morley remained absolutely unmoved, "standing with a patient smile on his face and his manuscript in his hand, apparently taking the most languid interest in the interruption." An anecdote of one of his colleagues has perhaps, as Reid observes, an American ancestry, but it loses nothing on that account:

The Conservatives have been laughing lately at a story about another Cabinet minister who is for the moment their *bête noire*, Lloyd George, the little Welsh lawyer who was suddenly made Chancellor of the Exchequer. Their story is that at a Welsh meeting somewhere a great admirer of George's was in a feverish state of excitement about his appearance. He kept pulling his neighbor by the shoulder, and asking, "Have you seen Lloyd George? Where is he?" Then a little later, "There he is! That little man—that's Lloyd George." And then a little later, "Do you see Lloyd George is going to speak. Let's get up closer." Finally, his more phlegmatic neighbor turned on him and said, "Can't you shut up? Lloyd George is not God Almighty." "Oh, well," said the excitable Welshman apologetically, "maybe not; but you know he's young yet."

The vignettes of public men scattered through Reid's correspondence are never more appreciative than when they deal with Asquith. He speaks of him as one of the strongest men in parliamentary life, commanding the admiration of both sides, but he depicts him also as the object of intense Conservative bitterness, exacerbated by the historic tussle between the Commons and the House of Lords. He was beset by anxieties, not all of them by any means of Conservative making. John Redmond and his forces were allies held as by a slender leash, and though the general election of 1909 wiped the political slate it left thereon, in grudging fashion, figures which imparted no really inspiring vigor to the Liberals' new lease of life. Asquith's cabinet had too many unruly elements. It continued in a state of confusion and alarm. "The situation under the surface here," Reid wrote to Knox in March, 1910, "may be better understood by a frank remark openly made by the Premier the other day at a large dinner, when the subject of the late general election was being talked about. 'One of my colleagues,' said Mr. Asquith, 'cost me thirty seats in the House.' Everybody understood the reference to be to Lloyd George, and there is probably no doubt that Lloyd George's Limehouse speech and other offensive utterances did do more than that amount of damage to the Liberal party at the last election." Between Redmond and Lloyd George, Asquith's position on the budget, the Lords' veto, and the whole question of the reformation of the Lords, was a thing requiring the endurance of a stoic and the agility of an acrobat. His demeanor in the House and the atmosphere surrounding him gain in Reid's description to Mrs. Taft from the backward glance it contains:

February 25, 1910.

Temper is beginning to control the general political situation. Mr. Asquith regrets bitterly the action of his own insubordinate followers, and with equal bitterness the taunts from the Irish. He settles back in his seat with a defiant air, grows red in the face, puffs out his cheeks, thrusts his hands in his pockets, and sinks lower and lower on the bench until he almost seems to be lying down. When an attempt is made to heckle him, he sometimes makes no response, and when a question has to be answered, answers it in his own way. Yesterday the questioner came back at him with this: "Am I to understand then that" so and so; and Mr. Asquith fairly flung back the reply, "The Hon. Member is to understand just what my answer said."

Naturally the free-lances on both sides take advantage of such opportunities to stir up more temper. Then the close division last night, only 31 Government majority where they used to have 354 last year, was taken as a practical triumph by the Unionists, who cheered and jeered in a way that would try the temper of a saint; and Mr. Asquith, with all his virtues, is not yet a saint.

All the while I cannot help contrasting the scenes now with what I witnessed at the debate on the King's speech four years ago. Then the Conservatives, after their long lease of power, had come back with the overwhelming majority of 354 against them, and their Premier, Mr. Balfour, was defeated outright. Until a vacancy in a safe constituency could be made for him, he had to keep out of the House, and the leadership of the party devolved on Mr. Chamberlain. Then the young man who seconded the address thought the Unionists so nearly extinguished that he threw the old ideas of Parliamentary courtesy to the winds, sneered at the absent leader and made a coarse reference, almost if not quite insulting, to the "tariff reform substitute." A moment later Mr. Chamberlain rose to reply, and in an instant the young man had found that he was a dangerous person to attack. He paid the usual compliments to the propriety and skill with which the mover of the resolution had discharged his task, and then referred in a single sentence to the extraordinary departure from the customary courtesy shown by the seconder. It was a sentence so bitter and so unanswerable that, as I looked at the young man, I saw him sink bodily into his seat, almost as if somebody had struck him on the head with a sledge hammer. Without another word of reference to him Mr. Chamberlain plunged into the various topics of the address, and was presently being howled down by the exultant Liberals, Labor men and Irish, all combined. They really acted as if they felt that Chamberlain had been so discredited by the defeat that he ought to hide his head in shame and slink out of the House.

Chamberlain continued making point after point, all thoroughly effective from his side of the argument, and at least calculated to sober his opponents; but every sentence only made them wilder in their cheers and insults. Finally he began a sentence with the words, "But when the pendulum swings back—." He got no farther. The Liberals fairly rose at him with insulting cheers and cries, as if they actually meant to drive him out of the House, or at any rate to refuse him a hearing. The slight figure stood perfectly erect at the box on the table which alone separated him from Campbell-Bannerman and Mr. Asquith, till the storm exhausted itself, and then continued, in tones so penetrating and incisive that for a moment the Liberals were sobered. "There is surely no one of these members so ignorant of the history of his country and of this body as not to know that the pendulum will surely swing back." He then went on with his argument as to what would then be thought of the present excesses of the Liberals. Even during the early days of our Civil War I never witnessed in either branch of Congress a more exciting scene.

Well, the pendulum has swung back with a vengeance, and with the exception of poor Campbell-Bannerman, nearly all the Liberal leaders are there to witness it, and to feel more intensely than would otherwise be possible the humiliation of being held in the hollow of their hand by the Irish contingent, and forced to bargain with them in the very presence of their foes for even a week's life.

Side by side with this picture of a scene in the House I must place one of a scene in the Lords. It occurs, like its predecessor, in a letter to Mrs. Taft, written only two or three weeks later. Chamberlain is the hero of the first. It is Lord Rosebery who is now portrayed.

March 15, 1910.

Yesterday everybody that could get into the House of Lords was there to hear the opening debate on Rosebery's resolutions for the reform of the Lords. When I arrived, ten minutes before the opening, the diplomatic gallery was already jammed; but one of the advantages of being an Ambassador is that the minor members of the corps make room for you. Directly below our gallery are the "cross benches" on which peers more or less detached from close party allegiance are apt to sit. Lord Cromer, Lord Milner, and many such may nearly always be found there. In the corner of the front cross bench nearest the Conservative side sat a slight, familiar bearded figure, with a silk hat tipped over the eye brows, preventing the features from being well seen from above. Presently you discover that it is the Prince of Wales, in animated conversation with a heavy figure by his side whose features are also obscured by a tall silk hat tipped over the forehead. The Lord Chancellor rises from the woolsack and reads two or three perfunctory notices. As he sits down, the hands of the clock are pointing to half past four, and one of the clerks, with a heavy curled, grey wig and black gown, rises from the table where he has been sitting with his back to the cross benches, and with a paper in his hand calls "Lord Rosebery." Then the stout figure beside the Prince of Wales rises quickly, walks to the center of the table in front of the Opposition row, takes his hat off and puts it on the table in front of him, leisurely fills a tumbler with water, puts that within convenient reach, draws from the breast-pocket of his tightly buttoned frock coat a sheaf of notes, written on loose leaves of note paper, adjusts these comfortably on a box with some sort of protection at one side, in front of him; and then, with his back to Lord Lansdowne, Lord Halsbury and Lord Londonderry, who sit immediately behind him on the front Opposition bench, with his side to the Lord Chancellor, sitting alone under his big wig on the woolsack beyond the end of the table, and facing directly Lord Morley, sitting in the center of the Ministers' bench on the other side of the table, and his own son-in-law, Lord Crewe, the Minister for the Colonies, he begins in a low tone with the conventional English pronunciation of "Me Luds"—the latter word not quite so short as this orthography indicates, but nothing like so long as the ordinary American pronunciation.

There had been a curious kind of movement and suppressed whisper as he took his place—a mere indication that the great feature of the day was on. The newspapers describe it as applause, and perhaps it was meant for that, though I should have considered it a much higher evidence of the strained attention of a highly expectant audience. His first sentences were very simple, showed no care in literary construction, and, in fact, had a good many repetitions of the phrases "this House" and "the House of Luds" and the like, which Lord Rosebery would have been the first to strike out with his pen if he had been revising an article for the press. The curious thing is that this indication of unpreparedness and avoidance of literary form was studied as carefully as any other part of the speech. It was the effort to conceal his art. Hardly half a dozen sentences had been uttered, however, till they began to flow in perfectly smooth and polished phrases, and he was propitiating his audience by a eulogy of its antiquity, its importance, its honors, and its great service. Then, with a dextrous turn, he referred to the higher eulogies passed by many great men whose eloquence and authority he could not hope to rival, and especially one comparatively recent one which, in spite of his knowledge of the dread with which audiences regarded extracts, he would venture to read. He read it effectively. At one of its swelling and extravagant periods, he stopped to say deprecatingly that he must say he thought this was a little overdrawn, and then went on to the finish leaving everybody still wondering who this unknown eulogist was. He proceeded to say a few words in recognition of the great knowledge and authority of the man he was quoting, and then quietly remarked it was Mr. Redmond.

As Redmond is the head and front of the war on the House of Lords, the hit was instantaneous and enormous. The whole House broke into roars of laughter on both sides.

For an hour and a half the speech went on, with frequent reference to the notes, and yet with the constant appearance of spontaneity, and with an extraordinary variety of elocution. The voice was sometimes so low and so conversational that we had to lean over the galleries to catch it. At other times, in moments of apparent passion it rang out so that it could have been heard easily in the lobbies. One rarely sees a more complete triumph of a great reputation sustained by an address generally thought worthy of it. Before the first half hour had passed the strained attention seemed to become almost painful. The Liberals watched him anxiously, as if they felt that their lost leader was their master still, and were apprehensive every moment of fresh chastisement in a new spot. Morley, Crewe and nearly everybody on the front bench had the same expression. Even they however could not fail to join in the universal hilarity when the remark dropped, in very low conversational tones, almost as it seemed unconsciously, as if thinking aloud, that he pitied the unfortunate Secretary for the Colonies when he had to communicate to the new Dominion in South Africa that the Mother Government was repudiating at home the second chamber which it had just inflicted upon them. The fact that this unfortunate secretary opposite was his son-in-law seemed to add to everybody's enjoyment of the hit. Presently he was speaking of the scorn with which the

United States, with its strong Senate and double veto on the action of the House of Representatives, would regard the present folly of the Mother of Parliaments. Some of the newspapers speak of his pointing the observation by turning to me, but I did not think it was so marked as to attract notice, though he certainly did look up at us and make a gesture towards our gallery.

It is a common remark about Rosebery that he speaks more like an American than like an Englishman. Nevertheless it is a remark that Americans would not be apt to make, especially at home. Everything that he does is more restrained than I can remember in any famous American speaker since Wendell Phillips. He is like Wendell Phillips in another respect. His literary taste is admirable, and, in spite of occasional attempts to conceal it, his sentences are as polished as if they were meant for his Life of Pitt or his Last Phase of Napoleon. Yet once or twice when he was interrupted, he showed that he was easily effective in retorts and replies which must have been extempore.

The American ambassador's observations throughout this year point to nothing save increasing virulence in the quarrel over parliamentary reform. In May, when King Edward died, it seemed as though the community of feeling produced by the event might lead to some sort of amiable composition of the trouble, but this hypothesis was short-lived. The dissolution that winter was faced by Asquith with militant confidence. He was sure that the bill affecting the House of Lords would have to be accepted by that body without the change of a word. But the general election proved a disconcerting blow. Conservatives and Liberals were exactly balanced in the new Parliament, and though the prime minister was continued in office, the people gave no encouragement to his more revolutionary proposals. As Reid put it to Secretary Knox, Asquith returned with no new mandate and no increased power.

There were both lights and shadows in the private life of the Reids at this period. In March, 1909, Mrs. Ward's son was born in London, an event sending ripples of rejoicing through his grandfather's correspondence. Then in January, 1910, Mr. Mills died. Mrs. Reid was with him in California when the end came. Her husband was at his post, and he sailed at once for New York. Knowledge of the heavy burden of Mr. Mills's years, and natural apprehensions for his health, still could not soften the shock of his death when it befell. On a brief visit home in the preceding summer they had observed an encouraging improvement in him, and at the camp in the Adirondacks a happy party of kinsfolk and friends had gathered around him on his birthday, happy and confident. The immediate future, at all events, had then seemed secure, with more of the companionship which was one of the stanchest pillars in the family life. Whenever leaves of absence permitted, the Reids spent their holidays with Mr. Mills, and he was with them more than once in England, where the King and many others in public and private life warmly welcomed him. His character was both strong and lovable, with a generous unselfishness at its base. At the time of the San Francisco disaster he cabled to his daughter in London and the distinction he draws between thought for himself and thought for others is so decisive that it may be cited here: "Mills Building and Millbrae destroyed. We lose sight of our own losses in the losses to the State and to our friends." That was eloquent of a civic sympathy rooted in true warmth of heart. Men in business, like Pierpont Morgan, who held his rectitude and judgment as indispensable bulwarks in the management of large transactions, delighted also in the traits revealed by his nature in intimate association. Philanthropy was accompanied in him by a sagacious practicality, as witness the Mills hotels, but the instinct to help came first, just as in his conception of capitalism an impulse toward absolute fairness was fundamental. It has been said of him that in a long life as a financier he never made an enemy or a detractor. Roosevelt, from Gondokoro, wrote: "I have always felt a peculiar regard for Mr. Mills; he is the type of 'captain of industry' whom I cordially respect; of whom I am proud as an American." For Reid he had been for nearly thirty years a tower of strength, bringing his weight to bear upon the fortunes of The Tribune, taking a leading part in the establishment of the linotype as a working investment, in many ways proving a master of counsel and aid in practical affairs. Through all this there ran an inspiring strain of mutual understanding and affection, the stimulus of true comradeship. Like Roosevelt, Reid admired his father-in-law, and, besides, he loved him.

CHAPTER XXI

THE DEATH OF EDWARD VII

In the period of political turmoil at which I have just glanced, the transition from one reign to another is not precisely foreshadowed by the American ambassador, but there are passages in his correspondence in the light of which this event comes not altogether without warning. The health of King Edward was uneven for some time before he died. He had an illness in January, 1909, which was considered rather serious, and those about him were anxious to have him as careful as possible. In the following April a bad cold, with an obstinate cough, led to alarmist despatches in the press, and though he seemed in good condition when he opened Parliament the court physicians sought to keep him as much out of the London climate as possible, and to moderate his passion for work.

For another year he held his own. When his defenses were broken down they went rapidly. The swift climax is thus described by Reid in letters to Mrs. Taft:

May 5th, 1910.

The King sent for me the other day to talk about Mr. Roosevelt's visit. I was startled to find that so soon after we had been assured by repeated despatches from Biarritz that he was in better health, and so soon after the newspapers had been commenting on his improved appearance on his return, he was suffering again from a bad bronchial attack. These give him more than usual trouble when they come on, because of his plethoric habit. Our talk was interrupted by spasms of coughing, and I found that he was suffering from a good many of the symptoms of which I had such painful experience myself during the winters when bronchial asthma banished me to Arizona. It seems to me that these attacks are coming on more frequently within the last two years, and that they are becoming harder to shake off. Still, he is a man of tremendous vigor of constitution, and of extraordinarily energetic habits. The general public think him in perfect health; but I am impressed with the notion that in the inner circles there is more anxiety about him lately than I have ever observed at any time before.

May 6th, 1910.

The above was dictated yesterday, in order to catch to-night's pouch. Since then the little news I gave you about the King has developed into the sensation of this morning's papers. Apparently the physicians consider the case far graver than I intimated.

The illness complicates the Roosevelt business enormously. Part of our invitations for the formal dinner at Dorchester House, which the King and Queen were to attend, had already gone out. Accordingly, I rushed down to the Palace to consult Lord Knollys as to what to do. After a moment's consideration, he said he thought it better to let the rest go out, and recall them later if the illness should be prolonged. He is ordinarily the most reticent of men in regard to the King's health, but in reply to my inquiries he shook his head sadly and said, "His condition is very grave." Then I drove around to the other end of the Palace, where the books are kept for what is called "inscription on the King and Queen." This is the substitute in their case for calling, or leaving cards. The courtyard was filled with red-coated Guards going through their usual morning evolutions, with banners and music, and outside were dense crowds pressing against the railings, not so much to watch the evolutions, which are a daily occurrence, but drawn by the excitement about the King's health, and busy watching the constant stream of carriages driving in with persons wishing to inquire and inscribe. It was a curious contrast; the showy parade, the throngs of people, the lines of carriages, the hushed inquiries as the callers came in, and the prompt replies of the red-coated servants in charge of the books that His Majesty was a little better this morning, when compared with the anxious scene I had just left at the other end of the Palace, in the private office of the man nearest the King and as familiar with his condition as the physicians themselves.

The excitement of the morning in court circles and around the Palace has now spread throughout London. It recalls and almost equals the intense anxiety and gloom which I witnessed here when the Coronation was postponed on account of the surgical operation. The bulletin of the physicians this afternoon is even more alarming than that of last night. One hesitates to consider the gravity of the effect in England and in Europe if the present forebodings are realized.

The King died in the night. His physicians united in a statement that his disease was entirely bronchial, but in one of the American ambassador's last notes on the subject there is a passage indicating that Edward VII had never spared himself, and that this fact was contributory to his death. A doctor of high standing who had at times treated him, broke out in Reid's hearing, saying: "The King killed himself. He would not take the proper precautions. After the severe warning at Biarritz, he came back to the more trying climate of England, worked himself to death, then rushed off to Sandringham for a day or two in the country, and spent this time paddling about in a dismal, raw day, and sometimes in the rain, till he brought on another attack, which his weakened throat and bronchial passages were not able to resist." The idea that Edward VII "worked himself to death" was easily shared by the ambassador. If he regarded the life of the King as of prime importance to Great Britain and to the peace of Europe, it was because his impressions of the ruler to whose court he was accredited centred on the traits of a statesman arduously serving his people up to the limits prescribed by the British system of government, and always exercising, in so far as that system permitted, a salutary influence upon international politics. Writing to me once about the relation to public affairs disclosed in the letters of Queen Victoria, and dwelling upon the growth of European appreciation of her character, Reid added: "I think, too, that the reputation of her son is likely to pass through very much the same course."

For two years Reid had been in correspondence with Roosevelt over the movements which the latter contemplated on leaving the White House, and had smoothed the way for his African venture, obtaining Lord Crewe's intercession with the authorities of Uganda, so that he might have a chance at a white rhinoceros, talking with the Sirdar of Egypt about access to the preserves under his control, and in various ways helping to facilitate the ex-President's plans. Later, as has been previously noted, he was occupied with matters involved in Roosevelt's journey through the capitals and courts of Europe. By the time the returning hunter had got through a good part of these ceremonious visits, the American ambassador had perfected an impressive sequence of engagements to be met in England. It was necessarily in striking contrast to what Roosevelt had fondly dreamed of when he first broached the African idea to Reid in the summer of 1908. Then he imagined that he could go abroad as a private citizen. "My present intention," he said, "is not to go to Europe at all until the memory of my presidency has faded, so as not to make the wretched sovereigns and statesmen feel obliged to see me or entertain me. When I stop being president I stop being president." He couldn't stop being Theodore Roosevelt, a circumstance of which Reid reminded him with mingled firmness and humor. Even before he left the United States he realized that it would be quite impossible for him to escape the cordialities which were piling up against his European tour. "I suppose you are right," he wrote to Reid, "and that even though I am a private individual it would look boorish for me not to pay my respects to the sovereigns or heads of governments of the countries through which I pass." It was like him, however, to receive with particular appreciation Curzon's request that he should deliver the Romanes lecture at Oxford. "This makes matters easy for me," he said, "because it gives me a genuine reason for going to England."

He looked forward to seeing the ambassador in London, "to talk over many things of both national and international consequence." How interesting he made the prospect, what inspiring talks his promised to be, may be judged from the following fragment:

> I am amused by the statements made to you that the difference between the Kaiser and myself was "that I made good." That is literally true. I have never yet failed to do what I said I would do if called upon to do it! On this point I wish some day to tell you for your own information the inside history of my relations with the Kaiser at the time of the Venezuela matter, of the message I finally felt obliged to send him, and of its instantaneous effect. The recent voyage of the fleet around the world was not the first occasion in which I have used it to bring about prompt resumption of peaceful relations between this country and a foreign power. But of course one of the conditions of such use is that it should be accompanied with every manifestation of politeness and friendship—manifestations which are sincere, by the way, for the foreign policy in which I believe is in very fact the policy of speaking softly and carrying a big stick. I want to make it evident to every foreign nation that I intend to do justice, and neither to wrong them nor to hurt their self-respect; but that on the other hand, I am both entirely ready and entirely able to see that our rights are maintained in their turn.

He was in Scandinavia, on the way to Berlin, when the King died. The ambassador wrote to him on May 10th about the funeral, which had been set for the 20th. Reid had learned that France and most of the important countries in Europe were going to send special representatives, and said: "I have taken measures to ascertain the exact facts as to this movement, and if it is as general as reported, I shall venture to tell the facts either to the Secretary or to Mr. Taft himself, and to say that under such circumstances I know your appointment for a similar duty would be well received here by the Government and people, and that it would be entirely agreeable to me." He cabled to Secretary Knox, and two days later Roosevelt had his appointment in his hands. "I am very much obliged to you," he wrote from Berlin, "for having suggested my name as special ambassador.

I did not know where it came from. At first I half hesitated about accepting, for I know nothing about such matters, and I suppose my function will be entirely separate from yours, although I hope it will still be convenient for you to have us with you." He arrived with Mrs. Roosevelt and three of their children at Dorchester House on May 16th, and entered upon three weeks of prodigious activity. A few hours after his arrival the Reids took him and his family to pass before the body of King Edward, lying in state at Buckingham Palace, and immediately afterward the ambassador went with him alone to Marlborough House, where they were expected for an audience with the new King. Thenceforth for a day or two the ex-President was fairly enveloped by royal personages, amongst whom he attracted enormous interest. As Reid said: "They are ordinarily so hedged about with etiquette that they don't have a chance for free talk with such a man, and this time they were all resolved to profit by their opportunity." The Kaiser's temper must have been sorely tried by attentions so liberally bestowed upon a republican, and a mere ex-President at that. That he grudged notice directed elsewhere than upon himself is drolly suggested in the *on dit* about him which ran through society at the time: "'What a disgusting fuss those English did make over that little terrier, Cæsar, that my uncle used to have." "Why? How?" "Why, they paid so much attention to it that the people actually took more notice of the dog than they did of me."

The Roosevelt visit came to an end on June 10th, when he left town early in the morning to spend the day with Sir Edward Grey in the New Forest, where they would sleep for the night and get up at four o'clock to listen to the notes of song-birds which could only be heard then and there. After that Roosevelt was to go on to Southampton for the steamer. The whole visit was extraordinarily successful. The English were in a mood not altogether uncritical, the candor of their guest's speeches in Egypt having evoked a breeze of comment. But his plain-spokenness found a justification not only in the conditions he traversed but in a fundamental personal character which elicited wide-spread sympathy and understanding. The famous speech at the Guildhall, in which he frankly admonished the British Empire on its policy in Egypt, would have been a blazing indiscretion in any one else, provoking a storm of resentment. From his lips it was received with remarkable amiability in some quarters, and the criticism it met in others was on the whole counterbalanced by its good effect. Not long after Reid's death, in a conversation about his work in London, Roosevelt told me how he had consulted the ambassador as to this speech, and how glad he was that his friend had made him consult Sir Edward Grey, going with him to the Foreign Office for discussion of the matter. He felt that that was a crucial point, and keenly appreciated the whole manner of Reid's collaboration in it. The American ambassador arranged all the precautionary conversations that Roosevelt had with Grey and other leading personages. He knew what was going to be said, and was exactly informed as to the real significance of the sensation produced at the Guildhall. A serviceable foot-note to the incident is provided in what he wrote to Secretary Knox:

> I was a witness to-day to his extraordinarily bold and unconventional address in the Guildhall. Arthur Balfour and Lord Cromer made no secret of their delight with it. I know confidentially that Sir Edward Grey was equally pleased (although under more necessity to conceal it), and is sure to take the same line in the House of Commons as soon as the subject comes up. Of course he is liable to a little chaff on account of it, since it can be construed as reading him and the Government a lecture on their failure hitherto to do their

duty; but he is too big a man to be annoyed about that. I think he would have been glad if he had had the opportunity to say the same thing first; but as he didn't, I think he is also glad to have such a powerful impression made in advance on the public mind by way of preparation for the Government's approaching change of attitude.

In traversing the papers of a diplomat established in London the significance of that metropolis as a kind of world's stage is sharply apprehended. Sooner or later every one of international fame appears thereon, and when the major figures like Roosevelt have had their hour, there are still plenty of minor ones who interestingly fill their briefer terms. The letters of the American ambassador keep pace with the weighty things of which political history is made. Also they constitute a vivacious chronicle of entrances and exits, picking out the salient actors in a thronging scene. Usually the more august personages are clothed in the aloofness which is part of their status. Royalty is enmeshed in the broideries of its own pageantry. But even through the pageantry some human naturalness peeps out. A great banquet given for the German Emperor by King Edward at Windsor Castle moves with unbroken stateliness until it culminates in toasts exchanged between the two monarchs. Then in the drawing-room the Kaiser's ambassador and various white-wanded court officers strive in desperation to adjust his conversational evening to the same formal gait. He makes them frantic by going on talking with Lloyd George as though he would never stop, and next, tired of having people tell him that this or that person must be presented, he seeks out interlocutors of his own choosing, in a series of unconventional dives across the room. One of the most courtly spectacles witnessed by the Reids in England was not at either Windsor Castle or at Buckingham Palace, but at Woods Norton, the residence of the Duc d'Orléans, where they attended in 1907 the marriage of the duc's sister. Not one detail of Bourbon splendor was omitted. Royal tradition prevailed, but Reid notes the young King of Spain's engaging refusal to be governed by it, his ease in conversation, and his altogether delightful bearing. In a letter to Mrs. Roosevelt there occurs this vivid portrait of the host:

> The Duc d'Orléans himself interested me as much as any of his guests. Although knowing some other members of the family, I had never seen him. He came to Paris while I was there, in what was thought by his followers a shrewd effort to gain popular favor by demanding the right to enlist as a private soldier in the French Army; but he was promptly arrested, convicted of having violated the law of France exiling those who consider themselves in a direct line of succession to the old throne, and after a few days' confinement escorted to the frontier. He was easily the best looking of the royalties—much larger and stronger than his kinsman, the Spanish King, with a fine well-shaped and rather large head and an open, manly countenance. The hair is light colored, and the beard, which he wears after the Spanish fashion, distinctly blond. He seems absolutely unaffected, and has a very frank, cordial manner. His shoulders and chest are rather unusually large, and altogether, as one looked at him in his perfectly fitting dress suit, standing with his arms folded, near his sister, the bride, one could not help thinking him as fine a figure of a man as is to be seen in months. He has had a stormy youth, as you know, and has made many mistakes; but he appears to be living very contentedly with his wife and is evidently greatly liked by his family. Whatever may be said against him, he certainly did things *en prince* for his sister, and with a disregard of expense which never used to be attributed to the earlier descendants of Louis Philippe.

When the King of Portugal was entertained at dinner at Windsor Castle in November, 1909, the American ambassador had there a brief conversation with the Queen of Norway, for whose charm of manner he had a special admiration. They discussed a subject making a signal appeal to Americans. He touches upon it in writing to Mrs. Taft:

She was full of talk, first about Nansen, who used to be one of my colleagues here. She said Nansen did not like diplomacy (although I am bound to say he certainly liked the social part of it when he was here, and was almost the last to be sent out of every ball room), and that he was now devoting himself to his duties as a professor. She was afraid the Copenhagen people had been a little premature in their recognition of Cook, but nevertheless said that one of their greatest Norwegian explorers fully believed in him, and had assured her of his conviction that Cook had been at the North Pole. Still she said they had been very much shaken by the Mt. McKinley business. As to Peary, she supposed of course that his record as an explorer was secure, but regretted that he had injured his personal standing by his despatches and talk about Cook.

Peary came to London in 1910, just on the eve of the King's death. In June the American ambassador presented him to George V, who asked him all sorts of questions about arctic exploration and sport, and drew him out with special interest on the edifying question of Cook. By this time even the Queen of Norway was doubtless persuaded that his standing had not, after all, been injured by his observations on his rival (!). Reid witnessed the bestowal upon Peary of the special gold medal of the Royal Geographical Society. The ceremony occurred in Albert Hall, before an audience of ten thousand, and the explorer's address left a fine impression. His short stay in London made him a multitude of friends. Its incidents had an exceptional interest for the American ambassador, connecting themselves as they did in his mind with a letter he had received from Peary six years before. At that time, in 1904, a cordial editorial in The Tribune had moved the explorer to express his thanks and he went on to ask Reid's co-operation in the difficult task of raising funds for his final dash to the pole. "This matter is not an idle dream," he said; "it is not a foolish fancy; it is today a big, broad, national proposition, with the support and approval of the President, the Navy Department, the press and the people of the country; and it is no exaggeration to say that both the President and the people are waiting, looking for some one to come forward and see the thing through and will greet such man with the liveliest acclaim, commendation, and approval. But time is vital. To insure the success of the expedition the question of the purchase of the ship must be settled within a few days." Reid's response was sympathetic. His paper all along had been, and it continued to be, enlisted in Peary's favor. Assisting in London at the triumph of the Columbus of the arctic he rejoiced in his countryman's development of that "big, broad national proposition" he had outlined in his letter with such ardent hope so long before.

Readers of Henry James, and especially of the memorabilia accumulated around his name since his death, well recall the perturbations of his ill-starred career as a playwright. The American ambassador took note of the curious fate which seemed to follow the author in this field. One of his comedies was produced in London in February, 1909. "I hope so much that you are lunching here to-morrow," Mrs. Charles Hunter wrote to Reid, "and that you will be able to go to Henry James's play. My box is very large and only your Excellency and I, with Mr. Sargent and Max Beerbohm, two great friends and admirers of Henry James, will be occupying it. Henry James himself will be lying *perdu.*" Reid went to the luncheon and found everybody hopeful. But in the undercurrents of talk flowing through London society the fate of the play was almost immediately declared. It had the usual *succès d'estime* and nothing more. Reid's chief literary interest at this moment was in the collection of John Hay's letters which Mrs. Hay had just sent him in their final form. He wrote to Mrs. Reid that they had kept him up for two or three nights till nearly midnight. In a letter to Mrs. Hay he says: "It is such a picture of a many-sided and most lovable man of genius—loyal beyond comparison to every friend he ever made, witty, gay, light-in-hand, and yet a prey to the most despondent notions at times about himself and others, marvellously well-informed, but wearing all his knowledge as easily and jauntily as a debonair young courtier of Louis XIV. wore his sword. All this and much more these letters show; but still they don't at all give the real measure of the man. For that we need many others, which no doubt you were right in thinking could not yet be published." Sir George Trevelyan was as absorbed by the book as Reid was himself. "I am deep in the 'Letters and Diaries of John Hay,'" he wrote, "and am now paying it the most sincere of compliments, that of counting the pages that are still to read—as I did lately with a second reading of James's 'Life of William Story.' What a period it was! What a policy! What men, and what a literature as the outcome of it! I had already gathered something about that inner circle from Henry Adams's autobiography, as I prefer to call the book that *he* names otherwise." The remark recalls one made to Reid by Henry Adams himself, apropos of the political *trouvailles* of the new generation. They didn't strike him as on the whole quite comparable to the men of an earlier day. "Apparently your lot," he said, "was a coruscation of genius. We are still living on the *disjecta membra.*"

Adams is interesting on one of the ambassador's own excursions into literature, the address on Byron delivered at University College, in Nottingham, in the winter of 1910. It was prepared with some hesitancy. Reid had plenty of appreciative things to say about the poet, but there were some other things he was disinclined to omit which he feared might prove unpalatable where

Byron was a local idol. But he received official assurance that he could be as critical as he liked, and the address remains one of the frankest of his always frank speeches in England. Adams wrote:

> Byron I envy you. One can hardly keep one's hands off him. His is one of the few really amusing figures in the British Pantheon. One can praise or criticize, admire or detract, as one likes, in perfect safety. One is sure to be more or less right. One need not even treat him seriously. He did not treat himself seriously, and would have jibed at us for it. He is the only complex figure, except perhaps Sheridan, in the whole galaxy. You saved yourself some ugly risks by keeping Shelley and Keats out of sight, who had nothing at all, that I can see, in common with Byron, whose only parallel is Châteaubriand or Voltaire. Curiously enough, the closest English parallel is certainly Disraeli. I wonder whether there was any Jew in Byron. There is certainly some Heine in him.

At the same time that the ambassador was framing his study of Byron he was engaged upon one of Lincoln, attacking at last a theme upon which he had received more than one request to speak since the first period of his long stay in England. The address which he delivered at the University of Birmingham only a week after his appearance at Nottingham belongs in the forefront of all his writings. Like the "Byron," it is dedicated to historical truth. Rising to its high theme, it is also a singularly human portrait, fashioned not only out of a lifetime's reflection on Lincoln's traits as a statesman but out of a sympathy dating from the old personal observations and contacts of which I have given some indications. Doctor Warren, the president of Magdalen College, whose father had stood fire on public platforms in England for the Union cause, and who himself had a cult for Lincoln, wrote to Reid: "Somehow I never felt that I had got at the real man until I read this lecture." I have forborne to swell these pages with many extracts from the congratulations which the ambassador was wont to receive on his speeches, but in this instance I may cite the appreciation of Roosevelt:

New York,
January 3, 1911.

DEAR MR. AMBASSADOR:

I have received your letter, and also the Lincoln address. I had already written to you about it on the strength of the newspaper reports and of what Laurence Abbot had told me. But I have now gone over the whole address, have asked that it be bound, and wish to tell you that I think it a very remarkable and really noteworthy address. I do not believe that as good a thing of the kind has ever been done by any American Ambassador, including Lowell; and at the moment I cannot think of as good a speech of just the same kind that is to the credit of any of our public men. It seems to me that you have done just what at the outset of the speech you said you could not do, and that is to give and develop one or two new thoughts of great importance. I wish that not merely our Wall Street friends but the sentimentalists on both sides, and the extremists on the other side, could be made to learn your address by heart. It is not only a finished and masterly piece of literary work, but it carries a weighty burden of insight and good sense for all serious politicians.

Give my love to Mrs. Reid. I wish I could write you about your address in a way to make you really feel how much I regard it.

Faithfully yours,
THEODORE ROOSEVELT.

His friends used to suggest to him that it would be desirable to collect his speeches in book form. He had done this in his "Problems of Expansion," when the whole question of the Spanish War gave a certain unity of purpose to the studies he then gathered together. The English addresses he never himself assembled for such publication; but he had them made into pamphlets, and he played with the idea of concentrating them in a volume, to the extent of inventing a title which would do for them all. He called them "Recreations of an Ambassador."

CHAPTER XXII

THE CLOSING YEARS

The phrase just cited, "Recreations of an Ambassador," in Reid's case hardly connotes rest. When he came home for a visit early in January, 1911, he wrote to a friend that the vacation was the first he had had in eighteen months, and the only one with any leisure in it for nearly three years. It lasted well into March, and was filled with delightful experiences, but it gave him very little chance for recuperation. In fact, he had rarely crowded so many things into so short a space of time. He was twice in Washington for meetings with the President and the secretary of state. He went down to Oyster Bay for a night with the Roosevelts. In Albany he attended a meeting of the Board of Regents. A month out of his leave of absence was spent in California, and although at Millbrae, as always, he found repose, there was no lack of activity. Business claimed him as a trustee of Leland Stanford, Jr., University, and at the banquet given in San Francisco in the interests of the Panama-Pacific Exposition he was duly called upon for a speech. In New York the days were marked by directors' meetings and the evenings by public and private dinners. All the time, in the back of his mind, were the problems left in London and soon to be resumed.

There was, however, one journey to be made which swept all diplomatic problems away and put public affairs into the background. This occurred when he went out to Wisconsin with Mrs. Reid in March. They went to Racine for the wedding of their son, whose engagement to Miss Helen Rogers had been announced not long before. It was the happiest imaginable rounding out of a sequence of years to which reference has already been made more than once in the course of this narrative. Hitherto the question had all been one of Ogden Reid's progress in preparing himself for the editorship of The Tribune. Now there intervened the matter which really establishes a man in life, and this wedding, like the one which had occurred in London three years before, brought to the Reids a rich contentment. They had felt in England the separation from their son. Thenceforth, though this continued, they could rejoice in the consciousness of the strength and happiness added to him as he was fixed in a new home.

Preparatory to the return to London Reid had some long talks in Washington. There he found Mr. Taft and Mr. Knox much occupied with Canadian and Central American negotiations, but they had time for exhaustive discussion of matters in his own budget—Liberia, the opium question, and, perennially, the Chinese railways. Salient, too, as especially important in the President's plans, was the projected general arbitration treaty with England. When Reid got back to London he learned that the Foreign Office was in sympathetic mood toward this. Sir Edward Grey had already communicated to the American Embassy his desire to consult as to the best means of profiting by the enthusiasm aroused in England by his public response to Mr. Taft's proposals. He feared that such popular demonstrations as he had elicited might have a bad effect if they seemed to outrun the feeling in the United States. With this thought he had discouraged an approach from both the Established Church and the Non-Conformists for a great mass-meeting in favor of the President's idea and his attitude toward it, to be held at the Royal Albert Hall; and had advised them to consult first with the churches in America, in order that, if thought wise, there might be reciprocal action in the United States. He wanted to be advised frankly if things were moving in our direction too fast or too conspicuously in England. It remained for Washington to let the American ambassador know if he was to "Go slow" or "Go ahead." But Washington, in turn, was in some dubiety, in the absence of light on the Anglo-Japanese treaty then pending and its possible bearing upon some future development concerning the two Western powers. Reid had gathered from conversations with senators and others during his recent visit to Washington that the only serious obstacle in the minds of a good many to the proposed arbitration treaty was the chance that it might be nullified by the clause in the British treaty with Japan compelling them to come to Japan's relief in case of attack. Sir Edward Grey's face brightened when the American ambassador explained this to him. The matter had all been arranged. He had foreseen the difficulty from the first, and it had been agreed upon that whenever a satisfactory treaty of general arbitration between Great Britain and the United States was negotiated, the article in question in the Anglo-Japanese treaty would be revised so as to make it of no effect with any country with which England had a treaty of general arbitration. The incident was closed with a cheerful agreement between the Foreign Office and the embassy to adopt Mr. Asquith's familiar formula, to "wait and see." Eventually the point was cleared up by an unequivocal article in the Anglo-Japanese treaty: "Should either high contracting party conclude a treaty of general arbitration with a third power, it is agreed that nothing in this agreement should entail upon such contracting party an obligation to go to war with the power with whom such treaty of arbitration is in force." It is interesting to see, behind this phraseology, the specific good-will toward America earlier disclosed in Sir Edward Grey's assurance to our ambassador. That much remained to console Reid for the untoward fortunes of the President's humane project at large.

I have noted the magnificent vitality of Chinese questions in the course of the American ambassador's relations with the Foreign Office, a vitality which carried them along month after month, indefinitely, and made him acquainted with endless windings and rewindings of international finance. When the entanglements surrounding the Hukuang Railway loan were straightened out, there supervened those belonging to loans for currency reform and other purposes. Reid was discussing the subject with Sir Edward Grey, off and on, all through 1911, and it carried over lustily into the following year. The chances for smooth progress through the Oriental thickets hardly seemed to be improved when the Manchu dynasty was displaced by a republic. Secretary Knox cabled to Reid in August, 1912, for the views of the British as regarded prompt recognition of the new government. His reply was not encouraging. "The President, Yuan Shih Kai," it ran in part, "himself admits that the Central Government are unable to enforce the observance of treaty obligations in certain provinces of China." That much he learned from Sir Edward Grey, and, further, that "His Majesty's Government have no reason to believe that recognition would add permanently to the stability of the existing administration." All of which boded ill for the peace of mind of any diplomat having anything to do with the loan, and it was not, indeed, until toward the close of his career in London that Reid was in a position to bid farewell to one of the most vexatious problems with which he had ever had to deal.

From international questions in general he was diverted, in the summer of 1911, by a decidedly interesting situation in English politics. Parliamentary reform was necessarily held in abeyance while preparations for the coronation of King George on June 22d were going forward, and shrewd observers were of the opinion that it would be delayed, in fact, until after the voyage to India and the Durbar. In the pause before the battle, Reid reflected a good deal on the new motive in political life which gained so much headway at this time, typified in Lloyd George's famous bill for the insurance of working men against disability or unemployment. He wondered if the Liberals knew precisely where they were going in proposing this enormous addition to the burden already inflicted by the old-age pensions. Reading in the "Telegraph" a philosophical analysis of the English constitutional crisis by his old friend M. Ribot, he expressed his appreciation in a letter from which I may take this statement of his own views on the policy at the heart of a momentous change:

> One thing seems to me plain. The old duty of the statesman was thought to be to economize the resources of his country, to avoid lavish expenditure, and look with alarm at every increase on the burdens of the tax-payers. The present duty of a statesman seems to be to search for new subjects of taxation, to find hitherto unknown economies which can be seized, hidden accumulations that can be extorted—all to swell the increasing sum which the state is eager to gather up from the thrifty and well-to-do, and pour out in a constantly increasing flood upon those who do not, and often do not want to, earn their own living.
>
> Don't think that I have grown to be a pessimist. No man who has traced the magnificent recuperation of his own country from the days of the Civil War to this time can fail to believe that somehow we shall pull through. Still one cannot help wondering how.

How far the making over of the House of Lords would serve in the perfecting of the new administrative dispensation hoped for by the Liberals he was at a loss to surmise, though it may be noted that his letters often reveal a strong conviction of the intellectual superiority of the upper house, and, in practical vein, he reminded Ribot that the much-abused chamber was the nearer to representing the classes that had to furnish the money. If that were really the case, would not the same reasons which originally reserved control over money bills for the Commons demand in the new crisis that that control should be given to the Lords? But he would not dogmatize about it any more than he would dogmatize "about the politics of the moon." He was content with the rôle of detached observer. It required some skill to preserve such an attitude in an environment as vibrant with excitement as was the environment of every public man in London when the time drew near for voting on a measure which would restrict the veto power held by the House of Lords. In the chapter on this subject in his "Recollections," Lord Morley indicates the gravity of feeling amongst parliamentary leaders. "The nation approached," he says, "what might prove a critical landmark in its annals." How he felt about it is indicated by Reid, who talked with him one Sunday at Nuneham, all the afternoon and after dinner, too, when the reform of the Lords was the great topic of the moment. "I found him, as I always do," he writes to Mrs. Reid, "a fascinating man." The talk went very pleasantly. "He seemed to want to discuss nearly everything under the sun, including the position of the Government, the unreason of the Conservatives, etc. On the question of single chamber government he had no defence, excepting that the mischief had been done years ago and that for a long time the House of Commons had been practically supreme. That would not be a defence, anyway, even if it were true; but, in view of their complaints against the tyranny of the Lords now, I am a little puzzled to see how an intelligent man can maintain, first, that the House of Commons has long been the sole authority, and, second, that the House of Commons has been deprived of all authority by the interference of the autocratic Lords."

This encounter at Harcourt's occurred late in July. A fortnight later came the vote on the question as to whether the Lords were to continue intrenched in a position to withstand the purposes of the Commons. Morley says that "no more exciting or dramatic scene had ever been beheld within the walls of the House of Lords," and compares the moment with that in 1640, when Pym moved the impeachment of Strafford. In a letter to Mrs. Taft, Reid thus describes the historic episode:

> There was absolute uncertainty as to how the vote would go, and in all my knowledge of the House of Lords I have never before seen it so turbulent. When we entered we were two stories below the diplomatic gallery, one below the actual level of the Chamber, and several hundred feet away from it. Yet even at this distance we heard the loud shouts and counter-shouts—so amazingly different from the usual tone of sober dignity which pervades the gilded chamber. As we entered Lord Halsbury was speaking in tones of great excitement and with rasping personal references to those of his own side who doubted the wisdom of his course. He was interrupted by cries and counter-cries from the two sides, almost as vehemently as if he had been in the Commons. Rosebery came to the table on a run, began in a very low tone, then when somebody rather tauntingly cried, "Speak up!" turned to face the larger body of tumultuous Lords and the reporters' gallery, and spoke in a louder tone than I had ever heard him use before, but extremely well. He closed with the statement that in spite of his disapproval and actual contempt for the bill, he should follow the Government into its lobby. He had hardly left the table when Lord Selborne came to it, quivering with excitement and waving aloft a scrap of paper. He began almost in a scream, and with wild gesticulation, to call the attention of the House to a recent speech of the noble Lord to whom they had just

listened, and then read with declamatory emphasis an extract in which Lord Rosebery had expressed in vehement language his disapproval of the Parliament bill. Then shaking his finger—it almost seemed shaking his fist—at Lord Rosebery, he shouted out, "When I heard those words from the noble Lord, I believed them; and in spite of his present course, I believe them still." The rest of his speech spluttered on for a little, but this was the point of it all.

I think I have never seen such a strained anxiety as appeared to fill everybody on both sides and in the galleries when the division was finally ordered, "Contents to the right of the Throne, Non-Contents to the left." Before this was carried out, Lansdowne's following of Conservatives, who simply abstained from voting, had to leave the chamber. If they had been there when the division began, they would have been compelled to vote on one side or the other. This withdrawal took a considerable time, and perplexed many spectators. Finally the real voters began to move to the two lobbies. To the amazement of most of us, the Archbishop of Canterbury and the Archbishop of York led the way to the Government lobby, followed by nearly all the entire flock of Lords Spiritual. Lord Rosebery and certain other peers who sit on the cross benches, or even on the Opposition side, moved in the same way. There was general surprise, however, at the number who followed Lord Halsbury. It looked at first as if there would be enough to overcome the Government, even with these reinforcements. It was not till the task of the tellers who stood at the gates and numbered the Lords as they returned was more than half over that it could be seen on which side the balance inclined. Before the last dozen Lords had returned through the Government gate, both sides saw what had happened, and applause ending in an actual cheer broke out on the Government side. During my stay here I have never seen or heard of a cheer in the House of Lords before.

Some idea of the strain under which men felt may be gathered from the fact that one of the Conservative peers who voted with the Government an hour later entered the Carlton Club. This, as you know, is the very sanctuary of Toryism and high breeding. As this man, whom the Halsbury people considered a traitor, entered, he was roundly hissed—given what they call here a good, old-fashioned "boo." To his credit be it said, that his aristocratic demeanor was not shaken, not a hair was ruffled, and he took no more notice of their unprecedented action than he did of the hooting of the motors outside.

The "strain" touched upon in the last paragraph was, of course, peculiarly a party strain. The American ambassador watched it with the interest natural to a lifelong participant in the ding-dong of Republican and Democratic controversy at home and there are frequent allusions in his correspondence to the downright hatred engendered by the vote on the Parliament bill. In the Conservative ranks there were bitter murmurings against Balfour's leadership, and though the revolt against him was quelled it was followed by his voluntary withdrawal. Party irritations, however, were overshadowed by larger issues. At the very moment in which something like state socialism appeared to be under way, industrial disturbances mocked the legislation nominally potent to pacify labor. Early in the Taft administration Reid answered an inquiry of the President's as to the working of trades-unionism in England by sending him a report giving a positively rosy account of the conciliation boards. It was justified by the conditions then prevailing. By the summer of 1911 British trades-unions were unblushingly breaking their agreements, rioting was going on in Liverpool, Manchester, and other centres, and, in short, the revolutionary atmosphere was spreading far beyond the confines of Parliament. Moreover, to troubles at home the British had added apprehensions abroad. On September 1st Reid wrote to Secretary Knox: "The general public is more apprehensive than I have seen them at any time since scares about Germany became the fashion. Serious business people and serious politicians are equally frank in speaking of war with Germany as a thing that may come at any time, and in fact is almost within measurable distance. They don't want it, but I doubt if they are as much disturbed by the prospect as they might be. Apparently they believe that if war comes, it will be England and France together against Germany, and that the German action has been so wanton and provocative that they will have the moral support not only of their own people, but to some extent of other nations." He was in the House in November when Sir Edward Grey made his noteworthy speech ratifying the firmness of the *entente* with France. It was an intensely exciting occasion. The speaker had to reckon with malcontents in his own party. The Laborites were ready to cut loose from the Liberals on foreign affairs in order to set up what they called "the solidarity of the labor classes" as a working political factor between English and German trades-unions. There were other elements of unrest on the floor of the House, and in the diplomatic gallery the nervousness of the moment was suggested by certain marked absences. As Reid expressed it to Secretary Knox, the people most vitally interested prudently stayed away, the German, French, and Russian ambassadors, who were all careful to avoid the chance of hearing something said which might be unpleasant to their respective countries. His own impression of the famous speech was that it was one of cautious and firm moderation. The net result of the debate was to leave it certain that England wanted no trouble with Germany, but would not be bullied into detaching herself from France.

The evidence at which I have just glanced of the increasing prospect of some vast military explosion is all a matter of public record. But in the letters of the American ambassador there is further and less familiar testimony to the fact that the Kaiser's conduct in 1914 was prefigured long before, at least to the extent of his disclosing a most unreasonable temper. When the German ambassador in London, Count Paul Wolf-Metternich, retired in 1912, he was given a brilliant banquet at Dorchester House, attended by all the members of the diplomatic corps and a number of the leading figures in English political life. His going excited some sympathy.

Lord Rosebery in his acceptance said: "Metternich will be lucky if he reaches Berlin alive, for he is being feasted every night for three weeks." The nature of the reception he was likely to get when he arrived in the Prussian capital may be inferred from the remarks on the true reasons for his retirement made by Reid to Secretary Knox:

Count Metternich was in the twelfth year of his service here as Ambassador, and before that he had already had a conspicuous career in the German diplomatic service. He was supposed to have the absolute confidence of his Government; and here he was always regarded with respect, though it could hardly be said that he had attained any particular popularity. His practical dismissal from the service and the substitution for him of the man who has so long kept Germany at the head in Constantinople came so suddenly and inexplicably that at the time the explanation was currently accepted that Metternich's retirement was at his own desire on account of his health as well as of his age, and that the other man had simply been seized upon as the readiest man at hand in their service and best equipped for their most important post.

I think, however, that I have learned authentically that the whole talk about Metternich's desire to retire has been a sham. When the Emperor came over here at the unveiling of the Victoria Memorial, just before the Coronation, he was received with more cordiality than the Germans expected, and it misled them and him alike. He instructed Metternich that the one thing for the Embassy here to accomplish was to break up the Anglo-French *entente*. Metternich has been very devoted to German interests and has gone pretty far in obeying orders; but he explained frankly to the Emperor that this was an impossible task. The Emperor is as headstrong as one or two American public men we know of, and was unwilling to be told that his plan was impossible.

Hence the change. It was accomplished with a brutality curiously characteristic of the German Foreign Office—almost as abrupt and indifferent to personal feelings or ordinary courtesy as the dismissal a few years ago (you will remember the details) of poor old Holleben, the German Ambassador in Washington. Various European members of the diplomatic corps here think they know these facts, and have been quietly resentful. Of course Metternich's recent service here has also been embarrassed by the scandals in which his nephew was involved in the notorious trial in Berlin, though it is not believed that in their rough and ready diplomatic service a trifle like this would have been allowed to interfere with his career.

Later, on an occasion when Reid was sojourning at Harrogate, the Beresfords came over to luncheon one day and Lord Charles, in confirming the cause of Metternich's dismissal, a cause which he had learned authoritatively from both English and German sources, added an interesting detail. The German ambassador, after long consideration of the problem set before him by the Kaiser, was believed to have reported that the one thing essential was to do something in Morocco which the French would consider intolerable, and yet which the English wouldn't want to back up the French in going to war about. Accordingly came the unexpected and almost inexplicable despatch of a German war-ship to Agadir. Only the trick did not work.

A story whispered in London on Metternich's retiring was that his successor, Baron Marschall von Bieberstein, had received in his turn a ticklish mandate. His business was to break up the more recent Anglo-Russian *entente*. Reid drew for Secretary Knox this sketch of him:

A greater contrast between the old Ambassador and the new could hardly be imagined. Metternich had the bearing and dignity of an accomplished man of the world and of the old diplomatic school. Marschall, but for a certain dignity of bearing, might be mistaken for a prosperous shopkeeper, or even butcher, who in his early days had gone through the ordeal of the German duello, with two or three ugly scars to show for it on his cheek, close to his mouth. His looks bear out his reputation in the Far East as a man accustomed to push diplomatic points with a strong hand and with the rattle of the Prussian sabre behind him.

The drollest observation I heard about him was that of my old colleague, the Spanish Ambassador. Said he, "Have you noticed the great change in German diplomacy since Metternich went and Marschall has come?" I said, "No, in fact, there hasn't been time for it." "Oh, yes. You have only to use your eyes to see it. Metternich's court costume, prescribed by his Emperor, always included trousers. Marschall is wearing breeches." And then the Ambassador went on to explain that at other European courts the German diplomatic costume included breeches but that trousers had been specially ordered by the Emperor at this court, "as a delicate means of annoying his uncle." The late King was always strict on the subject of knee breeches, even when you were invited to a dinner in ordinary London society, where the Queen was expected. I remember the Duke of Connaught being much embarrassed once at going to a dinner in trousers when he didn't know that his brother and sister-in-law were to be there. "I suppose," he said in an annoyed tone, "that I was the only man in London who did not know it."

It was not from the direction of Germany alone that mutterings of war came at this time. When the American ambassador gave his dinner to Metternich he was faced by a pretty little difficulty. After he had invited Imperiali, the Italian ambassador, he suddenly realized the embarrassment of asking the Turk and placing the two diplomats at the same table, when the whole world knew that their countries were at war. Some members of the diplomatic corps thought it would be risky, but Cambon, the dean, believed there would be no danger, and Sir Edward Grey was of the same opinion. Finally the French ambassador sounded Tewfik Pasha himself—"a fine old fellow," Reid calls him—and he promptly accepted, came, and was as happy as Imperiali or anybody else. Nevertheless, it was in the nature of a departure from precedent—like the dinner itself. The surprise of the Italian-Turkish War, by the way, was interpreted by the American ambassador, from the undercurrents he observed at the time, as precipitated by the Italian discovery that Germany was on the point of securing an important seaport on the Tripolitan coast. The Italian Government thereupon reasoned that the *coup* they had long been meditating must not be delayed, and that their associate in the Triple Alliance, when he attempted to steal a march on them on the opposite coast of the Mediterranean, which they had so long marked for their own, should find himself in the presence of *un fait accompli.* At one of the Wrest shooting-parties Imperiali explained to his host that neither the minister of foreign affairs in Italy nor the King could have prevented the war; that the temper of the Italians had been so aroused by a long succession of "pin pricks" that nothing could have held them back, especially after the amazing indiscretion of the German demonstration at Agadir. Of the overturn in Portugal few echoes of interest reached the American ambassador, but there is one incident which has a certain piquancy. The Marquis de Soveral, King Edward's great friend, formerly Portuguese minister in London, told Reid in May, 1911, that he regarded a monarchist revolution in his country as inevitable, and then likely to come very suddenly. The people, he said, were seething with discontent. There was, to be sure, a general belief in the air that a reaction against the republic had set in, and that the republican leaders had failed to "make good."

Europe was undoubtedly sick when the year 1912 dawned. At that time Lord Rosebery was frankly talking in a public speech about the early possibility, even the probability, of a war on the Continent greater than any in the Napoleonic era. It was like a passing release from an atmosphere charged with electricity for the Reids to come to America for their customary stay of a few winter weeks. The visit was marked this time by activities in their New York home such as were characteristic of Dorchester House. The Duke of Connaught had lately been appointed governor-general of Canada, and before leaving London he had casually spoken of the chance of seeing the Reids in their own country.

Whether the English authorities would permit him to leave his post for the purpose was, however, an open question, and the whole project, lightly touched in conversation, was left in a nebulous state. In Washington the American ambassador was pleasantly surprised to hear from Ottawa that the matter had been taken up in London, that the duke's application for leave had been granted, and that he would presently arrive in New York with the duchess and the Princess Patricia for a stay of three or four days. It was an unofficial visit, but the dance and other entertainments included in it, the calls at art galleries and public buildings, and all the incidents that served to rouse wide-spread interest, had results which had not been expected. The whole affair had occurred spontaneously, without the smallest thought that it could have any public significance. Yet that developed in the happiest manner. Smalley, writing from London, expressed the general view. "I suppose," he said, "you never did a better piece of work than when you asked the Connaughts to be your guests. It has proved in all ways a masterpiece of diplomacy. True, when the English first read the daily columns by cable they were amused at some of our enthusiasms. But it soon became clear to them that the American people were showing in a new way a new feeling toward the English; new in its universal cordiality and so obviously sincere that people here were touched by it and rejoiced in it; and so on this side also the visit had an equally good effect."

Side by side with the souvenirs of social diversions on this trip home there are others recalling Reid's wider interests in New York, never quite discontinued by his service abroad. He was glad of the opportunity to perform, as he so seldom could, his duties as a trustee of the Metropolitan Museum. He had a similarly welcome engagement at Columbia University. On the death of Joseph Pulitzer, in October, 1911, the several agreements he had entered into with that institution, relative to the establishment of a school of journalism, became operative. The editor of the "World" had, as I have shown, obtained the consent of his old friend to serve as a member of the advisory board. By great good fortune the organization meeting of this body was held while Reid was in New York, and he could, therefore, share in the deliberations paving the way for the formal opening of the school. From any participation in the conduct of his own paper he was, of course, detached by his diplomatic status, but there was a side to its affairs on which he could legitimately intervene, and in one of the little black-bound engagement books that he was wont to carry there is an entry from which a certain crucial action of his is to be inferred. Imbedded in a long series of notes, the interminable appointments of a diplomat's crowded life, there occur under the date of March 30th, 1912, these words, in which the reader will recognize an unuttered emotion of deep satisfaction: "Ogden began as Managing Editor of The Tribune."

They were written in London, after the ambassador had been for nearly a month back at his post. The date is near to one which had brought him another British honor. At Belfast, on the 28th, he repeated before the Historical Society the address he had delivered four months before at Edinburgh on "The Scot in America, and the Ulster Scot," and he was elected a freeman of the city. This was, again, a "Recreation." But it fell in a strenuous period. Strikes, with the consequent scarcity of coal, had disorganized railway traffic, and the journey home was a nightmare. England pulled through her spell of unrest, as we know, but it seemed at the moment as though she were plunged deep into a welter of social and economic troubles. In a letter to Mrs. Taft, written soon after his return from the United States, Reid touches upon the embarrassments of the government:

> In the Cabinet, Asquith is enormously overworked but up to the present seems to maintain his grip. He has been apparently doing his best to get some hold on the miners, but with precious little reward. Lloyd George seems the worst damaged of anybody in the Cabinet, and nobody appears to doubt that if the Government should be tripped up on some side motion and compelled to go before the people, his insurance bill would defeat it. Nobody can tell, however, which side is the more anxious to keep the Government from being thrown out at present, its members or the Opposition. The whole game of English politics at present is to select the ground on which to get their fall. Meantime I think the judgment of the man in the street is that the Government has bungled several things badly—particularly the insurance bill and the strike.

That hapless insurance bill was productive of mirth as well as rage. Domestic England was convulsed by the wrath of the servant-girls at a requirement that they and their mistresses should together put postage-stamps on a weekly card, indicating the amount of their taxation under this measure. Lady Sackville sent the American ambassador, in lieu of a Christmas card, a clever little statuette of Lloyd George, slightly caricatured but strikingly like him, with a big tongue much protruded, and on the pedestal this inscription: "Let him lick his own stamps."

A comprehensive study of the English political situation in 1912, pertinent, perhaps, in this place, but hardly necessary, would set Sir Edward Grey conspicuously in the Liberal foreground. We have seen him affirming the government's foreign policy in the House, and there were other occasions on which the American ambassador observed his activity as a party man. But in the story of Reid's last year in London the foreign minister figures almost exclusively as the negotiator of routine business, the friendly colleague in the advancement of interests common to Great Britain and the United States. Sometimes, no doubt, the interests of the two countries were not identical, but there remained always the same sympathetic understanding between the diplomat and the cabinet officer. Through long absorption in the records of a man's work his biographer comes to share in its atmosphere, to feel the actual pressure of those influences which helped or hindered it, and as I approach the close of Whitelaw Reid's embassy I cannot omit a reference to the personal elements in what was bound to be the determining factor in its success, his relation to the Foreign Office. The special qualities which he himself exercised upon that scene were the subject of some earnest remarks once made to me by the President who sent him to London in 1905. Roosevelt spoke of the peculiar confidence which he felt over any diplomatic matter which was in Reid's hands. Reid, he said, knew all about the suavities of English officials. He had these suavities himself. He knew just how to meet politeness of the highest degree of diplomatic fineness—with politeness and diplomacy of precisely the same character. But he never lost sight of the fact that American interests were the interests which he was in London to serve. When business developed like the negotiation of a *modus vivendi* in the Newfoundland controversy, his handling of it, said Roosevelt, was "simply perfection." Some diplomatic matters came up in our conversation which had been dealt with more particularly by Roosevelt himself at this end of the wire, the matter of the Alaskan boundary among them. He said frankly that if the Alaskan discussion had developed in Reid's time in London it would have been dealt with there. His whole tribute to the American ambassador testified to the peace of mind inspired in him by his sense of the thoroughness with which Reid mingled an unyielding Americanism with the arts of persuasion. Nothing could be more businesslike, more patriotic, than a typical conversation of his at the Foreign Office, and at the same time nothing could be more harmonious, more intellectually disinterested. In their official discussions of international topics one recognizes the same happy meeting of minds that is apparent when Reid and Grey are together in private life. To recall for a moment the significance of Metternich's rôle as it was assigned to him by the Kaiser is sufficient to make the more effective, by contrast, the American ambassador's mission and to deepen appreciation of that community of perfect good faith through which the friendship between England and the United States was strengthened. I have alluded to the slow and arduous labors connected with the Chinese loans. Negotiations over these ramified everywhere. Reid's despatches about them linked him not only to Washington but to Paris, Berlin, St. Petersburg, and, of course, Pekin. When he talked with Sir Edward Grey on this topic they handled, as it were, multifarious threads and each helped the other to clarify the confusion. Their dealings over the opium traffic made equally satisfactory progress. The Shanghai meeting early in 1909 bore good fruit, and though there was some little delay in fixing a date suitable to all the powers for the international conference at The Hague, that momentous gathering was at last admirably opened in December, 1911. If it did not accomplish absolutely all that was hoped from it, it at any rate justified the United States in having initiated the whole reformatory movement. The American ambassador was deeply concerned over the achievement of this great step toward the lessening of the opium evil. He had opened the original negotiations with Sir Edward Grey, and he had a special interest in the proceedings at The Hague because of the presence of his friend Bishop Brent among the American delegates. Allied in his mind with the opium question was another subject he had to discuss at the Foreign Office, the Putamayo atrocities, but these, as it happened, fell into a subordinate position in the tale of his diplomatic work.

With Liberia, as with the Chinese loans, he was long and very intimately occupied. Here, too, the theme was largely financial. He was instrumental in developing American co-operation where the economic affairs of the none too strong government were concerned. Also, he worked over the settlement of certain vexed Liberian boundary questions. It was a matter of finance, purely, that brought Chili upon his horizon. That republic was involved for something like twenty-five years in a controversy with the United States over a huge claim which the firm of Alsop & Company had asked our government to press. In 1909, as no solution had been arrived at, the contestants agreed to submit the whole problem to King Edward as an *aimable compositeur*. The task of obtaining his acquiescence was assigned to Reid. He was successful, but the King died shortly afterward, and the matter had to be arranged all over again with George V. That arbitrator made his award to the Alsops in July, 1911, and an account incredibly protracted was thus wiped off the books. The American ambassador rejoiced. The episode involved him in some tedious passages, even after the award was made, but the final disposition of it was clean-cut and decisive, the kind of settlement that a diplomat enjoys the more because it is so rare. Fate was to deny him anything like the same emotion over the last important question raised during his term in London. This developed in

1912, over President Taft's Panama Canal bill. Reid transmitted in July Sir Edward Grey's objections in the matter of tolls, objections which continued on the signing of the bill in the following month. In November he apprised Secretary Knox of the fact that an outline of the British views had been drawn up and was going forward to Ambassador Bryce in Washington. But this document was not handed in at the State Department until December 7th, a date which carries the subject beyond the limitations of our narrative.

In sketching Whitelaw Reid's work at the Foreign Office I have indicated the steady bearing it had upon the broad object of his diplomatic mission, the maintenance of Anglo-American good-will. The same purpose was furthered by his labors as a public speaker. Specific appearances of his in this capacity have been signalized in earlier chapters, but they form only part of an extraordinarily long list. From the moment of his arrival in London in 1905 he learned that the American ambassador was universally regarded as having a function apart, an obligation shared by no other member of the diplomatic corps, to speak at banquets and upon commemorative occasions. He found it, sometimes, a tax, but there was much in this duty that appealed to his literary instincts, and the care he lavished upon his addresses lifted them above the plane of ordinary ambassadorial "hands across the sea" oratory. He was at pains, of course, to emphasize, when it was appropriate, the international aspect of his discourse. One of the last speeches he made was delivered at the dinner given by the Boz Club in July, 1912, to celebrate the centenary of the birth of Charles Dickens. He recalled the words he had heard the great author utter at Delmonico's forty years before: "It would be better for this globe to be riven by an earthquake, fired by a comet, overrun by an iceberg, and abandoned to the Arctic fox and bear, than that it should present the spectacle of those two great nations, each of whom has, in its own way and hour, striven so hard and successfully for freedom, ever again being arrayed the one against the other." Reid's audience cheered his quotation. Audiences in England often had occasion to cheer him as a spokesman for the good feeling existing between the two countries. But his success as a speaker was based, also, on a wider and subtler appeal, that of a dispassionate historical and critical interpreter. Pure literature gave him many of his subjects—Shakespeare, Bacon, Milton, Thackeray, Byron, Dickens, and Poe. Others he drew from the world of statesmanship—Washington and Lincoln, Burke and John Bright. If in some instances the theme was set for him, in others he selected it himself, and when this was the case, he had some felicitous inspirations. One of them came when the Edinburgh Philosophical Institution asked him to make the opening address in November, 1911. He traced the influence of Scottish blood in American life and enriched the subject with a flood of light. Belfast, as I have noted, paid him the compliment of asking him to deliver his Edinburgh address over again there. His listeners in both places were profoundly interested by his elucidation of ties between their country and his own. Charles Francis Adams, writing to him about it from Boston, said: "Placed as you are, I do not see precisely how you did it. I could not have got together all those details and special instances." Industry had something to do with it, industry and a zest for historical research that he never lost. Of all the contacts with English literary interests that marked his life in London none appealed to him more strongly than his membership in the Roxburghe Club, an organization distinguished for its fine tradition of historical documentation.*

Besides the capacity for taking pains, the ardor of a man of letters, Whitelaw Reid had a quality on which I have paused again and again in these pages, and to which he gave free play in the last of his addresses, rounding out the large group belonging to his English activities. I refer to his independence, his love of intellectual exercise for its own sake. It won him appreciation from English hearers when it operated to such candid purpose as it did in his discussion of Byron at Nottingham, and I may remark in passing that the criticism was received with equal sympathy when it was soon after placed before a wider audience in the "Fort-

* The American ambassador was elected to the Roxburghe Club on the proposal of Lord Rosebery in 1909. Following custom, he sought some manuscript to print for distribution among his fellow members, and in his correspondence there are frequent traces of the efforts he made to find the right material, especially in American archives. Rosebery offered him in 1910, apropos of his quest, these characteristic observations: "As to the Roxburghe Club, a member, I fancy, prints what he chooses. I myself printed from a manuscript at the Bodleian. But if you print, I cannot help expressing the private and personal hope that it will be something historical, something that one can read. . . . Did you hear Huth say at the meeting that he purposed reading 'Amadis of Gaul'!"

Since her husband was not spared to carry his investigations to a successful conclusion, Mrs. Reid commissioned Lord Rosebery to act for her, and he found at Quaritch's the Coke papers, which on behalf and in memory of Whitelaw Reid she gave to the Roxburghe Club to print, later presenting the original documents to the New York Public Library. The volume appeared in 1915—"The Royal Commission on the Losses and Services of American Loyalists. 1783 to 1785. Being the Notes of Mr. Daniel Parker Coke, M.P., one of the Commissioners During That Period. Edited by Hugh Edward Egerton, Beit Professor of Colonial History in the University of Oxford." The work fulfils the condition commended to Reid. It is readable and it throws valuable light on the status of the loyalists. In certain copies there is inserted this note, written by Lord Rosebery:

"The surplus copies of this book, after the distribution to the Members of the Roxburghe Club and to a few libraries and individuals in England, were shipped to the donor, Mrs. Whitelaw Reid, in America by the s.s. '*Arabic*,' which was gratuitously torpedoed, outward bound, with much loss of civilian life, by a German sub-marine. A reprint was put in hand, and this slip is inserted in the copies of the reprint as a record of that incident which, it may be hoped, will remain unparalleled in the bibliographical history of the Roxburghe Club."

nightly." It shone forth with even richer implications when he spoke at the University College of Wales, at Aberystwyth, on October 31st, 1912, and chose as his theme "One Welshman." The man of Welsh origin to whom he dedicated one of the most polished analyses he ever wrote was the great exemplar of the American political faith to which he had been opposed from his youth up. His farewell appearance on the British platform was made for the utterance of a eulogy upon Thomas Jefferson. It was a tempered eulogy, no doubt. He spoke, as he had spoken of Byron, from an absolutely frank point of view, and there were some Democrats at home who did not relish all his words. "How he did take our hair off," Henry Adams said to me, in speaking of this address. "If the figure I have been presenting as an honor to Wales," Reid remarked in the course of it, "has a head of gold, just as clearly it will be seen to have had feet of clay." But Adams told me that he thought this address the best that Reid had ever made, and surely no Democrat could cavil at the closing sentences, spoken by a lifelong Republican:

> On the Fourth of July, 1826, John Adams was slowly dying, amid the noisy rejoicing already universal over nearly every recurrence of the great anniversary. In a final effort to make himself understood by the family, this old and fervid friend and opponent whispered, "Thomas Jefferson still lives." They were Adams's last words, and they were prophetic. That strange medley of inconsistency, extravagance, enthusiasm, and fervid patriotic devotion to whom he referred had in fact passed away a few hours earlier. But the author of the statute for religious liberty in Virginia and of the Declaration of Independence, the founder of the University of Virginia, and the purchaser of Louisiana "still lives" in the respectful memory of the world and in the affection of the people of the continent he served. I venture to appropriate for him the lines of Shelley—
>
> "till the Future dares
> Forget the Past, his fate and fame shall be
> An echo and a light unto eternity."

Physically the speech cost an effort which was to make itself felt the sooner because Reid had come to it already much fatigued. In the summer of 1912 the Board of Regents witnessed the fulfilment of its great ambition, the completion of the new Educational Building at Albany. The event had been anticipated when the ambassador was at home in the preceding winter, and pressure had been brought upon him to make another visit for the opening, to preside, and to speak, as chancellor. He crossed the Atlantic, performed his task on October 15th, and returned to London, all within a period of a month. The strain was too severe, and the Welsh speech, on the 31st, followed altogether too soon, especially in view of the journeying it involved. A sharp attack of his old bronchial trouble supervened, with the asthmatic accompaniment that he always dreaded. The sickness was complicated by a painful neuralgia. Sir William Osler stimulated him with the assurance that absolute rest and careful life in the open air would effect a cure. He had to remember, also, that he had passed his seventy-fifth birthday. But even a younger man might have felt the weight of the burden he had been carrying. "Osler tells me," he wrote to Mrs. Cowles, "that all my recent trouble is due entirely to overwork, and especially to my hurried trip to America, to do my duty as a member of the Board of Regents, and to my hurried trip back, to Aberystwyth, in Wales, to tell a small portion of the truth about Thomas Jefferson at their University College." He had overdrawn his vitality and the consequences swiftly ensued.

He had no forebodings. All through November he went on with the usual work of the embassy. There was a shooting-party at Wrest, with Sir Edward Grey among the guests, at the close of the month. On Monday, December 2d, he came up from this to Dorchester House, apparently in need of nothing more than rest, and the numerous entries in his engagement book bear mute witness to the confidence of his plans. Among them was one arranging for the Christmas holidays at his daughter's house in the country. Ogden Reid and his wife were coming over for this celebration. But when they came it was very suddenly, on a fast steamer, summoned by an anxious despatch. The ambassador's last illness began, quite unexpectedly, on December 3d. When the asthma overtook him it made disastrous inroads upon his strength. For ten days he kept to his room, or sat in Mrs. Reid's, talking with her. He grew very weak, until he could no longer rally from the exhaustion produced by the asthmatic strain. The end came on December 15th.

He died in harness, at a great diplomatic post, and the news of his death was received not only with a multitude of expressions of private grief but with signal evidences of a wide-spread recognition of the loss suffered by the public service. President Taft was apprised of the event by King George, who sent him this message:

It is with the deepest sorrow that I have to inform you of the death of Mr. Whitelaw Reid, at noon today. As your Ambassador in this country his loss will be sincerely deplored, while personally I shall mourn for an old friend of many years' standing for whom I had the greatest regard and respect. The Queen and I sympathize most warmly with Mrs. Whitelaw Reid in her heavy sorrow.

Between the lines this communication gave a heightened significance to the King's expression of regret. In making it he marked a departure from precedent, himself sending news which, as a rule, is transmitted by routine through the Foreign Office. Mr. Taft made the following reply:

Your Majesty's sad news of the death of Mr. Whitelaw Reid has just reached me. Mr. Reid's death is a loss to both countries, for his service as Ambassador was exceptional in the closer friendship that he secured between them through his own personality. His intimate knowledge of both countries, his profound respect and love for England, entirely consistent with the highest loyalty on his part to this country, gave him peculiar influence for good in his great station. I sincerely thank your Majesty for your message and your expressions of sympathy and respect.

"We regard him as a kinsman," said the prime minister of England in the House of Commons the next day, when he and ex-Premier Balfour joined in paying tribute to the dead ambassador, and Mr. Asquith stated his intention of suggesting to the American Government that one of his Majesty's war-ships should carry the body to the United States. This intimation was at once conveyed to Mrs. Reid by Sir Edward Grey, and the armored cruiser *Natal* was assigned to the duty. A few days would necessarily elapse before the embarkation, and in the meantime the Bishop of London suggested a memorial service in St. Paul's. The King, however, decided that Westminster would be preferable, and the service was accordingly held in the Abbey on Friday, December 20th, in the presence of representatives of the court, the diplomatic corps, and many political and other personages. On Saturday the body was conducted from Dorchester House on a gun-carriage draped with the American flag, proceeding under military escort. In recognition of the ambassador's Scotch ancestry a half battalion of Scots Guards formed part of the procession, which was headed by a troop of Household Cavalry in their scarlet cloaks. To the skirl of pipes and the beating of drums the march led to the railway-station, where the Admiralty had in readiness a special train for the journey to Portsmouth. During the departure from Dorchester House a battery in St. James's Park fired a salute of nineteen minute-guns, and at Portsmouth, as the body was taken on board the *Natal*, the guns of the *Victory* rendered the same honor. All the ships in the harbor flew the United States ensign as the cruiser left port.

A squadron of six American war-ships under Rear-Admiral Fiske, led by the *Florida*, met the *Natal* off Nantucket Light on its arrival here. On Friday, January 3d, the body was conveyed, again on a gun-carriage, to the Cathedral of St. John the Divine. It was guarded by a detachment of Marines and placed in the crypt. In the morning of the next day the funeral was held, the edifice thronged as the Abbey had been thronged, by an assemblage including the President of the United States, members of his cabinet, ex-President Roosevelt, and other leaders in public life. Then, once more under military guard, the ambassador was carried on his last journey, to be laid to rest in Sleepy Hollow, at Tarrytown.

THE END

INDEX

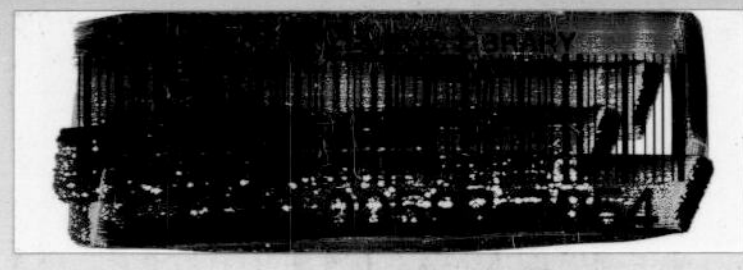

Cortissoz
Whitelaw Reid

	DATE DUE		